TRAILBLAZER

WINNING EDGE SERIES

RRB NTPC STAGE-I

Solved Papers (2016-17)

UNICORN BOOKS

www.unicornbooks.in • info@unicornbooks.in

CONTENTS

RRB NTPC stage-I Solved Paper

Held On 28th March 2016 (Shift-I)

1. The dance form Kuchipudi originated from which part of India?

(a) Tamil Nadu (b) Maharashtra

(c) Andhra Pradesh (d) Odisha

2. The number of bicycles sold by a shopkeeper in a particular week is shown below. How many bicycles were sold from Thursday to Sunday?

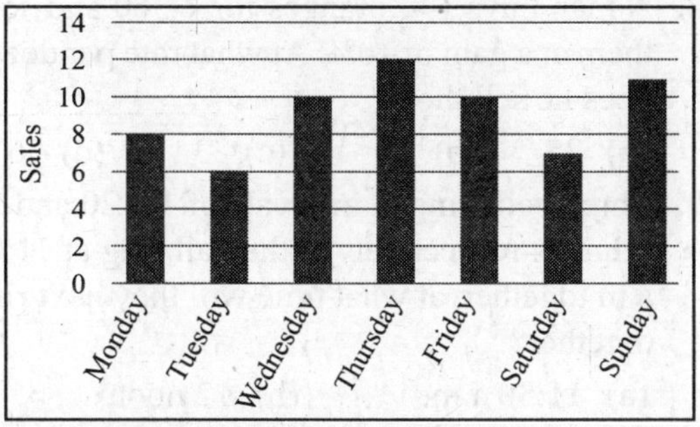

(a) 39 (b) 38 (c) 40 (d) 36

3. Which river used to be called the 'Sorrow of Bengal'?

(a) Brahmaputra (b) Hooghly

(c) Bhagirathi d) Damodar

4. How many moons does the planet Mars have?

(a) 1 (b) 2 (c) 3 (d) 4

5. The distance between two places, A and B, is 300 km. Two riders, on scooters start simultaneously from A and B towards each other. The distance between them after 2.5 hrs is 25 km. If the speed of one scooter is 10 km/hr more than the other, find the speed of each scooter in km/hr

(a) 50 and 60 (b) 30 and 40

(c) 40 and 50 (d) 60 and 70

6. If $(a^2 - b^2) \div (a + b) = 25$, find $a - b$.

(a) 15 (b) 18 (c) 25 (d) 30

7. What is the shape of the Earth?

(a) Perfect hemisphere (b) Mostly flat

(c) Perfect Sphere (d) Oblate Sphere

8. Who gave the slogan 'Do or Die' during India's freedom struggle?

(a) Veer Savarkar

(b) Netaji Subhas Chandra Bose

(c) Mahatma Gandhi

(d) Subramanya Bharati

9. Calculate the amount on ₹ 37,500 @ 8% p.a compounded half yearly for $1\frac{1}{2}$ years.

(a) ₹ 42,182.40 (b) ₹ 42,000

(c) ₹ 42,120 (d) ₹ 42,812.40

10. When did Vasco da Gama land in India?

(a) 1492 (b) 1498

(c) 1948 (d) 1857

11. In 2014, the ________ Lok Sabha was elected.

(a) 16th (b) 19th (c) 14th (d) 23rd

12. Arteries carry blood, that is filled with

(a) Oxygen (b) Carbon dioxide

(c) Toxins (d) Lipids

13. Pick the odd one out:

28, 44, 68, 80, 92

(a) 28 (b) 44 (c) 80 (d) 92

14. Find the product of square root of 16 and square of 4?

(a) 8 (b) 64 (c) 16 (d) 256

15. In a company 10 employees get a salary of ₹ 36,200 each and 15 employees get a salary of ₹ 33,550 each. What is the average salary per employee?

(a) 34,875 (b) 34,610

(c) 27,900 (d) 36,410

16. Find the odd one out. **1, 8, 27, 36, 125, 216**

(a) 1 (b) 8 (c) 36 (d) 216

17. What is the desert adjoining the Thar desert called in Pakistan?

(a) Gobi (b) Cholistan

(c) Sukkur (d) Mirpur

18. Mohan is taller than Rohan but shorter than Farhan. Kannan is shorter than Mohan but taller than Rohan Shankar is taller than Rohan and Farhan. Who is the tallest?

(a) Mohan (b) Farhan
(c) Shankar (d) Kannan

19. Which of the following is true?

(a) 1 Gigabyte = 1024 MB
(b) 1 Gigabyte = 1,000,000 Kilobytes
(c) 1 Gigabyte = 10,000 MB
(d) 1 Gigabyte = 100,000 KB

20. If **COW = 41, GOAT = 43,** then **DOG** =

(a) 47 (b) 38 (c) 25 (d) 26

DIRECTIONS (Qs. 21-23): *Read the following information and answer the following questions.*

Five girls are sitting in front, facing each other. Ruhi and Manali respectively are sitting to the right and left of Urja.

Dhwani is sitting between Manali and Tanya.

21. How many girls are there between Dhwani and Ruhi?

(a) 1 (b) 2 (c) 3 (d) 4

22. Who is sitting in the middle?

(a) Dhwani (b) Urja
(c) Manali (d) Tanya

23. Who is sitting to the right of Tanya?

(a) Ruhi (b) Manali
(c) Dhwani (d) Urja

24. Which among the below choices can cause a Tsunami (also known as harbor wave)

(a) Under sea earthquakes
(b) Typhoon
(c) Volcanic eruptions on land
(d) Drought

25. In the following number series, one missing term is shown by '?' choose the missing term from the options below.

6, 12, 20, 30, ?, 56, 72

(a) 40 (b) 42 (c) 44 (d) 48

26. Raj scored 67, 69, 78, and 88 in 4 of his subjects. What should be his score in the 5th subject so that his average equals 80?

(a) 88 (b) 90 (c) 96 (d) 98

27. Aruna Asaf Ali is remembered for hoisting the Indian National Congress Flag at

(a) Non-cooperation Movement.
(b) Civil Disobedience Movement
(c) Self-rule Movement
(d) Quit India Movement

28. A man buys 144 oranges for ₹ 360 and sells them at a gain of 10%. At what rate per dozen does he sell them?

(a) 25 (b) 30 (c) 33 (d) 36

29. Three bells ring at intervals of 15, 20 and 30 minutes respectively If they all ring at 11:00 a m together, at what time will they next ring together?

(a) 11:30 a.m. (b) 12 noon
(c) 12.30 p.m. (d) 1.00 p.m.

30 Aman and Ajay can build a wall in 9 days and 12 days respectively. In how many days can they finish the work if they work together?

(a) $5\frac{1}{7}$ (b) $11\frac{1}{2}$
(c) 2 (d) 7

31. Which of the following is also called Marsh Gas?

(a) Propane (b) Ethane
(c) Methane (d) Butane

32. Five students Priyanka, Mary, Sunil, Asha and Ryan are standing in a line. Priyanka and Sunil are standing ahead of Ryan. Sunil is standing between Ryan and Asha. Between Sunil and Mary, Ryan is standing. Who is the first in the line?

(a) Asha (b) Sunil
(c) Ryan (d) Priyanka

33. What should be subtracted from 107.03 to get 96.4?

(a) 1.63 (b) 10.63
(c) 10.53 (d) 9.63

34. Julia started walking towards North direction from her house. After a while she turned left and later on turned right. She further turned right. Which direction is she facing now?

(a) East (b) West
(c) North (d) South

35. How much is one decalitre?

(a) 10 kilolitre (b) 10 litre
(c) 100 litre (d) 10 centilitre

36. Anil bought 100 eggs at ₹ 6 per egg. He sold 25 eggs at 10% profit, another 25 eggs at 25% loss and the balance 50 eggs at 20% profit. Find the overall profit or loss percent Anil made?

(a) 6.25% loss (b) 6.25% profit
(c) 8% profit (d) 12% loss

37. Who is thought to have invented the thermoscope?

(a) Galileo Galilei (b) Copernicus
(c) Isaac Newton (d) J. Kepler

38. In a running race, if you overtake the last but one contestant, which position are you in?

(a) Last (b) Second from last
(c) Third from last (d) Fourth from last

39. Find the odd one out : **External Hard drive, Keyboard, Digital camera, Compact Disc**

(a) External Hard drive (b) Keyboard
(c) Digital camera (d) Compact Disc

40 Meena took a car loan for ₹ 275,000 from the bank. She paid an interest @ 8% p.a. and settled the account after 3 years. At the time of settlement she gave her old scooter to the bank plus ₹ 335,000. What price did the scooter fetch?

(a) 60,000 (b) 6,000
(c) 66,000 (d) 6,600

41. A tank can be filled by two taps X and Y in 5 hrs and 10 hrs respectively while another tap Z empties the tank in 20 hrs. In how many hours can the tank be filled if all 3 taps are kept open?

(a) 5 (b) 4 (c) 7 (d) 8

42. A man travelling by bus finds that the bus crosses 35 electric poles in 1 minute and the distance between 2 poles is 50 metres. Find the speed of the bus.

(a) 112 km/hr. (b) 102 km/hr.
(c) 110 km/hr. (d) 120 km/hr.

43. Blunt: Sharp as **Sow:**

(a) Reap (b) Seeds
(c) Farmer (d) Crop

44. If Cot A= $\frac{12}{5}$ then (Sin A + Cos A) therefore Cosec A is?

(a) 12/5 (b) 17/5
(c) 11/5 (d) 2

45. As the frequency of a wave increases, what happens to its wavelength?

(a) It increases
(b) It remains same
(c) It decreases
(d) There is no connection between the two

46. A seven-sided polygon is called

(a) Nonagon (b) Hexagon
(c) Heptagon (d) Octagon

47. In BRICS, which country is denoted by 'B'?

(a) Bangladesh (b) Belgium
(c) Brazil (d) Bahrain

48. Circle: Circumference as **Square:**

(a) Sides (b) Area
(b) Perimeter (d) Diagonal

49. Which is the capital of Cyprus?

(a) Nicosia (b) Polls
(c) Lamaca (d) Araddipou

50. If **AMERICA=1734651, INDIA=68961,** how will you write **CANADA**?

(a) 719181 (b) 518191
(c) 519581 (d) 715148

51. World Tuberculosis (TB) day is observed on?

(a) 28th March (b) 24th March
(c) 24th May (d) 28th May

52. A's height is 5/8th of B's height. What is the ratio of B's height to A's height?

(a) 5:8 (b) 3:8 (c) 5:3 (d) 8:5

53. The product of 2 numbers is 35828 and their HCF is 26. Find their LCM.
(a) 931788 (b) 689
(b) 1378 (d) 3583

54. Which number will be in the middle if the following numbers are arranged in descending order?
4456, 4465, 4655, 4665, 4565
(a) 4456 (b) 4465
(c) 4565 (d) 4655

55. In which State is Karla, famous for its Buddhist caves, located?
(a) Maharashtra (b) Uttar Pradesh
(c) Uttarakhand (d) Madhya Pradesh

56. Two-thirds of children are in the age group 1-12 years. Of this, if three-fourths are in the age group of 1-8 years, find the fraction of children in the age group of 9-12 years?
(a) 1/3 (b) 1/4 (c) 1/6 (d) 1/2

57. The Rowlatt Act was passed in which year?
(a) 1919 (b) 1921
(c) 1923 (d) 1916

58. Read statements 1 and 2. Also read the conclusions 3 and 4 drawn from the statements.
Statement:
1. Some birds are Donkeys.
2. All donkeys are stupid.

Conclusions:
3. All birds are stupid.
4. Some birds are stupid.

Choose which of the conclusions are right.
(a) Only 3 is correct
(b) Only 4 is correct
(c) Both 3 and 4 are correct
(d) Neither 3 nor 4 is correct

59. Which boxer is nicknamed The Real Deal'?
(a) Mike Tyson (b) Mohammed Ali
(c) Evander Holyfield (d) Joe Louis

60. Arrange the following word in alphabetical order and find the third word?
Singer, Single, Sinister, Simple.
(a) Single (b) Singer
(c) Sinister (d) Simple

61. A man sells a table for ₹ 4200 at 25% loss. At what price must he sell to get a profit of 25%?
(a) 1,400 (b) 8,400
(c) 7,000 (d) 5,600

62. Who is a hacker?
(a) A person who sells goods in the street.
(b) A person who uses computers to gain un authorized access to data.
(c) A person who only sells computers online
(d) A person who records phone calls.

63. If your father were your mother, your mother your brother, your brother your sister and your sister your father, how would you call your sister?
(a) Father (b) Mother
(c) Brother (d) Sister

64. Which of the following
(a) Angles totalling 180°
(b) Angles totalling 135°
(c) Angles totalling 75°
(d) Angles totalling 90°

65. What is the measure of the two equal angles of a right isosceles triangle?
(a) 30° (b) 45° (c) 60° (d) 90°

66. What percent of 1 hour is 1 minute and 12 seconds?
(a) 2% (b) 12% (c) 11% (d) 1.2%

67. Mrinalini Sarabhai passed away recently. Who was she?
(a) Film Actress (b) Scientist
(c) Classical Dancer (d) Playback Singer

68. Unscramble the letter 'CCITRKE' to form an English word and find the fifth letter of the unscrambled word?
(a) C (b) K (c) E (d) I

69. What was the name of Maharana Pratap's horse?
(a) Bulbul (b) Chetak
(c) Hayagriva (d) Badai

70. The function of the lens in our eyes is to
(a) Cover the eyes
(b) Send messages of images to the brain
(c) Change the focal distance of the eye
(d) Protects eyes from injury.

71. In India who is the executive head of the state?
(a) Prime Minister
(b) The President
(c) The Chief justice of Supreme Court
(d) The Governor

72. Who is believed to have built the Konark Temple?
(a) Raja Kulothunga (b) Narasimha Deva I
(c) Vishnugopa (d) Malnpala

73. Who invented Penicillin?
(a) Ian Fleming
(b) Alexander Fleming
(c) Stephen Hawking
(d) Alexander Graham Bell

74. **If TEACHER : BOOKS, DOCTOR: ?**
(a) Chalk (b) Cycle
(c) Stethoscope (d) Apron

75. Which was the first satellite to orbit our Moon?
(a) Luna2 (b) Luna 10
(c) Apollo 10 (d) Apollo 11

76. Find the odd one out:
Ostrich, Crow, Pigeon, Sparrow.
(a) Ostrich (b) Pigeon
(c) Crow (d) Sparrow

77. Science of the study of preserved remains or traces of animals, plants, and other organisms from the remote past is called
(a) Anthropology (b) Archaeology
(c) Paleontology (d) Pharmacology

78. With which sport is Karnam Malleswari associated?
(a) Tennis (b) Swimming
(c) Athletics (d) Weightlifting

79. How many prime numbers are there between 50 and 100?
(a) 6 (b) 10 (c) 13 (d) 5

80 If Christmas was on Sunday in 2011, what day will it be in 2012?
(a) Monday (b) Tuesday
(c) Wednesday (d) Thursday

81. Emperor Ashoka was the successor of:
(a) Chandragupta Maurya
(b) Bindusara
(c) Susima
(d) Dasharatha

82. If 'A' is the son of 'B' and is the father of 'C', how is 'B' related to 'C'?
(a) Father (b) Son
(c) Grandparent (d) Grandchild

DIRECTIONS (Qs. 83-85): *Amar, Babu, Cera and Diya were asked to solve a question paper with 4 multiple choice questions with choices 1, 2, 3, 4. The answer sheet as marked by them is reproduced here.*

	Amar	Babu	Cera	Diva
Ql	2	1	1	3
Q2	4	3	2	4
Q3	3	4	3	1
Q4	3	2	2	4

Babu got all answers wrong. Amar's first two answers were definitely wrong. Diva got two answers right but her fourth answer was definitely wrong. Amar and Cera each have got only one correct answer.

83. Which of Cera's question is correct?
(a) Ql (b) Q2 (c) Q3 (d) Q4

84. Whose answer to Q4 is correct?
(a) Amar (b) Babu
(c) Diya (d) None

85. Which two answers of Diva are correct?
(a) Ql and Q2 (b) Q1 and Q3
(c) Q2 and Q3 (d) Q3 and Q4

86. Simplify $\sqrt{(1 - \sin^2 \theta) \div (1 - \cos^2 \theta)}$
(a) Cot θ (b) Tan θ
(c) Sec θ (d) Cosec θ

87. Atomic weight of an element is compared with which of the following to get the atomic weight of that element?
(a) Oxygen (b) Carbon
(c) Hydrogen (d) Nitrogen

DIRECTIONS (Qs. 88-90): *Read the following information and answer the following questions.*

In a class of 40 students, 28 can speak Tamil and 30 can speak Telugu.

All students can speak at least one of the two languages.

88. Find the number of persons who can speak only Telugu?
(a) 8 (b) 10 (c) 12 (d) 14

89. Find the minimum number of students who can speak both Tamil and Telugu?
(a) 12 (b) 15 (c) 18 (d) 22

90. Find the number of students who can speak only Tamil.
(a) 8 (b) 10 (c) 12 (d) 14

91. Rajiv said pointing to a girl, "She is the only daughter of the father of my sister's brother". If so how is the girl related to Rajiv?
(a) Mother (b) Aunt
(c) Sister (d) Sister-in-law.

92. Ram is 4 times his son's age today. Five years hence, Ram will be thrice his son's age. Find their current ages?
(a) 60,15 (b) 40,10
(c) 20,5 (d) 32,8

93. Where can you find the Golden Temple of Dambulla?
(a) Amritsar (b) Sri Lanka
(c) Indonesia (d) Malaysia

94. From the following which is an example of a single-celled organism?
(a) Protozoa (b) Anthropods
(c) Echinoderms (d) Annelids

95. Which two teams played the first International match?
(a) England and Australia
(b) England and West Indies
(c) USA and Canada
(d) Australia and India

96. Which of this is not a memorial to a dead person?
(a) Bibi ka Maqbara (b) Taj Mahal
(c) Charminar (d) Itmad Ud Daulah

97. XCVI denotes
(a) 116 (b) 496 (c) 96 (d) 84

98. When was the Indian Constitution amended for the first time?
(a) 1949 (b) 1951
(c) 1952 (d) 1953

99. Find two consecutive numbers where thrice the first number is more than twice the second number by 5.
(a) 5 and 6 (b) 6 and 7
(c) 7and 8 (d) 9 and 10

100. Which is the smallest continent?
(a) Australia (b) South America
(c) Antarctica (d) Africa

Hints & Solutions

1. (c) Belonging to the Andhra Pradesh, Kuchipudi is probably the toughest form of classical dance in India. Kuchipudi includes both singing and dancing by the performer.

2. (c) From the given bar graph, we get

Number of bicycles sold on Thursday = 12

Number of bicycles sold on Friday = 10

Number of bicycles sold on Saturday = 7

Number of bicycles sold on Sunday = 11

Total number of bicycles sold from Thursday to Sunday = 12 + 10 + 7 + 11 = 40

3. (d)

4. (b) The two moons of Mars are Phobos and Deimos. Both are named after the Greek mythological twin characters Phobos (panic/fear) and Deimos (terror/dread).

5. (a) A ←——— 300 km ———→ B

Let speed of one vehicle is V km/hr

Then, speed of other vehicles is (V + 10) km/hr

Distance covered by one vehicles in 2.5 hr = 2.5V

Distance covered by other vehicles in 2.5 hr = 2.5 (V + 10)

ATQ, 2.5V + 2.5 (V + 10) + 25 = 300

$$2.5V + 2.5V + 25 + 25 = 300$$
$$5V + 50 = 300$$
$$V = \frac{300 - 50}{5} = \frac{250}{5}$$
$$V = 50$$

Hence, speed of one vehicle = 50 km/hr

speed of other vehicles = 50 + 10 = 60 km/hr

6. (c) $(a^2 - b^2) \div (a + b) = 25$

$$\frac{(a-b)(a+b)}{(a+b)} = 25 \Rightarrow (a-b) = 25$$

7. (d) The oblate ellipsoid is the regular geometric shape that most nearly approximates the shape of the Earth.

8. (c)

9. (a) Interest is compounded half yearly

so, $t = 1\frac{1}{2}$ year = 3 half year.

Rate r = 8% p.a. = 4% p. half year.

$$\text{Amount } A = P\left(1 + \frac{r}{100}\right)^t$$
$$= 37500\left(1 + \frac{4}{100}\right)^3$$
$$= 37500\left(\frac{104}{100}\right)^3$$
$$= \frac{37500 \times 104 \times 104 \times 104}{100 \times 100 \times 100}$$
$$= ₹\,42182.4$$

10. (b) On May 20, 1498, Portuguese explorer Vasco da Gama landed in what is now Kozhikode, to reach the trade centers of India by sea.

11. (a)

12. (a) An Artery is a blood vessel that takes blood away from the heart to all parts of the body. Most arteries carry oxygenated blood except pulmonary and the umbilical arteries, which carry deoxygenated blood.

13. (c) 28 = 4 × 7

44 = 4 × 11

68 = 4 × 17

80 = 4 × 20

92 = 4 × 23

Here, 7, 11, 17 and 23 are prime number. Whereas 20 is a compound number.

14. (b) Product of $\sqrt{16} \times 4^2 = \sqrt{4 \times 4} \times 4 \times 4$

$$= 4 \times 16 = 64$$

15. (b) Total salary of 10 employees = 36200 × 10

= 362000

Total salary of 15 employees = 33550 × 15

= 503250

Total salary of 25 (10 + 15) employees

= 362000 + 503250 = 865250

$$\text{Average salary per employee} = \frac{865250}{25} = 34610$$

16. (c)

1	8	27	36	125	216
↓	↓	↓	↓	↓	↓
$(1)^3$	$(2)^3$	$(3)^3$	$(6)^2$	$(5)^3$	$(6)^3$

Except '36' all others numbers are cube number.

17. (b) Cholistan desert is locally known as Rohi in Bhawalpur, Punjab, Pakistan adjoining the Thar deserts.

18. (c)

19. (a) 1 kilobyte = 1024 byte.

1 Megabyte = 1024 kilobyte.

1 Gigabyte = 1024 Megabyte.

20. (d) C O W = 41

↓ ↓ ↓

3 15 23 = 3 + 15 + 23 = 41

Letters position in alphabets

G O A T = 43

↓ ↓ ↓ ↓

7 15 1 20 = 7 + 15 + 1 + 20 = 43

Simply,

D O G

↓ ↓ ↓

4 15 7 = 4 + 15 + 7 = 26

(21-23) Sitting arrangement of five girls are like this:

Tanya — Dhwani — Manali — Urja — Ruhi

21. (b) There are two girls Manali and Urja are sitting between Dhwani and Ruhi.

22. (c) Manali is sitting in the middle.

23. (c) Dhawani is sitting right of Tanya.

24. (a) Most tsunami are caused by large earthquakes on the sea floor when slabs of rock move past each other suddenly, causing the overlying water to move and may cause a tsunami that will travel across the ocean.

25. (b) 6 , 12 , 20 , 30 , 42 , 56 , 72

(+6, +8, +10, +12, +14, +16)

26. (d) Let Raj score in the fifth subject is then, total score in the five subjects

$= 67 + 69 + 78 + 88 + x = 302 + x$

Average score in five subject = 80

$$\frac{302 + x}{5} = 80$$

$= 302 + x = 80 \times 5$

$x = 400 - 302 = 98$

27. (d) Aruna Asaf Ali is famous for hoisting the Congress flag at the Gowalia Tank maidan in Bombay during the Quit India Movement in 1942.

28. (c) Cost price of 144 orange = 360

profit = 10%

Selling price of 144 orange

$$= 360 \times \left(1 + \frac{10}{100}\right) = 396$$

$$144 \text{ orange} = \frac{144}{12} = 12 \text{ dozen}$$

Now, selling price of 12 dozen = 396

$$\therefore \text{Selling price per dozen} = \frac{396}{12} = ₹\ 33$$

29. (b) L.C.M. of 15, 20 and 30 = 60 minutes

So, time when all the three bell ring together = 11.00 + 1 hour = 12 noon.

30. (a) Wall built by Aman in one day $= \frac{1}{9}$

Wall built by Ajay in one day $= \frac{1}{12}$

When they work together, wall built by them in one day $= \frac{1}{9} + \frac{1}{12} = \frac{4+3}{36} = \frac{7}{36}$

Time required to build the wall

$$= \frac{1}{\frac{7}{36}} = \frac{36}{7} = 5\frac{1}{7} \text{ days}$$

31. (c) Marsh gas, (methane), is produced by the anaerobic bacterial decomposition of vegetable matter and the remains of herbivorous animals under water.

32. (d) Arrangement of five person in row:

Mary Ryan Sunil Asha Priyanka

Mary ↓ Last in the line; Priyanka ↓ First in the line

33. (b) Let us subtract x. then,

$107.03 - x = 96.4$

$\Rightarrow x = 107.03 - 96.4 = 10.63$

34. (a)

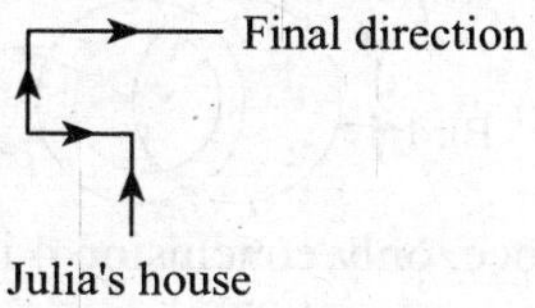

Hence, Julia is finally facing east direction

35. (b) 1 centilitre = 10 mililitre

1 decilitre = 10 centilitre

1 litre = 10 decilitre

1 decalitre = 10 litre

Hence, option (b) is correct.

36. (b) Cost price of 25 eggs = 25 × 6 = 150

Selling price of 25 eggs

$= 150 \times \left(1 + \frac{10}{100}\right) = ₹\, 165$

Selling price of another 25 eggs at 25% loss $= 150 \times \left(1 - \frac{25}{100}\right) = ₹\, 112.5$

Now cost price of 50 eggs = 50 × 6 = 300

Selling price of 50 eggs at 20% profit

$= 300 \times \left(1 + \frac{20}{100}\right) = ₹\, 360$

Total selling price of 100 eggs

= 165 + 112.5 + 360 = ₹ 637.5

Total cost price of 100 eggs 100 × 6 = 600

Profit% = 637.5 – 600 = 37.5

Profit% $= \frac{37.5}{600} \times 100 = 6.25\%$

37. (a) A thermoscope shows changes in temperature. Galileo Galilei discovered the specific principle and built the first thermoscope in 1593.

38. (b) In a running race, when you cross last but one player that means you are running at the last position. So, after crossing your just next ahead runner, your position would be second from the last.

39. (b) Keyboard is different from the other as it is computer essential device used in all computer.

40. (b) Interest after 3 years $= \frac{275000 \times 8 \times 3}{100}$

= 66000

Loan amount after 3 years

= 66000 + 275000 = 341000

∴ Price of scooter = 341000 – 335000

= ₹ 6000

41. (b) Portion of tank filled in 1 hour when all the three pipes open together

$= \frac{1}{5} + \frac{1}{10} - \frac{1}{20} = \frac{4 + 2 - 1}{20}$

$= \frac{5}{20} = \frac{1}{4}$

∴ Time required to fill the tank $= \frac{1}{\frac{1}{4}}$

= 4 hours.

42. (b) Distance between two poles = 50 m

Distance covered by crossing 35 poles

= 34 × 50 = 1700 m = 1.70 km

Time to travel = 1 minute $= \frac{1}{60}$ hours

∴ Bus speed (in km/hr) $= \frac{1.70}{\frac{1}{60}}$

= 1.70 × 60 = 102 km/hr

43. (a)

44. (b) (sinA + cosA) × cosecA

$= (\sin A + \cos A) \times \frac{1}{\sin A}$

$= \frac{\sin A}{\sin A} + \frac{\cos A}{\sin A} = 1 + \cot A$

$= 1 + \frac{12}{5} = \frac{17}{5}$

45. (c) The frequency and wavelength of a wave are related. As frequency increases, wavelength decreases.

46. (c) The heptagon is sometimes referred to as the septagon.

47. (c) BRICS is a grouping that refers to the countries of Brazil, Russia, India, China and South Africa. They have been identified as the fastest growing economics in the world.

48. (c) Circumference is a length measure of outermost boundary of any circular area as perimeter is the length measure of the outermost boundary of any square area.

49. (a)

50. (b)

Letter	A	M	E	R	I	C	N	D
Code	1	7	3	4	6	5	8	9

Hence, code of **CANADA** is **518191**

51. (b)

52. (d) Let A's height is x m.
and B's height is y m.
Then, $x = \frac{5}{8} \times y \Rightarrow \frac{y}{x} = \frac{8}{5}$

53. (c) We know that
L.C.M. × H.C.F. = Product of the two number
$= \text{L.C.M.} \times 26 = 35828$
$= \text{L.C.M.} = \frac{35828}{26} = 1378$

54. (c)
4665, 4655, 4565, 4465, 4456
↓
Middle number

55. (a) The Karla Caves are a conglomeration of enticing rock-cut caves of Buddhist origin situated at Karli close to Lonavala in Maharashtra. These were constructed between 2nd-5th centuries.

56. (c) Let total number of children is n.
Then, number of children in the age (1 - 12) $= \frac{2}{3}n$
Again, number of children in the age (1 - 8) $= \frac{3}{4} \times \frac{2}{3}n = \frac{n}{2}$
So, number of children in the age (9 - 12) $= \frac{2}{3}n - \frac{n}{2} = \frac{n}{6}$
Hence, $\frac{1}{6}$ of children are in age (9 - 12).

57. (a) Rowlatt Acts, (February 1919), legislation was passed by the Imperial Legislative Council, the legislature of British India. The acts allowed certain political cases to be tried without juries and permitted internment of suspects without trial.

58. (b)

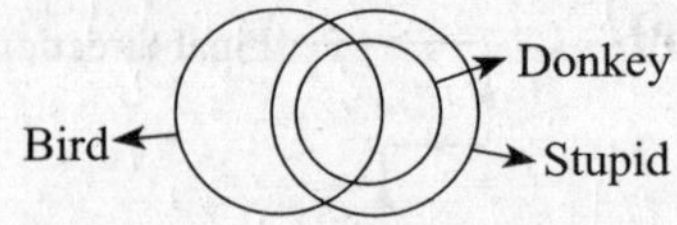

Hence, only conclusion 4 is correct

59. (c)

60. (a) Word arrangement in alphabetical order:
Simple, Singer, Single, Sinister
↓
Third word

61. (c) Selling price = 4200.
Loss% = 25%
∴ Cost price =
$\text{selling price} \times \left(\frac{100}{100 - \text{loss\%}}\right)$
$= 4200 \times \left(\frac{100}{100 - 25}\right) = 5600.$
Now, cost price = 5600
Profit% = 25%
$\therefore \text{Selling price} = 5600 \times \left(\frac{100 + 25}{100}\right)$
$= ₹\,7000$

62. (b) A hacker uses computer, networking or other skills to overcome a technical problem, and to gain unauthorized access to systems or networks.

63. (a) According to the given coding:
Sister is father. So, to call the sister, we call father.

64. (*)

65. (b) Let $\triangle ABC$ is a right isosceles triangle such that $\angle A = \angle C = \theta$ and $\angle B = 90°$

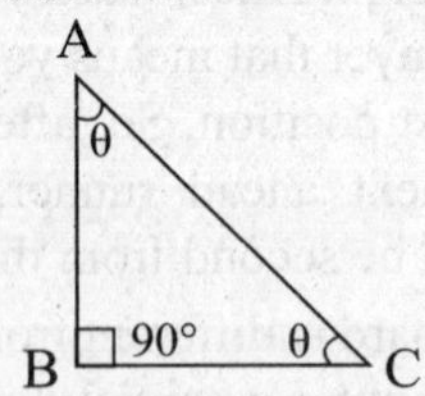

Now, in a triangle, sum of angles = 180°
$\angle A + \angle B + \angle C = 180$
$\theta + 90 + \theta = 180$
$2\theta = 180 - 90 \Rightarrow \theta = \frac{90}{2} = 45°$

66. (a) 1 hour = 3600 second

1 minute = 60 second

1 min. 12 second = 60 + 12 = 72 sec.

Required percent = $\frac{72}{3600} \times 100 = 2\%$

67. (c) Mrinalini Vikram Sarabhai was an Indian classical dancer, choreographer and instructor

68. (b) CCITRKE ⟶ CRICKET

↓ fifth letter

69. (b) Chetak is the horse ridden by Maharana Pratap at the Battle of Haldighati, fought on 21 June 1576, in the Aravalli Mountains of Rajasthan.

70. (c) The lens is located in the eye. It focuses the light rays that pass through it onto the retina in order to create clear images of objects. It works together with the cornea to refract, or bend, light.

71. (a) The President of India is the head of state and the commander-in-chief of the Indian Armed Forces whilst the elected prime minister acts as the head of the executive, and is responsible for running the union government.

72. (b) The Konark Sun Temple is one of the finest examples of Brahmin architecture and beliefs. This was built in the 13th century by King Narasimhadeva I (1238-1250 CE) of the Eastern Ganga Dynasty and dedicated to Sun God Surya.

73. (b) Penicillin antibiotics were the first medications to be effective against many bacterial infections caused by staphylococci and streptococci. It was discovered in 1928 by Scottish scientist Alexander Fleming.

74. (c) Teacher uses books to teach the students like that stethoscope is an acoustic medical device for listening to the internal sounds of an animal or human body.

75. (b) Luna 10 was the first spacecraft to go into orbit around the Moon, and the first human-made object to orbit any body beyond the Earth.

76. (a) **Ostrich** is flightless bird native to Africa. They are distinct with a long neck and legs and the ability to run at speed of about 65 km/h.

77. (c) Paleontology is the study of the history of life on Earth as based on fossils. Fossils are the remains of plants, animals, fungi, bacteria, and single-celled living things that have been replaced by rock material or impressions of organisms.

78. (d) Karnam Malleswari is an eminent Indian weight-lifter. She is famous for being the first Indian woman who won an Olympic bronze medal for India.

79. (b) Prime number between 50 and 100.:

53, 59, 61, 67, 71, 73, 79, 83, 89, 97

Hence, total number = 10.

80. (b) Year 2012 is a leap year. So, February will be 29 days and number of odd day in 2011 = 1 (365 days = 52 weeks + 1 day)

So, Christmas on 2012 = Tuesday.

81. (b)

82. (c) B is the father of A and A is the father of C so, B is grandfather of C.

(83-85) Babu's all answers were wrong.

So, answer for Q1 would be other than choice 1.

for Q2, correct choice would be either 1 or 2

for Q3, correct choice could be either 1, 2 or 3

for Q4, correct choice would be either 1 or 3.

Again, Diya fourth answer is wrong, so for Q4, correct choice could be either 1 or 3. Based on that, we can the table for correct answer as like this

	Amar	Babu	Cera	Diya
Q1	2×	1×	1×	3✓
Q2	4×	3×	2✓	4×
Q3	3×	4×	3×	1✓
Q4	3✓	2×	2×	4×

Hence, correct choice for Q1 $\longrightarrow$ 3, Q2 $\longrightarrow$ 2, Q3 $\longrightarrow$ 1 and Q4 $\longrightarrow$ 3

83. (b) Cera correct answer is Q2.

84. (a) For Q4 , Amar answer is correct.

85. (b) Diya Q1 and Q3 answer is correct.

86. (a) $\sqrt{(1-\sin^2\theta) \div (1-\cos^2\theta)}$

$\sqrt{\cos^2\theta \div \sin^2\theta} = \sqrt{\left(\frac{\cos\theta}{\sin\theta}\right)^2}$

$= \frac{\cos\theta}{\sin\theta} = \cot\theta$

87. (c)

(88-90)

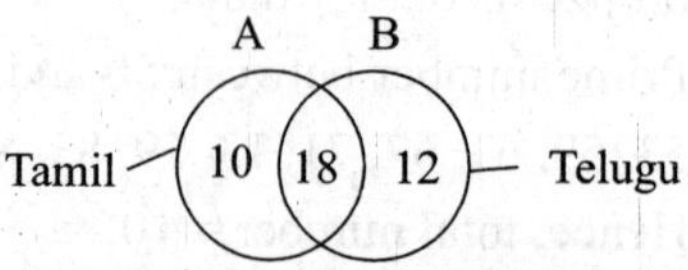

Number of students speak Tamil, n(A) = 28

" " " Telugu, n(B) = 30

Total number of students that speak either of Tamil or Telugu $n A\cup B = 40$

Number of students that speak both Tamil and Telugu $n(A\cap B) = n(A) + n(B) - n(A\cup B)$

$= 28 + 30 - 40 = 18$

88. (c) Number of students speak only Telugu

$= n(B) - n(A\cap B)$

$= 30 - 18 = 12$

89. (c) Number of students who can speak both Tamil and Telugu $= n(A\cap B) = 18$

90. (b) Number of students that can speak only Tamil $= n(A) - n(A\cap B)$

$= 28 - 18 = 10$

91. (c) My sister's brother means my brother. Now, father of my brother means my father and father's daughter is my sister. So, that girl is Rajiv's sister.

92. (b) Let x be Ramu's age and y be his son's age.

Now, $x = 4y$ ....(i)

$x + 5 = 3(y + 5)$ ...(ii)

$\Rightarrow 4y + 5 = 3y + 15$

$\Rightarrow y = 10$ and $x = 4\ (10) = 40$

93. (b) Located in Sri Lanka, the Golden Temple of Dambulla is a living Buddhist site inhabited by forest-dwelling Buddhist monks since the 3rd century BCE.

94. (a) A unicellular organism is an organism that consists of only one cell, unlike a multicellular organism that consists of more than one cell.

95. (c) "The first ever international cricket game was played between the USA and Canada in 1844 at the grounds of the St George's Cricket Club in New York."

96. (c) The Charminar is a massive arch built by Mohammed Quli Qutab Shah, in 1591 to commemorate the end of the plague in the city.

97. (c)

Roman		Language
X	$\longrightarrow$	10
C	$\longrightarrow$	100
VI	$\longrightarrow$	6

Now, CVI = 100 + 6 = 106

XCVI = 106 – 10 = 96

98. (b) First amendment was made through Constitution (First Amendment) Act,1951. It was moved by Pt. J.L. Nehru

99. (c) Let two consecutive numbers are n and (n + 1).

According to the question,

$3 \times n - 2\ (n + 1) = 5$

$3n - 2n - 2 = 5$

$n = 5 + 2 = 7$

So, first number n = 7

Second number (n + 1) = 7 + 1 = 8.

100. (a) There are seven continents in the world. Asia is the largest, Australia the smallest at almost a fifth of the size of Asia.

RRB NTPC stage-I Solved Paper

Held On 29th March 2016 (Shift-I)

1. Which Indian king used naval power to conquer parts of East Asia?
(a) Akbar
(b) Krishna deva Raya
(c) Rajendra Chola
(d) Shivaji

2. Pollination by wind is called?
(a) Hydrophily (b) Pollinophily
(c) Anemophily (d) Herbophily

3. Simplify $\sqrt{50} + \sqrt{18} - \sqrt{8}$
(a) $8\sqrt{2}$ (b) $7\sqrt{2}$ (c) $6\sqrt{2}$ (d) $5\sqrt{2}$

4. if a = ×, b = ÷ and c = +, find the value of **[7a5c1]b6**
(a) 4 (b) 6 (c) 5/3 (d) 7

5. Which revolutionary took his own life?
(a) Khudiram Bose
(b) Rash Behari Bose
(c) Bhagat Singh
(d) Chandrashekhar Azad

6. After allowing a discount of 20% on Marked price Kishore makes a profit of 12%. What percentage is the Marked price above the Cost price?
(a) 40% (b) 32% (c) 25% (d) 8%

7. Punched card is also called
(a) Hollerith card (b) Video card
(c) Sound card (d) Accelerator card

8. What smallest number should be added to the sum of squares of 15 and 14, so that the resulting number is a perfect square?
(a) 17 (b) 20 (c) 11 (d) 9

9. The ratio between the weights of gold and silver in an alloy is 17:3. If the weight of silver in the alloy is 2.7gm, find the weight of gold in the alloy?
(a) 12.6 gm (b) 15.3 gm
(c) 18 gm (d) 21.2 gm

10. Where was paper invented?
(a) China (b) India
(c) Zambia (d) Germany

11. Where is the Island of Seychelles located?
(a) Indian Ocean
(b) Pacific Ocean
(c) Atlantic Ocean
(d) The Southern Ocean

12. Find the odd one out: Chicken pox, Rubella, Flu, Meningitis
(a) Chicken pox (b) Rubella
(c) Flu (d) Meningitis

13. Find the value of:

$$\frac{(0.0112 - 0.0012) \text{ of } 0.14 + 0.25 \times 0.2}{0.02 \times 0.01}$$

(a) 257 (b) 25.7
(c) 2.57 (d) 0.0257

14. A points to B and says to a lady C "His mother is the only daughter of your father". If so, how is C related to B?
(a) Mother (b) Daughter
(c) Grandmother (d) Son

15. From where was Mangalyaan launched?
(a) Chennai (b) Sriharikota
(c) Trombay (d) Gopalpur, on sea

16. The sum of two digits of a number is 10. If the digits are interchanged, then its value increases by 18. Find the number.
(a) 46 (b) 64 (c) 19 (d) 28

17. In a certain code language. North = West, South = East. East = North, which direction does the sun rise?
(a) East (b) West
(c) North (d) South

18. **CAT : MOUSE** as **SNAKE :** ____________
(a) Reptile (b) Mongoose
(c) Hole (d) Poison

19. If △○ = 52, □# = 43 what is #△□?
(a) 523 (b) 245 (c) 432 (d) 354

20. Name the official language of Brazil?
(a) Portuguese (b) German
(c) Italian (d) Brazilian

21. Which number will fit both the series of numbers? **Series A: 1, 4, 9... Series B: 1, 8, 27...**
(a) 42 (b) 36 (c) 64 (d) 25

22. Which of the following is the name of a medieval Indian book on mathematics?
(a) Vastushastra (b) Leelavati
(b) Panchadashi (d) Roopmati

23. Din-i-llahi was promoted by
(a) Babur (b) Bahadur Shah
(c) Akbar (d) Humayun

24. If 1/4th of the wall is painted blue, 1/2 is painted yellow and remaining 3 m is painted white, what is the length of the wall?
(a) 10 (b) 8 (c) 16 (d) 12

25. The runs scored by two batsmen over 7 matches are given below. Which batsman's average was better?

Batsman 1	**42**	**51**	**09**	**78**	**63**	**20**	**12**
Batsman 2	**30**	**22**	**91**	**76**	**84**	**11**	**07**

(a) Batsman 1 - 39.3 (b) Batsman 1 - 45.9
(c) Batsman 1 - 43.2 (d) Batsman 2 - 45.9

26. In which year was RBI nationalized?
(a) 1969 (b) 1947 (c) 1949 (d) 1974

27. Which is the only organ in the human body that can regrow/regenerate?
(a) Spleen (b) Brain
(c) Liver (d) Pancreas

28. Which is the largest non-polar desert in the World?
(a) Kalahari (b) Gobi
(c) Sahara (d) Great Australian

29. Who wrote the National song of India?
(a) Rabindranath Tagore
(b) Bankim Chandra Chatterjee
(c) Mohammed Iqbal
(d) Chitragupta

30. If **3 : 27 :: 5 :?**
(a) 25 (b) 125 (c) 250 (d) 625

31. Find the value of $\sin^2 30\cos^2 45 + 4\tan^2 30 + (1/2)\sin^2 90 - 2\cos^2 90 + 1/24$
(a) 3 (b) 4 (c) 2 (d) 1

32. Where in the human body can you find the islets of Langerhans?
(a) Small intestine (b) Pancreas
(c) Stomach (d) Heart

33. Where can you find the Kunchikal waterfalls?
(a) Kerala (b) Karnataka
(c) Andhra Pradesh (d) Telangana

34. Which single discount will be equal to two successive discounts of 12% and 5%?
(a) 17% (b) 8.5%
(c) 16.4% (d) 15.2%

35. Which of the following gases are responsible for the greenhouse gas effect on Earth?
(a) Water Vapour and Carbon dioxide
(b) Carbon dioxide and Nitrogen
(c) Carbon dioxide and Methane
(d) Ozone and Methane

36. If **ALPHA = 36, BETA = 26**, then **DELTA = ?**
(a) 38 (b) 31 (c) 40 (d) 36

37. What is the technology used in a compact disc?
(a) Electrical (b) Laser
(c) Electro magnetic (d) Aeronautical

38. In a camp 180 students had ration for 20 days. How many students should leave the camp if the ration should last for 25 days?
(a) 36 (b) 24 (c) 28 (d) 40

39. Fill in the blanks: sinA = ____________ × cosA
(a) sin A (b) tanA
(c) cotA (d) cosA

40 If x is a prime number, LCM of x and its successive number would be

(a) x (b) x+1

(c) x(x +1) (d) $\frac{x}{x+1}$

41. Jimmy Wales and Larry Sanger are associated with?

(a) Wikipedia (b) Google

(c) Whatsapp (d) Facebook

42. The average age of 27 students of a class is 22. If the age of the teacher is also added to their ages, then the average increases by one. Find the age of the teacher.

(a) 42 (b) 48 (c) 50 (d) 52

43. Which is the brightest star in our night sky?

(a) Canopus (b) Sirius A

(c) Vega (d) Spica

44. Madhubani painting style is native to which state?

(a) Orissa (b) Andhra Pradesh

(c) Bihar (d) Madhya Pradesh

45. A certain sum when invested at 5% interest compounded annually for 3 years yields an interest of ₹ 2,522. Find the Principal?

(a) ₹ 12,522 (b) ₹ 15,200

(c) ₹ 16,000 (d) ₹ 17,200

46. If **SUN = 108, MOON = 114** what is **STAR** = ?

(a) 120 (b) 116

(c) 122 (d) 128

47. If **1= 2, 3 = 6, 4 = 8**, and + = –, what would be the value of **41 + 34 + 13 = ?**

(a) –88 (b) 88 (b) 12 (d) – 12

48. Which of the following is always present in organic compounds?

(a) Carbon (b) Nitrogen

(c) Sulphur (d) Potassium

49. In an equilateral triangle ABC, D, E, F are the mid points of AB, BC and AC respectively. The quadrilateral BEFD is a

(a) Square (b) Rectangle

(c) Parallelogram (d) Rhombus

DIRECTIONS (Qs. 50-52): *The below table gives rice production in each year. Read and answer the following questions.*

Year	Production in tons
2005	325
2006	438
2007	429
2008	258
2009	495

50. What percentage was the decline in production in year 2008 compared to 2007?

(a) 40% (b) 51%

(c) 67% (d) 45%

51. What is the increased percentage of production in 2009 compared to year 2005?

(a) 38.1% (b) 29.2%

(c) 52.3% (d) 46.3%

52. What was the average production of rice in the period 2005-2009?

(a) 378 (b) 389

(c) 399 (d) 412

53. Below are given statements followed by some conclusions. You have to take the given statements to be true even if they seem to be at variance with the commonly known facts.

Statements:

1. Health insurance in India caters only to rich.
2. Health insurance sector should be regulated.

Conclusion:

I. Health insurance sector should be nationalized

II. Health insurance is not required for the poor.

Decide which of the given conclusions logically follow(s) from the given statements.

(a) Neither I nor II follow

(b) Only conclusion I follows

(c) Either I or II follow

(d) Only conclusion II follow's

54. If Reena sold 12 mobile phones for ₹ 188,160 which cost ₹ 14,056 per phone, what was the total profit made by her?

(a) ₹ 19,488 (b) ₹ 17,621
(c) ₹ 21,014 (d) ₹ 18,958

55. Sita told her friend Gita "I am leaving today and will reach Mumbai tomorrow for my exams starting the day after tomorrow, which is Friday". What day is tomorrow in this conversation?

(a) Wednesday (b) Thursday
(b) Tuesday (d) Saturday

56. The perimeter of a rectangle is 28 cm. If the length is 5/2 times its breadth, find the length and breadth of the rectangle.

(a) 9 & 5 (b) 10 & 4
(c) 6 & 7 (d) 11 & 3

57. What comes next in the series?

B, D, H, N ?

(a) V (b) P (c) S (d) W

58. Which country has won maximum number of World cup titles in football?

(a) Italy (b) Argentina
(c) Brazil (d) France

59. Who was the first to score a perfect 10 in Olympics in gymnastics?

(a) Nadia Comaneci (b) Daniela Silivas
(c) Alexander Dityatin (d) Mary Lou Retton

60. Below are given statements followed by some conclusions. You have to take the given statements to be true even if they seem to be at variance with the commonly known facts.

Statements:

(1) Because of motor vehicles like cars, pollution has increased manifold.

(2) Respiratory diseases are increasing due to pollution.

Conclusions:

I. If cars were not there pollution would be nil.

II. Doctors earn a lot due to pollution.

Decide which of the given conclusions logically follow(s) from the given statements.

(a) Either I or II follow
(b) Neither I nor II follow
(c) Only conclusion I follows
(d) Only conclusion II follows

DIRECTIONS (Qs. 61-63): *Read the following information and answer the following questions below.*

In a class of 90 students, 80 students like burger or pizza. 62 like burger and 56 like pizza.

61. How many don't like burger?

(a) 18 (b) 28 (c) 38 (d) 48

62. How many like neither burger nor pizza?

(a) 10 (b) 28 (c) 16 (d) 14

63. How many like both burger and pizza?

(a) 24 (b) 38 (c) 32 (d) 18

64. If **COW ÷ CW = 13**, what might be the value of **COW**?

(a) 272 (b) 195
(c) 323 (d) 387

65. Find the mean of the first 6 prime numbers?

(a) 14/3 (b) 3
(b) 41/6 (d) 13/2

66. Which is the largest fresh water lake in the World?

(a) Lake Victoria (b) Lake Erie
(c) Lake Superior (d) Lake Ontario

67. Which of the following is called Aurum?

(a) Bronze (b) Gold
(c) Silver (d) Copper

68. If A's sister's husband is B's mother-in-law's son-in-law, how is A related to B?

(a) Father (b) Father-in-law
(c) Brother-in-law (d) Husband

69. Simplify: $\left[2\frac{1}{3} - 1\frac{1}{2}\right]$ of $\frac{3}{5} + 1\frac{2}{5} \div 2\frac{1}{3}$

(a) $\frac{1}{10}$ (b) $\frac{3}{10}$
(c) $1\frac{1}{10}$ (d) 1

70. 'Queensberry rules' is the code followed in which sport?
(a) Tennis (b) Cricket
(c) Boxing (d) Equestrian

71. World environment day is observed on
(a) February 28 (b) May 16
(c) June 05 (d) September 12

72. 'E' is related to 'BH' in the same way as 'N' is related to?
(a) IP (b) KQ (c) LP (d) DE

73. If angles of a quadrilateral are in the ratio 3:5:9:13, find the largest angle?
(a) 165 (b) 180
(c) 156 (d) 190

74. Headquarters of UNESCO is located at
(a) Moscow (b) New York
(c) London (d) Paris

75. Who was the last Mughal Emperor?
(a) Babur (b) Jehangir
(c) Akbar (d) Bahadur Shah

DIRECTIONS (Qs. 76-78): *Read the following information and answer the following questions below.*

Bindu is standing exactly in the middle of a line of girls. Asha is 6th to the left of Bindu and Ritu is 16th to Bindu's right.

76. What is Bindu's position in the line?
(a) 11 (b) 14 (c) 16 (d) 17

77. What should be the minimum number of girls in the line?
(a) 22 (b) 28 (c) 33 (d) 32

78. What is Asha's position in the line?
(a) 22 (b) 12 (c) 18 (d) 11

79. At a telephone exchange, three phones ring at intervals of 20 sec, 24 sec and 30 seconds. If they ring together at 11:25 a.m, when will they next ring together?
(a) 11:29am. (b) 11:27 a.m.
(c) 11:51 am. (d) 12:29 p.m.

80. The diagonals of a rhombus is 8m and 6m respectively. Find its area.
(a) 48 sq.m. (b) 24 sq.m.
(c) 12 sq.m. (d) 96 sq.m.

81. With which sport is the term 'Tee' connected?
(a) Hockey (b) Polo
(c) Golf (d) Badminton

82. Which of the following is reared for its fleece/ fiber?
(a) Alpaca (b) Alabama
(c) Apache (d) Alluvial

83. Below are given statements followed by some conclusions. You have to take the given statements to be true even if they seem to be at variance with the commonly known facts.

Statements:

1 Some kids are clever.
2 Some kids are players.

Conclusion:

I. Some players are clever
II. Some clever kids are players.

Decide which of the given conclusions logically follow (s) from the given statements.

(a) Only conclusion I follows
(b) Only conclusion II follows
(c) Both conclusion I and II follows
(d) Neither conclusion I nor II follows

84. If cost price of 5 cars is equal to selling price of 4 cars. Find the percentage of profit or loss
(a) 10% Profit (b) 10% Loss
(c) 25% Profit (d) 25% Loss

85. Divide 13,680 in three parts such that 1st part is 3/5th of the third part and the ratio between 2nd and 3rd part is 4:7. How much is the first part?
(a) 3780 (b) 6300
(c) 3600 (d) 4800

86. Geetha weighs 11.235 kg. Her sister weighs 1.4 times her weight. Find their combined weight?
(a) 15.729 kg. (b) 25.964 kg.
(c) 26.964 kg. (d) 26.946 kg.

87. Granite is an example of
(a) Metamorphic rock (b) Sedimentary rock
(c) Igneous rock (d) Artificial stone

88. Which of the following is the currency of Thailand?
(a) Rupee (b) Ringgit
(c) Baht (d) Yuan

89. Simplify $\frac{81x^2 - 49y^2}{9x + 7y}$
(a) $9x + 7y$ (b) $9x - 7y$
(c) $9x$ (d) $7y$

90. Which of the following is a land locked country?
(a) Azerbaijan (b) Kazakhstan
(c) Pakistan (d) Bangladesh

91. If ! = ÷, # = +, ^ = ×, then calculate the value of **32!44^7#5**
(a) 58 (b) 61 (c) 64 (d) 55

92. Smita can finish a work in 12 days and Sam can finish the same work in 9 days. After working together for 4 days they both leave the job. What is the fraction of unfinished work?
(a) 1/2 (b) 7/9 (b) 2/9 (d) 1/4

93. What did Edward Jenner pioneer?
(a) Vaccination
(b) Electrocution
(c) Dialysis
(d) Open heart surgery

94. Who is called the Frontier Gandhi?
(a) Muhammad All Jinnah
(b) Mahatma Gandhi
(c) Khan Abdul Ghaffar Khan
(d) Bal Gangadhar Tilak

95. What is the minimum age for getting elected to the Lok Sabha?
(a) 18 (b) 21 (c) 16 (d) 25

96. Azhar can complete a journey in 10 hours. He travels the first half of the journey at a speed of 21 km/hr. and the balance at 24km/hr. Find the total distance in km?
(a) 234 (b) 225
(c) 224 (d) 232

97. A deep crack in a glacier is called
(a) A crevice (b) A crevasse
(c) A crack (d) A cleft

98. Which number will fit in '?' place in the following series? **2, ?, 12, 20, 30, 42**
(a) 2 (b) 4 (c) 6 (d) 8

99. Where is the headquarters of Interpol located?
(a) Paris (b) London
(c) Lyon (d) Brussels

100. Ram and Rahim standing at a distance of 680m run towards each other at a speed of 8m/sec and 9m/sec respectively. After how long will they meet?
(a) 17 sec (b) 24 sec
(c) 40 sec (d) 36 sec

Hints & Solutions

1. (c) The Medieval Chola king Rajendra Chola I sent a naval expedition to Indochina, the Malay Peninsula and Indonesia in 1025 to subdue Srivijaya.

2. (c) Wind pollination ('Anemophily') is the process of the transfer of pollen from one individual plant to another, whereby the pollen is carried by air currents.

3. (c) $\sqrt{50} + \sqrt{18} - \sqrt{8}$

$= \sqrt{2 \times 5 \times 5} + \sqrt{2 \times 3 \times 3} - \sqrt{2 \times 2 \times 2}$

$= 5\sqrt{2} + 3\sqrt{2} - 2\sqrt{2} = 6\sqrt{2}$

4. (b) [7a5c1]b6 = [7 × 5 + 1] ÷ 6
= [35 + 1] ÷ 6 = 36 ÷ 6 = 6

5. (d) Chandra Shekhar Azad was an Indian revolutionary who reorganised the Hindustan Republican Association into Hindustan Socialist Republican Army (HSRA) after the death of Ram Prasad Bismil, Roshan Singh, Rajendra Nath Lahiri and Ashfaqulla Khan.

6. (a) Let marked price is ₹100.
discount = 20%
Then, selling price
$$= 100 \times \left(\frac{100-20}{100}\right) = 80$$
Now, profit% = 12%
$$\text{So, cost price} = 80 \times \frac{100}{100+12} = 71$$
Hence, required percent
$$= \frac{100-71}{71} \times 100 = 40\%$$

7. (a) Punch cards (Hollerith cards/IBM cards) were paper cards with several perforated holes that were punched by hand or machine to represent data. These cards were used to store and access information by entering the card into the computer.

8. (b) Sum of squares of 15 and 14
$= (15)^2 + (14)^2 = 225 + 196 = 421$
Now, $(20)^2 < 421 < (21)^2$
$400 > 421 < 441$
So, $441 - 421 = 20.$
Hence, number 20 should be added in 421 to make it perfect square.

9. (b)
$$\frac{\text{Weight of gold}}{\text{Weight of silver}} = \frac{17}{3}$$
$$\frac{\text{Weight of gold}}{2.7} = \frac{17}{3}$$
$$\therefore \text{Weight of gold} = \frac{17}{3} \times 2.7 = 15.3 \text{ gram}$$

10. (a) Paper was invented around 100 BC in China under the Han Dynasty.

11. (a) Seychelles is an archipelago country in the Indian Ocean. With a population of 94,228, it has the smallest population of any sovereign African country.

12. (d) Meningitis is an inflammation (swelling) of the protective membranes covering the brain and spinal cord.

13. (a)
$$\frac{(0.0112 - 0.0012) \text{ of } 0.14 + 0.25 \times 0.2}{0.02 \times 0.01}$$
$$= \frac{(0.0100) \times 0.14 + 0.25 \times 0.2}{0.02 \times 0.01}$$
$$= \frac{0.0014 + 0.050}{0.0002} = \frac{0.0514}{0.0002} = 257.$$

14. (a) According to A, B's mother is the only daughter of C's father means C is the mother of B.

15. (b) Mangalyaan was launched on board of PSLV C25 rocket from Sriharikota in Andhra Pradesh on November 5, 2013 with aim of studying Martian surface.

16. (a) Let the two digits number is 10m + n.
Where m and n are its two digit. (m = ten's place, n = unit's place)
When digit revers then, new number 10n + m.
According to the question, m + n = 10...(i)
and, 10n + m – (10m + n) = 18
9n – 9m = 18 ⇒ n – m = 2...(ii)
From equation (i) and (ii), we get
2n = 12 ⇒ n = 6
m = 10 – 6 = 4
Hence, number = 4 × 10 + 6 = 46

17. (c) We know that sun rises in the East direction. and in the given code language east is called North. So, sun rises in the North.

18. (b) CAT and MOUSE are pair words used in pair, like that SNAKE and MONGOOSE are pair word. And first word indicate one who can eat second one.

19. (d)

Symbol	△	○	□	#
Code	5	2	4	3

Hence, #△□ = 354.

20. (a) Portuguese is the official widely spoken language in Brazil. With 204 million speakers, Brazil is the world's most populated Portuguese-speaking country.

21. (c) Seriese A: 1, 4, 9, ... 64

$(1)^2, (2)^2, (3)^2, \ldots\ldots (8)^2,$

Seriese B: 1, 8, 27, ... 64

$(1)^3, (2)^3, (3)^3, \ldots\ldots (4)^3,$

Hence, number 64 will fit in both series.

22. (b)

23. (c) "Religion of God" was propounded by Akbar, intending to merge the best elements of the religions to reconcile the differences that divided his subjects.

24. (d) Let the length of total wall = L m

Then, $\frac{L}{4}$ is painted in blue.

$\frac{L}{2}$ is painted in yellow.

Remaining wall $= L - \frac{L}{2} - \frac{L}{4} = \frac{L}{4}$.

Now, $\frac{L}{4} = 3 \Rightarrow L = 3 \times 4 = 12$ m.

25. (d) Average run scored by batsman 1:

$= \frac{42 + 51 + 09 + 78 + 63 + 20 + 12}{7}$

$= 39.28$

Average run scored by batsman 2:

$= \frac{30 + 22 + 91 + 76 + 84 + 11 + 07}{7}$

$= 45.86$

Hence, average of batsman 2 is good.

26. (c) The RBI was nationalised on 1st January, 1949 on the basis of the Reserve Bank of India Act, 1948.

27. (c) The liver is the only organ that can regenerate itself. It can actually be split in half and transplanted into two different recipients, and both the portions will regenerate to original size.

28. (c) The largest desert in the world is the Sahara, in North Africa, measuring roughly 3.5 million square miles.

29. (b) Bankim Chandra Chattopadhyay was a Bengali, writer, poet and a journalist who composed our National Song 'Vande Mataram' during the freedom struggle.

30. (b) $3 : 27 :: 5 : 125$

$3 \rightarrow (3)^3 \qquad 5 \rightarrow (5)^3$

31. (c) $\sin^2 30° \cdot \cos^2 45° + 4\tan^2 30° + \frac{1}{2}\sin^2 90° - 2\cos^2 90° + \frac{1}{24}$

$\left(\frac{1}{2}\right)^2 \cdot \left(\frac{1}{\sqrt{2}}\right)^2 + 4\left(\frac{1}{\sqrt{3}}\right)^2 + \frac{1}{2}(1)^2 - 2.(0)^2 + \frac{1}{24}$

$= \frac{1}{4} \cdot \frac{1}{2} + \frac{4}{3} + \frac{1}{2} + \frac{1}{24}$

$= \frac{1}{8} + \frac{4}{3} + \frac{1}{2} + \frac{1}{24}$

$= \frac{3 + 32 + 12 + 1}{24} = \frac{48}{24} = 2$

32. (b) The pancreatic islets of Langerhans contain its endocrine (hormone-producing) cells, discovered in 1869 by German Paul Langerhans.

33. (b) The Kunchikal Falls is found in Shimoga, Karnataka, in the Agumbe Valley. It falls from a height of 1493 ft., making it the tallest waterfall in India.

34. (c) Let the original value is 100.

After first discount, value

$= 100 \times \left(\frac{100 - 12}{100}\right) = 88$

After second discount value

$= 88 \times \left(\frac{100 - 5}{100}\right) = 83.6$

Difference = 100 – 83.6 = 16.4%

35. (*) Greenhouse gases increase the temperature of the Earth's surface. Primary greenhouse gases are water vapour, CO_2, methane, N_2O and Ozone.

36. (c)

A	L	P	H	A
↓	↓	↓	↓	↓
1	12	16	8	1

Alphabet position

= 1 + 12 + 16 + 8 + 1 = 38

Now, $= 38 - 2 = 36$

Similarly, B → 2, E → 5, T → 20, A → 1

$= 2 + 5 + 20 + 1 = 28$

Now, $28 - 2 = 26$

Then, D → 4, E → 5, L → 12, T → 20, A → 1

$= 4 + 5 + 12 + 20 + 1 = 42,$

Now, $42 - 2 = 40$

37. (b) The compact disc is an evolution of LaserDisc technology, where a focused laser beam is used that enables the high information density required for high-quality digital audio signals.

38. (a) Let x be the number of students who remain in the camp.

Then, $180 \times 20 = x \times 25 \Rightarrow x = 144$

Number of student who left $180 - 144 = 36$

39. (b) $\sin A = x \times \cos A$

$$x = \frac{\sin A}{\cos A} = \tan A$$

40. (c) x is a prime number.

It's successive number $= (x + 1)$

L.C.M. of two number $= x \,.\, (x + 1)$.

41. (a)

42. (c) Total age of 27 students $= 27 \times 22$

Let the age of the teacher is x year.

Then, age of students and teacher $= (27 \times 22 + x)$

According to the question,

New average $= 22 + 1 = 23$ years

So, $\frac{(27 \times 22 + x)}{28} = 23$

$27 \times 22 + x = 23 \times 28$

$x = 23 \times 28 - 27 \times 22$

$x = 644 - 594 = 50$

Teacher's age $= 50$ years.

43. (b)

44. (c) Madhubani painting, also referred to as Mithila Art, is characterized by line drawings filled in by bright colours and contrasts or patterns. The work is done on freshly plastered or a mud walls.

45. (c) Let principal is ₹ x.

Then, $P\left[\left(1 + \frac{r}{100}\right)^t - 1\right] = \text{C.I.}$

$P\left[\left(1 + \frac{5}{100}\right)^3 - 1\right] = 2522$

$P[(1.05)^3 - 1] = 2522$

$P = \frac{2522}{0.157} = ₹\ 16{,}000.$

46. (b) S → 19, U → 21, N → 14 (Alphabet position)

$= 19 + 21 + 14 = 54$

Now, $54 \times 2 = 108.$

M → 13, O → 15, O → 15, N → 14

$= 13 + 15 + 15 + 14 = 57$

Now, $= 57 \times 2 = 114$

Then, S → 19, T → 20, A → 1, R → 18

$= 19 + 20 + 1 + 18 = 58$

Now, $= 58 \times 2 = 116.$

47. (d) $41 + 34 + 13 \Rightarrow 82 - 68 - 26 = -12$

48. (a) Organic compounds contain carbon. Often, other elements like, sulfur, nitrogen and oxygen, are bonded to the carbons.

49. (d)

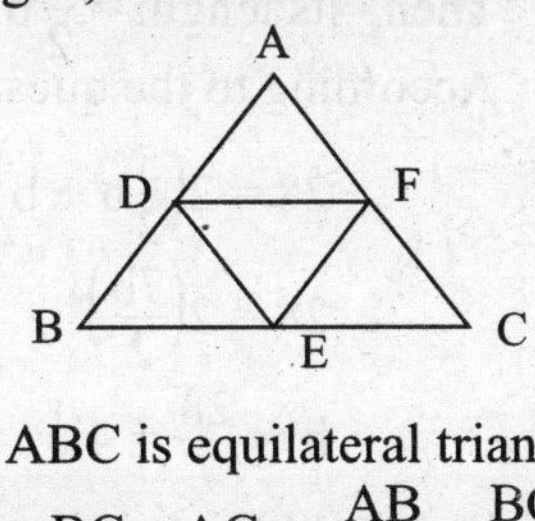

$\triangle$ABC is equilateral triangle,

So, $AB = BC = AC \Rightarrow \frac{AB}{2} = \frac{BC}{2} = \frac{AC}{2}$

$\Rightarrow BD = BE$

From $\triangle$ BDE, BD = BE and $\angle$DBE = 60°

So, $\angle$BDE = $\angle$BED = 60°

$\therefore$ BE = DE

Similarly, from $\triangle$ ECF, CE = EF.

In $\square$ BDFE, BD = DF = EF = BE

Hence, $\square$ BDFE is Rhombus.

50. (a) Decrease is production in year 2008 compared to 2007 = 258 – 429 = –171

Percentage decrease $= \frac{171}{429} \times 100 = 40\%$

51. (c) Increase in production in year 2009 compared to 2005 = 495 – 325 = 170

Percentage increase $= \frac{170}{325} \times 100 = 52.3\%$

52. (b) Average production of rice

$$= \frac{325 + 438 + 429 + 258 + 495}{5}$$

$$= \frac{1945}{5} = 389$$

53. (a) Neither conclusion I nor conclusion II follow.

54. (a) Cost price of 12 mobile phones

= 12 × 14056 = 168672.

Selling price of 12 mobile phones = 188160

Profit = 188160 – 168672 = 19488.

55. (b) Day after tomorrow is Friday

So, tomorrow will be Thursday.

56. (b) Perimeter of the rectangle = 2 (length + breadth)

Let the breadth of the rectangle is b

Then, its length $= \frac{5}{2}$b.

According to the question,

$$28 = 2\left(\frac{5}{2}b + b\right)$$

$$28 = 2\left(\frac{7b}{2}\right)$$

$$b = \frac{28}{7} = 4$$

breadth (b) = 4

length $= \frac{5}{2}b = \frac{5}{2} \times 4 = 10.$

57. (a) B , D , H , N , V (+2, +4, +6, +8)

58. (c) Brazil have won five times, and they are the only team to have played in every tournament.

59. (a) Perfect 10 refers to a score of 10.00 for a single routine in artistic gymnastics. The first person to score a perfect 10 was Romanian Nadia Comăneci, at the 1976 Olympic Games in Montreal.

60. (b) Here, from given statements, neither conclusion I nor II follow.

61-63:

Number of students like Burger or Pizza n(A$\cap$B) = 80

" " " Burger = n (A) = 62

" " " Pizza = n(B) = 56

" " " both Burger and Pizza

n(A$\cap$B) = n(A) + n(B) – n(A$\cup$B)

= 62 + 56 – 80 = 38.

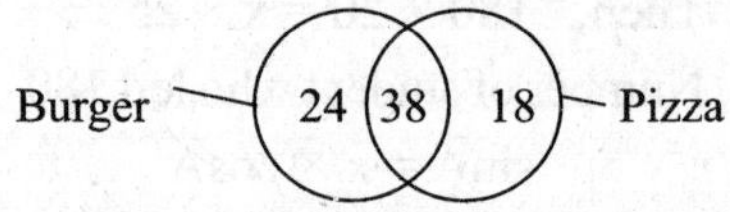

61. (b) Number of students don't like Burger

= n(A$\cup$B) – n(A) + (90 – 80)

= 80 – 62 + 10 = 28

62. (a) Number of students don't like any two of them = 90 – 80 = 10

63. (b) Number of students like both Burger and Pizza n(A$\cap$B) = 38

64. (b) Among the given options only 195 is divisible by 13.

Hence, COW = 195

65. (c) First 6 prime numbers are 2, 3, 5, 7, 11 and 13

$$\text{Mean} = \frac{2 + 3 + 5 + 7 + 11 + 13}{6} = \frac{41}{6}.$$

66. (c) Lake Superior is the largest lake in North America; largest freshwater lake in the world by surface area and the third-largest by volume. Its surface area is 31,700 square miles. The lake is 350 miles long, 160 miles wide, and 483 feet deep on average.

67. (b) Gold is also known as Aurum.

68. (d) Let A's sister is P and Q is P's husband and R is Q's mother.

Then,

(–)R
|
(+)Q ⟺ (–)P —— (+)A ⟺ (–)B
Spouse   Spouse

69. (c) $\left[2\frac{1}{3}-1\frac{1}{2}\right]$ of $\frac{3}{5}+1\frac{2}{5}\div 2\frac{1}{3}$

$\left[\frac{7}{3}-\frac{3}{2}\right]$ of $\frac{3}{5}+\frac{7}{5}\div\frac{7}{3}$

$\left[\frac{14-9}{6}\right]$ of $\frac{3}{5}+\frac{7}{5}\times\frac{3}{7}$

$\frac{5}{6}\times\frac{3}{5}+\frac{3}{5}=\frac{1}{2}+\frac{3}{5}=\frac{11}{10}=1\frac{1}{10}$

70. (c) The Marquess of Queensberry Rules are a code of generally accepted rules in the sport of boxing.

71. (c) World Environment Day is celebrated on the 5th of June every year, for encouraging awareness and action for the protection of our environment.

72. (b) B, E, H (+3, +3) Simply K, N, Q (+3, +3)

73. (c) Sum of all angles of any quadrilateral = 360°

$3x + 5x + 9x + 13x = 360$

$30x = 360 \Rightarrow x = \frac{360}{30} = 12$

Largest angle $13 \times 12 = 156°$.

74. (d) Located on the Place de Fontenoy, in Paris, the main building houses the Headquarters of UNESCO was inaugurated on 3 November 1958. The Y-shaped design was invented by three architects of different nationalities under the direction of an international committee.

75. (d) Bahadur Shah Zafar (24 October 1775–7 November 1862) was the last Mughal emperor. He was the second son of and became the successor to his father, Akbar II, upon his death on 28 September 1837.

76-78: Asha ←10 places→ Bindu ←6 places→ ←16 places→ Ritu

76. (d) Bindu's position in the line = 16 + 1 = 17.

77. (c) Minimum no. of girl = 17 + 17 – 1 = 33.

78. (d) Asha's position in the line = 10 + 1 = 11.

79. (b) L.C.M. of 20, 24 and 30 sec.

$20 = 2 \times 2 \times 5$

$24 = 2 \times 2 \times 2 \times 3$

$30 = 2 \times 3 \times 5$

$= 2 \times 2 \times 3 \times 5 \times 2 = 120$ sec. = 2 min.

Time when they ring together

= 11:25 + 2 = 11:27

80. (b) Area of the rhombus $=\frac{1}{2}\times$ (product of diagonals)

$=\frac{1}{2}\times(8\times 6)=24$

81. (c) A tee is a stand used to support a stationary ball so that the player can strike it, particularly in golf, tee ball, American football, and rugby.

82. (a)

83. (d)

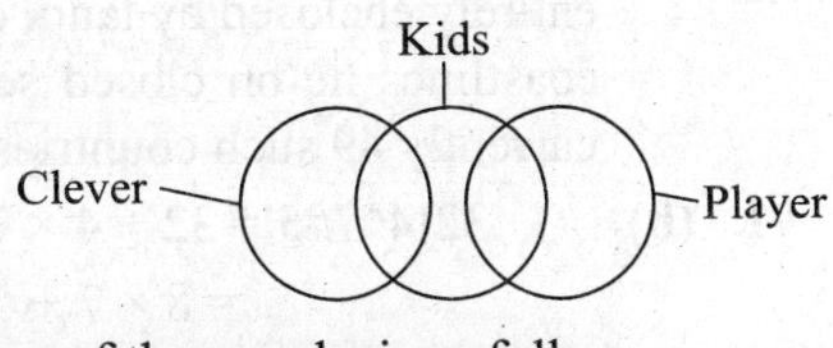

None of the conclusions follow.

84. (c) Let cost price of 5 cars = 500

Then, cost price of 1 car = 100

Again, selling price of 4 car = 500

Then, selling price of 1 car $=\frac{500}{4}=125$

Profit = 125 – 100 = 25

Profit% $=\frac{25}{100}\times 100 = 25\%$.

85. (a) Let second part is 4x, then third part is 7x

and first part $=\frac{3}{5}(7x)=\frac{21x}{5}$

According to the question,

$\frac{21x}{5}+4x+7x=13680$

$$\frac{76x}{5} = 13680$$

$$x = \frac{13680 \times 5}{76} = 900$$

$$\text{first part} = \frac{21x}{5} = \frac{21 \times 900}{5} = 3780$$

86. (c) Geetha sister weight = 1.4 × Geetha's weight

= 1.4 × 11.235 kg.

Combined weight = Geetha weight + her sister weight

= 11.235 + 1.4 × 11.235

= 11.235 + 15.729 = 26.964 kg

87. (c) Granite is a light-colored igneous, hard rock with grains large enough to be visible with the unaided eye.

88. (c) Baht banknotes and coins are issued by the Bank of Thailand. The baht is the official currency of Thailand.

89. (b) $$\frac{81x^2 - 49y^2}{9x + 7y} = \frac{(9x)^2 - (7y)^2}{9x + 7y} = \frac{(9x - 7y)(9x + 7y)}{9x + 7y} = (9x - 7y)$$

90. (b) A landlocked state is a sovereign state entirely enclosed by land, or whose only coastlines lie on closed seas. There are currently 49 such countries.

91. (b) 32!4^7#5 = 32 ÷ 4 × 7 + 5

= 8 × 7 + 5 = 61.

92. (c) Work finish by Smita in one day = $\frac{1}{12}$

" " Sam " " = $\frac{1}{9}$

Work finish by together working in one day = $\frac{1}{12} + \frac{1}{9} = \frac{3+4}{36} = \frac{7}{36}$

Work finish by together working in 4 days

$= 4 \times \frac{7}{36} = \frac{7}{9}$

Remaining work = $1 - \frac{7}{9} = \frac{9-7}{9} = \frac{2}{9}$

93. (a) Edward Jenner pioneered vaccination and invented, the first vaccine for smallpox, to create immunity.

94. (c) The Frontier Gandhi was Pashtun leader and nonviolent activist Abdul Ghaffar Khan, also known as Badshah Khan.

95. (d) Article 84(b) of Constitution of India provides that the minimum age for Lok Sabha election shall be 25 years.

96. (c) Let total distance to cover is 2d km.

Then, time taken to cover half distance (d km) = $\frac{d}{21}$

Time taken to cover second half distance (d km) = $\frac{d}{24}$

Total time taken = 10 hr

$$\therefore \frac{d}{21} + \frac{d}{24} = 10 \Rightarrow \frac{(24+21)d}{24 \times 21} = 10$$

$$d = \frac{10 \times 24 \times 21}{45} = 112$$

Hence, total distance 2d = 224

97. (b) A crevasse is a deep open crack in a glacier, formed when a magma chamber under a glacier causes melting and cracking and causes the glacier to slide into the ocean on the magma.

98. (c) 2 , 6 , 12 , 20 , 30 , 42

(+4, +6, +8, +10, +12)

Hence, required number is '6'.

99. (c)

100. (c) Ram → ←(680 – d)→ Rahim

← d m →

Let Ram meets Rahim after running d m.

Then, $\frac{d}{8} = \frac{(680-d)}{9}$

or $9d = 8(680 - d)$

$(9 + 8)d = 8 \times 680$

$d = \frac{8 \times 680}{17} = 320$ m.

Time taken to cover 320 = $\frac{320}{8}$ = 40 sec.

RRB NTPC stage-I Solved Paper

Held On 30th March 2016 (Shift-III)

1. Find the factors of $(x^2 - x - 132)$

(a) (x–11)(x – 12) (b) (x + 12)(x – 11)

(c) (x + 11)(x + 12) (d) (x –12)(x + 11)

2. A college council is auditioning students for a cultural festival. They must satisfy the following criteria -

1. Student must know at least one dance form.
2. Student must know' to play at least one musical instrument.
3. Student must have good acting skills.

Which one of the following will the council definitely select?

(a) Z is a Bharat Natyam dancer, a violinist but does not have any acting skills.

(b) P plays football, guitar, has acted in road shows and is a classical dancer.

(c) J is a contemporary dancer, a great actor and is planning to learn flute.

(d) A plays sitar, is a hip-hop dancer and does not have any acting skills.

3. If **RESEARCH** is $#!#%$&@ then **SCARE** is

(a) !&%$# (b) !$%#<&

(c) !@%$# (d) !@%#$

DIRECTIONS (Qs. 4-6): *The likes and professions of five friends Rosy, Mary, Lily, Andy and Daisy are given. Consider the following information and answer questions based on it.*

1. Rosy likes Yellow and is a Student.
2. The Librarian likes Green.
3. Mary and Andy like Purple and Blue respectively and neither of them is a Teacher.
4. Lily likes Brown and the Inspector likes Blue.
5. One of the five is a Principal.

4. Which colour does the Teacher like?

(a) Blue (b) Brown

(c) Purple (d) Green

5. Who is the Principal?

(a) Daisy (b) Andy

(c) Mary (d) Lily

6. Which among the following is the wrong pair?

(a) Andy — Inspector

(b) Purple — Principal

(c) Daisy — Green

(d) Rosy — Teacher

7. 1.123 + 11.23 + 112.3 = ?

(a) 123.453 (b) 132.343

(c) 124.653 (d) 134.643

8. The standard deviation of the set {10, 10, 10, 10, 10} is

(a) 0 (b) 1 (c) 5 (d) 10

9. Karan purchased one dozen pens for ₹ 120/- and sold a pack of 3 pens for ₹ 35/- each. What is his gain?

(a) 16.67% (b) 20%

(c) 15% (d) 33.33%

10. If **Deplete : Exhaust** then **Replenish :**

(a) Exhale (b) Inhale

(c) Reuse (d) Restore

11. What is the decibel level of normal conversation?

(a) About 60 dB (b) About 70 dB

(c) About 80 dB (d) About 90 dB

12. Statements followed by some conclusions are given below.

Statements:

1. X is 7 meters tall, Y is half as high and Z is 3 times the height of X,
2. P is taller than Z but shorter than A and B.

Conclusions:

I. B is the tallest of all.

II. The average height of X, Y and Z is less than 11 meters.

Find which of the given conclusions logically follows from the given statements.

(a) Only conclusion I follows.
(b) Only conclusion II follows.
(c) Both I and II follow.
(d) Neither I nor II follows.

13. G is twice as fast as S in doing work. If G can do a work in 30 days less than S, how many days will they take to complete the work together?
(a) 25 (b) 20 (c) 22 (d) 15

14. What is the ratio of simple interest earned on certain amount at the rate of 12% p. a. for 9 years and that for 12 years?
(a) 1:2 (b) 2:3 (c) 3:4 (d) 4:5

15.

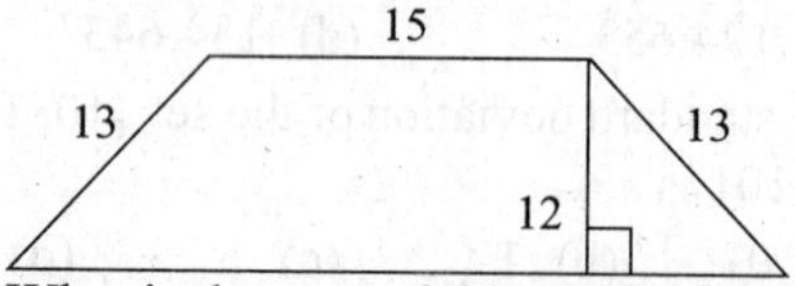

What is the area of this trapezoidal garden? (All measurements are in cm)
(a) 60 sq. cm (b) 180 sq. cm
(c) 210 sq. cm (d) 240 sq. cm

16. Select the alternative that shows a similar relationship as the given pair — **Mandatory : Compulsory**
(a) Philosophy : Idealism
(b) Thesis : Proposition
(c) Generosity : Narrow-mindedness
(d) Hypothesis : Supposition

17. For how many months is a cheque valid from the date of issue?
(a) 1 month (b) 2 months
(c) 3 months (d) 6 months

18. 'Ganga Action Plan' initiated
(a) Streamlining the flow of Ganga river.
(b) Reduction of pollution on Ganga river.
(c) Efficient use of Ganga water for irrigation.
(d) Using Ganga river for generating hydel energy.

19. Find the range and mode of the data 17, 18, 28, 19, 16, 18, 17, 29, 18
(a) 12 and 18 (b) 13 and 18
(c) 12 and 17 (d) 11 and 17

20. The percentage of nitrogen in the air is about
(a) 74% (b) 76% (c) 78% (d) 80%

21. K purchased a table for ₹ 11,000 and sold it for ₹ 13,500. What is his gain in percentage?
(a) 19.8% (b) 20.6%
(c) 22.7% (d) 22%

22. Shimla Agreement 1972 between India & Pakistan was signed in
(a) Barne's Court (b) Ellerslie Building
(c) Viceregal Lodge (d) Gorton Castle

23. The value of $(\sin\theta + \cos\theta)^2 =$
(a) $1+\sin^2\theta$ (b) $\sin^2\theta + \cos^2\theta$
(c) $1 + 2\cos\theta \sin\theta$ (d) $\cos^2\theta + 1$

24. The instrument used to regulate temperature to a particular degree is called
(a) Thermostat (b) Thermometer
(c) Pyrometer (d) Thermocouple

25. Pressure is measured in terms of
(a) Mass & Density (b) Work done
(c) Force and Area (d) Force and Distance

26. How many times does the number 3 occur in unit's place for numbers ranging from 1 to 100?
(a) 20 (b) 11 (c) 10 (d) 19

27. Between small and large human intestine which one is longer?
(a) Small intestine
(b) Large intestine
(c) Both are equal in length
(d) Depends on male or female

28. To conduct detailed study into disease causing organism in livestock, Biosafety Laboratory has been setup in India at
(a) Ludhiana (b) Bengaluru
(c) Anand (d) Allahabad

29. A pole is taller than a Giraffe which is taller than a tree. A signal is shorter than a pole but taller than a building which is taller than a Giraffe. Who is the shortest?

(a) Signal (b) Giraffe
(c) Tree (d) Building

30. Find the missing (?) in the series
NA, PC, RE, TG, ?, XK, ZM

(a) JV (b) VI (c) VII (d) VJ

31. Rearrange the jumbled letters to make a meaningful word and then select the one which is different.

(a) DNHA (b) EDAH
(c) THEA (d) IRHA

32. Sunil has a son Kama and a sister Sangeeta who is the mother of Jagdish and Vijay. Harnish is Jagdish's maternal uncle. How is Harnish related to Kama?

(a) Brother (b) Father
(c) Nephew (d) Paternal Uncle

33. International Maritime Organisation is concerned with

(a) Air pollution.
(b) Sea pollution.
(c) Adulteration in food.
(d) Deforestation.

34. Find the G.C.F. & L.C.M. of 20 and 28.

(a) 20.280 (b) 5.280
(c) 10.140 (d) 4,140

35. Astrosat is India's first

(a) Reconnaissance satellite
(b) Remote sensing satellite
(c) Space observatory
(d) Communication satellite

36. Ali travels a distance of 300 m in 2 minutes and 30 seconds. What is his speed in kmph?

(a) 6.9 (b) 7.1 (c) 7.2 (d) 7.3

37. Four pairs of words are given. Find the odd one out.

(a) Chalk : Slate
(b) Pencil : Notebook
(c) Pen: Ink
(d) Sketch Pen : Drawing Book

38. The Gandhi-Irwin pact was signed in the year

(a) 1930 (b) 1931
(c) 1932 (d) 1933

39. Twice the difference between two numbers is equal to their sum. If one number is 15, find the other number,

(a) 15 (b) 10 (c) 5 (d) 20

40. The sum of three consecutive numbers is 126. Find the highest number.

(a) 41 (b) 43 (c) 42 (d) 44

41. Surya is 25 years older than his son. In $ years, he will be twice as old as his son. What will be Surya's age after 3 years?

(a) 20 (b) 23 (c) 45 (d) 48

42. The name of the first bank established in India was

(a) Bank of Hindustan
(b) Reserve Bank of India
(c) Imperial Bank
(d) State Bank of India

43. If **M= 14, TANK = 62**, then **STARDOM** =

(a) 79 (b) 89 (c) 99 (d) 109

44. What is the 4th proportional of 3, 8,12, ?

(a) 36 (b) 26 (c) 32 (d) 16

45. Which of the following is a Space-Based Augmentation System?

(a) INSAT (b) GAGAN
(c) GSAT (d) SARAL

46. An assertion (A) and a reason (R) are given below.

Assertion (A): Forest cover in the country has gradually decreased.

Reason (R): Encroachment by humans is one of the concerns for the forest department.

Choose the correct option.

(a) Both A and R are true and R is the correct explanation of A
(b) Both A and R are true, but R is not the correct explanation of A

(c) A is true, but R is false
(d) A is false, but R is true

47. If the interior angle of a regular polygon is 108°, then it is a
(a) Octagon (b) Hexagon
(c) Pentagon (d) Tetragon

48. Rupee sign '₹' is a
(a) Devanagari letter
(b) Roman letter
(c) Sanskrit Script
(d) A combination of Roman & Devanagari letters

49. Which of the following does not belong to the group?
(a) Lakshadweep (b) Puducherry
(c) Nicobar (d) Andaman

50. The headquarters of ISRO is located at
(a) Bengaluru (b) New Delhi
(c) Pune (d) Mumbai

51. Which of the following will appear third, if they are arranged according to a dictionary?
(a) Autumn (b) Austere
(c) Assert (d) Auspicious

52. If $\sin\theta = 1/\sqrt{2}$ then $(\tan\theta + \cos\theta) =$
(a) $1/\sqrt{2}$ (b) $2/\sqrt{2}$
(c) $3/\sqrt{2}$ (d) $(1 + \sqrt{2})/\sqrt{2}$

53. The mean and median of 7, 5, 5, 2, 7, 6, 5, 3, 7, 6
(a) 5.3 and 5 (b) 5 and 6
(c) 5 and 5.5 (d) 5.3 and 5.5

54. Find the similarity in the following:
Olive Oil, Coconut Oil, Cod liver Oil, Sunflower Oil
(a) All of them are vegetable oils.
(b) All of them are rich in Vitamin A.
(c) All of them are rich in Vitamin
(d) All of them are oils.

55. Human nails are made of
(a) Pigment (b) Elastin
(c) Albumin (d) Keratin

56. Eastern boundary of Kashmir is
(a) LOC (b) Jammu
(c) POK (d) Ladakh region

57. The medicine paracetamol is
(a) An analgesic
(b) An antipyretic
(c) An analgesic and antipyretic
(d) A nonsteroidal anti-inflammatory drug

58. Sachin Tendulkar made his test debut in 1989 at
(a) Karachi, Pakistan
(b) Mumbai, India
(c) Kolkata, India
(d) Melbourne, Australia

59. Which key on a windows keyboard sets to full screen mode in most browsers?
(a) F1 (b) F10 (c) F11 (d) F12

60. The test for diagnosing HIV is
(a) Pap Smear (b) ELISA
(c) DNA (d) Mantoux

61. B has 32 pens, 24 pencils and 16 erasers. How many sets of these three items can B make without any left over?
(a) 6 (b) 7 (c) 8 (d) 9

62. Air Quality Index is
(a) A measuring instrument of air pollution.
(b) A number
(c) For measuring humidity level.
(d) For forecasting rain.

63. Who served as the first Deputy Prime Minister of independent India?
(a) K. Kamaraj
(b) Morarji Desai
(c) Sardar Vallabhbhai Patel
(d) C. Rajagopalachari

64. Gopal covers 100 km. He travels at a speed of 60 kmph for the first 40 km and the rest of the distance at 60 kmph. What is his average speed in kmph?
(a) 44.20 (b) 45.20
(b) 46.20 (d) 47.20

65. Secularism means
(a) Not practicing any religion.
(b) Practicing multiple religions.
(c) Freedom to join any satsang.
(d) Freedom of religion and worship.

66. A farmer purchased a piece of land for ₹ 18 lakh and spent ₹ 5 lakh for fencing it. He sold it for ₹ 24.57 lakh. Find his profit in percentage?
(a) 15% (b) 14.15%
(c) 16.5% (d) 6.82%

67. National Science Day falls on
(a) 26th February (b) 27th February
(c) 28th February (d) 29th February

DIRECTIONS (Qs. 68-70): *Study the following diagram and answer questions based on it.*

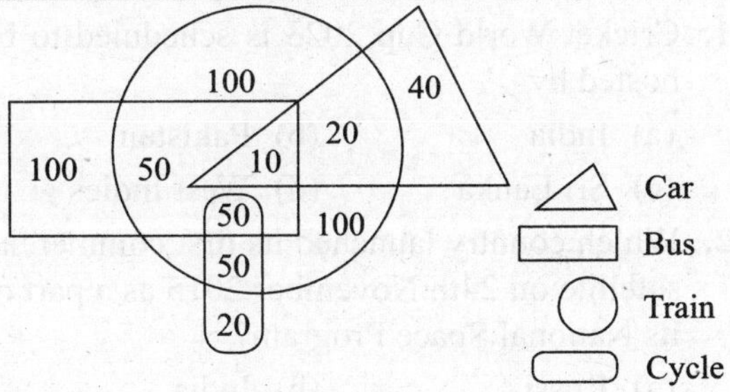

68. The ratio of total number of train travellers to the people who do not travel by train is
(a) 27/16 (b) 28/16
(c) 37/16 (d) 38/16

69. How many people who travel by train also travel by car or bus but not cycle?
(a) 50 (b) 70 (c) 80 (d) 100

70. Which two modes of transport used by people are mutually exclusive?
(a) Car — Bus (b) Car — Cycle
(c) Bus — Cycle (d) Cannot be determined

71. Find the missing (?) in the series 14, 28, 42, 56, ?, 84, 98
(a) 68 (b) 70 (b) 72 (d) 74

72. After 9/11 tragedy, the rebuilt World Trade Centre complex in New York is called
(a) New World Trade Centre
(b) Empire State Building
(c) One World Trade Centre
(d) World Trade Complex

73. The famous Nek Chand's Rock Garden is located in
(a) Srinagar (b) Jammu
(b) Chandigarh (d) Shimla

74. Expand: $(w - 9)^2$
(a) $(w^2 - 9w + 81)$ (b) $(w^2 - 9w + 18)$
(c) $(w^2 - 18w + 81)$ (d) $(w^2 - 18w - 81)$

75. On a certain principal, simple interest amounts to ₹ 1.000 in 1 year at the rate of 10% p.a. What will be the effective rate of interest if the same is compounded on half yearly basis?
(a) 10.10 (b) 10.15
(c) 10.20 (d) 10.25

76. In a certain code language if **41095** is **READY** and **840327** is **FRAILS** then **83145 419** is
(a) FEARY RED (b) FIERY RED
(c) FAIRY RED (d) FIREY RED

77. Which one of the following does not belong to the group?
(a) Monitor (b) Keyboard
(c) Webcam (d) Mouse

78. If **RATIONAL** is **CLETZYLW** then **EXPERIENCE** is
(a) OIZOCTOYMO (b) QIBDUQZOQ
(c) OHZBSOXMO (d) PIAPCTPYNP

79. 1\$ = ₹ 67.89. Money changer adds a margin of ₹ 1.11. What will be the cost of \$150?
(a) ₹ 10,183 (b) ₹ 10,350
(c) ₹ 10,330 (d) ₹ 10,450

80. If the area of a circle is 9π sq. cm then its circumference is
(a) 9 cm (b) 6π cm
(c) 3π cm (d) 6 cm

81. 'Maharatna' refers to a group of
(a) Emerging small and medium enterprises.
(b) Central public sector enterprises.
(c) Leading private sector enterprises.
(d) Leading multi-national companies.

DIRECTIONS (Qs. 82-84): *The bar chart represents number of fiction and non-fiction books in four libraries L1, L2, L3 and L4. Consider the bar chart and answer questions based on it.*

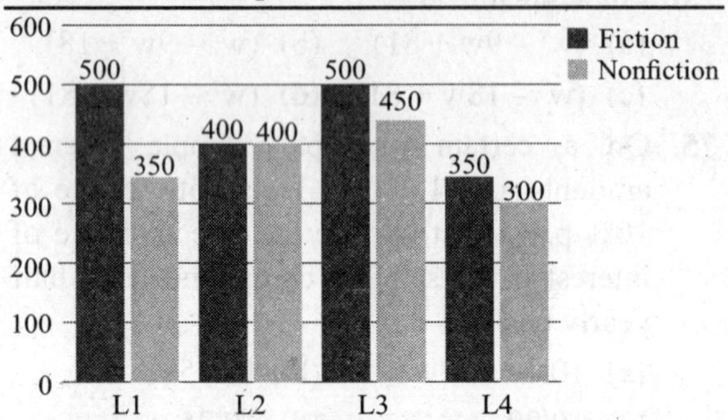

82. What is the percentage difference of total number of Fiction books in libraries L3 and L4 to the Non Fiction books in L3 and L4?
(a) 13.34% (b) 11.76%
(c) 6.67% (d) It is the same

83. The ratio of total books of libraries L1 and L3 to L2 and L4 is
(a) 29/36 (b) 33/32
(b) 36/29 (d) 32/33

84. The ratio of total number of Non-Fiction to Fiction books in all libraries is:
(a) 7/6 (b) 6/7
(c) 15/17 (d) 17/15

85. Which of the following statements is true with respect to ASCII?
(a) A programming language
(b) ASCII chart is not for decimals
(c) American security code for information interchange
(d) A character encoding scheme

86. The first Olympics games was held in
(a) U.K. (b) U.S.A.
(c) Greece (d) Italy

87. A person carries ₹ 165/- in the form of currency notes of denominations ₹ 5, ₹ 10 & ₹ 20 in the ratio of 3:2:1. What is the value of currency notes of ₹ 20 denomination?
(a) ₹ 60 (b) ₹ 100 (c) ₹ 40 (d) ₹ 80

88. Which of the following fractions is the highest of all?
(a) 5/4 (b) 4/3 (c) 3/2 (d) 6/5

89. Name the Indian who became the CEO of Google in 2015.
(a) Satya Nadella (b) Cyrus Mistry
(b) Sundar Pichai (d) Vishal Sikka

90. The periodicity of the Commonwealth games is
(a) No fixed interval (b) 4 years
(c) 5 years (d) 6 years

91. Cricket World Cup 2023 is scheduled to be hosted by
(a) India (b) Pakistan
(c) Sri Lanka (d) West Indies

92. Which country launched its first commercial satellite on 24th November 2015 as a part of its National Space Program?
(a) Russia (b) India
(c) Japan (d) China

93. Which of the following is not a Union Territory?
(a) Puducherry (b) Chandigarh
(c) Lakshadweep (d) Sikkim

94. If '+' and '÷'; 'x' and '–' are interchanged in the equation: **17 ÷ 7 – 27 + 7 x 37,** then its value will be
(a) 7 (b) 17 (c) 27 (d) 37

95. If the mathematical operator '+' means division, '–' means multiplication, '×' means subtraction and '÷' means addition, then the value of
1 × 7 + 21 × 2 ÷ 2 + 3 – 4 is
(a) 8/3 (b) 4/3
(c) –4/3 (d) –8/3

96. 10 people can do a work in 30 days. In how many days, can 15 people complete double the work?
(a) 20 (b) 25 (c) 40 (d) 45

97. Look carefully at the sequence of symbols to find the pattern.

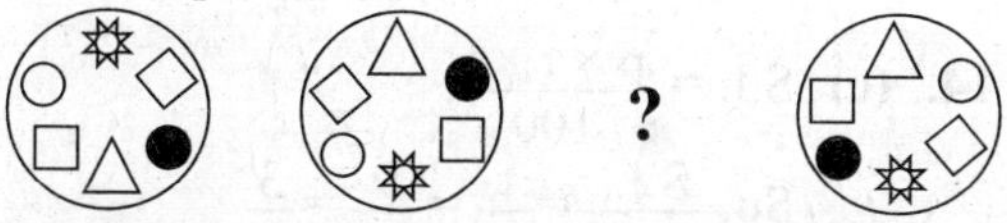

Which of the following will replace the (?) in the sequence?

(a) 
(b) 

(c) 
(d) 

98. Statements followed by some conclusions are given below.

Statements:

1. Most people have orange scooters while some have red ones.
2. People like bright coloured scooters.

Conclusions:

I. People cannot afford bright coloured cars.
II. Most people prefer orange over other bright colours.

Find which of the given conclusions logically follows from the given statements.

(a) Only conclusion I follows.
(b) Only conclusion II follows.
(c) Both I and II follows.
(d) Neither I nor II follows.

99. Which of the following is not a bleaching agent?
(a) Sodium hypochlorite
(b) Calcium hypochlorite
(c) Hydrogen peroxide
(d) Hydrogen sulphide

100. Which movement was called off following the violence at 'Chauri Chaura' incident?
(a) Khilafat Movement
(b) Quit India Movement
(c) Non co-operation Movement
(d) Home Rule Movement

Hints & Solutions

1. (d) $(x^2 - x - 132)$
$= (x^2 - 12x + 11x - 132)$
$= x(x - 12) + 11(x - 12)$
$= (x - 12)(x + 11)$

2. (b) Based on given three criteria,
P plays football and guitar — criteria- 2
P acted in a road show — criteria- 3
P is a classical dancer — criteria- 1
Hence, P will definitely be selected.

3. (a)

Letter	R	E	S	A	C	H
Code	$	#	!	%	&	@

Hence, code of **SCARE** is **!&%$#**

Solution (4-6)

Persons	Profession	Colour
Rosy	Student	Yellow
Mary	Principal	Purple
Lily	Teacher	Brown
Andy	Inspector	Blue
Daisy	Librarian	Green

4. (b) Lily is a teacher, who likes brown colour.
5. (c) Mary is principal.
6. (d) Rosy is a student.

7. (c)

$$\begin{array}{r} 1.123 \\ 11.23 \\ 112.3 \\ \hline 124.653 \end{array}$$

8. (a) Formula for standard deviation

$= \sqrt{\dfrac{\sum(x-\overline{X})^2}{N-1}}$

Where, N = Number of observation.

From question. $\overline{X} = \dfrac{\sum X}{N}$

$= \dfrac{10+10+10+10+10}{5} = \dfrac{50}{5} = 10.$

Now, as the $(X - \overline{X}) = 0$ for all observation, S.D. is zero.

9. (a) Cost of 12 pens = 120

$\therefore$ Cost of 1 pen = 10

Selling price of 3 pens = 35

" " " 1 " $= \dfrac{35}{3} =$ ₹ 11.66

profit = 11.66 – 10 = 1.66

profit % $= \dfrac{1.66}{10} \times 100 = 16.66\%$

10. (d) Deplete : Exhaust :: Replenish : Restore

11. (a) Normal conversation is about 60 dB, a lawn mower is about 90 dB, and a loud rock concert is about 120 dB. Sounds above 85 are harmful.

12. (b) From statement (i) X = 7 m

$Y = \dfrac{7}{2}$ m

$Z = 3 \times 7 = 21$ m

Conclusion II : Average height of X, Y

and Z $= \dfrac{7 + \frac{7}{2} + 21}{3} = \dfrac{63}{6} = 10.5$ m

From given statement I, conclusion II follows.

13. (b) Let S can complete a work in d days.

Then, G can complete the same work in $\dfrac{d}{2}$ days.

Now, $d - \dfrac{d}{2} = 30$

$2d - d = 30 \times 2 \Rightarrow d = 60$ days

$\therefore$ S can complete a work in 60 days

and G can " " same " in 30 days

Let x be the no. of days they work together.

Then, $= \dfrac{x}{30} + \dfrac{x}{60} = 1 \Rightarrow \dfrac{2x + x}{60} = 1$

$= 3x = 60 \Rightarrow x = 20$ days.

14. (c) S.I. $= \dfrac{p \times r \times t}{100}$

So, $\dfrac{S.I._1}{S.I._2} = \dfrac{t_1}{t_2} = \dfrac{9}{12} = \dfrac{3}{4}$

15. (d)

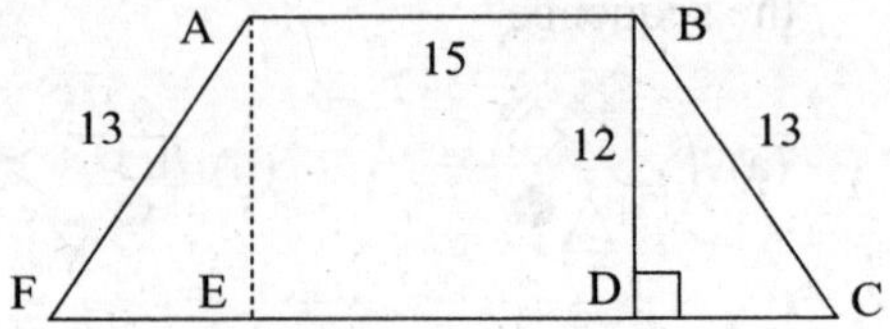

As AB = DE (by symmetry)

$\therefore$ AB = DE = 15

Again from $\triangle$AEF,

$EF = \sqrt{(AF)^2 - (AE)^2}$

$= \sqrt{(13)^2 - (12)^2} = 5$ cm

Again from symmetry, EF = CD = 5 cm

CF = 5 + 15 + 5 = 25 cm.

$\therefore$ Area of trapezoidal garden

$= \dfrac{1}{2}(AB + CF) \times AE$

$= \dfrac{1}{2}(15 + 25) \times 12 = 240 \text{ cm}^2$

16. (d)

17. (c) From April 1, 2012, the validity period of Cheques, Demand Drafts, Pay Orders and Banker's Cheques is reduced from 6 months to 3 months.

18. (b) The Ganga action plan was, launched to improve the water quality by Interception, diversion and treatment of domestic sewage and present toxic and industrial chemical wastes from polluting units entering in to the river.

19. (b) Arranging the given data in ascending order : 16, 17, 17, 18, 18, 18, 19, 28, 29.

Here, Mode = Number which is repeated most number of times,

So, mode = 18 (as it is repeated 3 times) and range = difference in Maximum value – Min. value = 29 – 16 = 13

Hence, Range = 13, Mode = 18.

20. (c)

21. (c) Gain % = $\frac{\text{Selling price} - \text{Cost price}}{\text{Cost price}} \times 100$

$= \frac{13500 - 11000}{11000} \times 100$

$= \frac{2500}{11000} \times 100 = 22.7\%$

22. (a) The Shimla Agreement, was signed between India and Pakistan on 2 July 1972. It followed from the Bangladesh Liberation war in 1971 that led to the independence of Bangladesh.

23. (c) $(\sin\theta + \cos\theta)^2 = \sin^2\theta + \cos^2\theta + 2\sin\theta\cos\theta$

$= 1 + 2\sin\theta\cos\theta$

24. (a) A thermostat senses the temperature of a physical system and performs actions so that the system's temperature is maintained near a desired set-point.

25. (c) Pressure is the perpendicular force per unit area, or the stress at a point within a confined fluid. The weight of the atmosphere pushing down on each unit area of Earth's surface constitutes atmospheric pressure.

26. (c) In 1 to 100, 3 occurs 10 times at unit place.

That are, 3, 13, 23, 33, 43, 53, 63, 73, 83 and 93.

27. (a) The small intestine is narrower than the large intestine, it is the longest section of the digestive tube, measuring 22 feet on average.

28. (b) A biosafety level is a set of precautions required to isolate dangerous biological agents in a laboratory facility. The levels of containment range from the lowest biosafety level 1 (BSL-1) to the highest at level 4 (BSL-4).

29. (c) Arrangement in decreasing height :

Pole > Signal > Building > Giraffe > Tree

↓ Tallest ... ↓ Shortest

30. (b) NA , PC , RE , TG , VI , XK , ZM

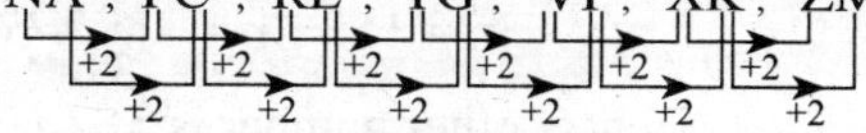

31. (c) DNHA ⟶ HAND, EDAH ⟶ HEAD, THEA ⟶ HEAT and IRHA ⟶ HAIR

Hence, THEA is different among the given words.

32. (d)

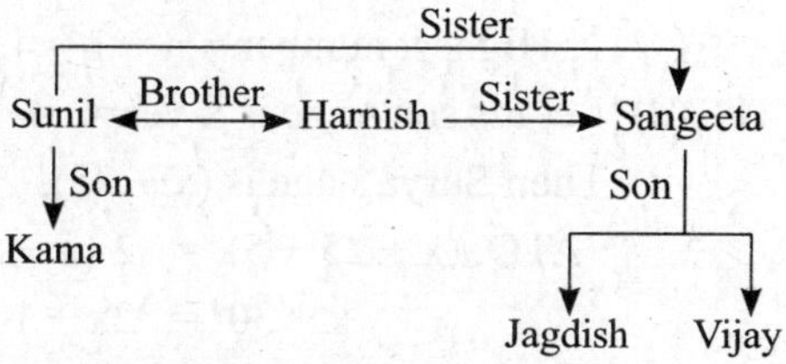

Hence, Harnish is paternal uncle of Kama.

33. (b) The International Maritime Organization (IMO) of the United Nations is responsible for measures to improve the safety and security of international shipping and to prevent marine pollution.

34. (d) 20 = | 2 × 2 | × 5

28 = | 2 × 2 | × 7

G.C.F. = 2 × 2 = 4

L.C.M. = 2 × 2 × 5 × 7 = 140

35. (c) Astrosat is India's first dedicated multi-wavelength space telescope.

36. (c) Time of travel = 2 min. 30 second

= 2 × 60 + 30 = 150 sec.

Distance covered = 300 m

Speed (m/sec.) = $\frac{300}{150} = 2$ m/sec.

Speed (km/hr) = $2 \times \frac{18}{5} = 7.2$ km/hr

37. (c)

38. (b) Gandhi-Irwin Pact, signed on March 5, 1931 marked the end of a period of civil disobedience (satyagraha) in India against British rule that Gandhi and his followers had initiated with the Salt March (March–April 1930).

39. (c) Let other number be n then.

$$2(15 - n) = 15 + n$$
$$30 - 2n = 15 + n$$
$$n + 2n = 30 - 15$$
$$3n = 15 \Rightarrow n = \frac{15}{3} = 5$$

Hence, other number is 5.

40. (c) Let three consecutive numbers are n – 1, n and (n + 1). Sum of the numbers

$$n - 1 + n + n + 1 = 126$$
$$3n = 126 = 42$$

$\therefore$ Highest number = n + 1 = 42 + 1 = 43

41. (d) Let his son's age is x years.

Then Surya's age is (x + 25).

$$\text{ATQ, } (x + 25 + 5) = 2(x + 5).$$
$$x + 30 = 2x + 10$$
$$\therefore x = 20$$

Surya's age after 3 years = (x + 25 + 3)

= 20 + 25 + 3 = 48 years

42. (a) The first bank established in India was Bank of Hindustan, in 1770. Second was The General Bank of India, in 1786. The oldest bank still in existence in India is the State Bank of India which originated from Bank of Calcutta in June 1806.

43. (c) M = 14 (M's letter position in reverse alphabet)

TANK = 7 + 26 + 13 + 16 = 62

but it is 61.

So, this question is not correct.

STARDOM = 8 + 7 + 26 + 9 + 23 + 12 + 14 = 99

44. (c) 3, 8, 12, ?

Product of means = Product of extremes

Now, $3 \times x = 8 \times 12 \Rightarrow x = \frac{3 \times 12}{3} = 32.$

45. (b) The GPS-aided GEO augmented navigation (GAGAN) is a regional Satellite-based Augmentation System by the Indian government. It is the first step towards introduction of modern Communication, navigation and surveillance/Air Traffic Management system over Indian airspace.

46. (a) Encroachment by humans is one of the concerns for gradual decrease in the forest cover in the country.

47. (c) Since interior angle = 108°

exterior angle = 180 – 108 = 72°

Sum of exterior angels of a polygon = 360°

$\Rightarrow 72 \times$ no. of sides = 360°

$\Rightarrow$ no. of sides $= \frac{360°}{72°} = 5$

Hence, it is pentagon

48. (d) The new rupee sign is a combination of the Devanagari letter '₹' and the Latin capital letter 'R'.

49. (b)

50. (a) The secretariat of ISRO is located at Antariksh Bhavan in Bangalore. ISRO coordinates the programmes like satellite communication, earth observation, launch vehicle, space science, disaster management support etc.

51. (b) Arrangement according to the dictionary.

Assert, Auspicious, Austere, Autumn

52. (d) $\sin\theta = \frac{1}{\sqrt{2}} \Rightarrow \sin\theta = \sin 45° \Rightarrow \theta = 45°$

$$\tan\theta + \cos\theta = \tan 45° + \cos 45°$$
$$= 1 + \frac{1}{\sqrt{2}} = \frac{\sqrt{2} + 1}{\sqrt{2}}$$

53. (d) $\text{Mean} = \frac{\sum x}{n}$

$$= \frac{7 + 5 + 5 + 2 + 7 + 6 + 5 + 3 + 7 + 6}{10}$$
$$= \frac{53}{10} = 5.3$$

Arranging the data in ascending order:

2, 3, 5, 5, 5, 6, 6, 7, 7, 7.

$$\text{Median} = \frac{\left(\frac{n}{2}\right)^{th} \text{term} + \left(\frac{n}{2} + 1\right)^{th} \text{term}}{2}$$
$$= \frac{5^{th} \text{term} + (5 + 1)^{th} \text{term}}{2}$$
$$= \frac{5 + 6}{2} = 5.5$$

54. (d)

55. (d) The nails are composed of keratin, a hardened protein. As new cells grow, the older cells are pushed out, compacted and take on the familiar flattened, hardened form of the fingernail.

56 (d)

57. (c) Paracetamol, known as analgesic, or painkiller, is used to relieve pain and lowering a raised temperature (fever).

58. (a) Tendulkar made his Test debut against Pakistan in Karachi in November 1989 aged 16 years and 205 days.

59. (c)

60. (b) ELISA, enzyme-linked immunosorbent assay, is used to detect HIV infection. If an ELISA test is positive, the Western blot test is administered to confirm the diagnosis. If negative and patient thinks he may have HIV, he should be tested again in 1-3 months.

61. (c) Number of Pens = 32

" " Pencils = 24

" " Erasers = 16

H.C.F. of 32, 24, 16 $\Rightarrow 32 = 8 \times 4$

$24 = 8 \times 3$

$16 = 8 \times 2$

H.C.F. = 8

$\therefore$ Number of sets can be made = 8

62. (b) An air quality index is used to communicate to the public how polluted the air currently is or how polluted it is forecast to become. Public health risks increase as the AQI rises.

63. (c) The first Deputy Prime Minister of India was Vallabhbhai Patel, who was also home minister in Jawaharlal Nehru's cabinet. The office has since been only intermittently occupied. The last deputy prime minister was L.K. Advani, who took on the role from 2002 to 2004 in Vajpayee's government.

64. (*) Time taken to cover 40 km with speed 60 kmph $= \frac{40}{60} = \frac{2}{3}$ hours.

Time taken to cover 60 km with speed 60 kmph $= \frac{60}{60} = 1$ hour.

Total time of travel $= \frac{2}{3} + 1 = \frac{5}{3}$ hours.

Average speed $= \frac{100}{\frac{5}{3}} = 60$ kmph.

65. (d) Secularism, as defined in the Merriam-Webster dictionary,[1] is the "indifference to, or rejection or exclusion of, religion and religious considerations." In certain context, the word can refer to anticlericalism, atheism, desire to exclude religion from social activities or civic affairs, banishment of religious symbols from the public sphere, state neutrality toward religion, the separation of religion from state, or disestablishment.

66. (d) Total cost price = 18 + 5 = 23 lakhs.

Total selling price = 24.57 lakhs.

Profit % $= \frac{24.57 - 23}{23} \times 100$

$= \frac{1.57}{23} \times 100 = 6.82\%$

67. (c)

68. (d) Number of train traveller

$= 100 + 10 + 20 + 50 + 50 + 50 + 100$

$= 380$

Number of people that are not train traveller $= 100 + 40 + 20 = 160$

Required ratio $= \frac{380}{160} = \frac{38}{16}$.

69. (c) Number of people travelled by train and bus or car but not by cycle is represented by number inside triangle and circle or circle and rectangle but not in the cylinder. So, required number is $50 + 10 + 20 = 80$

70. (b) From given fig. car and cycle do not have common number. So, they are mutually exclusive.

71. (b) Table of 14 $14 \times 5 = 70$.

72. (c)

73. (c) Nek Chand Saini (15/12/1924 – 12/6/2015) was a self-taught Indian artist, known for building the Rock Garden of Chandigarh.

74. (c) $(w - 9)^2 = w^2 + 9^2 - 2.w.9$

$= w^2 - 18w + 81$

75. (d) Principle (P) $= \frac{S.I. \times 100}{rate \times time}$

$= \frac{1000 \times 100}{10 \times 1} = 10000$

When, interest compounded half yearly $t = 2$ Let rate of interest $= r\%$

then, on solving, we get $r = 10.25\%$

76. (b)

Letter	R	E	A	D	Y	F	I	L	S
Digit	4	1	0	9	5	8	3	2	7

Hence, 83145 419 is FIERY RED

77. (a)

78. (d)

R A T I O N A L

+11↓ +11↓ +11↓ +11↓ +11↓ +11↓ +11↓ +11↓

C L E T Z Y L W

Simply,

E X P E R I E N C E

+11↓+11↓+11↓+11↓+11↓+11↓+11↓+11↓+11↓+11↓

P I A P C T P Y N P

79. (b) Total value of 1\$ = 67.89 + 1.11 = ₹ 69

So, total value of 150\$ = 150 × 69

= ₹ 10,350

80. (b) Let the radius of the circle is r cm then, its area $\pi r^2 = 9\pi \Rightarrow r^2 = 9 \Rightarrow r = 3$

It is perimeter $P = 2\pi r = 2\pi.3 = 6\pi$ cm.

81. (b) Maharatna status is given to select central public sector enterprises to give them greater autonomy to compete in the global market.

82. (b) Total number of fiction books in L3 & L4 = 500 + 350 = 850.

Total number of non-fiction books in L3 and L4 = 450 + 300 = 750.

Percentage difference

$= \frac{850 - 750}{850} \times 100 = 11.76\%$

83. (c) Ratio of total books in L1 and L3 to L2 and L4 $\Rightarrow \frac{(500 + 350) + (500 + 450)}{(400 + 400) + (350 + 300)}$

$= \frac{1800}{1450} = \frac{36}{29}$

84. (b) Total number of non-fiction books

$= 350 + 400 + 450 + 300 = 1500$

Total number of fiction books

$= 500 + 400 + 500 + 350 = 1750$

Required ratio $= \frac{1500}{1750} = \frac{6}{7}$

85. (d) ASCII is a character encoding standard for electronic communication. These codes represent text in computers, telecommunication equipments, and other devices.

86. (c)

87. (a) Let the no. of ₹ 20 notes = x

Number of ₹ 5, ₹ 10, ₹ 20 notes are 3x, 2x and x respectively.

Then,

$5 \times 3x + 10 \times 2x + 20 \times x = 165$

$55x = 165 \Rightarrow x = 3$

So, value of ₹ 20 denomination

$= 20 \times 3 = 60$

88. (c) $\frac{5}{4} = \frac{5 \times 15}{4 \times 15} = \frac{75}{60}$, $\frac{4}{3} = \frac{4 \times 20}{3 \times 20} = \frac{80}{60}$,

$\frac{3}{2} = \frac{3 \times 30}{2 \times 30} = \frac{90}{60}$, $\frac{6}{5} = \frac{6 \times 12}{5 \times 12} = \frac{72}{60}$

Hence, $\frac{3}{2}$ is is highest.

89. (c) Pichai became the CEO of Google on August 10, 2015 after previously being appointed Product Chief by CEO, Larry Page.

90. (b) The Commonwealth Games are multi-sport event involving athletes from the Commonwealth of Nations. It was first held in 1930, and every four years since then.

91. (a) The 2023 Cricket World Cup will be the 13th edition, scheduled to be hosted by India, from 9 February to 26 March 2023.

92. (c)

93. (d) Sikkim is a state in northeastern India. It borders Tibet in the north and northeast, Bhutan in the east, Nepal in the west, and West Bengal in the south.

94. (a) $17 \div 7 - 27 + 7 \times 37$

$= 17 + 7 \times 27 \div 7 - 37$

$= 17 + 27 - 37 = 7$

95. (b) $1 \times 7 + 21 \times 2 \div 2 + 3 - 4$

$= 1 - 7 \div 21 - 2 + 2 \div 3 \times 4$

$= 1 - \frac{1}{3} - 2 + \frac{2}{3} \times 4$

$= -\frac{4}{3} + \frac{8}{3} = \frac{4}{3}$

96. (c) 10 people can do a work in 30 days.

then, 5 people can do the same work in 60 days.

so, 15 people can do the same work in $\frac{60}{3} = 20$ days $\therefore$ Double work = 40 days.

97. (c) In the given figure we see that △ and ✡ interchange their position and rest of the elements rotate anti-clockwise.

98. (b) From given statement only conclusion II follows, that most people prefer orange colour are other colour.

99. (d)

100. (c) The Chauri Chaura incident, took place on February 5, 1922, in the Gorakhpur district of British India. During the non-cooperation movement, a group of protestors clashed with police and as a result of this, policemen opened fired on the protestors. Provoked by this shooting incident, the demonstrators burnt down a police station, killing all its occupants. Resulting in the death of 22 or 23 policemen and three civilians, the incident also turned many against Mahatma Gandhi as he called off the 'Non-cooperation Movement' after the incident.

RRB NTPC stage-I Solved Paper

Held On 3rd April 2016 (Shift-I)

1. What among the following is FALSE about the Richter scale?
   (a) It was developed by Charles Richter and Gutenberg in 1935.
   (b) It is a logarithmic scale
   (c) It can be measured using a seismometer
   (d) Magnitude of 8-9 on a Richter scale means it is a micro earthquake.

2. The following graph represents marks obtained in mathematics, out of 10, of five students.

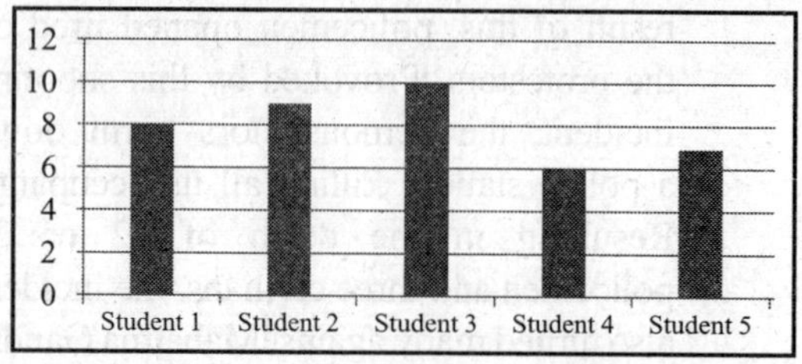

   Student 3 and 5 get how many more marks than student 4 and 1
   (a) 2 (b) 1 (c) 3 (d) 4

3. Which device is used to convert digital signal to analog.
   (a) WiFi (b) Modem
   (c) Port (d) USB

4. If N : 38 :: 3 : 57, Find N.
   (a) 2/3 (b) 1/3 (c) 3 (d) 2

5. The distance between two points A and B is covered in 5 1/2 hours at a speed of 50 km/hr. If the speed is increased by 5 km/hr. how much time would be saved?
   (a) 5 minutes (b) 15 minutes
   (c) 50 minutes (d) 30 minutes

6. If $x = 7 - 4\sqrt{3}$ find the value of $\sqrt{x} + \frac{1}{\sqrt{x}}$
   (a) 0 (b) 1 (c) 4 (d) –4

7. Which is India's longest river that does not flow into the sea?
   (a) Ganga (b) Jamuna
   (c) Tapti (d) Kaveri

8. What is the most cultivated crop in India?
   (a) Ragi (b) Wheat
   (c) Cora (d) Rice

9. In which city is the value of Gold determined?
   (a) California (b) Sydney
   (c) Rome (d) London

10. Find the similarity in the following:
    Elephant, Camel, Buffalo, Giraffe
    (a) The milk produced by all of them cannot be consumed by people.
    (b) All of them have horns.
    (c) None of them are mammals,
    (d) The young ones of all of them are called calf.

11. If $y = \frac{2x - 1}{x + 3}$ find x when y = 1
    (a) 4 (b) –4 (c) 3/2 (d) 4/3

12. Which vitamin among the following is crucial for blood clotting?
    (a) Vitamin K (b) Vitamin D
    (c) Vitamin A (d) Vitamin E

13. If the mathematical operators, '+' and '×' are interchanged, what will he the value of the equation $9 \div 5 + 10 - 23 \times 2$
    (a) 3 (b) 2 (c) –3 (d) –5

14. A wire is in the shape of a rectangle. Its length is 42.7 m and breadth is 21.8 m. If the same wire is re-bent in the shape of a square, what will be the measure of the side of the square?
    (a) 16.125 (b) 32.25
    (c) 11.35 (d) 22.70

15. According to the Swachchh Bharat 2015 survey, which is the cleanest city in India?
    (a) Chennai (b) Delhi
    (c) Ahmedabad (d) Mysore

16. Which is the most peaceful country according to the 2015 Global Peace Index?

(a) Iceland (b) Bhutan
(c) Austria (d) New Zealand

17. Where did the Chipko movement begin?

(a) Rajasthan (b) Assam
(c) Arunachal Pradesh (d) Mizoram

18. Rearrange the jumbled letters to make a meaningful word and then select the one which is different.

(4) ORIN (b) NADS
(c) POPCER (d) DLOG

DIRECTIONS (Qs. 19-21): *Study the following diagram and answer questions based on it. The diagram represents the likes of kids of a class.*

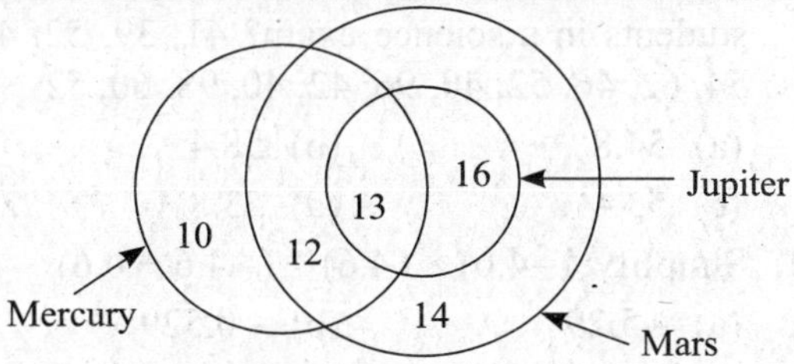

19. The ratio of kids who like only Mars to those who like all the three

(a) 7/5 (b) 7/8
(c) 7/6 (d) 14/13

20. What is the difference between the kids who like Mercury and Jupiter?

(a) 6 (b) 8 (c) 10 (d) 12

21. How many people who Like Mars like Jupiter also?

(a) 45 (b) 29 (c) 26 (d) 13

22. Name the capital of Uganda?

(a) Mogadishu (b) Kampala
(c) Lusaka (d) Bulenga

23. What is Madhubani art?

(a) The art of Storytelling
(b) The art of Gujarat
(c) A folk art practiced in Bihar
(d) The art of honey extraction

24. What is 'Planet Nine'?

(a) A planet in the Comet Galaxy
(b) A planet in Andromeda Galaxy
(c) A planet where the 'Star Wars' series took place
(d) A large icy planet proposed in the outer Solar System

25. Which is NOT an Operating System?

(a) OS X (b) Windows 7
(c) DOS (d) C++

26. What is the smallest number of 5 digits which is exactly divisible by 12. 24, 48, 60 and 96?

(a) 10000 (b) 10024
(c) 10160 (d) 10080

27. Find the cost in rupees for carpeting a room 65dm × 30dm at Rs 45 per sq.m

(a) 877.50 (b) 87750
(c) 87.75 (d) 8775

28. What is most common treatment for bacterial infections in humans?

(a) Aspirin (b) Antibodies
(c) Antibiotics (d) Antigen

29. The ratio of ages of Jai and Joy is 5:2. The sum of their ages is 63. After 9 years what will be the ratio of their ages?

(a) 5 : 2 (b) 2 : 1 (c) 3 : 2 (d) 4 : 3

30. By selling 90 chocolates for ₹ 160, a chocolate trader loses 20%. How many chocolates should he sell for ₹ 96 to make a profit of 20%?

(a) 45 (b) 36 (c) 54 (d) 28

31. What is an archipelago?

(a) Group, chain cluster or collection of Islands
(b) The meeting of Land and Sea
(c) An Architect's paradise
(d) A type of Church

DIRECTIONS (Qs. 32-34): *Six animals - horse, cow, pig, dog. donkey and goat are tied to a pole each, in a circle, facing each other, in random order. Consider the following information and answer the questions based on it.*

1. Goat is to the immediate right of pig.
2. Cow is not tied next to either donkey or dog.
3. If the animals mark the vertices of a hexagon, then the horse is diagonally opposite to the pig.

32. The cow is tied to the immediate left of
(a) Goat (b) Pig
(c) Horse (d) Dog

33. Which pair is tied next to each other?
(a) Horse and Goat (b) Pig and Cow
(c) Goat and Dog (d) Donkey and Dog

34. Which animal is tied to the immediate left of pig?
(a) Goat (b) Donkey
(c) Dog (d) Cannot be determined

35. Who is Sabari Karthik?
(a) Famous Indian Karate Champion
(b) Rugby Player
(c) Cricket Player
(d) Kabaddi Champion

36. Which among the following is popularly called Laughing Gas?
(a) Nitric oxide (b) Nitrogen dioxide
(c) Nitrous oxide (d) Nitrogen peroxide

37. Four pairs of words are given. Find the odd one out.
(a) 65th anniversary : Diamond Jubilee
(b) 50th anniversary : Golden Jubilee
(c) 40th anniversary : Ruby Jubilee
(d) 25th anniversary : Silver Jubilee

38. A lady wants to buy the following items in the given price range —
1. Tomato between ₹ 40 and ₹ 45 per kg.
2. Grapes in the price range of ₹ 80 and ₹ 90 per kg.
3. Milk packets at ₹ 23 per litre.

In which shop from the following will she definitely get all her items?
(a) Shop S sells tomato at ₹ 22.5 per half kg, grapes at ₹ 82 per kg and milk at ₹ 24 per litre.
(b) Shop H sells grapes at ₹ 21 per quarter kg. milk at 12.5 per half litre and tomato at ₹ 22 per half kg.
(c) Shop O sells milk at ₹ 11.5 per half litre, tomato at ₹ 21 per half kg and grapes at ₹ 43 per half kg.
(d) Shop P sells tomato at ₹ 23.5 per half kg, grapes at ₹ 85 per kg and milk at ₹ 23 per litre.

39. What did M. S. Swaminathan, an Indian geneticist, play a leading role in?
(a) Yellow Revolution
(b) White Revolution
(c) Green Revolution
(d) Black Revolution

40. What is the mean of the marks scored by students in a science exam? 41, 39, 52, 48, 54, 62, 46, 52, 40, 96, 42, 40, 98, 60, 52
(a) 54.8 (b) 58.4
(c) 53.4 (d) 53.8

41. Simplify: $(-4.6) \times (4.6) \div (-4.6 + 0.6)$
(a) -5.29 (b) -0.529
(c) -4.06 (d) 5.01

42. Indian currency notes. are printed in which place?
(a) New Delhi (b) Bombay
(c) Nashik (d) Agra

43. The price of 4 1/2 m of cloth is ₹ 60 3/4. Find the cost per meter
(a) 15 1/2 (b) 13 1/2
(c) 14 3/4 (d) 13 3/4

44. What is the number of Galilean moons of Jupiter discovered by Galileo Galilei in January 1610?
(a) 2 (b) 3 (c) 4 (d) 5

45. Mica is available abundantly in which state?
(a) West Bengal (b) Madhya Pradesh
(c) Bihar (d) Rajasthan

46. If X = 24 and BE = 7, then RING = ?
(a) 41 (b) 47 (c) 48 (d) 49

47. The product of two consecutive odd numbers is 399. Find the lower of them

(a) 17 (b) 19 (b) 21 (d) 23

48. Between which stations does India's longest train run?

(a) Kanyakumari - Baramulla
(b) Dibrugarh - Naliya
(c) Dibrugarh - Kanyakumari
(d) Thiruvanathapuram - New Delhi

49. With reference to classification of fundamental rights, which of the following is true?

1. Right to exploitation
2. Right against equality
3. Cultural and economic rights

Select the correct statements from the following codes

(a) Only 1 (b) Only 1 and 2
(c) 1,2 and 3 (d) None of these

50. What is The Siberian ibex?

(a) Mountain Lions
(b) Large and heavily built goats
(c) Mountain Deer
(d) A Type of Horse

51. Cost price of 25 chairs equals the selling price of 20 chairs. Find the profit %.

(a) 20% (b) 33%
(c) 25% (d) 12.5%

52. A trader marks his goods at 20% above cost price. If he allows a discount of 5% what is his final profit?

(a) 12% (b) 14% (c) 15% (d) 18%

53. What is Swadeshi?

(a) Made in India, from materials that have also been produced in India
(b) Made in Foreign Lands from materials that are foreign
(c) A Charkha that is used to spin cotton wool
(d) A Country Flag that is made of Cotton

54. Which among the following happens in an oxidation reaction

(a) Electrons are gained
(b) Electrons are lost
(c) Protons are gained
(d) Protons are lost

55. Where is the Masai Mara National Reserve?

(a) Mali (b) Kenya
(c) Gabon (d) Zambia

56. Find the compound interest to the nearest rupee on ₹ 7500 for 2 years 4 months at 12% p.a. reckoned annually?

(a) 2284 (b) 2176 (c) 2097 (d) 2235

DIRECTIONS (Qs. 57-59): *The following table represents the percentage marks of four students in six subjects. Consider the table and answer questions based on it.*

Student	Maths	Science	History	Geography	English	Hindi
Shamita	75	80	65	68	72	65
Smita	80	85	75	65	70	70
Shilpa	82	88	70	69	71	70
Sheela	78	87	65	70	75	74

57. The average marks obtained by the students in Geography and History are

(a) 68.75 and 68 (b) 70.5 and 69
(c) 68 and 68.75 (d) 68.75 and 68.5

58. Average marks obtained in Science is higher than that of Maths by

(a) 15 (b) 20 (c) 25 (d) 40

59. Who has the highest total marks?

(a) Shamita (b) Smita
(c) Shilpa (d) Sheela

60. If $\cos\theta + \sin\theta = m$, $\sec\theta + \text{cosec}\,\theta = n$, what is m/n

(a) 1 (b) $\sin\theta\cos\theta$

(c) $\sec\theta\ \text{cosec}\,\theta$ (d) $\cot\theta\tan\theta$

61. M is the son of N. O is the father of N. P is the father of M. How is N related to P?

(a) Wife (b) Husband

(c) Father (d) Mother

62. What is Sepak Takraw?

(a) A Bird

(b) An ancient hunting team in Malaysia

(c) Kick Volleyball

(d) A type of Combat Flight

63. X, Y and Z take 18 days to complete a piece of work. If X works alone he finishes the work in 36 days and if Y works alone he finishes it in 60 days. How long will it take Z to complete the work alone?

(a) 78 days (b) 90 days

(c) 96 days (d) 14 days

64. Which is the capital of Sri Lanka?

(a) Colombo

(b) Kandy

(c) Jayawardenepurs Kotte

(d) Anuradhapura

65. Solve: $\frac{\sin\theta}{1+\cos\theta} + \frac{1+\cos\theta}{\sin\theta} = ?$

(a) $\tan\theta$ (b) $\cot\theta$

(c) $\frac{2}{\sin\theta}$ (d) $\frac{2}{\cos\theta}$

66. The Panchatantra fables are thought to be composed by

(a) Mullah Nasruddin

(b) Vishnu Sharma

(c) King Sudharshan

(d) Tenali Raman

67. What was the code name of the nuclear tests conducted by India in Pokhran in 1998

(a) Operation Desert Storm

(b) Operation Vijay

(c) Operation Shakti

(d) Operation Kaboom

68. An assertion (A) and a reason (R) are given below.

Assertion (A): Penguins are birds, found in the hottest regions of the earth.

Reason (R): Birds in hot regions do not have wings.

Choose the correct option.

(a) Both A and R are true and R is the correct explanation of A

(b) Both A and R are true, but R is not the correct explanation of A

(c) Ais true, but R is false

(d) Both A and R are false

69. Who is Anjolie Ela Menon?

(a) An Indian politician

(b) Bharatanatyam dancer

(c) A popular musician

(d) Indian Female Artist

70. The sum of the digits of a 2 digit number is 9. When 27 is added to the number, the digits get interchanged. Find the number.

(a) 45 (b) 36 (c) 18 (d) 27

71. Find the missing (?) in the series

13, 14, 18, 27, ?, 68, 104 ....

(a) 36 (b) 41 (c) 43 (d) 54

72. Kitty said, "Uthara is one of the two daughters of my mother's brother's wife". How is Kitty's mother related to Uthara's sister?

(a) Maternal Aunt (b) Mother

(c) Grandmother (d) Sister

73. One angle of a triangle is 55°. If the other two angles are in the ratio 9:16, find the angles-

(a) 65 and 115 (b) 90 and 160

(c) 55 and 165 (d) 45 and 80

74. Which contemporary painter made a series of paintings on Mahatma Gandhi?

(a) Amrita Shergill (b) Ram Kinkar

(c) M.F. Hussain (d) Atul Dodiya

75. The income of a person is represented by the pie-chart below. If his total income is ₹ 360,000 then find his income of the second week.

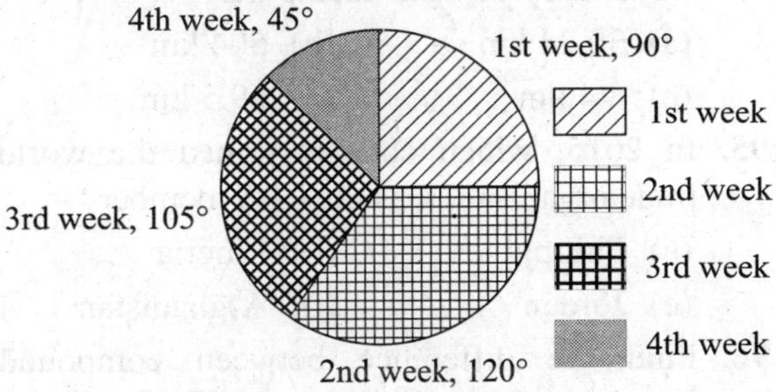

(a) ₹ 90,000 (b) ₹ 120,000
(c) ₹ 46,000 (d) ₹ 105,000

76. If **HOUSES = GNAYDR**, then **DIARY** =
(a) CHGXZ (b) CHEWZ
(c) CHGXX (d) CHEWX

77. What does "Satyameva Jayate" mean?
(a) "Truth alone triumphs"
(b) "True Faith is Rare"
(c) "Truth is Divine"
(d) "Truth is a Treasure"

78. Male is the capital of which Country?
(a) Mauritius (b) Lakshadweep
(c) Maldives (d) Malaysia

79. Select the alternative that does not have a similar relationship as the given pair - **Forward : Backward**
(a) Hope : Despair (b) Love : Hate
(c) Anger : Wrath (d) Light : Dark

80. A statement followed by some conclusions are given below.
Statement: Religions teach the guiding principles for leading one's life.
Conclusions:
I. Religion is a way of life.
II. Religion is a teacher.
Find which of the given conclusions logically follow from the given statement.
(a) Only conclusion I follows.
(b) Only conclusion II follow's.
(c) Both I and II follow.
(d) Neither I nor II follows.

81. If **H_2O : Hydrogen,** than **KOH :**
(a) Cobalt (b) Phosphorous
(c) Potassium (d) Krypton

82. Simplify: $\frac{9}{13} \div \frac{18}{26} \div \frac{90}{52}$
(a) 45/26 (b) 13/45
(c) 26/45 (d) 45/13

83. Zero degree centigrade is equal to what degree Fahrenheit?
(a) 100°F (b) 30°F (c) 34°F (d) 32°F

84. If **SHFIF** is **FUSVS**, then **ZEBRA** is
(a) NRMEO (b) MRNEO
(c) NROEM (d) MROEN

85. What is the normal resting heart rate range for adults (beats/min)?
(a) 60 to 100 (b) 50 to 80
(c) 120 to 180 (d) 75 to 120

86. Q's father is B's son-in-law. C is Q's sister and the daughter of P. P is the maternal aunt of D. How is P related to B?
(a) Son (b) Daughter
(c) Grandson (d) Granddaughter

87. Who was the first woman to reach summit of Mt. Everest?
(a) Bachendri Pal (b) Junko Tabei
(c) Aruniina Sinha (d) Premlata Agarwal

88. 6 carpenters make 96 windows in 6 days. If 8 carpenters work for 4 days how many windows will they make?
(a) 16 (b) 28 (c) 36 (d) 32

89. A factory produced 18,58,509 cassettes in the month of January. 7623 more cassettes in the month of February and owing to short supply of electricity produced 25,838 less cassettes in March than in February. Find the total production in all?
(a) 55,57,312 (b) 59,83,245
(c) 55,64,935 (d) 56,08,988

90. What is Makar Sankranti?
(a) Lunar Eclipse (b) Harvesting Festival
(c) Kite Festival (d) Puppet Show

91. Statements followed by some conclusions are given below.
Statements:
(a) Confusion causes mental tension.
(b) Mental tension causes anxiety.
Conclusions:
I. Anxiety is a disease.
II. Confusion leads to anxiety.
Find which of the given conclusions logical! follow from the given statements.
(a) Only conclusion I follow's.
(b) Only conclusion II follows.
(c) Both I and II follow.
(d) Neither I nor II follows.

92. If 'Mango, lemon and melon are fruits', is written as 439516: "Mango and lemon are yellow' is 04396 and "Melon is green' is 857, which digit represents "melon"?
(a) 5 (b) 8
(c) 7 (d) Cannot be determined

93. Find the missing (?) in the series
AIQ, BJR, CKS, DLT, ?, ...
(a) ENU (b) EMV
(c) ENV (d) EMU

94. Sanjay and Jacob start running in opposite directions from the same point at speeds of 7m/s and 5m/s. After 42 minutes, how far would they be from each other?
(a) 30.24 km (b) 504 km
(c) 8.4 km (d) 69.5 km

95. In 2015, which country joined the world trade organisation as the 44th member?
(a) Philippines (b) Liberia
(c) Jordan (d) Afghanistan

96. Find the difference between compound interest and simple interest on ₹ 5000 for 2 years at 8% p.a payable annually,
(a) 45 (b) 32 (c) 57 (d) 84

97. Solve: $12 - [26 - \{2 + 5 \times (6 - 3)\}]$
(a) 2 (b) 3 (c) 7 (d) 8

98. Abdul prepared 42 litres of medicine and filled it in bottles of 280 ml each. Find how many bottles would be required?
(a) 15 (b) 1500
(c) 150 (d) 300

99. The LCM of two consecutive even numbers is 144, find the numbers
(a) 16 and 18 (b) 14 and 16
(c) 18 and 20 (d) 22 and 24

100. The Dibru-Saikhowa, Nameri and Orang National Park are all found in which State?
(a) Andhra Pradesh (b) Assam
(c) Arunachal Pradesh (d) Uttarakhand

Hints & Solutions

1. (d) Earthquakes vibrations travel through Earth; they are recorded on seismographs. Seismographs record a zigzag trace that shows the varying amplitude of ground oscillations (richter scale).

2. (c) Marks obtained by student 3 and 5
$= 10 + 7 = 17$
Marks obtained by student 4 and 1
$= 6 + 8 = 14.$
Difference $= 17 - 14 = 3.$

3. (b) Modems convert digital signals to analog signals, and vice versa. They allow people to connect their computers with other computers, corporate office LANs, and the Internet.

4. (d) N : 38 :: 3 : 57 $\Rightarrow \frac{N}{38} = \frac{3}{57}$

$57 \times N = 38 \times 3 \Rightarrow N = \frac{38 \times 3}{57} = 2.$

5. (d) Distance = speed × time

$= 50 \times \frac{11}{2} = 275$ km.

When speed increases by 5 km/hr

Time $= \frac{\text{Distance}}{\text{Speed}} = \frac{275}{55} = 5$ hours.

Time difference = 5.5 – 5 = 0.5 hours = 30 minutes.

6. (c) $x = 7 - 4\sqrt{3} = 4 + 3 - 2.2(\sqrt{3})$

$= (2)^2 + (\sqrt{3})^2 - 2 \times 2.(\sqrt{3})$

$= (2 - \sqrt{3})^2$

$\therefore \quad \sqrt{x} = (2 - \sqrt{3})$

and $\frac{1}{\sqrt{x}} = \frac{1}{2 - \sqrt{3}}$

$= \frac{2 + \sqrt{3}}{(2 - \sqrt{3})(2 + \sqrt{3})} = \frac{2 + \sqrt{3}}{4 - 3} = 2 + \sqrt{3}$

Now, $\sqrt{x} + \frac{1}{\sqrt{x}} = 2 - \sqrt{3} + 2 + \sqrt{3} = 4.$

7. (b) The Yamuna the largest river in the country that does not ever flow to the sea. It is one of the Ganges main tributaries.

8. (d)

9. (d) The London Gold Market Fixing Limited, consists of five major London banks, was established to determine the fair market price of the gold. The group has continued to fix gold prices since Sept. 12, 1919.

10. (d) The young one of all of them is called calf.

11. (a) $y = \frac{2x - 1}{x + 3} \Rightarrow 1 = \frac{2x - 1}{x + 3}$

$x + 3 = 2x - 1$

$2x - x = 3 + 1 \Rightarrow x = 4.$

12. (a) Vitamin K is one of the factors which is required for blood clotting.

13. (c) $9 \div 5 + 10 - 23 \times 2$

After interchange : $9 \div 5 \times 10 - 23 + 2$

$= 9 \times 2 - 23 + 2 = -3.$

14. (b) Perimeter of the rectangle = 2 × (42.7 + 21.8) = 129 m

Here, Perimeter of the square = Perimeter of the rectangle

$\therefore$ 4 × side of the square = 129

$\therefore$ Side of the square $= \frac{129}{4} = 32.25$ cm

15. (d) **16. (a)**

17. (a) The Chipko movement started in the 18th century in Rajasthan. A local woman, Amrita Devi, risked her life along with 84 villagers to protect the forest trees from being cut on the order of the king.

18. (b) ORIN → IRON, NADS → SAND

POPCER → COPPER, DLOG → GOLD

Except SAND, other three IRON, GOLD and COPPER are metal.

19. (d) $\frac{\text{Kids like only Mars}}{\text{Kids like all the three}} = \frac{14}{13}$

20. (a) Difference = Kids like Mercury – Kids like Jupiter

= (10 + 12 + 13) – (13 + 16)

= 6

21. (b) Kids like Mars and Jupiter both = 29.

22. (b)

23. (c) Madhubani paintings are usually created by women on walls and floors of homes during festivals, ceremonies or special occasions. Originated in the Mithila region in Bihar; has been in practice in areas around Bihar and Nepal.

24. (d) A massive ice planet (planet nine) is hypothetically proposed to be travelling outer solar system beyond Pluto.

25. (d) C++ is a general-purpose object-oriented programming (OOP) language and is an extension of the C language.

26. (d) L.C.M. of 12, 24, 48, 60 and 96.

$12 = 12 \times 1$

$24 = 12 \times 2$

$48 = 12 \times 4$

$60 = 12 \times 5$

$96 = 12 \times 8$

$\therefore$ L.C.M. $12 \times 8 \times 5 = 480$

Smallest 5-digit number divisible by 480

$= 480 \times 20 = 9600$ (4 digit number)

$\therefore 480 \times 21 = 10080$. (5 digit number)

27. (a) Floor area of the room = 65 dm × 30 dm

$= 6.5 \text{ m} \times 3.0 \text{ m}$

$= 19.5$

Cost of carpeting $= 19.5 \times 45$

$= 877.5 \text{ m}^2$.

28. (c) Antibiotics are powerful medicines that fight infections and can save lives when used properly. They either stop bacteria from reproducing or destroy them.

29. (b) Let Jai and Joy's age are 5x and 2x respectively.

Sum of their age $= 5x + 2x = 63$

$7x = 63 \Rightarrow x = 9$

After 9 years Jai's age $= 5x + 9$

$= 5 \times 9 + 9$

$= 54$ years

After 9 years Joy's age $= 2 \times 9 + 9$

$= 27$ years

Ratio of their age $= \frac{54}{27} = 2 : 1$.

30. (b) Cost price of 90 chocolates

$= 160 \times \frac{100}{(100-20)} = 160 \times \frac{100}{80} = ₹\ 200$

Cost price of 1 chocolate $= \frac{200}{90} = ₹\ \frac{20}{9}$

Selling price 1 chocolate with 20% profit

$= \left(\frac{20}{9} \times \frac{20}{100}\right) + \frac{20}{9} = \frac{24}{9}$

$\therefore$ Number of chocolate he sell in ₹ 96.

$= \frac{96}{24} \times 9 = 36$

31. (a) An archipelago is a specific geological land formation made up of a number of islands. The various islands are located relatively close together.

(32-34) : Circular arrangement of six animals in a circle is like this:

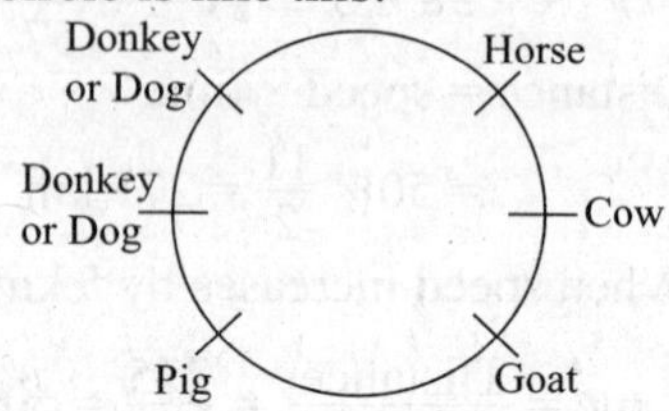

32. (c) Cow is immediate left of Horse.

33. (d) Donkey and dog are next to each other.

34. (d) We can not determined.

35. (a) Sabari Karthik is a South Asian Karate champion (2014), Three times National champion and a National Games (2011) Gold medalist. He holds two bronze medals in Commonwealth Karate Championship (2009- South Africa).

36. (c) Nitrous oxide, (laughing gas N_2O) is an oxide of nitrogen. It is a colourless non-flammable gas, with a slight metallic scent and taste.

37. (a)

38. (c) Price range of tomato = ₹ 40 to ₹ 45

Price range of grapes = ₹ 80 to ₹ 90

Price range of Milk = ₹ 23 per litre.

Shop c sells : 1 litre milk $= 11.5 \times 2 = ₹\ 23$

1 Kg tomato $= 21 \times 2 = ₹\ 42$

1 Kg grapes $= 43 \times 2 = ₹\ 86$

Hence, Lady will get all his item at shop C.

39. (c) MS Swaminathan is an Indian geneticist known as the father of India's Green Revolution, a program under which high-yield varieties of wheat and rice were planted.

40. (a) Mean Marks = $\frac{\text{Sum of all marks}}{\text{Number of exams}}$

From question, sum of Marks = 822

and number of students = 15

$\therefore$ Mean = $\frac{822}{15} = 54.8$

41. (a) $(-4.6) \times (-4.6) \div (-4.6 + 0.6)$

$= \frac{(-4.6) \times (-4.6)}{-4} = -5.29$

42. (c)

43. (b) Price of $4\frac{1}{2}$ m $= \frac{9}{2}$ m of cloth

$= ₹\ 60\frac{3}{4} = \frac{243}{4}$

$\therefore$ Cost of 1 m of cloth $= \frac{243}{4} \times \frac{2}{9} = ₹13\frac{1}{2}$

44. (c) The Galilean moons are the four largest moons of Jupiter—Io, Europa, Ganymede, and Callisto. They were first seen by Galileo Galilei and recognized by him as satellites of Jupiter in 1610.

45. (c)

46. (c) X = 24 (position in English alphabets)

BE = 2 + 5 = 7

Similarly, RING = 18 + 9 + 14 + 7 = 48.

47. (b) Let two constitutive odd numbers are n and (n + 2).

Now, $n(n + 2) = 399$

$n^2 + 2n - 399$

$\Rightarrow (n + 21)(n - 19) = 0$

$\therefore n = 19.$

48. (c) Dibrugarh–Kanyakumari Vivek Express is a weekly Express train which runs from Dibrugarh in Assam to Kanyakumari (Tamil Nadu). In 96.30 hours the train covers a distance of 4,262 kilometres and traverses seven states in India.

49. (d)

50. (b) Siberian ibexes are large and heavily built goats that live in central Asia.

51. (c) let cost price of 25 chair = 100

then, cost price of 1 chair $= \frac{100}{25}$ ₹ 4

Selling price of 20 chair = 100

$\therefore$ Selling price of 1 chair $= \frac{100}{20} = ₹\ 5$

Profit % $= \frac{5-4}{4} \times 100 = 25\%$

52. (b) Let cost price of the goods is ₹ 100.

Marked price of the goods $= 100 \times \frac{120}{100}$

$= 120$

Selling price $= 120 \times \left(\frac{100-5}{100}\right) = ₹\ 114$

Profit % $= \left(\frac{114-100}{100}\right) \times 100 = 14\%$

53. (a) Swadeshi means that each and every thing in a country should be our own not of any other country or society. In hindi swadeshi means:"Apne desh ka".

54. (b) Oxidation occurs when a reactant loses electrons during the reaction. Reduction occurs when a reactant gains electrons during the reaction. This often occurs when metals are reacted with acid.

55. (b) Maasai Mara National Reserve is a large game reserve in Narok County, Kenya. It is globally famous for its exceptional population of lions, leopards and cheetahs, and the annual migration of zebra, Thomson's gazelle, and wildebeest.

56. (a) First we calculate compound interest for 2 years at 12% per annum. Then we calculate 4 month's interest on total amount.

7500@12% = 900 – first year

Total amount after one year = 7500 + 900 = ₹ 8400

For second year

8400 × 12% = 1008

Total amount 8400 + 1008 = 9408

Now for 4 months

$$9408 \times \frac{12}{100} \times \frac{4}{12} = 376.32 = 376$$

Total amount 9408 + 376 = 9784

Net interest after 2 years 4 months

9784 – 7500 = 2284

(57-59) :

57. (c) Average marks in geography

$$= \frac{68 + 65 + 69 + 70}{4} = 68$$

Average marks in history

$$= \frac{65 + 75 + 70 + 65}{4} = 68.75$$

58. (*) Average marks in science

$$= \frac{80 + 85 + 88 + 87}{4} = 85$$

Average marks in math

$$= \frac{75 + 80 + 82 + 78}{4} = 78.75$$

Required percentage difference

$$= \left(\frac{85 - 78.75}{78.75}\right) \times 100 = 8\%$$

59. (c) Shamita = 75 + 80 + 65 + 68 + 72 + 65 = 425

Smita = 80 + 85 + 75 + 65 + 70 + 70 = 445

Shilpa = 82 + 88 + 70 + 69 + 71 + 70 = 450

Sheela = 78 + 87 + 65 + 70 + 75 + 74 = 449

∴ Shilpa has got highest total marks.

60. (b) $\sin\theta + \cos\theta = m$

$$\sec\theta + \operatorname{cosec}\theta = n \Rightarrow \frac{1}{\cos\theta} + \frac{1}{\sin\theta} = n$$

$$= \frac{\sin\theta + \cos\theta}{\sin\theta.\cos\theta} = n$$

$$= \frac{m}{\sin\theta.\cos\theta} = n$$

$$\therefore \frac{m}{n} = \sin\theta.\cos\theta$$

61. (a) N is the wife of P. And both have one son M.O is the father-in-law of P.

62. (c) Sepak takraw or kick volleyball, is a sport native to Southeast Asia. Sepak takraw differs from the similar sport of foot volley in its use of a rattan ball and only allowing players to use their feet, knee, chest and head to touch the ball.

63. (b) Let Z alone can finish the work in n days.

$$\text{Then, } \frac{1}{36} + \frac{1}{60} + \frac{1}{n} = \frac{1}{18}$$

$$\frac{1}{n} = \frac{1}{18} - \frac{1}{36} - \frac{1}{60} = \frac{10 - 5 - 3}{180}$$

$$\frac{1}{n} = \frac{1}{90} \Rightarrow n = 90$$

Hence, Z alone can finish it in 90 days.

64. (c) Colombo, the capital of Sri Lanka, has a long history as a port on ancient east-west trade routes, ruled successively by the Portuguese, Dutch and British. That heritage is reflected in its architecture, mixing colonial buildings with high-rises and shopping malls.

65. (c) $$\frac{\sin\theta}{1 + \cos\theta} + \frac{1 + \cos\theta}{\sin\theta} = \frac{\sin^2\theta + (1 + \cos\theta)^2}{(1 + \cos\theta)\sin\theta}$$

$$\frac{\sin^2\theta + \cos^2\theta + 1 + 2\cos\theta}{(1 + \cos\theta)\sin\theta}$$

$$\frac{1 + 1 + 2\cos\theta}{(1 + \cos\theta)\sin\theta} = \frac{2 + 2\cos\theta}{(1 + \cos\theta)\sin\theta}$$

$$\frac{2(1 + \cos\theta)}{(1 + \cos\theta)\sin\theta} = \frac{2}{\sin\theta}$$

66. (b) The Panchatantra is an ancient Indian collection of interrelated animal fables in Sanskrit verse and prose. The surviving work is dated to roughly 200 BCE. The text's author is unknown, but has been attributed to Vishnu Sharma.

67. (c) The Pokhran-II tests were a series of five nuclear bomb test explosions conducted by India at the Indian Army's Pokhran Test Range in May 1998. It was the second instance of nuclear testing conducted by India; the first test, code-named Smiling Buddha, was conducted in May 1974.

68. (d) Penguins are found in coldest regions in the world and also birds found in hot region have wings.

69. (d) Anjolie Ela Menon (born 1940) is one of India's leading contemporary artists.

Her paintings are in several major collections. In 2006 her work "Yatra" was acquired by the Asian Art Museum of San Francisco, California. Her preferred medium is oil on masonite, though she has also worked in other media, including glass and water colour. She is a well known muralist. She was awarded the Padma Shree in 2000.

70. (b) Let the two digits of the number are x and (9 – x).

Number is $10x + (9 - x) = 9(1 + x)$

(2-digit at ten place 1-digit at unit place)

ATQ, $9(1 + x) + 27 = 10(9 - x) + x$

(digits interchanges)

$9x + 36 = 90 - 9x$

$18x = 54 \Rightarrow x = 3$

Number $= 10 \times 3 + (9 - 3) = 36$

71. (c) 13 , 14 , 18 , 27 , 43 , 68 , 104

$+(1)^2$ $+(2)^2$ $+(3)^2$ $+(4)^2$ $+(5)^2$ $+(6)^2$

72. (a) Kitty's mother is Uthara's maternal aunt.

73. (d) Let other two angles are 9x and 16x.

Then, $9x + 16x + 55 = 180$

$25x = 125 \Rightarrow x = 5$

Hence, two angles are $9 \times 5 = 45°$

$16 \times 5 = 80°$

74. (d) Atul Dodiya is one of the most sought after contemporary artists today. Atul came into prominence in 1999 with his series on Mahatma Gandhi, where the painter sought to reconstruct images from a forgotten biography of the leader. His watercolours led the Mahatma out of the tumultuous pages of history into the gentle sepia-washed terrain of his canvas.

75. (b) 2nd week income $= \frac{120°}{360°} \times 360000$

$= ₹\ 120000$

76. (c)

H O U S E S

↓–1 ↓–1 |+6 ↓+6 ↓–1 ↓–1

G N A Y D R

Similarly,

D I A R Y

↓–1 ↓–1 |+6 ↓+6 ↓–1

C H G X X

77. (a) Satyameva Jayathe translates to "Truth Alone Triumphs" This Mantra shows the power of truth and how it ultimately wins. These words are inscribed on the Ashok Stambh, which was built by Emperor Ashoka and reflects the ideals of the great emperor.

78. (c) Malé is the densely populated capital of the Maldives, an island nation in the Indian Ocean. It's known for its mosques and colourful buildings.

79. (c) Forward : Backward are opposite word. Except Anger : Wrath, other three pairs of words are opposite pair.

80. (a) Religions teach the guiding principles for leading one's life implies that religion is a way of life.

81. (c) In H_2O, H is Hydrogen and O is Oxygen. Similarly in KOH, K is Potassium and OH is Hydroxide group.

82. (c) $\frac{9}{13} \div \frac{18}{26} \div \frac{90}{52} = \frac{9}{13} \times \frac{26}{18} \times \frac{52}{90} = \frac{26}{45}$

83. (d) $\frac{0-0}{100-0} = \frac{F-32}{212-32}$

$0 = \frac{F-32}{180} \Rightarrow F - 32 = 0$

$\therefore F = 32°F$

84. (d)

S H F I F

↓+13 ↓+13 ↓+13 ↓+13 ↓+13

F U S V S

Similarly,

Z E B R A

↓+13 ↓+13 ↓+13 ↓+13 ↓+13

M R O E N

85. (*) A normal resting heart rate for adults ranges from 60 to 100 beats per minute. Generally, a lower heart rate at rest implies more efficient heart function and better cardiovascular fitness.

86. (b) Here Q and C are children of P. And P is the wife of Q's father. So, P is daughter of B.

87. (b) Junko Tabei was a Japanese mountaineer. She was the first woman to reach the summit of Mount Everest, and the first woman to ascend all Seven Summits on every continent.

88. (*) Number of windows made by 8 carpenter for working 6 days $= \frac{96 \times 8}{6} = 128$ windows

So, Number of window made in 4 days

$= \frac{128}{6} \times 4 = 85.33$ windows

89. (c) Production of cassettes in month

January = 1858509

February = 1858509 + 7623 = 1866132

March = 1866132 – 25838 = 1840294

Total productions in three months

= 1858509 + 1866132 + 1840294

= 5564935

90. (b) Makara Sankranti, or Maghi, is a festival day in the Hindu calendar, dedicated to the deity Surya. It is observed each year in January. It marks the first day of the sun's transit into the Makara, marking the end of the month with the winter solstice and the start of longer days.

91. (b) Confusion causes mental tension which causes anxiety.

92. (a) (i) Mango, lemon and melon are fruits — 439516

(ii) Mango and lemon are yellow — 04396

(iii) Melon is green — 857

From (i) and (ii), we get 'Melon' code is '5'.

93. (d)

A I Q, B J R, C K S, D L T, E M U,

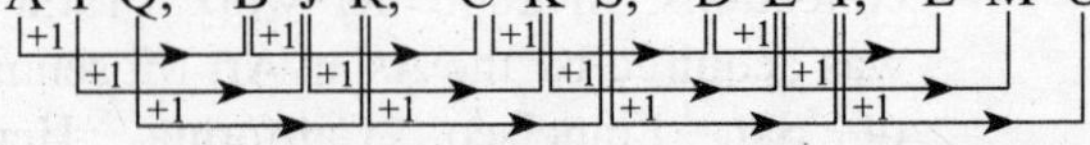

94. (a) Both are running in opposite direction, so relative speed = 7 + 5 = 12 m/sec

Distance between then in 42 minutes.

$= 12 \times 42 \times 60$ m

$= \frac{12 \times 42 \times 60}{1000}$ km = 30.24 km

95. (d) In 2015 Afghanistan joined the world trade organization as the 44th member.

96. (b) Difference between C.I. and S.I. when time is 2 years.

$$\text{S.I.} = \frac{5000 \times 8 \times 2}{100} = ₹\,800$$

$$\text{C.I.} = 5000\left[\left(1 + \frac{8}{100}\right)^2 - 1\right]$$

$= ₹\,832$

$\therefore$ Difference = 832 – 800 = ₹ 32

97. (b)

$12 - [26 - \{2 + 5 \times (6 - 3)\}]$

$12 - [26 - \{2 + 15\}]$

$12 - [26 - 17] = 12 - 9 = 3$

98. (c) Number of bottles required $= \frac{42 \times 1000}{280}$

= 150.

99. (a) Let two consecutive numbers are n and (n + 2).

Their L.C.M. = 144

H.C.M. = 2(as both are consecutive even number)

So, L.C.M. × H.C.M = Product of numbers

$144 \times 2 = n \times (n + 2)$

$n^2 + 2n = 288 \Rightarrow n^2 + 2n - 288 = 0$

$(n - 16)(n + 18) = 0$

$n = 16$

$n + 2 = 18$

Hence, two numbers are 16 and 18.

100. (b) Dibru-Saikhowa National Park is a national park in Assam, India. It is located in Dibrugarh and Tinsukia districts and was designated a Biosphere Reserve in July 1997.

RRB NTPC stage-I Solved Paper
Held On 3rd April 2016 (Shift-II)

1. The make In India's' Logo is made up of what?
(a) Lion made of Cogs
(b) Eagle Made of Steel
(c) Chakra Made of Cotton
(d) Tiger Made of Khadi

2. The median of the following numbers arranged in ascending order is 2.5, if so find x?
0, 0, 1, 1, 2, 2, x, 3, 3, 4, 5, 7
(a) 2 (b) 3 (c) 4 (d) 0

3. How do Indians celebrate Holi?
(a) By playing pranks on each other
(b) By throwing coloured powder and water on each other
(c) By lighting lamps
(d) By setting pigeons free

4. X is the only daughter of Y's grand father's only son, Y's grandfather has only one child. How is X related to Y?
(a) Mother (b) Sister
(c) Paternal aunt (d) Grand mother

5. In Indian sport what does HIL stand for?
(a) Himachal Indian Lions
(b) Haryana Indus League
(c) Hockey India League
(d) Hyderabad India League

Directions (Q. Nos. 6-8) *Study the following diagram and answer questions based on it.*

The diagram represents the likes of children in a society.

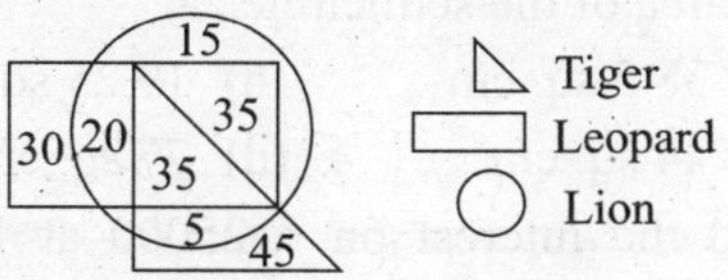

6. The difference between children who like leopard to those who like tiger is
(a) 50 (b) 35 (c) 30 (d) 5

7. How many children like both lion and leopard?
(a) 35 (b) 55 (c) 90 (d) 95

8. How many children who like lion, also like tiger?
(a) 5 (b) 15 (c) 35 (d) 40

9. Find the missing (?) in the series 50, 49.5, ?, 45.5, 42, 37.5, ...
(a) 49 (b) 48 (c) 47.5 (d) 46

10. Malgudi Days is based on the works of which Indian Writer?
(a) Shankar Nag (b) RK Lakshman
(c) RK Narayan (d) Girish Karnad

11. Statements followed by some conclusions are given below.

Statements
1. Employees are well paid.
2. Rajan earns well.

Conclusions
I. Rajan is an employee.
II. Rajan is self-employed.

Find which of the given conclusions logically follows from the given statements.
(a) Only Conclusion I follows.
(b) Only Conclusion II follows.
(c) Both I and II follow.
(d) Neither I nor II follows.

12. At what time did India Gain Independence of 15th August, 1947.
(a) Morning (b) Mid-evening
(c) Mid-night (d) Noon

13. A train having a length of 500 m passes through a tunnel of 1000 m in one minute. What is the speed of the train in km/h?
(a) 75 km/h (b) 90 km/h
(c) 87 km/h (d) 96 km/h

14. What is the science or Art of designing and accelerating projectiles so as to achieve a desired performance Called?

(a) Ballistic (b) Catapulting

(c) Ejection (d) Rocket Science

15. Find the similarity in the following: Orange Peach, Olive, Chrome

(a) All of them are fruits.

(b) All of them are names of seasons.

(c) All of them are colours

(d) All of them are shades of orange.

16. What does WLAN stand for?

(a) Wireless Local Area Network

(b) Wide Local Area Network

(c) Wind Light Atmospheric Nature

(d) Wireless Local Area Node

17. What does "Bicameral Legislature" mean?

(a) Legislators are divided into 4 separate assemblies

(b) Legislators are grouped as 1 assembly

(c) Legislators are divided into 2 separate assemblies

(d) Legislators are divided into 8 separate assemblies

18. Find the missing (?) in the series ... HG, IJ, LK, MN, ?, ...

(a) OP (b) PO (c) QP (d) PQ

19. A small shop owner keeps inventory satisfying the following criteria

(a) Shampoo Sachets that are priced between ₹ 4 and ₹ 10 per sachets.

(b) Chocolates in the price range of ₹ 1 and ₹ 60 per piece

(c) Dry fruits priced more than ₹ 125 per 100 gm

(d) Milk packets in the price range of ₹ 21 and ₹ 29 per litre

20. Which is the most abundant combustible natural gas?

(a) Propane (b) Methane

(c) Ethane (d) Butane

21. Which among the following is the largest Freshwater Lake in India?

(a) Dal Lake (b) Thol Lake

(c) Pushkar Lake (d) Wular Lake

22. Manu sold a dozen watches for 1454.64 per watch and made a profit of 16%. Find the cost price of the watches

(a) 1254.00 (b) 1362.36

(c) 15048.00 (d) 16348.32

23. The famous camel trading event is a part of this annual fair.

(a) Udaipur Mela (b) Thar Mela

(c) Kumbh Mela (D) Pushkar Mela

24. What is the rate of change of position of an object with respect to a frame of reference, which is a function of time called?

(a) Mechanics (b) Vector

(c) Velocity (d) Magnitude

25. If DELHI is QRYUV, then BOMBAY is

(a) OBZNOL (b) OZBNOL

(c) OZBONL (d) OBZONL

26. If GOING is 38253 and CASUAL is 409106, then LOGICAL is

(a) 6034286 (b) 6834206

(c) 6032486 (d) 6832406

27. Manju takes 16 days to complete a work. If she works with her friend Jenny they complete it in 12 days. How many days will it take for Jenny to complete the work alone?

(a) 48 (b) 32 (c) 36 (d) 24

28. Solve : $10^9 \times 10^2 \div 10^3$

(a) 10^8 (b) 10^6 (c) 10^2 (d) 10^5

29. If the circumference of a circle is 22 cm, find the area of the semicircle.

(a) 38.5 sq. cm (b) 19.25 sq.cm

(c) 44 sq. cm (d) 77 sq. cm

30. Find the interest on ₹ 25000 at 12% p.a. compounded annually for 3 yr.

(a) 9,000 (b) 9,833.40

(c) 10,123.20 (d) 10,678.90

31. The LCM and HCF of two numbers are 168 and 6 respectively. If one of the numbers is 24. Find the other

(a) 36 (b) 38 (c) 40 (d) 42

32. Seeta said, " Ram's only brother is the father of my son's father". How is Ram's brother related to Seeta's son?

(a) Father (b) Grandfather
(c) Maternal uncle (d) Paternal uncle

33. 78 books, 114 crayons and 141 note books were distributed to school children equally. It was found that 6 were left undistributed in each. What was the total number of children?

(a) 9 (b) 8 (c) 13 (d) 12

34. What are Viviparous?

(a) Vertebrates that are born live
(b) Type of cactus
(c) Type of algae
(d) A mollusk

Directions (Q. Nos. 35-37)

The bar chart represents percentage marks scored by four students U, V, W and X in History and Geography. Consider the bar chart and answer questions based on it.

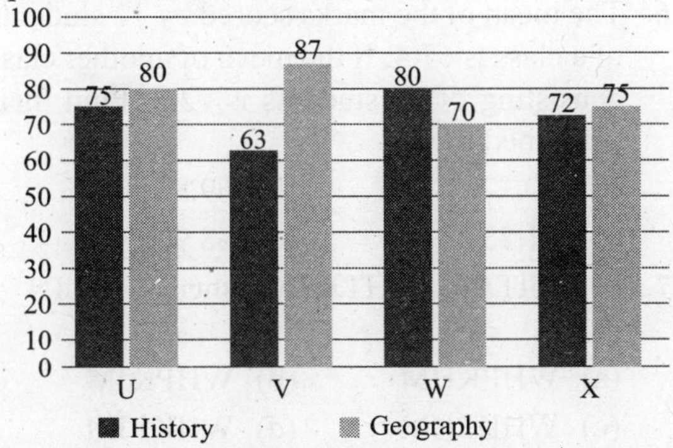

35. Who scored the highest percentage in both the subjects combined?

(a) Both V and W (b) V
(c) W (d) U

36. What is the percentage difference in the total marks obtained in Geography and History?

(a) 7.8% (b) 22%
(c) 4.13% (d) 5%

37. What is the average percentage marks obtained in History by all students?

(a) 78% (b) 75%
(c) 72.5% (d) 70%

38. If $a^{x+y} = a^6$ and x > y by 2 find x.

(a) 1 (b) 2 (c) 3 (d) 4

39. What is a Limerick ?

(a) A type of Lime Stone
(b) A form of poetry mostly in five-lines
(c) A type of Theatre Play
(d) A type of Word game

40. If **Annual : One year**, then **Quinquennial : ....**

(a) Five years (b) Ten years
(c) Hundred years (d) Thousand years

41. Andromeda is a

(a) Galaxy neighbouring the Milky Way
(b) Planet
(c) Name of a black hole
(d) Comet

42. Whose quote is "In practice of tolerance, one's enemy is the best teacher"?

(a) Gautama Buddha (b) Mahatma Gandhi
(c) Barack Obama (d) The Dalai Lama

43. What is Shigmo?

(a) A Goa Spring Festival
(b) The tallest peak in Nilgiris
(c) A type of Rangoli
(d) One of the names of Lord Shiva

44. In computers, what does Yosemite, Mavericks, Mountain Lion, Lion Snow Leopard, Leopard, Tiger, Tiger Panther, Jaguar, Puma and Cheetah stand for?

(a) Versions of Mac OS X
(b) Types of Storage Servers
(c) Macintosh Clones
(d) None of the above

45. Rearrange the jumbled letters to make a meaningful word and then select the one which is different.

(a) ENNI (b) NEO
(c) EPPI (d) REETH

46. Solve $\frac{12}{13} \times \frac{285}{96} \div \frac{171}{169} = ?$

(a) $3\frac{2}{3}$ (b) $2\frac{17}{24}$
(c) $\frac{7}{8}$ (d) $\frac{11}{24}$

47. LIGO, Laser Interferometer Gravitational Wave Observatory was recently in the news. Why?

(a) Discovery of water in Mars
(b) Discovery of a diamond-filled star
(c) Detection of Gravitational waves
(d) Proving Big Bang theory as wrong

48. In which century did Portuguese merchants first land in Goa?

(a) 14th (b) 15th (c) 16th (d) 17th

49. In 1999 who was the Prime Minister of Pakistan who was overthrown by a Military coup led by General Pervez Musharraf?

(a) Zulfiqar Ali Bhutto (b) Zia ul-Haq
(c) Nawaz Sharif (d) Yusuf Raza Gilani

50. What is C_6H_6?

(a) Hydro Carbon (b) Hydro Chloric Acid
(c) Benzene (d) Toluene

51. What is Oneirology, the study of ?

(a) Gods (b) Dreams
(c) Sleep (d) Colour

52. Which was the host city of the first modern summer Olympic games held in 1896 ?

(a) Athens (b) Paris
(c) London (d) Amsterdam

53. I take a book from a library containing 378 pages to be returned in a week's time. If I can read 14 pages an hour for three hours daily, for how long should it be renewed so that the book can be fully read?

(a) 1 day (b) 3 days
(c) 4 days (d) 2 days

54. Carl Sagan was

(a) An American astronomer
(b) British Physicist
(c) French Astronaut
(d) American President

55. Eggs sold by a shopkeeper over a week is given in the table below. Eggs sold in dozens

Day	Sales in dozen
Sunday	12
Monday	8
Tuesday	11
Wednesday	5
Thursday	9
Friday	10
Saturday	10

If the price of one dozen egg was ₹ 2.50, how much more did he earn on Friday than on Monday?

(a) ₹ 25 (b) ₹ 2.50
(c) ₹ 5.00 (d) ₹ 3.25

56. The mean of the marks scored by 12 students of a class is 67.4. If the mean of another class consisting of 15 students is 72.3. Find their combined mean.

(a) 70.12 (b) 69.85
(c) 71.23 (d) 68.94

57. If GUITAR = HTJSBQ, then VIOLIN = ____________

(a) WHPKHM (b) WHPKJM
(c) WHKPHM (d) WHKPJM

58. Aman walks at a certain speed and reaches his destination which is 6 km in 1h 40 min. If he runs the same distance, she reaches in 1 hour 20 min. What is the difference in speed?

(a) 1 km/h (b) 0.9 km/h
(c) 1.5 km/h (d) 1.9 km/h

59. What is "Binary Electronic Sequence Calculator'(BESK), created in 1953 ?

(a) Electronic Computer
(b) Analogous Computer
(c) Digital Computer
(d) A Banker's Calculator

60. Find $\sin(90° - \theta)$

(a) $\cos 90°$ (b) $\frac{1}{2}$ (c) 1 (d) $\cos\theta$

61. What is India's famous comic series started by Anant Pai called?

(a) Raj comics (b) Amar Chitra Katha
(c) Tinkle (d) Chandamama

62. Find $(x + y)^2 - (x - y)^2$.

(a) $2x^2y^2$ (b) $4xy$
(c) $2x^2 + 2y^2$ (d) $x^2 - y^2 + 2xy$

63. The area of a rectangle is 42 sq. cm and its length is 7 cm. Find its perimeter.

(a) 14cm (b) 21 cm
(c) 26 cm (d) 24 cm

64. If by selling 20 cycles vinay incurs a loss equal to the selling price of 2 cycles. Find his loss percentage.

(a) 10% (b) 11%
(c) $13\frac{1}{3}\%$ (d) $9\frac{1}{11}\%$

65. Read the following and answer the questions based on it.

Proteins are used by the body for energy, metabolism, gene growth and maintenance 10 to 35 percent of the daily calorie intake should ideally consist of proteins. They are found in all cells of the body. Hair and nail are made up of protein called keratin, having sulphur bonds. Curly hair has more sulphur links. Too much intake of proteins can sometimes lead to body weight gain. Proteins ....

(a) Are not used by the body for any of its functions
(b) Are required by the body in adequate quantities
(c) Makes hair shiny, lengthy and black
(d) Do not caus¢ weight gain

Directions (Q. Nos. 66-68) *Consider the following information and answer questions based on it.*

Five pickles - mango, lime, tomato, goose-berry and garlic are kept in five jars, in a row, in a random order, from left to right.

1. Goose-berry is not on either extremes.
2. There is one jar between mango and garlic.
3. Tomato is placed on the left side of lime.
4. The second jar from the left contain garlic.

66. There are two jars between which of the following

(a) Lime and Goose-berry
(b) Goose-berry and Tomato
(c) Mango and Lime
(d) Tomato and Mango

67. Lime is in the......... jar from left.

(a) Fifth (b) Fourth
(c) Third (d) First

68. The middle jar contains

(a) Mango (b) Tomato
(c) Goose-berry (d) Lime

69. What is an interstellar cloud of dust, hydrogen, helium and other ionized gases called?

(a) Galaxy (b) Supernova
(c) Nebula (d) Black Hole

70. Where is the mosque, Adhai Din Ka Jhopra located?

(a) Agra (b) Ajmer
(c) Ahmedabad (d) Mount Abu

71. What is the official language in Bhutan ?

(a) English (b) Hindi
(c) Dzongkha (d) Khmer

72. If the mathematical operator '+' means '×', '÷' means '–', '–' means '+' and '×' means '÷' find the value of $1 \times 2 + 6 - 2 \div 7$

(a) 2 (b) –2 (c) 3 (d) –1

73. When did Sikkim become a state of India?

(a) 1975 (b) 1973 (c) 1972 (d) 1950

74. What does PNR stand for ?

(a) Public Number in Railway

(b) Passenger Name Record

(c) Passenger Number Reservation

(d) Priority Number in Reservation (3) D

75. A politician distributed 285 kg of sugar among the people of a village counting 1487. Find out how much sugar does each person get.

(a) 1.91 kg (b) 191 kg

(c) 0.191 kg (d) 19.1 kg

76. A sum borrowed at 6% per annum earns an interest which is $\frac{1}{3}$ rd of its principal in x years. Find x

(a) $5\frac{5}{9}$ (b) $4\frac{2}{9}$ (c) $6\frac{3}{7}$ (d) $5\frac{3}{4}$

77. +91 is the country calling code for which nation?

(a) Canada (b) USA

(c) India (d) China

78. What plant has the scientific name Solanum Tuberosum?

(a) Potato (b) Tomato

(c) Pumpkin (d) Onion

79. Which signs should be interchanged if the equation below needs to be true?

$2 \div 16 - 2 + 6 \times 1 = 0$

(a) × and – (b) – and +

(c) – and ÷ (d) + and ×

80. Who is called 'India's Child Surgeon'?

(a) Akrit Pran Jaswal

(b) Tathagat Avtar Tulsi

(c) Nischal Narayanam

(d) Sudhma Verma

81. Yash sells vegetables at 40 per kg and incurs a loss of 10%. If the total loss incurred is 144, what is the weight of vegetables sold ? (Rounded off)

(a) 36 kg (b) 32.40 kg

(c) 35 kg (d) 39.2 kg

82. Name the inter-governmental organisation to promote International Co-operation?

(a) NATO (b) UN

(c) WHO (d) IGO

83. 1.08 tonne = ? kg

(a) 10800 (b) 108

(c) 1080 (d) 1.08

84. Looking at a photo, Anand said, "This man is the eldest son of my father's mother-in-law". How is Anand's mother related to this man?

(a) Mother (b) Daughter

(c) Maternal Aunt (d) Sister

85. An Assertion (A) and a Reason (R) are given below.

Assertion (A) Leaves are green in colour.

Reason (R) Chlorophyll, a green pigment is present in leaves.

Choose the correct option.

(a) Both (A) and (R) are true and (R) is the correct explanation of (A).

(b) Both (A) and (R) are true but (R) is not the correct explanation of (A).

(c) (A) is true, but (R) is false.

(d) (A) is false, but (R) is true.

86. What is the opposite of Dharma?

(a) Adharma (b) Karma

(c) Moksha (d) Maya

87. A statement followed by some conclusions are given below.

Statement

The price of pulses has increased steeply.

Conclusions

I. People cannot buy pulses.

II. Pulses have become a rare commodity.

Find which of the given conclusions logically follow from the given statement.

(a) Only conclusion I follows.

(b) Only conclusion II follows.

(c) Both I and II follows.

(d) Neither I nor II follows.

88. Who has never been a Vice-President of India?
(a) Mohammad Hamid Ansari
(b) APJ Abdul Kalam
(c) Ramaswamy Venkataraman
(d) Shankar Dayal Sharma

89. Solve :$1+\tan^2\theta = ?$
(a) $\cos^2\theta$ (b) $\sec^2\theta$ (c) $\tan^2\theta$ (d) 2

90. If x is an even number, what is the consecutive odd number?
(a) x – 1 (b) x + 1 (c) x + 2 (d) x – 2

91. Select the alternative that shows a similar relationship as the given pair. Truthful : Honest
(a) Notwithstanding : Nevertheless
(b) Including : Excluding
(c) Winning : Losing
(d) Procuring : Disposing

92. Four pairs of words are given. Find the odd one out.
(a) Ear: Hearing (b) Tongue: Taste
(c) Mouth : Speech (d) Light : Vision

93. If INSECT = @ &*!#$ and OR= %?, then CISTERN = ...
(a) #@*$!%& (b) #@*$?!&
(c) #@*$!?& (d) #@*$%!&

94. How many litres of water can be stored in a tank of 1 m length; $\frac{1}{2}$ m breadth and; $\frac{1}{2}$ m tall?
(a) 25,000 (b) 250
(c) 25 (d) 2,500

95. What was recently discovered hidden under ice in Antarctica?
(a) A massive mountain range
(b) A lost Kingdom
(c) A massive canyon system and lake
(d) A huge Dinosaur Skeleton

96. Jane won a lottery and gets $\frac{1}{3}$rd of the winning amount and donates = 6000 which is $\frac{1}{6}$th, find how much the lottery was worth.
(a) 36000 (b) 18000
(c) 54000 (d) 108000

97. Find the difference between the place value and face value of the digit 9 in the number 229301 ?
(a) 9292 (b) 8991 (c) 0 (d) 220

98. The sum of two numbers is 437 and their product is 21982. Find the numbers.
(a) 399 and 38 (b) 295 and 142
(c) 58 and 379 (d) 323 and 114

99. What is the gravitational force exerted on a mass called?
(a) Stress (b) Inertia
(c) Weight (d) Work

100. A bank agrees to lend a loan to Arvind of ₹ 2,38,75,697. Which falls short by 17% for starting his business. How much more loan would he need ?
(a) 4890203 (b) 4375303
(c) 5700108 (d) 5125533

Hints & Solutions

1. (a) The logo of 'Make-in-India' is the silhouette of a lion, made entirely of cogs, symbolising manufacturing, strength and national pride.

2. (a) Number in ascending order:
1, 1, 2, 2, x, 3, 3, 4, 5, 7
Number of forms = 10
Median = mean of 5th and 6th term
$2.5 = \frac{x+3}{2} \Rightarrow x + 3 = 5 \Rightarrow x = 2$

3. (b) Holi is a popular ancient Hindu festival of colours, where people smear and drench each other with colours.

4. **(b)** Y's grand father only son is Y's father. Now, Y's father's daughter is x. So, x is the sister of Y.

5. **(c)** Hockey India League, is a professional field hockey league in India, organized by Hockey India, the governing body for the sport in India.

6-8:

6. **(b)** Required difference = 30 + 20 + 35 – 5 – 45 = 35

7. **(c)** Number of children like both leopard and lion = 20 + 35 + 35 = 90

8. **(d)** Required number = 35 + 5 = 40

9. **(b)** Series is

50, 49.5, 48, 45.5, 42, 37.5

–0.5 –1.5 –2.5 –3.5 –4.5

10. **(c)** Malgudi Days is a collection of short stories by R. K. Narayan published in 1943. The book includes 32 stories, all set in the fictional town of Malgudi.

11. **(d)** All well earner are not employee. So it is not compulsory true that Rajan is an employee. Also, we can not say about his employment.

12. **(c)** India became a free country at midnight between August 14 and August 15, 1947. It was then that the free India's first prime minister Pandit Jawaharlal Nehru gave his famous "Tryst with Destiny" speech.

13. **(b)** Speed of the train $= \frac{500 + 1000}{60\,(\text{sec})} = \frac{1500}{60}$

$= 25\text{m/sec} = 25 \times \frac{18}{5} = 90$ km/hr.

14. **(a)** Ballistics is the science of mechanics that deals with the flight, behaviour, and effects of projectiles, especially bullets, unguided bombs, rockets, etc.

15. **(c)**

16. **(a)** A wireless local area network is one in which multiple computers can communicate with each other through a wireless connection.

17. **(c)** A bicameral legislature has legislators in two separate assemblies, chambers, or houses i.e. Upper house and Lower house.

18. **(b)**

+1 +1 +1

H G, I J, L K, M N, P O

+1 +1 +1 +1 +1 +1

19. **(*)**

20. **(b)** Methane is the most abundant component of pure natural gas; is highly combustible and can be used for a wide range of energy purposes.

21. **(d)** Wular Lake, located in Jammu and Kashmir, is a natural lake which is a major part of the Jhelum River basin.

22. **(a)** $\text{Cost price} = \text{selling price} \times \frac{100}{100 + \text{profit}\%}$

$= 1454.64 \times \frac{100}{100 + 16} = ₹\ 1254$

23. **(d)** The Pushkar Fair, also called Pushkar Camel Fair is an annual multi-day livestock fair held in Pushkar (Rajasthan).

24. **(c)** The velocity or speed of an object is the rate of change of its position with respect to a frame of reference, and is a function of time.

25. **(d)**

D E L H I

↓+13 ↓+13 ↓+13 ↓+13 ↓+13

Q R Y U V

Similarly,

B O M B A Y

↓+13 ↓+13 ↓+13 ↓+13 ↓+13 ↓+13

O B Z O N L

26. **(d)**

Letter	G	O	I	N	C	A	S	U	L
Code	3	8	2	5	4	0	9	1	6

Hence, code of 'LOGICAL' is '6832406'.

27. **(a)** Let Jenny done can complete the whole work in n days. Then, $\frac{1}{n} + \frac{1}{16} = \frac{1}{12}$

$\frac{1}{n} = \frac{1}{12} - \frac{1}{16} \Rightarrow \frac{4-3}{48} \Rightarrow \frac{1}{n} = \frac{1}{48}$

n = 48 days

28. (a) $10^9 \times 10^2 \div 10^3 = 10^{9+2-3} = 10^8$

29. (b) Circumference of the circle = $2\pi r$

$$22 = 2\frac{22}{7}r \Rightarrow r = \frac{7}{2}$$

Area of the semicircle = $\frac{1}{2}\pi r^2$

$$= \frac{1}{2} \times \frac{22}{7} \times \left(\frac{7}{2}\right)^2 = \frac{77}{4} = 19.25 \text{ cm}^2$$

30. (c) Compound interest = $P\left[\left(1 + \frac{r}{100}\right)^t - 1\right]$

$$= 25000\left[\left(1 + \frac{12}{100}\right)^3 - 1\right]$$

$= 25000[1.4 - 1] = ₹\ 10123.2$

31. (d) Product of two numbers = L.C.M. × H.C.F

$\therefore$ Second number = $\frac{168 \times 6}{24} = 42$

32. (b) Father of my son's father mean my son's grandfather. Hence, Ram's only brother is Seeta's son's grandfather.

33. (a) Number of distribution of each items = (78 – 6) = 72 book; (114 – 6) = 108 crayons and (141 – 6) = 135 note books. Number of children = H.C.F. of 72, 108 and 135 = 9

34. (a) An animal that is viviparous gives birth to developed live young ones.

35. (d) 'U' scores in both subjects = 75 + 80 = 155 Which is highest among all the students.

36. (b) Required percentage difference

(80 + 87 + 70 + 75) – (75 + 63 + 80 + 72)

312 – 290 = 22%

37. (c) Average percent in History

$$= \frac{290}{4} = 72.5\%$$

38. (d) $a^{x+y} = a^6 \Rightarrow x + y = 6$ ...(i)

and $x - y = 2$ ...(ii) {given in the question}

From (i) and (ii),

$2x = 6 + 2 \Rightarrow x = \frac{8}{2} = 4.$

39. (b) A limerick is a humorous poem consisting of five lines.

40. (a) One year is also called annual, similarly five years is also called quinquennial.

41. (a) The Andromeda Galaxy, is our closest neighbour spiral galaxy, which is two and one-half million light-years away.

42. (d)

43. (a) The Shigmo festival takes place in Goa, during the spring season. It is a beautiful and auspicious festival of Hindus that celebrates the vibrancy of colours.

44. (a)

45. (c) ENNI — NINE, NEO — ONE

EPPI — PIPE, REETH — THREE.

46. (b) $\frac{12}{13} \times \frac{285}{96} \div \frac{228}{169} = \frac{12}{13} \times \frac{285}{96} \times \frac{169}{228}$

$$= \frac{5 \times 13}{6 \times 4} = 2\frac{17}{24}$$

47. (c) The Laser Interferometer Gravitational-Wave Observatory is a large-scale physics experiment and observatory to detect cosmic gravitational waves.

48. (c) Portuguese merchants first landed in Goa in 16th Century. In 1510, Portuguese conquered Goa from Adil Shah of Bijapur.

49. (c)

50. (c) Benzene is an organic chemical compound with six carbon atoms joined in a ring with one hydrogen atom attached to each.

51. (b)

52. (a) On April 6, 1896, the first modern Olympic Games were held in Athens, Greece, with athletes from 14 countries participating. The International Olympic Committee met for the first time in Paris in June 1894 and chose Greece as the site of the inaugural modern Olympiad.

53. (d) Number of pages one can read per day

14 × 3 = 42 pages

Number of days required = $\frac{378}{42}$ = 9 days

Number of days renewed = 9 – 7 = 2 days

54. (a) Carl Edward Sagan was an American astronomer, cosmologist, astrophysicist and author. He is best known as a science popularizer and communicator.

55. (c) Required amount = $(10 - 8) \times 2.5 =$ ₹ 5.00

56. (c) Total marks obtained by 27(12 + 15) students = $67.4 \times 12 + 72.3 \times 15$

Combined mean = $\dfrac{67.4 \times 12 + 72.3 \times 15}{27}$

$= \dfrac{808.8 + 1087.5}{27} = 71.23$

57. (b) G U I T A R — H T J S B Q

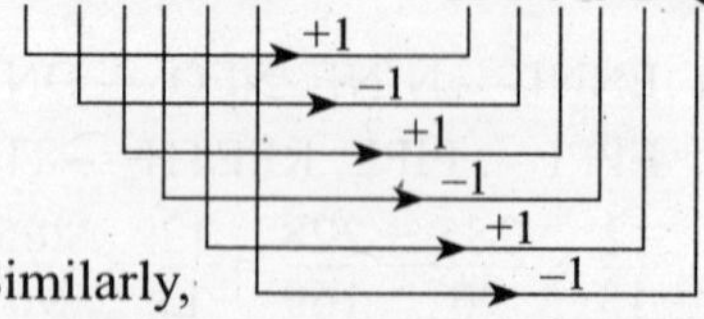

Similarly,

V I O L I N — W H P K J M

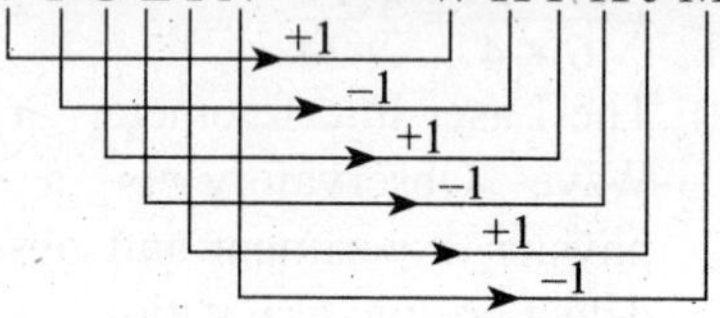

58. (b) Difference in speed = $\dfrac{6}{1 + \frac{20}{60}} - \dfrac{6}{1 + \frac{40}{60}}$

$\dfrac{6 \times 3}{4} - \dfrac{6 \times 3}{5} = \dfrac{18}{4} - \dfrac{18}{5} = \dfrac{18}{20} = 0.9$ km/hr.

59. (a) Binary Electronic Sequence Calculator was Sweden's first electronic computer, using vacuum tubes instead of relays; developed by Swedish Board for Computing Machinery. It was the fastest computer in the world.

60. (d) $\sin(90 - \theta) = \cos\theta$

61. (b) Anant Pai was an Indian educationist and pioneer of the Indian Comic Industry. Amar Chitra Katha and Tinkle are two of his most famous comic book series that is enjoyed by all age groups.

62. (b) $(x + y)^2 - (x - y)^2 = x^2 + y^2 + 2xy - x^2 - y^2 + 2xy = 4xy$

63. (c) Area of rectangle = Length × Breadth

$42 = 7 \times \text{Breadth} \Rightarrow \text{Breadth} = \dfrac{42}{7} = 6$ cm.

Perimeter = 2(Length + Breadth)

$= 2(7 + 6) = 2 \times 13 = 26$ cm

64. (d) Let selling price of each cycle = ₹ 100

Then, loss = 2 × selling price = $2 \times 100 = 200$

Total cost price = $2000 + 200 = 2200$

Loss% = $\dfrac{200}{2200} \times 100 = 9\dfrac{1}{11}\%$

65. (b) Proteins are required by the body in adequate quantities.

66-68: Arrangement of five pickles in a row:

Tomato — Garlic — Goose-berry — Mango — Lime

66. (d) **67. (a)** **68. (c)**

69. (c) A nebula is an interstellar cloud of dust, hydrogen, helium and other ionized gases.

70. (b) Adhai Din Ka Jhonpra is located in Ajmer, Rajasthan. It is one of the oldest mosques in India, and the oldest surviving monument in Ajmer.

71. (c) Dzongkha, or Bhutanese, is a Sino-Tibetan language spoken by over half a million people in Bhutan; it is the sole official and national language of the Kingdom of Bhutan.

72. (b) $1 \times 2 + 6 - 2 \div 7 = 1 \div 2 \times 6 + 2 - 7$

$= \dfrac{1}{2} \times 6 - 5 = -2$

73. (a)

74. (b) In the airline and travel industries, a passenger name record (PNR) in the database of a computer reservation system consists of the personal information for a passenger and also contains the itinerary for the passenger.

75. (c) In take of each person = $\dfrac{285}{1487} = 0.191$ kg

76. (a) Time = $\dfrac{\text{S.I.} \times 100}{P \times r} = \dfrac{1}{3} \times \dfrac{100}{1 \times 6} = 5\dfrac{5}{9}$ years.

77. (c) The India country code 91 allows you to call India from another country.

78. (a) The potato is a root vegetable that is part of the plant Solanum tuberosum.

79. (c) $2 \div 16 - 2 + 6 \times 1 \Rightarrow 2 - 16 \div 2 + 6 \times 1$

$\Rightarrow 2 - 8 + 6 = 0$

80. (a) Akrit Jaswal performed his first surgery at the age of 7. Akrit has an IQ of 146.

81. (b) Loss% = 10%

Cost price of 1 kg $= 40 \times \frac{100}{100-10} = 44.44$

Loss = 44.44 – 40 = 4.44

Now total loss = ₹ 144 (given)

Hence, weight of vegetable Yash sold

$= \frac{144}{4.44} = 32.4$ kg.

82. (b)

83. (c) 1 tonne = 1000 kg

1.08 tonnes = 1.08 × 1000 = 1080 kg.

84. (d) Son of my father's mother-in-law will be my mother's brother. Hence, my mother will be his sister.

85. (a) Due to chlorophyll a green pigment present in the leave, leaves are green in colour.

86. (a)

87. (d) People could have more money and demand increase could have caused price rise.

88. (b) APJ Abdul Kalam was an aerospace scientist who served as the 11th President of India from 2002 to 2007 but never as vice-president. It was intimately involved in India's civilian space programme and military missile development efforts.

89. (b) $1 + \tan^2\theta = 1 + \frac{\sin^2\theta}{\cos^2\theta} = \frac{\cos^2\theta + \sin^2\theta}{\cos^2\theta}$

$= \frac{1}{\cos^2\theta} = \sec^2\theta$

90. (b) Its x is a even number, then next odd number will be x + 1. For example, '6' is even number and 6 + 1 = 7 is next odd number.

91. (a)

92. (d) Ear, Tongue and Mouth are human body parts and by that one can hour, taste and speech respectively. Hence, light and vision are mismatch pair.

93. (c)

Letter	I	N	S	E	C	T	O	R
Symbol	@	&	*	!	#	$	%	?

Hence, code of 'CISTERN' is '#@*$!?&'

94. (b) We know that 1 m³ = 1000 litres

Now, volue of tank = length × breadth × height

$= 1 \times \frac{1}{2} \times \frac{1}{2} = \frac{1}{4}$ m3

$= \frac{1}{4} \times 1000$ litres = 250 litres.

95. (a) A team of researchers (UK) found a massive canyon by analysing satellite data of the ice sheet covering Princess Elizabeth Land in East Antarctica. While not visible to the eye, faint traces of the sub-glacial landscape can be detected in satellite imagery.

96. (d) Let lottery worth was ₹ x.

Then, $x \times \frac{1}{3} \times \frac{1}{6} = 6000$

$\Rightarrow x = 3 \times 6 \times 6000 =$ ₹ 108000

97. (b) Required difference = 9000 – 9 = 8991

98. (c) Let two numbers are x and y.

ATQ, x + y = 437 ...(i)

and xy = 21982

$(x-y)^2 = (x+y)^2 - 4xy = (437)^2 - 4 \times 21982$

= 190969 – 87928 = 103041

Now, $(x - y) = \sqrt{103041} = 321$ ...(ii)

From (i) and (ii)

$x = \frac{437+321}{2} = 379, \quad y = \frac{437-321}{2} = 58$

99. (c) In a uniform gravitational field, the gravitational force exerted on an object is directly proportional to its mass and is called its weight.

100. (a) Let Arvind needs ₹ x is start a business.

ATQ, $x - 23875697 = x \times \frac{17}{100}$

$\frac{100-17}{100}x = 23875697$

$\Rightarrow \frac{83}{100}x = 23875697$

$x = \frac{23875697 \times 100}{83} = 28765900$

Hence, required amount

= 28765900 – 23875697 = 4890203.

RRB NTPC stage-I Solved Paper

Held On 6th April 2016 (Shift-I)

1. Rearrange the jumbled letters to make meaningful words and then select the one which is different.

(a) LOWELY (b) IFER
(c) THIWE (d) WRONB

2. Find the value of '?', if the mean of the data set 18, 16, 22, 13, ? = 16

(a) 9 (b) 11 (c) 10 (d) 12

3. Which of the following will fit in '?' place the following series?

AN, BO, CP, DQ, ?

(a) ES (b) RE (c) FS (d) ER

4. The planet Mars is also known as the

(a) morning star (b) evening star
(c) red planet (d) blue planet

5. What is the common name of the solution of calcium hydroxide?

(a) Lime water (b) Diet soda
(c) Salt solution (d) Vinegar

6. Nurse : Ward :: Teacher : ?

(a) Student (b) Board
(c) Class (d) Lesson

7. 'Smiling Buddha' was the code name for

(a) The rescue and relief operations after the cloudburst in Uttarakhand in 2013.
(b) The rescue and relief operations after an earthquake hit Nepal in
(c) Pokhran-II nuclear test conducted by India in 1998.
(d) Pokhran-I nuclear test conducted by India in 1974.

Directions (Q. Nos. 8-10) *Consider the following information and answer questions based on it.*

Six cars S, T, V, W, X and Y are parked in a parking lot, in a random order, from left to right, such that

(A) T is parked on the extreme right.
(B) V is parked to the immediate right of Y and is one car away from W.
(C) X is to the immediate left of T and is three cars away from S.

8. Which of the following statement is true?

(a) There are two cars between T and V.
(b) There is one car between X and Y.
(c) There are three cars between Y and S.
(d) There is no car between X and W.

9. W is in the immediate right of

(a) S (b) Y
(c) V (d) Cannot be determined

10. Which car is parked to the immediate left of X?

(a) V (b) Y (c) W (d) T

11. Jantar Mantar in Delhi is historically important for

(a) Public meetings.
(b) Hunger strikes.
(c) Ancient sculptures.
(d) Astronomical observatory.

12. 'Bharat Stage Emission Standards' refers to

(a) Vehicular pollution
(b) Industrial pollution
(c) Water pollution
(d) Soil pollution

13. Statements followed by some conclusions are given below.

Statement

1. $M > L > N$
2. $N = R$

Conclusion

I. $R > L$
II. $R < M$

Find which of the given conclusions logically follows from the given statements

(a) Only conclusion I follows.
(b) Only conclusion II follows.
(c) Both I and II follow.
(d) Neither I nor II follows.

14. Find the odd statement. Two lines are perpendicular to each other, if they are
(a) Adjacent sides of a rectangle.
(b) Diagonals of a rhombus.
(c) Hypotenuse and one side of a right-angle triangle.
(d) Adjacent sides of a square.

15. A certain number of men agreed to do a work in 20 days. 5 men did not come for work. Other completed the work in 40 days. Find the number of men who had agreed to do the work originally.
(a) 8 (b) 10 (c) 12 (d) 15

16. How many prime numbers are there between the positive integers 60 and 100?
(a) 9 (b) 6 (c) 7 (d) 8

17. A migrating bird flies 40 km North, then turns East and flies 50 km, then turns North and flies 110 km, and turns to its left and flies 50 km.
Where is it now with reference to its starting position?
(a) 150 km South (b) 150 km North
(c) 70 km North (d) 70 km South

18. What do you mean by mixed economy?
(a) Economy of many nation mixed together
(b) Agricultural and Industrial sector together
(c) Combination of Private and state enterprises
(d) Industrial and service sector together

19. Find the value of $y(y^4 - y^2 - y)$, when $y = 5$.
(a) 2900 (b) 2975
(c) 2925 (d) 2995

20. The sum of two positive integers is 34 and their difference is 8. Find their product.
(a) 308 (b) 273 (c) 209 (d) 345

21. The LCM of two numbers is 66. The numbers are in the ratio 2 : 3. The sum of the numbers is
(a) 60 (b) 55 (c) 50 (d) 65

22. If P means '÷', R means '×', Q means '+'and S means '–', then 36 P 6 Q 7 R 8 S 11 =
(a) 45 (b) 51 (c) 52 (d) 62

23. Multitasking system specifically refers to
(a) More than one user.
(b) More than one process.
(c) More than one hardware.
(d) More than one IP address.

24. Union Government's School Nursery Yojana is about
(a) Creating environmental awareness in young minds.
(b) Streamlining admissions in nursery schools.
(c) Bringing nursery schools under regulations.
(d) Creating awareness about safety of children.

25. Ms. Chandra said that Laxmi's husband is the only son of my grandfather. How is Ms. Chandra related to Lakshmi?
(a) Mother (b) Daughter
(c) Cousin (d) Niece

26. Chief Election Commissioner of India can be removed from the office by
(a) Both houses of Parliament.
(b) Union council of Ministers.
(c) President of India.
(d) Chief Justice of India.

27. $\cos^2 90° + \text{cosec}^2 90° - \cot^2 45° = ?$
(a) 2 (b) –1 (c) 1/2 (d) $\sqrt{3}/2$

28. As per Census of India 2011, the population density was about
(a) 382 people per sq km
(b) 353 people per sq km
(c) 402 people per sq km
(d) 428 people per sq km

29. The difference between the ages of two sisters is 4 years when father's age is 54. Father is elder by 2 years to mother. Younger sister's age is half of mother's age. Find the age of the elder sister.

(a) 26 (b) 27 (c) 29 (d) 30

30. $2^2 - 3^3 + 4^3 - 6^2 = ?$

(a) 2 (b) 3 (c) 4 (d) 5

31. Syed Modi International Grand Prix Gold Championship is held every year at

(a) Chandigarh (b) Lucknow
(c) Delhi (d) Hyderabad

32. Name the first woman to head a paramilitary force

(a) Divya Ajith
(b) Archana Ramasundaram
(c) Punita Arora
(d) Ashwini Pawar

33. Who was known as Badshah Khan?

(a) Mohammed Ali Jinnah
(b) Abul Kalam Azad
(c) Khan Abdul Ghaffar Khan
(d) Khan Abdul Wali Khan

Directions (Q. Nos. 34-36) *The following table represents the rainfall (in mm) of five states from June to September in a year.*

	June	July	August	September
JK	1100	1100	1000	1200
HP	1100	1100	1000	1300
WB	1400	1300	1200	1000
GA	1000	1300	1500	1700
TN	1200	1050	1000	1100

Consider the information and answer questions based on it.

34. Which state has the lowest average rainfall?

(a) JK (b) HP (c) WB (d) TN

35. Which state shows a gradual increase in its rainfall from June to September?

(a) HP (b) GA (c) WB (d) TN

36. Which month received the lowest rainfall in the year?

(a) June (b) July
(c) August (d) September

37. The weights of 4 boxes are 90, 30, 20 and 50 kg. Which of the following cannot be the total weight in kg, of any combination of these boxes and in a combination a box can be used only once?

(a) 190 (b) 100
(c) 170 (d) 150

38. During morning walk, a man covers a distance of 3 km, 4 km, 3.5 km and 5 km and 4.5 km from Monday to Friday, respectively. How much distance should he cover on two more days, So that his average per week: becomes 4 km per day?

(a) 4 (b) 8 (c) 5 (d) 6

39. Find the HCF and LCM of 16, 24.

(a) 8, 48 (b) 4, 12
(c) 2, 24 (d) 4, 48

40. Saffron is produced in a large scale in

(a) Himachal Pradesh (b) Gujarat
(c) Jammu and Kashmir (d) Kerala

41. Aman purchased a cycle for ₹ 3,000 and agreed to pay 12% on the amount as interest. He repaid principal and interest in 12 equal monthly instalments. Find the amount of each instalment.

(a) ₹ 260 (b) ₹ 240
(c) ₹ 280 (d) ₹ 300

42. The political system in Afghanistan is known as

(a) Islamic State of Afghanistan
(b) Islamic Republic of Afghanistan
(c) Islamic Emirate of Afghanistan
(d) Islamic Government of Afghanistan

43. If 'are you sam' = 'ri ai ki', 'all hate you' = 'vi li ri' and 'all are fake' = 'mi ai li' then which represents 'hate'?

(a) ri (b) li (c) vi (d) ai

44. Pointing to K, M said that she was the daughter of the only son of his grandfather. How M is related to K?

(a) Mother (b) Maternal Aunt
(c) Daughter (d) Sister

45. Find the mean value of 2,3, 3, 4,6, 7

(a) 4.17 (b) 4.15 (c) 4.13 (d) 4.70

46. Who won majority of the men's singles tennis grand slam tournaments in 2015?

(a) Andy Murray (b) Novak Djokovic
(c) Roger Federer (d) Stanislas Wawrinka

47. The ratio of present ages of two brothers is 1 : 2 and 5 yr back the ratio was 1 : 3. What will be the ratio of their ages after 5 yr?

(a) 1 : 4 (b) 2 : 3
(c) 3 : 5 (d) 5 : 6

48. If CABINET = EIACBTN, then COMPUTE =

(a) TPOMECU (b) TPOCMEU
(c) PTOCMEU (d) CMUEOPT

49. The constituent Assembly adopted Indian national flag on

(a) 22nd July 1947
(b) 22nd August 1947
(c) 22nd January 1948
(d) 22nd October 1947

50. When milk becomes sour, ... is produced.

(a) Lactose (b) Lactic acid
(c) Salicylic acid (d) Linoleic acid

51. A shopkeeper purchased 10 kg of rice and 20 kg of sugar at ₹ 75 and ₹ 85/kg respectively. On selling, he gained 20% on rice and 10% on sugar. What was the total sale price?

(a) ₹ 2695 (b) ₹ 2770
(c) ₹ 2800 (d) ₹ 2750

52. Yellow fever is mainly transmitted among humans by

(a) Female mosquito bite
(b) Male mosquito bite
(c) Water
(d) Air

53. Read the given statements carefully and answer the question. The main reasons for vehicles crawling on city roads during peak hours are increasing number of private vehicles and double parking, which is a very common sight. A survey reveals that vehicles move on an average at 20 kmph during peak hours. Which of the following is true according to the given statement?

(a) Vehicles move at 20 kmph during 5 pm to 9 pm.
(b) Double parking is not a violation of traffic rules in the city.
(c) The number of private vehicles have gone up.
(d) The number of Government vehicles remain the same.

54. Which of the following is in ascending order?

(a) 0.65, 0.76, 0.67, 0.86
(b) 0.65, 0.86, 0.67, 0.76
(c) 0.65, 0.67, 0.76, 0.86
(d) 0.67, 0.65, 0.76, 0.86

55. Which one does not belong to the group?

(a) Zee (b) Screen
(c) Colors (d) Sony

56. A path of 2.5 m width surrounds a rectangular garden of length 10 m and Breadth 8 m. Area of the garden, inclusive of the path is

(a) 13.25 sqm (b) 131.25 sqm
(c) 195.00 sq m (d) 162.50 sq m

57. Find the similarity in the following

Leopard, Tiger, Jaguar, Lion

(a) All of them are found in India.
(b) All of them belong to the cat family.
(c) All of their young ones are called kittens.
(d) There is no similarly.

58. The end of British rule in India came in the year

(a) 1946 (b) 1947
(c) 1948 (d) 1950

59. A trader bought 10 kg of tea @ 400/kg. He sold half the quantity at 20% loss and remaining at 10% profit. What was his net profit or loss in percentage?
(a) 5% loss (b) 5% gain
(c) 10% loss (d) 10% gain

60. Aayush's birthday is on Monday 22nd May. On what day of the week will be Neerav's birthday in the same year if Neerav was born on 30th October?
(a) Monday (b) Wednesday
(c) Friday (d) Thursday

61. Nephrology is 'study of'
(a) NOSE (b) KIDNEY
(c) LIVER (d) HEART

62. Who was the first chairman of ISRO?
(a) Kasturirangan (b) Vikram Sarabhai
(c) Homi K. Bhabha (d) CV Raman

63. Find the odd statement out in relation to fire wall
(a) Fire wall can be a software
(b) Fire wall can be a hardware
(c) Fire wall can be a combination of software and hardware
(d) Fire wall protects computer from fire

64. What will be the cost of levelling a circular ground of diameter 28 m, if the charges are ₹ 125/sq m? ($\pi = 22/7$)
(a) ₹ 76000 (b) ₹ 76400
(c) ₹ 76800 (d) ₹ 77000

65. The popular Yankee Stadium in USA is located at
(a) Boston (b) New York
(c) Las Vegas (d) Washington

66. $\operatorname{cosec}(90° - \theta) = ?$
(a) $\tan\theta$ (b) $\cot\theta$
(c) $\sec\theta$ (d) $\cos\theta$

67. An article was sold for ₹ 2100 at a profit of 25%. What is its cost price?
(a) ₹ 1620 (b) ₹ 1640
(c) ₹ 1660 (d) ₹ 1680

68. In a certain code, 327 means "don't cut tree', 635 means "Plant on tree", 138 means "tree gives shade"and 4953 means "We must plant tree" Which digit represents "shade"?
(a) 1 (b) 4
(c) 8 (d) Cannot be determined

69. Read the given statements carefully and answer the question.
Spending money should be based on logical decision and not compulsive or impulsive behaviour. One should not fall prey to possible hidden agenda of the sellers who come out with 'sale' 'free offer' etc. Price is what you pay, value is what you should get.
(a) When you pay for something look for value
(b) Any discounted sale has a hidden agenda against the consumer
(c) People do compulsive or impulsive and not logical spending
(d) Sellers are cheating the public

70. An electric motor converts
(a) Mechanical energy into electrical energy
(b) Thermal energy into electrical energy
(c) Electrical energy into mechanical energy
(d) Radiant energy into electrical energy

71. When the car takes a bend, the force that pushes us to the outside of the curve is the
(a) Centripetal Force
(b) Centrifugal Force
(c) Frictional Force
(d) Tension Force

72. The Prime Minister is the ex-officio President of
(a) CLRI (b) CSIR
(c) ISRO (d) DRDO

73. The name of the newest Antarctica research base commissioned in 2015 is
(a) Dakshin Gangotri (b) Maitri
(c) Bharati (d) Lotus

74. A car covers the first 30 km at a speed of 60 kmph and the next 20 km at 80 kmph. Find the average speed.

(a) 65.67 kmph (b) 65.33 kmph
(c) 66.33 kmph (d) 66.67 kmph

75. Indian sports person Gagan Narang is associated with

(a) Archery (b) Air rifle shooting
(c) Wrestling (d) Badminton

76. Which number will fit in'?' place in the following series? **12, 23, 45, 89, ?**

(a) 175 (b) 176 (c) 177 (d) 178

77. Micro-soft Corporation was founded in

(a) 1979 (b) 1981
(c) 1975 (d) 1965

78. If F = 6, THE = 33 then, WOMAN = ?

(a) 64 (b) 65 (c) 66 (d) 67

79. If the mathematical operators, '×' means '+' '÷' means '×' '+' means '–' and '–' means '÷' then $22 + 36 - 12 \times 6 \div 4 = ?$

(a) –21 (b) 43 (c) 68 (d) 53

80. Which organ is not a gland?

(a) Adrenal (b) Liver
(c) Pituitary (d) Gall bladder

81. Who was conferred the Arjuna Award for wrestling in 2015

(a) Babita Kumari
(b) Abhilasha Shashikant
(c) Yumnam Sanathoi Devi
(d) M. R. Poovamma

82. Every set in the dotted format of IP address is called

(a) Subnet (b) Octet
(c) Subset (d) IP set

83. If $x + y = 19$ and $x - y = 7$, then $xy = ?$

(a) 13 (b) 48 (c) 78 (d) 72

84. A tap can fill a tank in 20 minutes. If a leakage is capable of emptying the tank in 60 minutes, the tank will be filled in

(a) 1 h (b) 45 min
(c) 30 min (d) 50 min

85. The arithmetic mean of the marks scored by students of a class is 58. 20% of them secured a mean score of 60. The mean score of another 30% of the students was 40. The mean score of the remaining students is

(a) 65 (b) 66 (c) 68 (d) 70

86. Parliament House in Delhi was constructed during

(a) 1895-1900 (b) 1901-1909
(c) 1921-1927 (d) 1931-1935

87. Anaemic condition is due to

(a) Deficiency of platelets
(b) Deficiency of RBC
(c) Deficiency of WBC
(d) Deficiency of oxidants

Directions (Q. Nos. 88-90) *Consider the following information and answer the questions based on it.*

Out of 50 kids in a colony, 10 like only basketball, 25 like only football, 10 like both volleyball and football and 5 like only volleyball.

88. How many kids do not like volleyball?

(a) 15 (b) 25 (c) 35 (d) 45

89. The ratio of kids who like only football to those who like only basketball is

(a) 5/2 (b) 7/2 (c) 4 (d) 5

90. How many kids like only one sport?

(a) 50 (b) 40 (c) 35 (d) 25

91. Four pairs of words are given. Find the odd one out.

(a) White : Snow (b) Red : Blood
(c) Brown : Sky (d) Green : Grass

92. The recent trial run of 'odd-even' traffic scheme for Delhi was based on

(a) odd-even calendar months
(b) odd-even calendar dates
(c) vehicle registration numbers
(d) odd-even hours during 8 am

93. Read the given statements carefully and answer the question.

Taxes on eating out have been increased. Eating out is not an act of the luxurious. Over-worked and time-pressed poor also need to eat out.

(a) The poor enjoy the luxury of eating out.
(b) Eating out is luxury for the poor.
(c) Eating out is need-based for the poor also.
(d) Tax on eating our must be reduced.

94. The ratio of marks obtained by a student in 3 subjects was 1 : 2 : 3. The school decided to allow grace marks of 5% for each subject. Find the students new ratio.

(a) 1 : 2 : 3 (b) 2 : 3 : 4
(c) 2 : 3: 1 (d) 3 : 2 : 1

95. A bus runs at 50 kmph. If the speed is increased by 10 kmph, it will cover 20 km more in the same time. Find the actual distance covered?

(a) 100 km (b) 150 km
(c) 200 km (d) 250 km

96. The Hornbill festival is celebrated in

(a) Arunachal Pradesh
(b) Nagaland
(c) Odisha
(d) West Bengal

97. Four pairs of words are given. Find the odd one out.

(a) Rhombus : Four-sided polygon
(b) Nonagon : Seven-sided polygon
(c) Octagon : Eight-sided polygon
(d) Hexagon : Six-sided polygon

98. Find the 4th proportional to 9, 17 and 27

(a) 57 (b) 48 (c) 51 (d) 53

99. Union Government Budget deficit for a particular financial year represents.

(a) Total amount of revenue receipts
(b) Total amount of capital receipts
(c) The amount of money that the Government has to borrow
(d) Total amount of estimated Government expenditure

100. Which aircraft carrier was formally inducted into the Indian Navy by Prime Minister Narendra Modi in the year 2014?

(a) INS Vikrant
(b) INS Vikramaditya
(c) INS Viraat
(d) INS Chakra

Hints & Solutions

1. (b) LOWELY—YELLOW; THIWE—WHITE; WRONB—BROWN; IFER—FIRE

Here, yellow, white, brown are colours where as fire is not a colour.

2. (b) Mean $= \dfrac{\text{sum of data}}{\text{number of data}}$

$$16 = \frac{18 + 16 + 22 + 13 + ?}{5}$$

$80 = 69 + ? \Rightarrow ? = 80 - 69 = 11$

3. (d) A N B O, C P, D Q E R

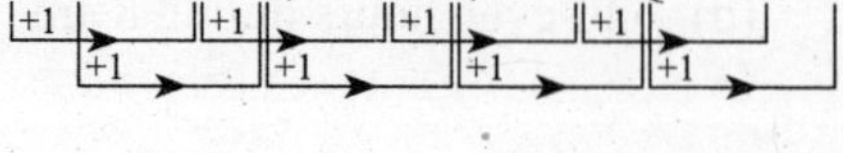

4. (c) Mars is often called the 'Red Planet' because it appears in the sky as an orange-red star which is due to rust in the Martian rocks.

5. (a) Calcium hydroxide, when mixed with water, partly gets dissolved, forming limewater, the rest remaining as a suspension called milk of lime.

6. (c) All nurse dispense his/her duties at hospital wards like that all teachers teach students in the class room.

7. (d) Smiling Buddha was the code name of India's first successful nuclear bomb test on 18 May 1974 at Pokhran in Rajsthan.

8-10 : Parking of six cars in 9 row is like this:

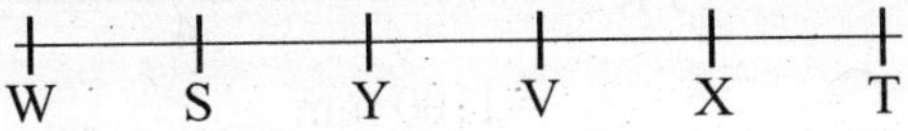

8. (b) There is only one car V between X and Y.

9. (d)

10. (a) V is immediate left of X.

11. (d) Jantar Mantar is astronomical monument in the form of a sundial. Built in 1724 by Maharaja Jai Singh II of Jaipur, the motive of the observatory was to gauge and collate the astronomical charts, and to estimate the time by tracking the movements of the planets, moon and the sun.

12. (a) Bharat Stage Emission Standards (BSES) are emission standards instituted by the Government of India to regulate the output of air pollutants from internal combustion engines and Spark-ignition engines, including motor vehicles.

13. (b) $M > L > N = R \Rightarrow M > R$

hence, only conclusion II follows.

14. (c) Adjacent sides of square and rectangle are always perpendicular. And also Diagonals of rhombus are always perpendicular but hypotenuse and one side of a right angle triangle can never be perpendicular.

15. (b) Let originally there were n men to do the work.

then, work done by n men in 1 day $= \frac{1}{20}$.

Work done by 1 man in 1 day $= \frac{1}{20 \times n}$

Similarly, work done by 1 man in 1 day when whole work finished in 40 days $= \frac{1}{(n-5)\,40}$.

Now, $\frac{1}{20 \times n} = \frac{1}{40 \times (n-5)}$

$\Rightarrow \quad 2(n-5) = n$

$2n - n = 10$

$n = 10.$

16. (d) Prime number between 60 to 100 are 61, 67, 71, 73, 79, 83, 89 and 97

Hence, number of required number = 8.

17. (b) Bird is finally, 110 + 40 = 150 km North from starting point.

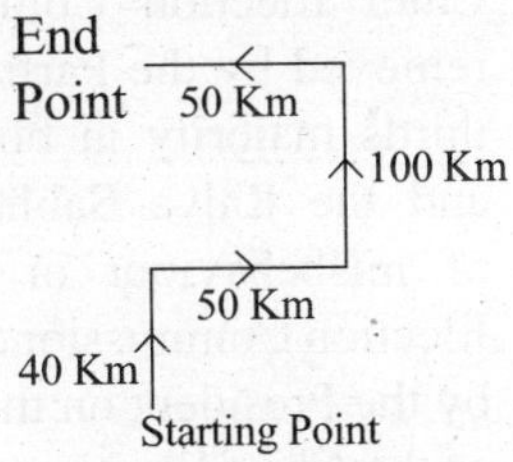

18. (c) Indian economy is a mixed economy because it consists of both private and public sectors enterprises side by side.

19. (b) $f(y) = y(y^4 - y^2 - y)$

$f(5) = 5(5^4 - 5^2 - 5)$

$= 5(625 - 25 - 5) = 2975.$

20. (b) Let two integers are x and y.

then, $x + y = 34$ and $x - y = 8$

Now, add $\quad 2x = 42 \Rightarrow x = 21$

$y = 13$

$\therefore x.y = 273$

21. (b) Let two numbers are 2x and 3x.

then, L.C.M. $= 2x \times 3x = 66.$

$x = \frac{66}{6} = 11.$

Sum of two numbers $= 2x + 3x$

$= 5x = 5 \times 11 = 55.$

22. (b) 36 P 6 Q 7 R 8 S 11

$= 36 \div 6 + 7 \times 8 - 11 = 6 + 56 - 11$

$= 62 - 11 = 51.$

23. (b) Multitasking, in an operating system, is allowing a user to perform more than one computer task at a time. The operating system is able to keep track of where you are in these tasks and go from one to the other without losing information.

24. (a) Union Government has launched the School Nursery Yojana in a bid to bring school students closer to nature by involving them in raising of plant saplings in school nurseries.

25. (b) Ms. Chandra is Laxmi's daughter and Laxmi's husband would be her father.

26. (a) Chief Election Commissioner can be removed by the Parliament with a two-thirds majority in both the Lok Sabha and the Rajya Sabha on the grounds of misbehaviour or incapacity. Other Election Commissioners can be removed by the President on the recommendation of the Chief Election Commissioner.

27. (*) $\text{Cos}^2 90° + \text{Cosec}^2 90° - \text{Cot}^2 45°$

$(0)^2 + (1)^2 - (1)^2 = 0$

28. (a) Population density records show that the density has increased from a figure of 324 to that 382 per square kilometer. Bihar is the most thickly populated state (1106 persons/sq km.) followed by West Bengal-1028 and Kerala 860.

29. (d) Mother's age $= \text{father's age} - 2$

$= 54 - 2 = 52$

Younger sister age $= \dfrac{\text{Mother age}}{2} = \dfrac{52}{2}$

$= 26$ years.

Elder sister age $= 26 + 4 = 30$ years

30. (d) $2^2 - 3^3 + 4^3 - 6^2 = 4 - 27 + 64 - 36 = 5.$

31. (b)

32. (b) Archana Ramasundaram created history by becoming the first woman to head a paramilitary force. She assumed charge as the Director General, Sashastra Seema Bal, which guards the 1,751-km Indo-Nepal and 699-km Indo-Bhutan borders.

33. (c) Khan Abdul Gaffar Khan was known as Badshah Khan and "Sarhadi Gandhi" and Frontier Gandhi. He was a Pashtun leader and ardent follower of Mahatma Gandhi and known for his nonviolent opposition to British Rule. He started Khudai Khidmatgar movement.

34. (d) Average rainfall in following state:.

J.K. $= \dfrac{1100 + 1100 + 1000 + 1200}{4}$

$= 1100$ mm

G.A. $= \dfrac{1000 + 1300 + 1500 + 1700}{4}$

$= 1125$ mm

H.P. $= \dfrac{1100 + 1100 + 1000 + 1300}{4}$

$= 1125$ mm

W.B. $= \dfrac{1400 + 1300 + 1200 + 1000}{4}$

$= 1225$ mm

T.N. $= \dfrac{1200 + 1050 + 1000 + 1100}{4}$

$= 1087.5$ mm

Hence, TN has lowest average rainfall.

35. (c) GA shows a gradual increase in its rainfall from June to September.

36. (c) Rain fall in following months:

June : $1100 + 1100 + 1400 + 1000 + 1200 = 5800$ mm

July : $1100 + 1100 + 1300 + 1300 + 1050 = 5850$ mm

August : $1000 + 1000 + 1200 + 1500 + 1000 = 5700$ mm (Lowest).

September : $1200 + 1300 + 1000 + 1700 + 1100 = 6300$ mm (highest).

37. (d) $90 + 30 + 20 + 50 = 190$ Kg.

$30 + 20 + 50 = 100$ Kg.

$90 + 30 + 50 = 170$ Kg.

But we can not get 150 Kg by these combination.

38. (b) Let man has covered distance x Km in next two days.

ATQ, $\dfrac{3 + 4 + 3.5 + 5 + 4.5 + x}{7} = 4$

$20 + x = 28$

$x = 28 - 20 = 8$ Km.

39. (a) $16 = 2 \times 8, 24 = 3 \times 8$

$\therefore$ H.C.F. = 8

L.C.M. $= \dfrac{16 \times 24}{8} = 48.$

40. (c)

41. (c) Amount after 1 year

$= 300 + \dfrac{3000 \times 12 \times 1}{100} = 3360.$

Instalment $= \dfrac{3360}{12} = ₹\ 280$

42. (b)

43. (c) are you Sam = ri ai Ki

all hate you = vi li ri

all are fake = mi ai li

Hence, code for 'hate' — 'vi'

44. (d) M's grandfather has only son who is father of K.

45. (a) Mean $= \dfrac{2+3+3+4+6+7}{6} = \dfrac{25}{6}$

$= 4.17$

46. (b) Novak djokovic won majority of the men's singles tennis grand slam tournaments in 2015. He won 82 matches in 2015 and became only the third man in the Open era to reach the final of each Grand Slam.

47. (c) Let present age of two brothers are x and 2x years.

ATQ, $\dfrac{x-5}{2x-5} = \dfrac{1}{3} \Rightarrow 3(x-5) = 2x-5$

$3x - 2x = -5 + 15$

$x = 10$

Ratio of their age after 5 year's $\dfrac{15}{25} = \dfrac{3}{5}$

48. (c) C A B I N E T — E I A C B T N

Similarly,

C O M P U T E — T P O C M E U

49. (a) The National Flag of India was adopted in its present form during by Constituent Assembly on the 22 July 1947.

50. (b) Milk contains a sugar called lactose. It also contains harmless bacteria called lactobacillus, which uses lactose for energy and creates lactic acid as a by-product which makes milk taste sour.

51. (b) Cost price of 10 kg rice = $75 \times 10 = 750$

Cost price of 20 kg sugar = 20×85

$= 1700$

Selling price of 10 kg of rice $= 750 \times \dfrac{120}{100}$

$= 900$

Selling price of 20 kg of sugar

$= 1700 \times \dfrac{110}{100} = 1870$

Total selling price = 900 + 1870

= ₹ 2770

52. (a) Yellow fever is caused by yellow fever virus and spread by the bite of an infected female mosquito Aedes aegypti, found throughout the tropics and subtropics.

53. (c)

54. (c) Ascending order : 0.65, 0.67, 0.76, 0.86.

55. (b) Zee, Colors and Sony are different TV channels where of screen is different.

56. (c) Area of the garden (inclusive of the path)

$= (10 + 2 \times 2.5) \times (8 + 2 \times 2.5)$

$= 15 \times 13 = 195$ sq. m.

57. (b) Leopard, Tiger, Jaguar and Lion all belongs to cat family.

58. (b) British rule ended in India in 1947.

59. (a) Total cost price of 10 kg Tea

$= 10 \times 400 = 4000.$

Selling price of 5 kg at 20% loss

$= 5 \times 400 \times \dfrac{80}{100} = 1600.$

Selling price of 5 kg at 10% profit

$= 5 \times 400 \times \dfrac{110}{100} = 2200.$

Loss % $= \left(\frac{4000 - 3800}{4000}\right) \times 100$

$= 5\%$ Loss

60. (a) Number of days between 22nd May and 30th October

$= 9 + 30 + 31 + 31 + 30 + 30 = 161$ days

$= 23$ weeks.

Hence, 30th October will be Monday.

61. (b) A nephrologist specializes in kidney care and treats diseases of the kidneys.

62. (b)

63. (a) Fire wall protects computer of malware and virus. It is a software.

64. (d) Cost of levelling of circular ground

$= \pi\left(\frac{d}{2}\right)^2 \times 125 = \frac{22}{7} \times \left(\frac{28}{2}\right)^2 \times 125$

$=$ ₹ 77000

65. (b) Yankee Stadium is a baseball park located in Bronx, New York. It is the home field for the New York Yankees of Major League Baseball, and New York City FC of Major League Soccer.

66. (c) $\text{Cosec}\,(90° - \theta) = \frac{1}{\text{Sin}\,(90° - \theta)}$

$= \frac{1}{\text{Cos}\,\theta} = \text{Sec}\,\theta.$

67. (d) Cost price $= \text{Selling Price} \times \frac{100}{(100 - \text{loss\%})}$

$= 2100 \times \frac{100}{120} =$ ₹ 1680.

68. (d) ③ 2 7 — don't cut (tree)

6 ③ 5 — plant on (tree)

1 ③ 8 — (tree) gives shade

4 9 5 ③ — we must plant (tree)

Hence, code of 'Shade' may be '1' or '8'

69. (a) When we pay for something look for value of money.

70. (c) A generator converts mechanical energy into electrical energy, while a motor does the opposite. Both devices work on electromagnetic induction in which voltage is induced by changing magnetic field.

71. (b) In Newtonian mechanics, the centrifugal force is an inertial force that act on all rotating objects. It is directed radially outwards from the axis.

72. (b) The CSIR is largest public funded R&D organisation, covering science and technology areas. CSIR has the Prime Minister of India as the it's head.

73. (b) Bharati is 3rd Antarctic research station commissioned by India alongside Maitri. and Dakshin Gangotri.

74. (d) Average speed of the car

$= \frac{\text{total distance covered}}{\text{total time taken}}$

$= \frac{30 + 20}{\frac{30}{60} + \frac{20}{80}} = \frac{50}{\frac{1}{2} + \frac{1}{4}} = \frac{50}{0.75}$

$= 66.67$ km/hr.

75. (b) Gagan Narang is an Indian shooter, the first Indian to qualify for the London Olympics. He won the Bronze Medal in the Men's 10 m air rifle event.

76. (c) 12 → 23 → 45 → 89 → 177

(each step $\times 2 - 1$)

77. (c) Microsoft Corp, registered in 1975, is an American technology company that supports the invention, manufacturing, and licensing of goods and services related to computing.

78. (c) F - 6, T H E → 20 8 5 (Letter's position) $= 20 + 8 + 5 = 33,$

W O M A N → 23 15 13 1 14 (Letter's position) $= 23 + 15 + 13 + 1 + 14 = 66$

79. (b) $22 + 36 - 12 \times 6 \div 4$

$= 22 - 36 \div 12 + 6 \times 4$

$= 22 - 3 + 24 = 43.$

80. (b) The gallbladder stores bile produced by the liver. It is not a gland.

81. (a)

82. (b) An IP address is a 32-bit binary address. This 32-bit address is subdivided into four 8-bit segments called octets.

83. (c) $xy = \frac{(x+y)^2 - (x-y)^2}{4} = \frac{(19)^2 - (7)^2}{4}$

$= \frac{12 \times 26}{4} = 78.$

84. (c) Time to fill the tank $= \frac{60 \times 20}{60 - 20} = \frac{60 \times 20}{40}$

$= 30$ min.

85. (c) Let there are 100 students in the class.

then, total marks of the class $= 58 \times 100 = 5800$

total marks of 20 students $= 20 \times 60 = 1200.$

total marks of 30 students $= 30 \times 40 = 1200.$

total marks of remaining 50 students

$= 5800 - 1200 - 1200 = 3400$

Mean marks of remaining 50% students

$= \frac{3400}{50} = 68$

86. (c)

87. (b) Anaemia is decrease in the total amount of red blood cells or haemoglobin in the blood, or a lowered ability of the blood to carry oxygen.

88-90:

88. (c) Number of kids do not like Volleyball

$= 50 - 10 - 5 = 35.$

89. (a) Required ratio $= \frac{25}{10} = \frac{5}{2}$

90. (b) Number of kids like only one sport

$= 10 + 25 + 5 = 40.$

91. (c) Sky colour is blue not brown.

Hence, Brown sky is mismatch pair.

92. (c) The new scheme involved private vehicles to run across the city based on their registration numbers. For example, if a vehicle's registration number ends with an odd digit, it will be allowed on the road on 1st, 3rd, 5th...., while those ending with an even number can be driven on the 2nd, 4th, 6th ... and so on.

93. (c)

94. (a) Let total marks obtained in three subjects are 100.

then, marks obtained are $\frac{100}{6}$, $\frac{100}{3}$ and $\frac{100}{2}$ respectively.

After allowing grace marks,

their marks

$= \frac{100}{6} \times \frac{105}{100} : \frac{100}{3} \times \frac{105}{100} : \frac{100}{2} \times \frac{105}{100}$

$= 1 : 2 : 3.$

95. (a) Let actual distance to cover is d km.

then, $\frac{d}{50} = \frac{d+20}{50+10}$

$\Rightarrow \frac{d}{50} = \frac{d+20}{60}$

$\Rightarrow (60 - 50)\, d = 50 \times 20$

$d = 100$ Km.

96. (b) The Hornbill Festival is held every year in December, in Nagaland. Nagaland is home to several tribes, which have their own distinct festivals. More than 60% of the population of Nagaland depends on agriculture and therefore most of their festivals revolve around agriculture.

97. (b) Nonagon is a nine side polygon.

98. (c) Let 4th proportional is x.

then, $\frac{9}{17} = \frac{27}{x} \Rightarrow x = \frac{27 \times 17}{9} = 51.$

99. (c) A government budget is a financial statement of proposed revenues and spending for a financial year. A positive balance is called budget surplus, and a negative balance is budget deficit.

100. (a)

RRB NTPC stage-I Solved Paper

Held On 6th April 2016 (Shift-II)

1. A recently discovered bird species named 'Himalayan Forest Thrush' was found in ________.
   (a) Dehradun (b) Northeast India
   (c) Uttarakhand (d) Ladakh Region
2. Leprosy is also known as
   (a) Angina (b) Hansen's disease
   (c) Gaucher disease (d) Hodgkin disease
3. Find the odd one out in relation to world heritage sites.
   (a) Rashtrapati Bhavan
   (b) Chatrapati Shivaji Terminus
   (c) Taj Mahal
   (d) Sun Temple
4. One side of a rectangle is 12 m and its diagonal is 13 m. Find its area.
   (a) 60 sq.m (b) 55 sq.m
   (c) 50 sq.m (d) 45 sq.m
5. Who was the coach for U-19 World Cup (2016) held in Bangladesh?
   (a) Rahul Dravid (b) Virendra Sehwag
   (c) Sourav Ganguly (d) Anil Kumble
6. Read the given statements carefully and answer the question. Statement:
   I. Domestic price of petrol has gone down.
   II. International price of crude oil has decreased.
   (a) I is the cause and II is the effect.
   (b) II is the cause and I is the effect.
   (c) I and II are independent of each other.
   (d) I and II are effects of independent causes.
7. In a map drawn to a scale of 1 cm = 18.5 km, the distance between places A and B = 22.25 cm. Find the actual distance in kilometer.
   (a) 411.625 (b) 425.615
   (c) 412.625 (d) 405.615
8. Find the odd one out.
   (a) Silent valley (b) Silicon valley
   (c) Indus valley (d) Damodar valley
9. Who was conferred the Arjuna Award for badminton in 2015?
   (a) Kidambi Srikanth (b) Saina Nehwal
   (c) Chetan Anand (d) Rohit Sharma
10. If **'you are john'** is written as **'net let fat'**, **'who are you'** is **'let wet net'** and **'john is good'** is **'get set fat'**, which represents 'is'?
    (a) set (b) get
    (c) fat (d) cannot be determined.
11. Till the end of 2015, India has established research stations in Antarctica.
    (a) 2 (b) 3 (c) 4 (d) 5
12. A train running at 60 kmph crosses a pole in 30 seconds. What is the length of the train?
    (a) 250 m (b) 750 m
    (c) 500 m (d) 450 m
13. Jantar Mantar in Delhi was built by Maharaja ________.
    (a) Jai Singh I of Jaipur (b) Jai Singh II of Jaipur
    (c) Ram Singh I (d) Bishan Singh
14. A statement followed by some conclusions is given below.
    Statement: Customer service cannot be enforced. It has to come from within.
    Conclusions:
    I. Customer service should be voluntary.
    II. Employees do not serve customers.
    Find which of the given conclusions logically follow from the given statement.
    (a) Only conclusion I follows.
    (b) Only conclusion II follows.
    (c) Both I and II follow.
    (d) Neither I nor II follows.

15. As per the India State Forest Report 2015, ____________ has the largest forest cover in terms of its area.

(a) Assam (b) Jammu and Kashmir
(c) Madhya Pradesh (d) Arunachal Pradesh

16. 9876 + 34.567– ? = 9908.221

(a) 23.45 (b) 234.6
(c) 2.345 (d) 2.346

17. A's share is 2 times that of B whose share is 3 times that of C. ₹ 1800/- is to be given to them in that ratio. B's share is

(a) ₹ 1080 (b) ₹ 540
(b) ₹ 180 (d) ₹ 900

18. Cell phone : Communication :: Cycle : ?

(a) Walking (b) Gym
(c) Mechanization (d) Transportation

19. Name the security force which does not fall under Union Home ministry.

(a) Sashastra Seema Bal
(b) Border Security Force
(c) Railway Protection Force
(d) Indo-Tibetan Border Police Force

20. The greenhouse gas which is called laughing gas is

(a) Methane (b) Carbon dioxide
(c) Nitrous oxide (d) Sulphur dioxide

21. If (a + b + c) = 6 and a' + b' + c' = 14, then (ab + bc + ca) = ?

(a) 22 (b) 11 (c) 33 (d) 44

22. Which one is called the dwarf planet?

(a) Venus (b) Mercury
(c) Moon (d) Pluto

23. Major part of biogas is ____________.

(a) Hydrogen (b) Nitrogen
(c) Methane (d) Carbon dioxide

24. Mac OS was introduced by

(a) IBM (b) Microsoft
(c) Apple (d) Micromax

25. Find the missing (?) in the series.

BDACE, GIFHJ, ? , QSPRT ....

(a) LMKNO (b) NLKOM
(c) LNKMO (d) KLNOM

26. Find the least number required to be added to 3105 so that it is exactly divisible by 3, 4, 5 and 6.

(a) 15 (b) 120 (c) 115 (d) 125

27. Two vessels of equal volume contain milk and water in the ratio 1:3 and 2:1. If they are mixed together, what is the new ratio?

(a) 11:13 (b) 13:11
(c) 9:11 (d) 11:9

28. ____________ extinguishes fire.

(a) O_2 (b) CO_2 (c) SO_2 (d) NO_2

29. Four pairs of words are given. Find the odd one out.

(a) Saturn : Planet
(b) Sun : Star
(c) Milky Way : Constellation
(d) Titan : Satellite

30. After entering Bangladesh. the main branch of the Ganges is known as

(a) Hooghly river (b) Jamuna river
(c) Meghna river (d) Padma river

31. The efficiency of work of P and Q are in the ratio 5 : 7. What will be the ratio of number of days taken by them to finish the work?

(a) 7 : 5 (b) 3 : 4 (c) 4 : 3 (d) 5 : 7

DIRECTIONS (Qs. 32-34): *Consider the following information and answer questions based on it.*

Among 60 students, 12 like only algebra, 13 like only geometry, 10 like only trigonometry, 5 like both algebra and trigonometry, 8 like only physics, 5 like both physics and geometry and the remaining like both algebra and physics.

32. The number of students who like physics but not geometry is

(a) 8 (b) 13 (c) 15 (d) 17

33. How many students like more than one subject?

(a) 5 (b) 10 (c) 12 (d) 17

34. The ratio of students who like algebra to those who like geometry is

(a) 12:13 (b) 4:3
(c) 17:18 (d) 17:13

35. Sagar has two daughters, Lata and Asha. Asha's only paternal aunt's son's grandfather is Aniket. How is Sagar related to Aniket's wife?

(a) Father (b) Son
(c) Grandson (d) Grandfather

36. If **OWL = 50 and N = 14.** then **TIME** is

(a) 45 (b) 47 (c) 43 (d) 49

37. In a certain code, **'RIDE' = 3218, 'TALK' = 4756, 'DIRT' = 1234 and 'LIKE' = 5268.** Which digit represents "A"

(a) 9 (b) 3 (c) 5 (d) 7

38. Which of the following is not true in relation to the Global Positioning System?

(a) It is a space-based navigation system.
(b) It can predict cyclones.
(c) It can be used to map vehicular traffic.
(d) It can be used for in-car navigation.

39. If the posts of the President and Vice-president fall vacant, who will act as the President of India?

(a) Speaker of Lok Sabha
(b) Prime Minister of India
(c) Chief Justice of India
(d) Union Council of Ministers

40. The average of first three out of four numbers is 18. The average of last three numbers is 14. The sum of first and last number is 16. The last number is

(a) 17 (b) 13 (c) 9 (d) 2

41. The difference between the ages of two sisters is 2 years when father's age was 52. Father is elder by 2 years to mother. Elder sister's age is half of mother's age. Find the age of younger sister.

(a) 27 (b) 21 (c) 25 (d) 23

42. The maturity value after three years, of a certain sum at 15% p.a. simple interest, is ₹ 8,700/-. Find the principal amount.

(a) ₹ 5,000 (b) ₹ 6,000
(c) ₹ 5,500 (d) ₹ 6,500

43. If **PIXIE** is **OHXHD** then **ELEANOR** is

(a) DKDAMNQ (b) DDKAMNR
(c) DKDANMR (d) DJDAMNQ

44. The marked prices of small and big note books are ₹ 10 and ₹ 15 respectively. A student bought 5 dozen small and 10 dozen big note books at a total discount of 5%. Find the total discount amount.

(a) ₹100 (c) ₹ 120
(c) ₹ 110 (d) ₹ 130

45. An event happening once in 4 years is described as

(a) Biennial (b) Quadrennial
(c) Triennial (d) Perennial

46. Read the following data carefully and answer the question based on it.

(i) 'A + G' means 'A is mother of G'
(ii) 'A ÷ G' means 'A is daughter of G'
(iii) 'A – G' means 'A is husband of G'
(iv) 'A × G' means 'A is maternal aunt of G

If L+ M × N then how is L related to N?

(a) Aunt (b) Mother
(c) Daughter (d) Grandmother

47. Find the value of $[(525 + 252)^2 - (525 - 252)^2]/(525 \times 252)$.

(a) 3 (b) 4 (c) 5 (d) 6

48. If $2\cos\theta = +3$, $\cos\theta \times \tan\theta = ?$

(a) 1 (b) $\sqrt{3}/3$ (c) $\sqrt{3}/2$ (d) 1/2

49. A generator converts

(a) mechanical energy into electrical energy.
(b) electrical energy into chemical energy.
(c) thermal energy into electrical energy.
(d) electrical energy into light energy.

50. A man has equal number of five, ten and twenty rupee notes amounting to ₹ 385. Find the number of each notes?

(a) 13 (b) 11 (c) 15 (d) 21

51. Which key combination is used for pasting text in MS Word?
(a) Ctrl + v (b) Ctrl + z
(c) Alt + r (d) Alt + F4

52. Find the median of the data set: **1.9, 8.4, 3.6, 5.8**
(a) 5.1 (b) 4.7 (c) 5.2 (d) 5.6

53. In the following equation, if the mathematical operators '–' and '×' are interchanged then the value of $\mathbf{4 - 6 + 1 \times 15 \div 3}$ will be
(a) 24 (b) 20 (c) –5 (d) –4

54. Which one is not a network protocol?
(a) SSH (b) HTML
(c) PPP (d) POP

55. The mean of first 11 natural numbers is
(a) 5.5 (b) 6 (c) 6.6 (d) 5

56. National Air Quality Index is determined on the basis of concentration of _____ pollutants.
(a) 5 (b) 6 (c) 7 (d) 8

57. Starting from her house a woman walks 15 km towards South. She turns right and walks 35 km. Again she turns right and walks 15 km. Then she turns left and walks 5 km. How far is her house now?
(a) 35 (b) 40 (c) 50 (d) 15

58. Motion of a spinning 'top' is an example of
(a) Centripetal Force
(b) Centrifugal Force
(c) Gravitational Force
(d) Frictional Force

59. Read the given statements carefully and answer the question.
Statements:
1. All teachers get angry.
2. Some teachers are sad.
3. Sad people may cry.
Which of the following conclusion is true?
(a) All sad people cry.
(b) Some teachers may cry.
(c) All angry people are teachers.
(d) All sad people get angry.

60. If the mathematical operator '×' means by A, '+' means by R, '÷' means by E and '–' means by B, then the value of **24 B 6 E 2 A 9 R I7** is
(a) 14 (b) –3 (c) 17 (d) –10

61. Which one is anti-virus?
(a) Code Red (b) Melissa
(c) Crypto Locker (d) Dr. Web

62. PM inaugurated the XII South Asian Games on 5 February 2016 at
(a) Lucknow (b) Guwahati
(c) Kolkata (d) Ahmadabad

63. Name the. chess champion against whom Viswananthan Anand lost in 2014 World Chess Championship.
(a) Vladimir Kramnik (b) Veselin Topalov
(c) Boris Gelfand (d) Magnus Carlsen

64. Which one is different from the other three?
(a) Spinach (b) Lentil
(c) Coriander (d) Lettuce

65. Expand $(a - 4)^3$
(a) $a^3 - 12a^2 + 48a + 64$
(b) $a^3 - 48a^2 + 12a - 64$
(c) $a^3 + 12a^2 - 48a - 64$
(d) $a^3 - 12a^2 + 48a - 64$

66. B does 50% of a work in 20 days. C joins B and they together finish the remaining work in 4 days. C alone can do the whole work in _____ days.
(a) 10 (b) 8 (c) 12 (d) 9

67. Losoong festival is popular in
(a) Himachal Pradesh (b) Sikkim
(c) Arunachal Pradesh (d) Tripura

68. The most popular folk dance of Tamil Nadu
(a) Karagam (b) Koodiyattam
(c) Yakshagana (d) Kathakali

69. The loss in selling an article for ₹ 1235 was 5%. At what price should it be sold to get a profit of 10%?
(a) ₹ 1,335 (b) ₹ 1,380
(c) ₹ 1,430 (d) ₹ 71,300

70. If $22x - 40 = 207 + 3x$, then x =?

(a) 14 (b) 13 (c) 12 (d) 11

71. The ratio of two numbers is 4 : 3 and their HCF is 8. Find their LCM.

(a) 48 (b) 96 (c) 64 (d) 84

72. The technique used for printing "RESERVE BANK OF INDIA' appearing on the face of the Indian currency notes is

(a) Intaglio printing (b) Micro lettering
(c) Latent printing (d) Screen printing

73. The aim of the Civil Disobedience Movement of 1929 was

(a) complete disobedience of the orders of the British Government.
(b) to protest the Chauri Chaura incident.
(c) partial disobedience of the orders of the British Government.
(d) to ensure all civil rights of the citizens are granted by the Government.

74. The British Government agreed to grant independence to India in

(a) 1944 (b) 1945 (c) 1946 (d) 1947

75. Y is R's mother's mother-in-law's only daughter and Q's wife. How is Q related to R?

(a) Paternal Uncle (b) Nephew
(c) Husband (d) Father

76. Find the similarity in the following:

Ginger, Turnip, Carrot, Radish

(a) All are red in colour.
(b) All are round in shape.
(c) All of them grow above the soil.
(d) All are roots.

77. Rearrange the jumbled letters to make a meaningful word and then select the one which is different.

(a) SUVNE (b) APTLE
(c) ARMS (d) RUJIIPE

78. The surface-to-air, Akash missile, was test fired from

(a) Sriharikota (b) Abdul Kalam Island
(c) Thumba (d) Pokhran

79. An article was sold at ₹ 920 at a profit of 15%. Find the selling price to get a profit of 20%.

(a) ₹ 1,000 (b) ₹ 980
(c) ₹ 960 (d) ₹ 940

80. Yeast used in making bread

(a) acts as a catalyst for fermentation.
(b) does not help the process of fermentation.
(c) makes it tasty.
(d) acts as a preservative.

81. The area of a triangle is 456 sq.cm and its height is 24 cm. The length of its base is

(a) 32 (b) 36 (c) 34 (d) 38

82. Louis Pasteur was known for discovery of

(a) Polio vaccine
(b) Chicken pox vaccine
(c) Small pox vaccine
(d) Rabies vaccine

83. Find the missing (?) in the series:

1, 1, 8, 4, 27, 9, ?, 16...

(a) 32 (b) 48 (c) 64 (d) 72

DIRECTIONS (Qs. 84-86): *Consider the following information and answer questions based on it.*

Seven students J, K, L, M, N, O and P are standing in a row, in random order, from left to right, such that—

1. P, O, K and N do not stand on any of the extreme ends.
2. J is to the immediate left of P and immediate right of O.
3. M is not at the center.
4. K is to the immediate right of N and immediate left of L.

84. The student standing to the immediate left of O is

(a) L (b) J (c) M (d) P

85. Who is at the center of the row?

(a) N (b) J (c) P (d) K

86. Who stands fifth from the left of the row?

(a) K (b) P (c) N (d) J

87. What is the difference between the maturity value of two deposits of ₹ 5,000 each invested for 2 years (i) at 5% simple interest and (ii) at the same interest compounded annually?

(a) ₹ 11.00 (b) ₹ 11.50
(c) ₹ 12.00 (d) ₹ 12.50

88. The area of a trapezium is 18 sq.cm. Its height and base are 3 cm and 5 cm respectively. Find the length of the side parallel to the base.

(a) 4 cm (b) 6 cm (c) 8 cm (d) 7 cm

89. There are ________________ zones in Indian Railways.

(a) 8 (b) 18 (c) 16 (d) 12

90. Evaluate: $(\sin\theta / \cos\theta) \times (\cot\theta / \operatorname{cosec}\theta)$.

(a) $\cos\theta$ (b) $\sin\theta$
(c) $\tan\theta$ (d) $\sec\theta$

DIRECTIONS (Qs. 91-93): *The following table represents the category wise count of books in four local libraries.*

Category	ABL	GHL	MNL	PQL
Self-help	150	170	200	200
Nonfiction	500	600	550	600
Fiction	750	610	700	600
Management	100	130	100	110
Comics	175	100	100	75
Technical	115	100	150	200

Consider the table and answer questions based on it.

91. The self-help books in library GHL is how much less than its fictional books?

(a) 340 (b) 430
(c) 440 (d) 330

92. Which library has the highest total count of books?

(a) ABL (b) GHL (c) MNL (d) PQL

93. The difference between the total number of nonfiction and management books of all four libraries is

(a) 1850 (b) 1810
(c) 2250 (d) 1800

94. A statement followed by some conclusions is given below.

Statement: Unlike Aryabhata, moon is a natural satellite of the Earth. Conclusions:

I. Aryabhatta is not a satellite.

II. Moon is star and Aryabhatta is a satellite.

Find which of the given conclusions logically follow from the given statements.

(a) Only conclusion I follows.
(b) Only conclusion II follows.
(c) Both I and II follow.
(d) Neither I nor II follows.

95. The recently approved, LIGO-India project, is related to

(a) Research on use of solar energy
(b) Research on laser technologies
(c) Research on gravitational waves
(d) Research on relocation of lions

96. A statement followed by some conclusions is given below.

Statements:

1. Medical profession has become the most unethical.
2. People are afraid of falling sick.

Conclusions:

I. Medical is the only unethical profession.

II. Unethical people fall sick.

Find which of the given conclusions logically follow from the given statements.

(a) Only conclusion I follows
(b) Only conclusion II follows
(c) Both I and II follow
(d) Neither I nor II follows

97. Name of the 8th UN Secretary General is

(a) B. Ghali (b) Kofi A. Annan
(c) Ban Ki-moon (d) Dr. Jim Yong Kim

98. K walked at 3 kmph for a certain distance with L and thereafter at 6 kmph with M to cover a total distance of 27 km in 7 hours. Find the distance travelled with M.

(a) 15 km (b) 12 km
(c) 10 km (d) 9 km

99. Who is considered to be the 'father of modem genetics"?

(a) Charles Darwin (b) Gregor Mendel
(c) Alexander Fleming (d) Otto Hahn

100. Name the country whose currency is not called 'Rupee'.

(a) Nepal (b) Pakistan
(c) Sri Lanka (d) Myanmar

Hints & Solutions

1. (b) A new species of bird has been discovered from northeastern India and China, named Himalayan Forest Thrush (Zoothera **salimalii**). The scientific name honours the great Indian ornithologist Dr Sálim Ali (1896–1987).

2. (b) Leprosy, (Hansen's disease) a chronic disease, affects the skin, peripheral nerves, mucosal surfaces and the eyes.

3. (a)

4. (a)

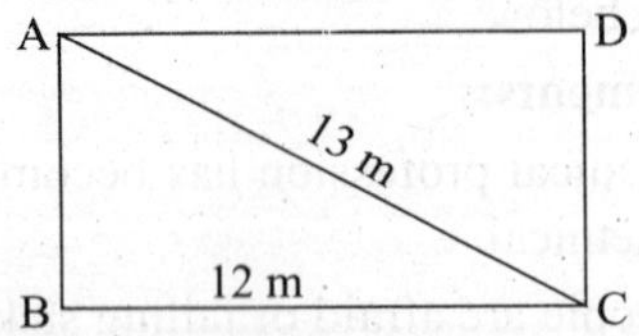

Let ▭ ABCD is a rectangle such that BC = 12m, AC = 13m

Then, from △ABC,

$AB = \sqrt{(AC)^2 - (BC)^2} = \sqrt{(13)^2 - (12)^2}$

$AB = \sqrt{169 - 144} = \sqrt{25} = 5m^2$

Area of the rectangle = AB × BC

$= 5 \times 12 = 60\ m^2$

5. (a)

6. (b) Global crude oil price decrease caused domestic petrol price to go down. Hence, II is cause and I is the effect.

7. (a) 1 cm = 18.5 km

$\therefore$ 22.25 cm = 18.5 × 22.25 = 411.625 km

8. (b) Silicon valley (San Francisco) is the home to many technology companies.

9. (a) Kidambi captured Swiss Open Grand Prix Gold in 2015 and became the first Indian to do it. Next was the India Superseries. He was conferred the prestigious Arjuna Award in 2015.

10. (d) you are john — net let fat

who are you — let net wet

john is good — get set fat

Hence, code for 'is' could be. 'get' or 'set'. So, we can not determined it.

11. (b) Under the environmental Antarctic Treaty (1959), India has set up three research stations - Dakshin Gangotri, Maitri and Bharti 1st, 2nd and 3rd stations.

12. (c) Length of the train

= time to cross the pole × speed

$= 30 \times 60 \times \frac{5}{18} = 500$ m

13. (b) Jantar Mantar (Delhi) consists of 13 architectural astronomy instruments. The site is one of five built by Maharaja Jai Singh II of Jaipur.

14. (a) Customer service can not be enforced. It has to come from within. It should be voluntary.

15. (c)

16. (d) 9876 + 34.567 – x = 9908.221

x = 9876 + 34.567 – 9908.221 = 2.346

17. (b) Let C's share is ₹ x.
Then, B's share is ₹ 3x.
and A's share is ₹ 6x.
According to the question,
$$x + 3x + 6x = 1800$$
$$10x = 1800 \Rightarrow x = 180.$$
B's share = 3 × 180 = ₹ 540.

18. (d) As cell phone is used for communication like that cycle is used for transportation.

19. (c) The Railway Protection Force (RPF) is established for protection and security of railway property. It has the power to search, arrest, investigate and prosecute.

20. (c) Nitrous oxide, (laughing gas N_2O) is an oxide of nitrogen. It is colourless non-flammable gas, with a slight metallic scent and taste.

21. (b) $(a + b + c)^2 = a^2 + b^2 + c^2 + 2(ab + bc + ca)$
$$(6)^2 = 14 + 2(ab + bc + ca)$$
$$36 - 14 = 2(ab + bc + ca)$$
$$(ab + bc + ca) = \frac{22}{2} = 11$$

22. (d) A dwarf planet is neither a true planet nor a natural satellite. There are 5 dwarf planets: Ceres, Pluto, Haumea, Makemake, and Eris in the outer Solar System.

23. (c) Methane, a biogas is also the main component in natural gas, a fossil fuel.

24. (c)

25. (c)

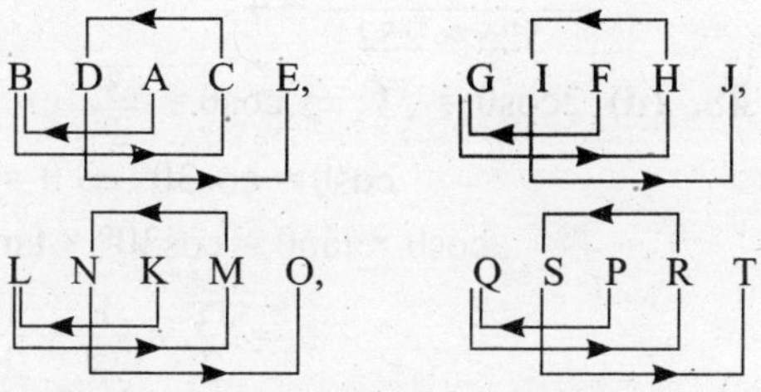

26. (a) L.C.M. of 3, 4, 5 and 6 = 3 × 2 × 5 = 30.
Now, 30 × 103 + 15 = 3105
Hence, required number = 15.

27. (a) Let volume of each vessel = 12 litre
Now, in the first vessel milk : water = 1 : 3
So, $\text{milk} = 12 \times \frac{1}{4} = 3$ litre
$\text{water} = 12 \times \frac{3}{4} = 9$ litre
In the second vessel milk : water = 2 : 1.
So, $\text{milk} = 12 \times \frac{2}{3} = 8$ litre
$\text{water} = 12 \times \frac{1}{3} = 4$ litre
In the mixture,
$$\text{milk} : \text{water} = (3 + 8) : (9 + 4)$$
$$= 11 : 13.$$

28. (b) CO_2 act as a fire extinguisher. It is a colourless and odourless gas, doesn't react with burning materials, doesn't create any toxic or other by-products when used to suppress a fire.

29. (c) Here, first word is the example of second type. Saturn is a planet, Sun is a Star, and Titan is a satellite. Milky way is not a constellation.

30. (d) The Padma (Bangladesh) is the main distributary of the Ganges, flowing southeast for 120 Km to join the Meghna River near the Bay of Bengal.

31. (a) Time taken to do the work is inversely proportional to their efficiency.
Hence, ratio of number of days = 7 : 5.

32-34:

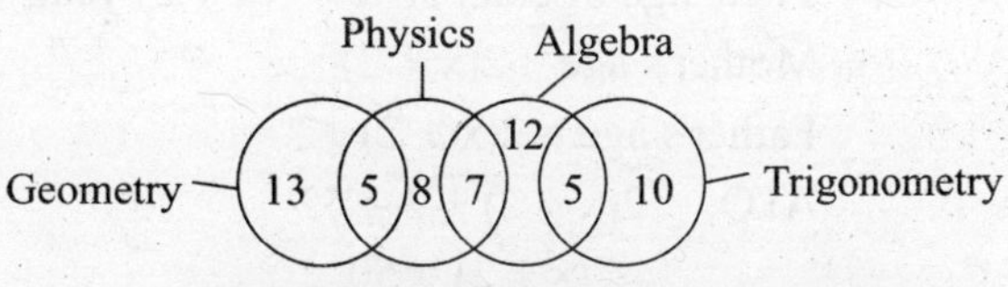

Total number of students = 60 (given)
So, remaining like both algebra and physics = 60 – 53 = 7.

32. (c) Number of students who like physics but not geometry = 8 + 7 = 15.

33. (d) Number of students who like more than one subject = 5 + 7 + 5 = 17.

34. (b) Required ratio $= \frac{12 + 7 + 5}{13 + 5} = \frac{24}{18} = 4 : 3.$

35. (b) Aniket's wife is the mother of Sagar. Hence, Sagar is son of Aniket's wife.

36. (b) N = 14 (Letter 'N' position in English alphabet)

OWL = 15 + 23 + 12 = 50.

Similarly, TIME = 20 + 9 + 13 + 5 = 47.

37. (d) From TALK = 4756 ....(i)

DIRT = 1234 ....(ii)

LIKE = 5268 ....(iii)

Hence, code of A = 7.

38. (b)

39. (c) The President Act, 1969 provides that the Chief Justice of India shall act as the President of India in the event of the offices of both the President and the Vice President being vacant.

40. (d) Let last number is x.

Then, first number is 16 – x

Sum of first three number = 3 × 18 = 54.

Sum of last three number = 3 × 14 = 42.

Difference of first and last number (Since the middle two digits are common)

= 54 – 42 = 12.

So, $16 - x - x = 12$

$2x = 16 - 12 = 4$

$\therefore$ Last number $x = \frac{4}{2} = 2$

41. (d) Let younger sister age = x year.

Then, age of elder sister = (x + 2) year.

Mother's age = 2(x + 2).

Father's age = 2(x + 2) +2

ATQ, $2(x + 2) + 2 = 52$

$2(x + 2) = 50$

$x = 25 - 2 = 23$ years

42. (b) Let principle amount is P.

Then, age of students and teacher

$$\text{Amount} = \frac{P \times r \times t}{100} + P.$$

$$8700 = \frac{P \times 15 \times 3}{100} + P \Rightarrow \frac{9P + 20P}{20}$$

$$8700 = \frac{29P}{20}$$

$$\therefore P = \frac{20 \times 8700}{29} = ₹\ 6000$$

43. (a)

P	I	X	I	E
↓–1	↓–1	0	↓–1	↓–1
O	H	X	H	D

Similarly,

E	L	E	A	N	O	R
↓–1	↓–1	↓–1	0	↓–1	↓–1	↓–1
D	K	D	A	M	N	Q

44. (c) Cost price of 1 dozen small book

= 12 × 10 = 120

Cost price of 1 dozen big book

= 12 × 15 = 180

Total cost of 5 dozen small and 10 dozen bog book = 5 × 120 + 10 ×180 = 2400.

$\text{Discount} = 2400 \times \frac{5}{100} = ₹\ 120$

45. (b) Any event happening in 4 years called quadrennial.

46. (d) L + M × N L is the mother of M and M is maternal aunt of N.

So, L is grandmother of N.

47. (b) $\frac{(525 + 252)^2 - (525 - 252)^2}{(525 \times 252)}$

$\frac{(a + b)^2 - (a - b)^2}{a \times b}$

$\frac{a^2 + b^2 + 2ab - (a^2 + b^2 - 2ab)}{ab} \Rightarrow \frac{4ab}{ab}$

$\frac{4 \times 525 \times 252}{525 \times 252} = 4$

48. (d) $2\cos\theta = \sqrt{3}, \Rightarrow \cos\theta = \frac{\sqrt{3}}{2}$

$\cos\theta = \cos 30° \Rightarrow \theta = 30°$

$\cos\theta \times \tan\theta = \cos 30° \times \tan 30°$

$= \frac{\sqrt{3}}{2} \times \frac{1}{\sqrt{3}} = \frac{1}{2}$

49. (a) A generator converts mechanical energy into electrical energy, while a motor does the opposite. Both work on electromagnetic induction, which is when a voltage is induced by a changing magnetic field.

50. (b) Let number of each denomination is x.

Then, $(5 + 10 + 20) \times x = 385$

$$35x = 385$$

$$x = \frac{385}{35} = 11.$$

51. (a)

52. (b) Arrangement of data in increasing order: 1.9, 3.6, 5.8, 8.4.

$$\text{Median} = \frac{3.6 \times 5.8}{2} = 4.7$$

53. (b) $4 - 6 + 1 \times 15 \div 3 = 4 \times 6 + 1 - 15 \div 3$

$$= 24 + 1 - 5 = 20.$$

54. (b)

55. (b) $\text{Mean} = \frac{\text{sum of first 11 natural number}}{11}$

$$= \frac{\frac{11}{2} \times (1 + 11)}{11} = 6.$$

56. (d) Eight parameters (PM10, PM2.5, NO_2, SO_2, CO, O_3, NH_3, and Pb) having short-term standards have been considered for near real-time dissemination of AQI.

57. (b)

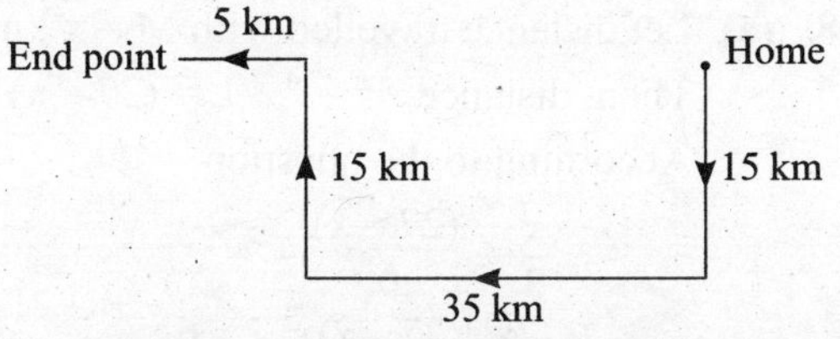

Hence, distance from home = 35 + 5 = 40 km.

58. (a)

59. (b) From statement 2 and 3, Some teachers are sad and sad people may cry.

So, Some teachers may cry.

60. (a) $24B6E2A9R17 = 24 - 6 \div 2 \times 9 + 17$

$$= 24 - 3 \times 9 + 17$$

$$= 24 - 27 + 17 = 14$$

61. (d)

62. (b) The XII South Asian Games, 2016 was a major multi-sport event (5 to 16 February) in Guwahati and Shillong.

63. (d)

64. (b) Lentil is a pulse but spinach, coriander and lettuce are species.

65. (d) $(a - 4)^3 = (a - 4)(a^2 + (4)^2 - 2a4)$

$$= (a - 4)(a^2 + 16 - 8a)$$

$$= a^3 - 12a^2 + 48a - 64$$

66. (a) Remaining work $= 1 - \frac{1}{2} = \frac{1}{2}$ day.

B alone can do the work in $20 \times 1 = 40$ days

C alone can do the whole work

$$\Rightarrow \frac{20}{40} + \left(\frac{1}{40} + \frac{1}{C}\right) \times 4 = 1$$

$$\left(\frac{1}{2} + \frac{1}{10}\right) + \frac{4}{C} = 1$$

$$\frac{6}{10} + \frac{4}{C} = 1$$

$$\frac{4}{C} = 1 - \frac{6}{10} = \frac{4}{10}$$

$\therefore$ C = 10 days

67. (b) The Lasoong is a popular festival of Sikkim, celebrated at the end of the tenth Tibetan lunar month (December). It is marked by the traditional Chaan dancing and merry-making.

68. (a) Karagam is a folk dance with musical accompaniment, performed balancing a pot on the head by villagers in praise of the rain goddess Mari Amman and river goddess, Gangai Amman.

69. (c) $\text{Cost price} = 1235 \times \frac{100}{100 - 5}$

$$= 1235 \times \frac{100}{95} = 1300$$

$$\text{Selling price} = 1300 \times \frac{100 + 10}{100} = ₹\ 1430$$

70. (b) $22x - 40 = 207 + 3x$

$$19x = 207 + 40$$

$$x = \frac{247}{19} = 13.$$

71. (b) Let two numbers are 4x and 3x.

Then, H.C.F. of 4x and 3x = x = 8 (given)

L.C.M. = $4 \times 3 \times x = 4 \times 3 \times 8 = 96$

72. (a) **73. (a)** **74. (d)**

75. (a) Q is paternal uncle of R

76. (d) Ginger, Turnip, Carrot and Radish all are example of roots.

77. (b) SUVNE — VENUS, ARMS — MARS
RUJITPE — JUPITER, APTLE — PLATE

78. (b)

79. (c) Cost price of the article

$$= 920 \times \frac{100}{100+15}$$

$$= 920 \times \frac{100}{115} = 800$$

$$\text{Selling price} = 800 \times \frac{100+20}{100} = ₹\,960$$

80. (a) Yeast is commonly used in bread baking for fermentation. It requires food, moisture and a controlled warm environment.

81. (d) Area of the triangle $= \frac{1}{2} \times \text{height} \times \text{Base}$

$$456 = \frac{1}{2} \times 24 \times \text{Base}$$

$$\therefore \text{Base} = \frac{456 \times 2}{24} = 38.$$

82. (d)

83. (c)

$$\begin{array}{cccccccc} 1, & 1, & 8, & 4, & 27, & 9, & 64, & 16 \\ \downarrow & \downarrow & \downarrow & \downarrow & \downarrow & \downarrow & \downarrow & \downarrow \\ (1)^3 & (1)^2 & (2)^3 & (2)^2 & (3)^3 & (3)^2 & (4)^3 & (4)^2 \end{array}$$

84-86:

M O J P N K L

84. (c) M is immediate left of O.

85. (c) P is at the centre.

86. (c) N is fifth from the left.

87. (d) Difference in C.I. and S.I. when time is 2 year $= P\frac{(r)^2}{(100)^2} = 5000 \times \frac{(5)^2}{(100)^2} = ₹\,12.5.$

88. (d) Area of trapezium

$$= \frac{1}{2} \times h \times (\text{sum of parallel sides})$$

$$18 = \frac{1}{2} \times 3(5+x)$$

$$(5+x) = \frac{18 \times 2}{3} = 12 \Rightarrow x = 7 \text{ cm.}$$

89. (b)

90. (b) $\frac{\sin\theta}{\cos\theta} \times \frac{\cot\theta}{\operatorname{cosec}\theta} = \frac{\sin\theta}{\cos\theta} \times \frac{\cos\theta}{\sin\theta} \cdot \sin\theta$

$$= \sin\theta$$

91. (c) Self help book in GHL = 170.
Fiction book in GHL = 610.
Difference = 610 – 170 = 440.

92. (c) MNL has highest total count of books.

93. (b) Required difference

$$[500+600+550+600] - [100+130+100+110] = 2250 - 440 = 1810$$

94. (d) Aryabhatta is a setellite and moon is not a star. Hence, none of the conclusion is correct.

95. (c) LIGO-India is a advanced gravitational-wave observatory to be located in India as part of the worldwide network.

96. (d) Nonc of thc conclusion follow.

97. (c) Ban Ki-moon is a South Korean politician and diplomat who served as the eighth Secretary-General of the UN from January 2007 to December 2016.

98. (a) Let distance travelled with M = x km
Then, distance " " L = (27 – x) km
According to the question,

$$\frac{x}{3} + \frac{(27-x)}{6} = 7$$

$$(2x + 27 - x) = 7 \times 6$$

$$x = 42 - 27 = 15$$

Hence, distance travel with M = 15 km.

99. (b) Gregor Mendel, is called the father of modern genetics. He crossed pea plant varieties having different heights, colours, pod shapes, seed shapes, and flower positions. Mendel's experiments revealed how traits are passed down from parents to off springs.

100. (d)

RRB NTPC stage-I Solved Paper

Held On 11th April 2016 (Shift-I)

1. Read the statements and select conclusion from the given alternatives.

Statements

All Apples are leaves. Some leaves are lemons. No lemon is house.

Conclusions

I. All houses are apples.

II. Some Lemons are apples.

III. No house is apple

(a) Only I follows

(b) Only II follows

(c) Only III follows

(d) Either I or III follows

2. In a certain code, TRIPPLE is written as SQHOOKD. How is EXOTIC coded in that code?

(a) DWNHSB (b) DNWHSB

(c) DWNSHB (d) DNWSHB

3. X-rays, which are now used on a day to day basis for diagnosis in medicine, was discovered by?

(a) Wilhelm Rontgen (b) Niels Bohr

(c) Enrest Rutherford (d) Max Bon

4. Which company has been associated with the development of Post-It and Scotch Tape.

(a) Johnson and Johnson (b) 3M

(c) Unilever (d) Amazon

5. Simplify: 5x (x +2) + 4x

(a) $5x^2 + 10$ (b) $9x + 10$

(c) $5x^2 - 14x$ (d) $5x^2 + 14x$

6. In a computer, what is the name of the high speed memory used

(a) Cache (b) RAM

(c) BIOS (d) Hard Disk

7. A shopkeeper cheats to the extent of 11% while buying and selling fruits, by using tampered weights. His total gain in percentage is

(a) 23.25 (b) 23.21 (c) 23.75 (d) 23.5

8. The cash difference between the selling price of an article at a profit of 2% and 18% is ₹3. The ratio of two selling prices is

(a) 51 : 59 (b) 51 : 53

(c) 51 : 60 (d) 55 : 59

9. The value of 0.592 ÷ 0.8 = ?

(a) 7.4 (b) 0.74

(c) 740 (d) 0.074

10. Laura was going with a boy and is asked by a woman about the relationship between them. Laura replied, "My maternal uncle and the uncle of his maternal uncle is the same.' How is Laura related with that boy?

(a) Mother and Son

(b) Aunt and Nephew

(c) Grandmother and Grandson

(d) Cannot be determined

11. Compute of 69696 × 9999 = ?

(a) 696980304 (b) 666890304

(c) 696809304 (d) 696890304

12. In a certain code, RIPPLE is written as 613382, PREACH is coded as 362454. How is PILLER written in that code? :

(a) 318826 (b) 318286

(c) 618826 (d) 338816

13. A flask has two holes. The Ist hole alone makes the flask empty in 9 minutes and 2nd hole alone makes the flask empty in 16 minutes. If water leaks out at a constant rate, how long in minutes does it take if both the holes together empty the flask?

(a) $\frac{19}{25}$ (b) $4\frac{19}{25}$

(c) $5\frac{20}{25}$ (d) $5\frac{19}{25}$

14. Who was appointed as the head of the Jury of the International Film Festival of India in November 2015?

(a) Anil Kapoor (b) Shekhar Kapoor
(c) Anupam Kher (d) Naseeruddin shah

15. Which of the following is a Tsunami warning sign?

(a) Stormy weather
(b) Hailstorm
(c) Water falling back quickly from the beach.
(d) Pets acting strangely

16. Answer the questions based on the below information.

If '+' is '×', '–' is '+', '×' is '÷' and '÷' is '–' then $6 + 7 \times 3 - 8 \div 20 = ?$

(a) –3 (b) 7 (c) 2 (d) 1

17. The most abundant of the rare gases is

(a) Helium (b) Argon
(c) Neon (d) Nitrogen

18. Read the statements and select a conclusion from the given alternatives.

Statement Sukhvinder emphasized the need to replace the present training programme by other methods which will bring out the real merit of the candidates.

Conclusions

I. It is not important to bring out the real merit of the candidates.
II. The present training programme does not bring out the real merit of the candidates.

(a) Only conclusion I follows
(b) Only conclusion II follows
(c) Both I and II follow
(d) Neither I nor II follows

19. The variance of a set of data is 196. Then the standard deviation of the data is

(a) ±14 (b) 14 (c) 96 (d) 98

20. The Indian National Army reclaimed the Andaman and Nicobar Island from British rule and named them?

(a) Swaraj Islands
(b) Shaheed and Swaraj Island
(c) Free Islands
(d) Swatantra and Swaraj Island

21. Compute $4923 \div 547 - 10$

(a) 1 (b) –1
(c) $\frac{1641}{179}$ (d) $\frac{1614}{179}$

22. A protruding part of the throat that is responsible for growing voice box in boys is called?

(a) Larynx (b) Testosterone
(c) Pharynx (d) Adam's Apple

23. Which country is going to organise the FIFA U-17 World cup in the year 2017?

(a) Chile (c) Nigeria
(c) UAE (d) India

24. The mean of the data $1, \frac{1}{2}, \frac{1}{2}, \frac{3}{4}, \frac{1}{4}, 2, \frac{1}{2}, \frac{1}{4}, \frac{3}{4}$ is

(a) $\frac{15}{18}$ (b) $\frac{13}{18}$ (c) $\frac{7}{9}$ (d) $\frac{8}{9}$

25. Variance of the data 2, 4, 5, 6, 8, 17, is 23.33. Then the variance of 4, 8, 10, 12, 16, 34, will be.

(a) 11.66 (b) 46.66
(c) 93.33 (d) 4.83

26. Mr. Mahesh sold a bus for ₹ 22100 with a loss of 15%. At what price should the bus be sold to get profit of 15%.

(a) 29,700 (b) 30,000
(c) 29,800 (d) 29,900

27. Read the statements and select a conclusion from the given alternatives.

Statements

All pens are pencils. Some pencils are erasers. Some erasers are ropes. All ropes are tents.

Conclusions

I. Some tents are trams.
II. Some ropes are pens.
III. Some erasers are pens.

IV. Some pencils are pens.

(a) Only I and II follow
(b) Only I, II and III follow
(c) Only I and III follow
(d) Only IV follows

28. Which is the correct ascending order of the given numbers?

(a) $\frac{2}{3}, \frac{5}{6}, \frac{3}{4}$ (b) $\frac{3}{4}, \frac{2}{3}, \frac{5}{6}$

(c) $\frac{2}{3}, \frac{3}{4}, \frac{5}{6}$ (d) $\frac{5}{6}, \frac{3}{4}, \frac{2}{3}$

29. If $\tan A = \frac{15}{8}$ and $\tan B = \frac{7}{24}$, then $\cos(A+B) = ?$

(a) $\frac{87}{425}$ (b) $\frac{304}{425}$

(c) $\frac{297}{425}$ (d) $\frac{416}{425}$

30. Which country among the following voted in 2015 to be the first country to allow three parent in vitro fertilisation?

(a) Britain (b) USA
(c) France (d) Italy

31. The basic concept of Montessori education is

(a) Discovery by travelling
(b) Dreaming
(c) Communicating
(d) Self-discovery through experiment

32. The term polyarchy was used by Robert Dahl to describe a form of government in which?

(a) It reduces the multitudinous differences of opinion to relatively simple alternatives.
(b) It takes individual as the basic unit of democratic model
(c) People can participate through their representations.
(d) People act both through the electoral system and the group process.

33. $(8)^{2/3} = ?$

(a) $\sqrt{4}$ (b) 2 (c) 4 (d) 64

34. Mr. Kavitha borrowed & 950 at 6% per annum simple interest. What amount will she pay to clear her debt after 4 years?

(a) 282 (b) 1187
(c) 1178 (d) 228

35. Divide ₹ 368 in the ratio 1:5:8:9. The rupees in the respective ratios are given by

(a) 16, 80, 127 and 145
(b) 16, 80, 129 and 143
(c) 16, 80, 128 and 144
(d) 16, 80, 128 and 143

36. Which of the following is a probe to the Kuiper belt bodies?

(a) Voyager 1 (b) Van Allen Probe
(c) New Horizon (d) Pioneer 11

37. Dried fruit like raisins when soaked in water, bulge and get filled with water. What is the scientific reason that explains this daily life event?

(a) Osmosis (b) Active transport
(c) Diffusion (d) Passive Transport

38. India participated in the 2014 commonwealth games at ________.

(a) Gold Coast, Australia
(b) New Delhi, India
(c) Samoa, Pacific Island
(d) Glasgow, United Kingdom

39. The order of rotational symmetry of a rectangle is

(a) 1 (b) 4 (c) 2 (d) 0

40. If the product of two numbers is 2400 and then LCM is 96 then their HCF is

(a) 35 (b) 240 (c) 24 (d) 25

41. Josna takes 4h 30 min in walking a distance and riding back to same place where she started. She could walk both ways in 5h 40 minutes. The time taken by her to ride back both ways is

(a) 3 h 20 min (b) 3h 35 min
(c) 3h 45 min (d) 3h 15 min

42. Birth control pills contain
(a) Progesterone only
(b) Oestrogen only
(c) Mixture of progesterone and oestrogen derivative
(d) Neither progesterone nor oestrogen

43. Two cycles start from a house with a speed of 24 km/h, at interval of 15 min. With how much more speed (km/h) the women coming from the opposite direction towards the house has to travel to meet the cycles at an intervals of 10 min.
(a) 13 (b) 11 (c) 12 (d) 14

44. Harappan people did not worship one of the following God
(a) Shiva (b) Vishnu
(c) Pigeon (d) Swastik

45. The theory behind stars twinkling is that
(a) The refractive index of the different layers of earth's atmosphere changes continuously the position of the star's image changes with time.
(b) The intensity of light emitted by them changes with time.
(c) The light from the star is scattered by the dust particles and air molecules in the earth's atmosphere.
(d) The distance of the stars from the earth changes with time.

46. Complete the figure X from the given alternatives, 1, 2, 3,4

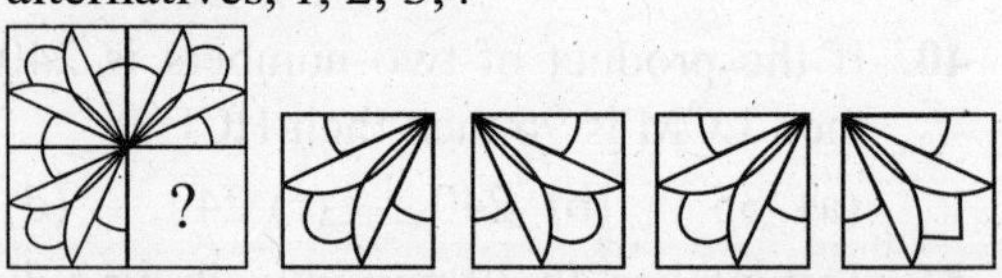

(X) (1) (2) (3) (4)

(a) 1 (b) 2 (c) 3 (c) 4

47. Who was awarded the Harvard Humanitarian Award for 2015?
(a) Malala Yousafzai (b) Kailash Satyarthi
(c) Tommy Hilfiger (d) Lionel Richie

Direction (Q. Nos. 48-50) *Read the data given and answer the following questions*

In a class of 60 students: 42 like Maths, 32 like English, 12 like neither Maths nor English.

48. Students who like only Maths forms what percentage of the total number of students in the class?
(a) 26.67% (b) 24.22%
(c) 28.80% (d) 32.82%

49. How many students like both Maths and English?
(a) 28 (b) 26 (c) 16 (d) 12

50. How many students like exactly one subject?
(a) 16 (b) 12 (c) 6 (d) 22

51. The famous Golconda Fort is situated in the state of
(a) Madhya Pradesh (b) Telangana
(c) Karnataka (d) Bihar

52. If $\sin x = \frac{4}{5}$, then $\sec^2 x - 1 = ?$
(a) $\frac{16}{25}$ (b) $\frac{25}{9}$
(c) $\frac{9}{16}$ (d) $\frac{16}{9}$

53. If the letters in PRABA are coded as 27595 and HITAL are coded as 68354 how can BHARATHI be coded?
(a) 37536689 (b) 57686535
(c) 96575368 (d) 96855368

54. Find the HCF of 1757, 2259.
(a) 231 (b) 241 (c) 251 (d) 261

55. Which country in the month of November 2015 was ranked No. 1 men's team for the first time in FIFA rankings?
(a) Nigeria (b) Belgium
(c) Russia (d) Portugal

56. Given $w = -2$, $x = 3$, $y = 0$ and $z = -\frac{1}{2}$, find the value of $w^2\sqrt{(z^2 + y^2)}$
(a) ± 2 (b) –2 (c) 2 (d) 4

57. Ram said, "This girl is the wife of the grandson of my mother". Who is Ram to the girl?

(a) Husband (b) Father
(c) Father-in-law (d) Grandfather

58. Which is the oldest High Court in India?

(a) Bombay High Court
(b) Madras High Court
(c) Allahabad High Court
(d) Calcutta High Court

59. ________ is the transition of a substance directly from the solid to the gas phase without passing through the intermediate liquid phase.

(a) Sublimation (b) Evaporation
(c) Condensation (d) Liquidation

60. Solve: $x - 3 = 3x + 7$.

(a) 5 (b) –5 (c) 1 (d) $\frac{10}{4}$

61. Who was the first Muslim woman to higher judiciary?

(a) Justice M Fathima Beevi
(b) Justice V Khalida
(c) Justice Benazir Islam
(d) Justice M Farooq

62. Vernal equinox occurs on,

(a) June 22 (b) March 20
(c) May 20 (d) June 20

63. Compute 33800/520/5.

(a) 31 (b) 325 (c) 13 (d) 352

64. In which direction does the tail of a comet point toward?

(a) Away from the sun
(b) Towards the sun
(c) Away from earth
(d) Towards the earth

65. What title did the British confer Gandhi with which was, relinquished by him?

(a) Rai Bahadur (b) Rai Sahib
(c) Hind Kesari (d) Kaiser-e-Hind

66. Read the statements given below and derive the conclusion.

Statements

No window is monkey.
All the monkeys are cats.

Conclusions

I. No window is cat.
II. No cat is window.
III. Some cats are monkeys.
IV. All the cats are monkeys.

(a) Only II and IV (b) Only I and III
(c) Only III and IV (d) Only III

67. Complete the figure X from the given alternatives 1, 2, 3, 4.

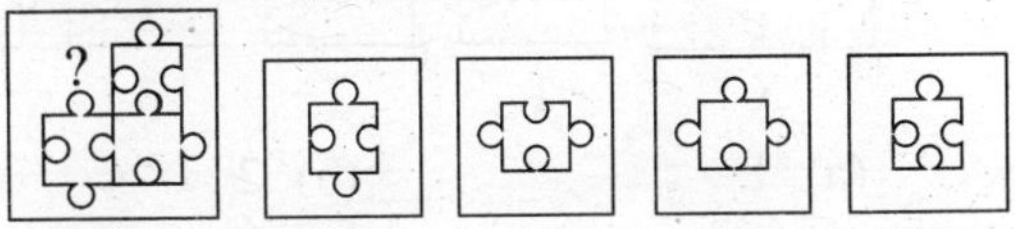

(X) (1) (2) (3) (4)

(a) 1 (b) 2 (c) 3 (d) 4

68. Answer the questions based on the below information.

If '+' is '×', '–' is '+', '×' is '÷' and '÷' is '–' then $6 - 9 + 8 \times 3 \div 20 = ?$

(a) –2 (b) 6 (c) 10 (d) 12

69. One of the best preserved Budhist caves, Karla, is in which of the following states?

(a) Bihar (b) Uttar Pradesh
(c) Maharashtra (d) Uttarakhand

70. While watching 3D movies at the theatre, we have to wear special glasses because?

(a) The glasses allow out left and right eyes to see different images.
(b) 3-D movies use special colours which cannot be sensed by the human eye.
(c) 3-D movies are brighter than ordinary movies and can hurt our eyes if seen directly.
(d) The glasses allow both the eyes to see similar images.

71. Which river originates from Amarkantak?
(a) Betwa (b) Chambal
(c) Damodar (d) Narmada

72. Who has the distinction of serving as the chief Justice of India, President and Vice President?
(a) Justice M Hidayatullah
(b) Justice Bhagwati
(c) Justice H J Kania
(d) Justice Mehr Chand Mahajan

73. Complete the Figure X from the given alternatives 1, 2, 3, 4.

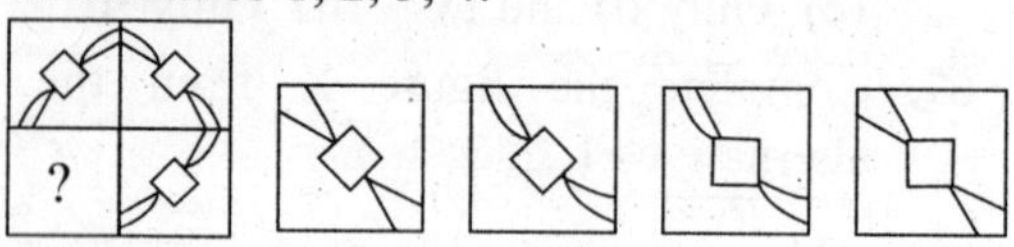

X 1 2 3 4

(a) 1 (b) 2
(c) 3 (d) 4

Direction (Q. Nos. 74-76) *Study the; following table and answer the questions based on it.*

Following table gives the expenditures of a company (in lakh rupees) per annum over the given years.

Year	Items of Expenditure				
	Salary	Fuel and Transport	Bonus	Interest on loan	Taxes
1998	288	98	3.00	23.4	83
1999	342	112	2.52	32.5	108
2000	324	101	3.84	41.6	74
2001	336	133	3.68	36.4	88
2002	420	142	3.96	49.4	98

74. The ratio between the total expenditure on taxes for all the years to the total Bonus for all the years respectively is
(a) 9 : 40 (b) 25 : 13
(c) 451 : 17 (d) 1 : 25

75. Expenditure on fuel and transport forms the percentage of expenditure on salary for the year 2001.
(a) 34.54% (B) 39.22%
(c) 33.57% (d) 39.58%

76. The total expenditure of the company over the items during the year 2001 is
(a) ₹ 590 lakhs (b) ₹ 598 lakhs
(c) ₹ 597 lakhs (d) ₹ 957.08 lakhs

77. Pointing to a boy in a photograph Rani said, "His mother's only daughter is my mother." How is Rani related to that boy?
(a) Wife (b) Sister
(c) Niece (d) Brother

78. The first gasoline run car engine was developed by
(a) Henry Ford (b) Carl Benz
(c) Hugh Chalmers (d) Horace Elgin Dodge

79. The first democratically elected woman President of Africa is from
(a) Nigeria (b) Liberia
(c) Tanzania (d) Kenya

80. Answer the question based on the below information
If '+' is '×', '–' is '+', '×' is '÷' and '÷' is '–' then $9 \div 5 + 4 - 3 \times 2 = ?$
(a) 2 (b) –9 (c) –3 (d) –9.5

81. The length of a diagonal in cms of a rectangle of length 5 cm and width 3 cm is
(a) $\sqrt{34}$ (b) $\pm\sqrt{34}$
(c) 4 (d) ± 4

82. The number of sides of a regular polygon whose exterior angles are each 72° is
(a) 7 (b) 6 (c) 5 (d) 8

83. Which among the following is not an environment friendly mode of producing electricity?
(a) Thermal Power (b) Solar Power
(c) Wind Energy (d) Bio-waste

84. The G-20 Summit in November 2015 was organised in which European Country?
(a) Germany (b) France
(c) Turkey (d) Spain

85. Read the statements and select a conclusion from the given alternatives:

Statements

The health care system has expanded in terms of number of hospitals. But the fact is that most of them are not well equipped and unable to make significant progress in the field of patient care.

Conclusions

I. We should provide good doctors and equipment to existing hospitals now onwards.

II. Now, it is not necessary to open any new hospitals.

(a) Only conclusion I follows
(b) Only conclusion II follows
(c) Both I and II follow
(d) Neither I nor II follows

86. Mr. Ibrahim borrowed ₹ 7500 at 5% per annum compound interest. The compound interest compounded annually for 2 yr is

(a) 768.75 (b) 8286.75
(c) 8268.75 (d) 786.75

87. ________ was the first woman Prime Minister of Sri Lanka.

(a) Ranasinghe Premadasa
(b) Dingiri Banda Wijetunge
(c) Sirimavo Bandaranaike
(d) Chandrika Kumaratunga

Direction (Q. Nos. 88-90) *Study the following instruction and answer the questions based on it.*

Five boys are sitting on a beach to be photographed. Sachin is to the left of Ram and to the right of Bin. Monty is to the right of Ram. Rony is between Ram and Monty.

88. Who is in the middle of the photograph?

(a) Bin (b) Ram
(c) Rony (d) Sachin

89. Who is second from the right in the photograph?

(a) Monty (b) Ram
(c) Rony (d) Bin

90. Who is second from the left in the photograph?

(a) Rony (b) Monty
(c) Bin (d) Sachin

91. Answer the question based on the below information.

If '+' is '×' '–' is '+', '×' is '÷' and '÷' is '–' then $3 \times 2 + 4 - 2 \div 9 = ?$

(a) –1 (b) 1
(c) –2 (d) 3

92. What is the meaning of an ECOTONE?

(a) ECOTONE is where two biomes meet
(b) It's an area with low survival for species
(c) An area with limited flora and fauna
(d) An area with high biomass production

93. Rakshanth is twice as good a trademan as Verma and together they finish a piece of work in 19 days. In how many days will Verma alone finish the work?

(a) 38 (b) 57
(c) 76 (d) 50

94. Read the statements and select a conclusion for the given alternative.

Statement

To cultivate interest in debate the school has made it compulsory from December, 2015 for each student to attend two debate classes per week and submit a weekly report on the debate discussed.

Conclusions

I. Interest in debating can be created by force.

II. Some students eventually will develop interest in debating.

(a) Only conclusion on I follows
(b) Only conclusion II follows
(c) Both I and II follow
(d) Neither I nor II follows

95. Bill Gates co-founded 'Microsoft Corporation' in 1975 with?

(a) Chris Hughes (b) Tim Berners-Lee

(c) Steve Paul Jobs (d) Paul G. Allen

96. Two numbers are in ratio 2:5 and their HCF is 18. Their LCM is

(a) 180 (b) 36 (c) 90 (d) 188

97. How many constellations have been named ?

(a) 88 (b) 99 (c) 90 (d) 87

98. Complete the figure X from the given alternatives 1, 2, 3, 4.

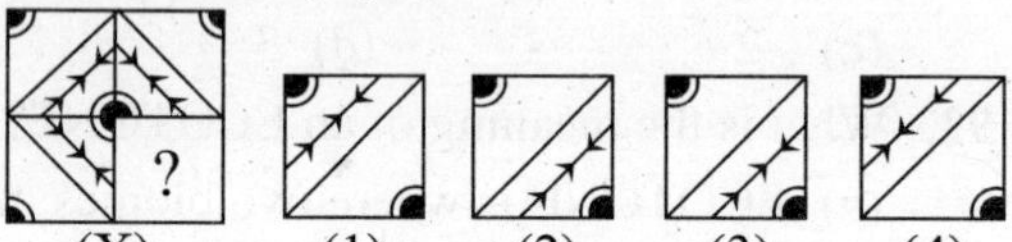

(X) (1) (2) (3) (4)

(a) 1 (b) 2 (c) 3 (d) 4

99. ____________ jointly launched International Solar Alliance (ISA) at conference of parties (Cop 21) climate conference held in Paris, France on Ist December, 2015.

(a) India and China

(b) India and France

(c) India and USA

(d) India and Russia

100. If in a certain language KINDLE is coded as ELDNIK, how is IMPOSING coded in that code?

(a) GNIOSPMI (b) GNSIOPMI

(c) GNISPOMI (d) GNISOPMI

Hints & Solutions

1. (*)

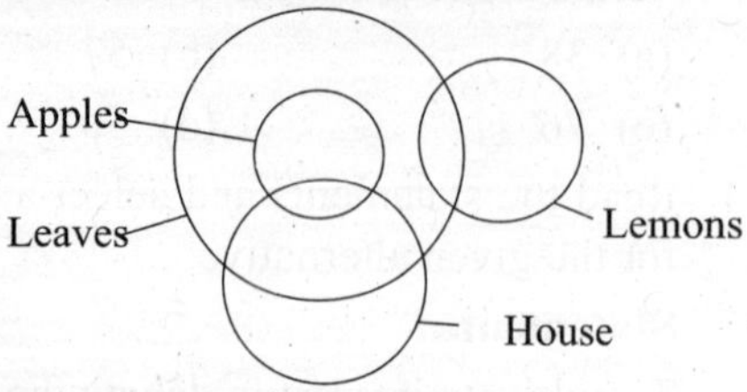

Here, no answer is correct.

2. (c)

T R I P P L E

↓ ↓ ↓ ↓ ↓ ↓ ↓

–1 –1 –1 –1 –1 –1 –1

S Q H O O K D

Similarly,

E X O T I C

↓ ↓ ↓ ↓ ↓ ↓

–1 –1 –1 –1 –1 –1

D W N S H B

3. (a) German physicist Wilhelm Röntgen accidentally discovered X-rays. These are electromagnetic radiation capable of penetrating most solid objects.

4. (b) 3M's Post-it Note is a small piece of paper with a strip of glue on its back, for temporarily attaching notes to documents and other surfaces.

5. (d) $5x(x+2)+4x = 5x^2+10x+4x$

$= 5x^2+14x$

6. (b) A cache, is memory made of high-speed static RAM (SRAM) instead of the slower and cheaper dynamic RAM (DRAM) used for main memory.

7. (b) Gain %

$$= \left(\frac{(100+\text{common gain\%})^2}{100} - 100\right)$$

$$= \left(\frac{(100+11)^2}{100} - 100\right)$$

$$= (123.21 - 100) = 23.21\%$$

8. (a)

$$\frac{(\text{Selling Price) 1}}{(\text{Selling Price) 2}} = \frac{\left(1+\frac{2}{100}\right)}{\left(1+\frac{18}{100}\right)}$$

$$= \frac{102}{118} = \frac{51}{59}$$

9. (b) $\frac{0.592}{0.8}=\frac{592}{800}=\frac{74}{100}=0.74$

10. (b) Laura is the Aunt of that boy. So, relations is Aunt and Nephew.

11. (d) $69696 \times 9999 = 69696 \times (10000 - 1)$
$= 696960000 - 69696 = 696890304$

12. (a)

Letter	R	I	P	L	E	A	C	H
Code	6	1	3	8	2	4	5	4

Hence, code of 'PILLER' is '318826'

13. (d) In one minute, the flask will be empty by

$\frac{1}{9}+\frac{1}{16}=\frac{16+9}{144}=\frac{25}{144}$

So, time required to empty full flask

$=\frac{144}{25}=5\frac{19}{25}$ minutes

14. (b)

15. (c) A few natural warning signs to predict tsunami are: Strong ground shaking on the coast; Unusual sea-level fluctuations: a rapid rise or fall in coastal waters; Abnormally huge wave; Loud ocean roar.

16. (c) $6+7\times 3-8\div 20=6\times 7\div 3+8-20$

$=\frac{6\times 7}{3}+8-20=14+8-20=2.$

17. (b) Argon is the third-most abundant gas in the Earth's atmosphere, and crust.

18. (b) The present training programme does not bring out the real merit of the candidates. So, it need to be changed by some other training programme.

19. (b) S.D. $=\sqrt{\text{Variance}}=\sqrt{196}=14$

20. (b) Netaji hoisted the national flag at Port Blair on December 30, 1943, and established the Azad Hind government and renamed Andaman & Nicobar Islands to Shaheed & Swaraj Islands.

21. (b) $4923 \div 547 - 10 = 9 - 10 = -1$

22. (d) At puberty, the voice box or the larynx begins to grow. Boys develop larger voice boxes (Adam's apple).

23. (d)

24. (b) Mean $=\frac{\text{Sum of datas}}{\text{Number of data}}$

$=\frac{1+\frac{1}{2}+\frac{1}{2}+\frac{3}{4}+\frac{1}{4}+\frac{1}{2}+2+\frac{1}{2}+\frac{1}{4}+\frac{3}{4}}{9}$

$=\frac{\frac{13}{2}}{9}=\frac{13}{18}$

25. (b) If variance (σ^2) of the data: 2, 4, 5, 6. 8, 17 is 23.33.

Then variance of the data: 4, 8, 10, 12, 16, 34

$= 2 \times 23.33 = 46.66$

26. (d) Cost Price $=$ Selling Price $\times \frac{100}{(100-\text{loss}\%)}$

$=22100\times\frac{100}{(100-15)}=\frac{22100\times 100}{85}$

Selling Price

$=$ Cost Price $\times\frac{100+\text{Profit}\%}{100}$

$=\frac{22100\times 100}{85}\times\frac{(100+15)}{100}$

$=\frac{22100\times 100\times 115}{85\times 100}=$ ₹ 29900

27. (d)

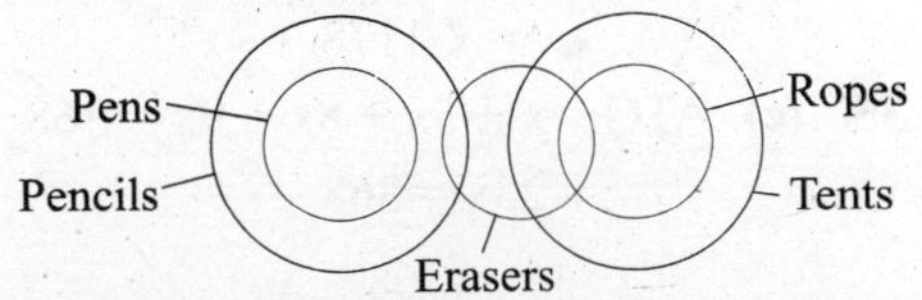

Only conclusion (iv) follows.

28. (c) $\frac{2}{3}=\frac{2\times 4}{3\times 4}=\frac{8}{12}$ Now, $\frac{8}{12}<\frac{9}{12}<\frac{10}{12}$

$\frac{3}{4}=\frac{3\times 3}{4\times 3}=\frac{9}{12}$ i.e., $\frac{2}{3}<\frac{3}{4}<\frac{5}{6}$

$\frac{5}{6}=\frac{5\times 2}{6\times 2}=\frac{10}{12}$

29. (a) Cos (A + B)

$=$ Cos A . Cos B – Sin A . Sin B

Now, tan A $=\frac{15}{8}$, then Cos A

$= \frac{8}{17}, \text{Sin A} = \frac{15}{17}.$

and tan B $= \frac{7}{24}$, then Cos B

$= \frac{24}{25}, \text{Sin B} = \frac{7}{25}.$

$\text{Cos (A + B)} = \frac{8}{17} \times \frac{24}{25} - \frac{15}{17} \times \frac{7}{25}$

$= \frac{192 - 105}{425} = \frac{87}{425}$

30. (a)

31. (d) The Montessori Method, is based on self-education. Rather than sitting still and absorbing lessons, the child in the Montessori classroom educates himself with the teacher as his guide.

32. (d) Polyarchy is a form of government in which power is invested in multiple people. It takes the form of neither a dictatorship nor a democracy.

33. (c) $8^{\frac{2}{3}} = (2^3)^{\frac{2}{3}} = 2^2 = 4.$

34. (c) Amount $= P + \frac{prt}{100} = 950 + \frac{950 \times 6 \times 4}{100}$

$= ₹\ 1178$

35. (c) ATQ, $x + 5x + 8x + 9x = 368$

$23x = 368$

$x = \frac{368}{23} = 16.$

Hence, respective rupees are

16, 80, 128 and 144.

36. (c) New Horizons is an interplanetary space probe launched by NASA in 2006-to perform a flyby study of the Pluto system in 2015, and a secondary mission study one or more other Kuiper belt objects (KBOs) in the decade to follow.

37. (a) Water moves into a raisin through osmosis when there is a lower concentration of water inside the cell than outside.

38. (d)

39. (c) The rotational symmetry is the number of times the shape maps onto itself on a rotation of 360°. A rectangle has rotational symmetry of 2 at 180° and 360°.

40. (d) L.C.M. × H.C.F. = Product of two numbers

96 × H.C.F. $= 2400$

H.C.F. $= \frac{2400}{96} = 25$

41. (a) Let the one way distance is d km and walking and riding speeds are x and y km/hr respectively.

ATQ, $\frac{d}{x} + \frac{d}{y} = 4.5$ ...(i)

and $\frac{d}{x} + \frac{d}{x} = 5.66$ ...(ii)

from (ii), $\frac{d}{x} = \frac{5.66}{2}$

then, from (i), $\frac{5.66}{2} + \frac{d}{x} = 4.5$

$5.66 + \frac{2d}{y} = 9$

$\frac{2d}{y} = 9 - 5.66 = 3.34$

Hence, required time = 3 hr 20 min.

42. (c)

43. (c) The women has to travel with speed x km/h. Distance between two cycliest

$= 24 \times \frac{15}{60} = 6 \text{ km}.$

Now, Distance travelled by cycliest in 10 min.

$= 24 \times \frac{10}{60} = 4 \text{ km}.$

Hence, women speed $= \frac{6 - 4}{\frac{10}{60}} = \frac{2 \times 60}{10}$

$= 12 \text{ km/hr}$

44. (b) Harappans worshipped mother goddess, shiva, peepal, pigeon and swastik.

45. (a) The twinkling of a star is due to refraction of starlight which on entering the earth's atmosphere, undergoes refraction continuously before it reaches the earth.

46. (b) Fig. given in number (2) will complete the fig. X.

47. (b) The Harvard Foundation presented Mr. Satyarthi, Nobel Peace award for his dedication to protecting children's rights.

48-50: Number of students like Maths = 42.

Number of students like English = 32

Number of students like neither Math nor English, $n(\bar{A} \cap \bar{B}) = 12$

$\therefore$ Number of students like either Math or English

$n(A \cup B) = 60 - 12 = 48$

$\therefore$ Number of students who like both

$$n(A \cap B) = n(A) + n(B) - n(A \cup B)$$
$$= 42 + 32 - 48$$
$$= 26.$$

48. (a) Number of students like only Math

$$= n(A) - n(A \cap B) = 42 - 26 = 16$$

Required percent $= \frac{16}{60} \times 100 = 26.67\%$

49. (b) Number of students like both subjects

$$n(A \cap B) = 26.$$

50. (d) Number of students like exactly one subjects = 16 + 6 = 22.

51. (b) Golconda is a citadel and fort in Southern India and was the capital of the medieval Qutb Shahi dynasty (c.1512–1687), is situated 11 km west of Hyderabad.

52. (d) $\text{Sin } x = \frac{4}{5}$, $\text{Cos } x = (1 - \sin^2 x)^{\frac{1}{2}}$

$$= \left(1 - \frac{4}{5}^2\right)^{\frac{1}{2}} = \left(\frac{9}{25}\right)^{\frac{1}{2}} = \frac{3}{5}$$

$\text{Sec } x = \frac{5}{3}$

Now, $\text{Sec}^2 x - 1 = \left(\frac{5}{3}\right)^2 - 1 = \frac{25 - 9}{9} = \frac{16}{9}$

53. (c)

Letter	P	R	A	B	H	I	T	L
Code	2	7	5	9	6	8	3	4

Hence, code of 'BHARATHI' is '9 6 5 7 5 3 6 8'

54. (c)

$$1757 = 7 \times 251$$

and $2259 = 9 \times 251$

Hence, H.C.F. = 251

55. (b)

56. (c)

$$w^2\sqrt{(z^2 + y^2)} = (-2)^2\sqrt{\left(-\frac{1}{2}\right)^2 + (0)^2}$$
$$= 4 \times \frac{1}{2} = 2$$

57. (c) Ram is the father-in-law of that girl.

58. (d) The Calcutta High Court is the oldest high court in the country, established on 2 July 1862.

59. (a) Sublimation is the transition of a substance directly from the solid to the gas phase without the liquid phase.

60. (b) $x - 3 = 3x + 7 \Rightarrow 3x - x = -3 - 7$

$$2x = -10$$
$$x = -\frac{10}{2} = -5$$

61. (a) M. Fathima Beevi was the first woman and first Muslim woman to be appointed as judge of the Supreme Court of India in 1989.

62. (b) An equinox is the time when the plane of Earth's equator passes through the centre of the Sun. This occurs twice each year: around 20 March and 23 September. It is the moment at which the centre of the visible Sun is directly above the Equator.

63. (c) $\frac{33800}{\frac{520}{5}} = 33800 \times \frac{1}{520} \times \frac{1}{5} = 13.$

64. (a) When the comet gets closer to the Sun, the solar winds cause the comet's tail to point away from the Sun.

65. (d) Kaiser-e- Hind title was conferred on Gandhi but he relinquished it.

66. (d)

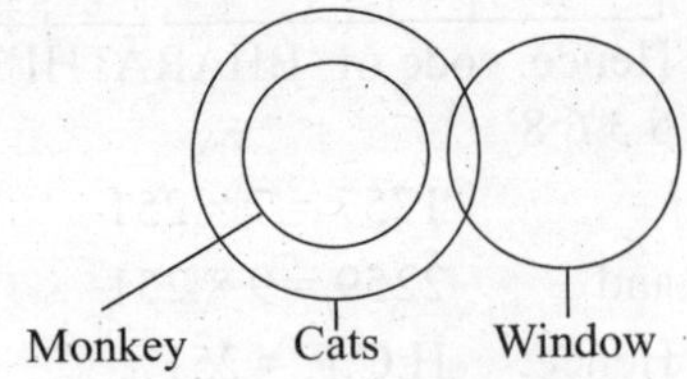

Only conclusion III follow.

67. (b) Fig.(2) will complete the fig (X)

68. (c) $6-9+8\times3\div20 \;=6+9\times8\div3-20$
$=6+8\times3-20$
$=6+24-20=10$

69. (c) Karla Caves located near Lonavala (Mumbai) originated back in the 2nd century BC. The 16 caves are connected to the Hinayana period of Buddhism and the three belong to the Mahayana stage. Their best-preserved cave is a prayer hall, chaityagriha or Grand Chaitya

70. (a) 3D glasses make it possible for your left eye to see the left eye image, and the right eye to see the right eye image only, which they do very effectively.

71. (d) The source of the Narmada is a small reservoir, Narmada Kund, at Amarkantak in Madhya Pradesh. The river descends from Sonmud, then falls over a cliff as Kapildhara waterfall and flowing through a tortuous course crossing the rocks and islands up to the palace of Ramnagar.

72. (a) M. Hidayatullah was the 11th Chief Justice the sixth Vice President of India. He also served as the Acting President of India from 20 July to 24 August 1969 and from 6 October to 31 October 1982.

73. (b) Fig.(2) will complete the fig. (X).

74. (c) Required ratio $=\dfrac{\text{total exp. on taxes}}{\text{total exp. on bonus}}$

$$=\frac{83+108+74+88+98}{3+2.52+3.84+3.68+3.96}=\frac{451}{17}$$

75. (d) Required percent

$$=\frac{\text{Exp. on fuel and transport in 2001}}{\text{Exp. on salary in 2001}}\times100$$

$$=\frac{133}{336}\times100=39.6\%$$

76. (d) Total exp. in 2001

$=336+133+3.68+36.4+88$

$=$ ₹ 957.08 lakhs

77. (c) Rani is the niece to that boy.

78. (b) Karl Benz is credited for inventing the automobile because his car was practical, used a gasoline-powered internal-combustion engine and worked like modern cars do today.

79. (b)

80. (d) $9\div5+4-3\times2 \;=9-5\times4+3\div2$
$=9-20+1.5=-9.5$

81. (a) Let ABCD is a rectangle with length BC = 5 cm. Width AB = 3 cm.

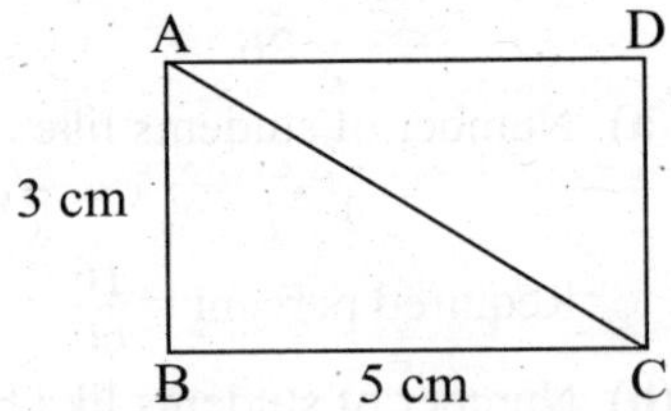

then, Diagonal AC $=\sqrt{(AB)^2+(BC)^2}$

$=\sqrt{(3)^2+(5)^2}$

$=\sqrt{34}$ cm

82. (c) For a polygon of n sides,
Sum of its exterior angles = 360°

$$n\times72=360°\Rightarrow n=\frac{360}{72}=5$$

83. (a) Electric power systems consist of different energy sources, transmission networks, and distribution lines. Each of these components can have environmental impacts at multiple stages of their development. Thermal power is not an environment friendly mode of producing electricity.

84. (c)

85. (a) With increase in the number of hospitals, govt. should also increase the number of good doctors and equipment to existing hospitals.

86. (a) C.I. $= P\left[\left(1+\frac{r}{100}\right)^t - 1\right]$

$$= 7500\left[\left(1+\frac{5}{100}\right)^2 - 1\right]$$

$$= 7500\,[1.1025 - 1] = ₹\,768.75$$

87. (c) Sirimavo Bandaranaike served as prime minister three times and was the leader of the Sri Lanka Freedom Party. She was the first woman to be elected head of government in the world.

88-90: Sitting arrangement of five boys on a bench is like this:

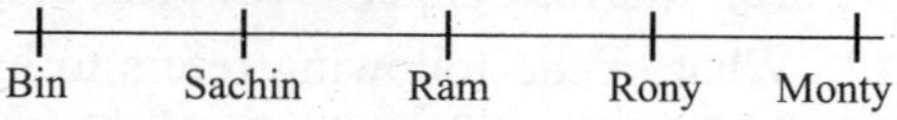

88. (b)

89. (*) Sachin is second from right

90. (a)

91. (a) $3 \times 2 + 4 - 2 \div 9 = 3 \div 2 \times 4 + 2 - 9$

$$= 3 \times 2 + 2 - 9 = -1$$

92. (a) An ecotone is a transition area where two communities meet and integrate. An ecotone may appear on the ground as a gradual blending of the two communities across a broad area, or it may manifest itself as a sharp boundary line.

93. (b) Let Verma alone can finish the work in x day then, Rakshanth will finish the work in x/2 days.

ATQ, $\frac{2}{x} + \frac{1}{x} = \frac{1}{19}$

$$\frac{3}{x} = \frac{1}{19} \Rightarrow x = 3 \times 19 = 57 \text{ days.}$$

94. (b) Only conclusion II follows. Some students eventually will develop interest in debating.

95. (d) Paul Gardner Allen, an American business magnate, investor, researcher, humanitarian, and philanthropist, co-founded Microsoft with Bill Gates in 1975, which sparked the microcomputer revolution and later became the world's largest PC software company.

96. (a) Let two number are 2x and 5x.

then, their H.C.F. = x = 18.

So, L.C.M. = 2 × 5x = 10x

= 10 × 18 = 180.

97. (a) A constellation is a group of stars that forms an imaginary pattern on the celestial sphere, typically representing an animal, mythological person or creature, a god, or an inanimate object.

98. (d) Fig. (4) will complete the fig. (X).

99. (b) ISA was jointly launched by Indian Prime Minister and French President on November 30, 2015 in Paris to the United Nations Framework Convention on Climate Change.

100. (d)

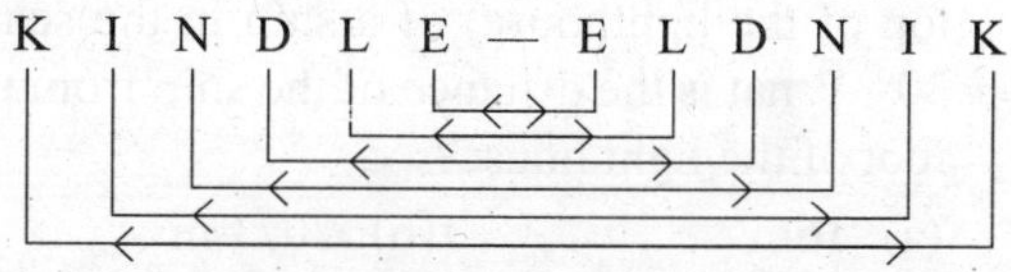

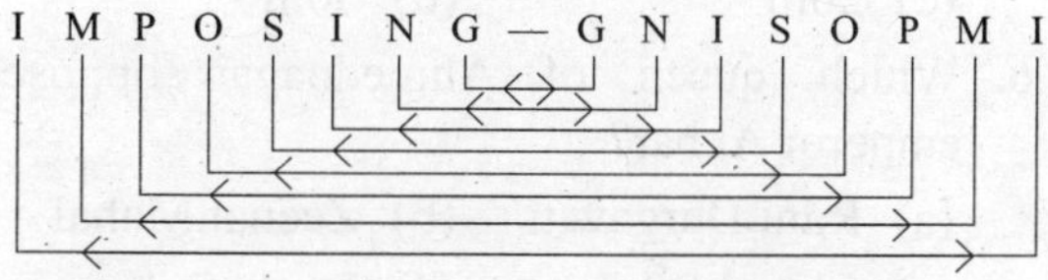

RRB NTPC stage-I Solved Paper

Held On 12th April 2016 (Shift-III)

1. Ritesh sold a pen for ₹ 36 with a profit of 20%. If it were sold for ₹ 33, then what could be the percentage of profit or loss?
   (a) 10% Profit (b) 15% Profit
   (c) 12% Loss (d) 18% Loss
2. Which sport has the highest rank of Yokozuna?
   (a) Sumo wrestling (b) Judo
   (c) Jujitsu (d) Kendo
3. Rearrange the jumbled up letters in their natural sequence and find the odd one out.
   (a) SAMR (b) MOETC
   (c) USVNE (d) PUJIERT
4. What does UFO stand for?
   (a) Under Fire Object
   (b) Unidentified Flying Object
   (c) Unapproved Foreign Object
   (d) Unidentified Free Object
5. The height of a light house is 20 meters above sea level. The angle of depression (from the top of the lighthouse) of a ship in the sea is 30°. What is the distance of the ship from the foot of the light house?
   (a) 16m (b) $20\sqrt{3}$ m
   (c) 20m (d) 30m
6. Which queen of Ahmednagar opposed emperor Akbar?
   (a) Rani Durgavati (b) Zeenat Mahal
   (c) Chand Bibi (d) Razia Sultan
7. When is International day for Preservation of Ozone layer observed?
   (a) September 16 (b) July 4
   (c) January 23 (d) May 1
8. Who invented the bifocal glasses?
   (a) Thomas Alva Edison
   (b) Benjamin Franklin
   (c) Evangelista
   (d) Isaac Newton
9. Identify the odd one from the list below.
   (a) Snake (b) Lizard
   (c) Reptiles (d) Crocodile
10. What denotes learned and shared beliefs and behaviours?
    (a) Culture (b) Ethnicity
    (c) Group (d) Descent
11. Who invented the mobile phone?
    (a) Joseph Wilson (b) Edwin Land
    (c) Martin Cooper (d) John Lloyd Wright
12. What of the following refers to hypotheses which are confirmed by varied tests?
    (a) Assumption (b) Theory
    (c) Answer (d) Opinion
13. What does PDA stand for?
    (a) Personal Data Assistant
    (b) Personal Digital Assistant
    (c) Prime Data Assistant
    (d) Prime Digital Assistant
14. If the angles of a triangle are in the ratio of 1 : 4 : 7, then find the ratio of the greatest angle to the smallest angle.
    (a) 7 : 2 (b) 2 : 3 (c) 7 : 1 (d) 3 : 5
15. Name the architect who designed New Delhi.
    (a) Le Corbusier (b) Sir Edwin Lutyens
    (c) Andrew Paul (d) George Baker
16. The mean of 10 observations is 17. One more observation is included and the new mean becomes 16.
    (a) 16 (b) 8 (c) 6 (d) 12
17. Battle of Plassey was fought by the British under the leadership of
    (a) Robert Clive (b) Lord Dalhousie
    (c) Warren Hastings (d) James Heartly

18. Arun and Amit can do a piece of work in 9 days and 12 days respectively. If they work for alternate days and Amit starts the work first, then in how many days 35/36 parts of whole work will be completed?

(a) 10 days (b) 12 days
(c) 5 days (d) 8 days

19. Aparna changes the marked price of an item to 50% above its C.P. What % of discount allowed (in approximately) to gain 10%?

(a) 27% (b) 25%
(c) 35% (d) 37%

20. A wholesaler purchased 7 hair clips for a rupee. How many for a rupee must he sell to get profit of 40%

(a) 6 (b) 5 (c) 4 (d) 3

21. If E = 5, GUN = 42 and ROSE = 57, then what is the value of GATE?

(a) 23 (b) 32 (c) 33 (d) 35

22. In which state is the Valley of Flowers National park situated?

(a) Uttarakhand
(b) Himachal Pradesh
(c) Jammu and Kashmir
(d) Assam

23. Three numbers are given in which the second is triple the first and is also double the third. If the average of the three numbers is 66. Find the first number.

(a) 36 (b) 54 (c) 108 (d) 72

24. Pihu and Aayu are running on a circular track of diameter 28 m. Speed of Pihu is 48 m/s and that of Aayu is 40 m/s. They start from the same point at the same time in the same direction. When will they meet again for the first time?

(a) 8 seconds (b) 11 seconds
(c) 13 seconds (d) 14 seconds

25. Who replaced B. S. Bassi as Police Commissioner

(a) Alok Kumar Verma
(b) Rakesh Maria
(c) Dattatray Padsalgikar
(d) Neeraj Kumar

DIRECTIONS (Qs. 26-28): *In the following questions answers are to be based on the details given below:*

A salesman visits 274 houses in a town to find out the views about three products X, Y and Z. He found that 157 use X, 98 use only X, 22 use all the three, 14 use X and Z but not Y, 39 use Y and Z, 48 use only Y.

26. Which product is the most popular one?

(a) X (b) Y
(c) Z (d) Both X and Z

27. How many use product Z only?

(a) 10 (b) 50 (c) 52 (d) 25

28. What fraction used at least two products?

(a) 67/274 (b) 76/274
(c) 73/274 (d) 37/274

29. A superfast Duronto express running at 90 kmph overtakes a bike running at 36 kmph in 25 seconds. What is the length of the train in meters?

(a) 375 m (b) 225 m
(c) 275 m (d) 325 m

30. If EFMIJ means DELHI, then the last letter of the word got by decoding IQBOS is

(a) R (b) T (c) K (d) M

31. An Assertion (A) and Reason (R) are given below:

Assertion (A): We prefer to wear white clothes in winter.

Reason (R): White clothes are good reflectors of heat.

Choose the correct option.

(a) Ais true but R is false.
(b) A is false but R is true.
(c) Both A and R are true and R is the correct explanation of A.
(d) Both A and R are true and R is not the correct explanation of A.

32. Select the pair in which the numbers are similarly related as in the given pair:

9 : 27 : : ______ : ______

(a) 5 : 125 (b) 8:64

(c) 15: 135 (d) 81: 729

33. How many princely states were there in India at the time of Independence?

(a) 347 (b) 490

(c) 565 (d) 418

34. Given that x + (I/x) = 15, then find the value of $\frac{5x}{5x^2 - 20x + 5}$

(a) 1/3 (b) 1/4

(c) 1/5 (d) 1/11

35. Who is considered as the Father of Modern Indian Renaissance?

(a) Mahatma Gandhi

(b) Sardar Vallabhbhai Patel

(c) VinobaBhave

(d) Raja Ram Mohan Roy

36. Find the largest number of three digits exactly divisible by 15. 18, 27 and 30.

(a) 870 (b) 900

(c) 810 (d) 780

37. Who invented the Band-aid?

(a) Earle Dickson (b) Alan Gant

(c) Louis Pasteur (d) Frank Epperson

38. If (x + 1/x) = 2, then find the value of $(x^3 + 1/x^3) \div (x^{18} + 1/x^{18})$

(a) 2/9 (b) 5 (c) 1 (d) 1/9

39. Find the approximate simple interest on ₹2000 from March 9, 2010 to May 21, 2010 at 8.25% per annum.

(a) ₹ 43 (b) ₹ 37

(c) ₹ 33 (d) ₹ 40

40. The angle of elevation of the top of tower at a distance of 25 m from its foot is 60°. The approximate height of the tower is -

(a) 20.3 m (b) 15.3m

(c) 36.3m (d) 43.3m

41. Which of the following refers to the number of pixels per inch, printed on a page?

(a) Print Margin (b) Resolution

(c) Filter (d) Colour mode

42. In which generation of computer was the mechanical language for programming used?

(a) First (b) Second

(c) Third (d) Fourth

43. Which is the fastest land animal in the World?

(a) Dog (b) Cheetah

(c) Tiger (d) Horse

44. If @ means +, # means – , $ means × and * means ÷, then what is the value of **16 @ 4 $ 5 # 72 * 8 =**

(a) 27 (b) 26 (c) 36 (d) 35

45. 4 years ago, the ratio of Vikah's to Rahul's age was 3: 5. After 6 years, this ratio would become 4:5. Find the present age of Rahul.

(a) 10 (b) 15 (c) 14 (d) 17

46. If in a certain code language, PROMOTION is written as 365458957, how will the word MONITOR be written in that code language?

(a) 4579856 (b) 4578956

(c) 4597866 (d) 4578596

47. If '+' means 'multiplication', '–' means 'division', 'x' means 'subtraction' and '÷' means 'addition', then 9 + 8 ÷ 8 – 4 × 9 is

(a) 65 (b) 11 (c) 26 (d) 56

48. Who was the American astronaut who returned to Earth after spending 340 days in International Space Station?

(a) Scott Kelly (b) Mikhail Kornienko

(c) Eric Boe (d) Douglas Hurley

49. Knife is an example for

(a) Lever (b) Wedge

(c) Inclined plane (d) Pulley

50. The famous tennis player Steffi Graf belongs to which of the following countries?

(a) USA (b) England

(c) Germany (d) Switzerland

51. When two liquids do not mix with each other to form a solution, what is it called?

(a) Solvent (b) Solute
(c) Immiscible (d) Decantation

DIRECTIONS (Qs. 52-54): *Study the following information carefully and answer the questions given below it.*

(i) There are six members in a family in which there are two married couples.
(ii) Sandhya, a lawyer, is married to the engineer and is mother of Charu and Suraj.
(iii) Bhuvanesh, the teacher, is married Aruna.
(iv) Aruna has one son and one grandson.
(v) Of the two married ladies one is a housewife.
(vi) There is also one student and one male doctor in the family

52. How is Aruna related to Charu?

(a) Sister (b) Mother
(c) Grandfather (d) Grandmother

53. Who among the following is the housewife?

(a) Charu (b) Aruna
(c) Sandhiya (d) None

54. Which of the following is true about the grand daughter in the family?

(a) She is a Doctor (b) She is a Teacher
(c) She is a Student (d) Data inadequate

55. Find the correct option which has a similar relationship.

Produce : Waste :: Contrast : ?

(a) Correct (b) Match
(c) Contradict (d) Oppose

56. An Assertion (A) and a Reason (R) are given below.

Assertion (A): Beriberi is a viral infection.
Reason (R): Vitamin deficiency causes diseases.
Choose the correct option.

(a) A is false but R is true.
(b) A is true but R is false.
(c) Both A and R are false
(d) Both A and R are true and R is the correct explanation of A.

57. Glaciers are formed by

(a) Melting snow
(b) Accumulation of snow
(c) Heavy hail fall
(d) High rainfall

58. 12 men and 16 women together can complete a work in 4 days. It takes 80 days for one man alone to complete the same work, then how many days would be required for one woman alone to complete the same work?

(a) 160 (b) 150
(b) 130 (d) 175

59. Jalal, Amit and Feroz enter into partnership. Jalal invests 4 times as much as Amit and Amit invests three-fourth of what Feroz invests. At the end of the financial year, the total profit earned is ₹19,000. Find the share for Jalal.

(a) ₹ 15,000 (b) ₹ 12,000
(c) ₹ 13,000 (d) ₹ 10,000

60. How many astronauts have walked on the moon?

(a) 2 (b) 5 (c) 8 (d) 12

61. Identify the odd one from the list below.

(a) Stream (b) Bridge
(c) Canal (d) River

62. An Assertion (A) and Reason (R) are given below.

Assertion (A): Leakages in household gas cylinders can be detected.
Reason (R): LPG has a strong smell.
Choose the correct option.

(a) Both A and R are true and R is the correct explanation of A.
(b) Both A and R are true and R is not the correct explanation of A.
(c) Both A and R are false
(d) A is true but R is false.

63. Who was sworn in as the Prime Minister of Nepal in 2015?
(a) Sushil Koirala
(b) Bidhya Devi Bhandari
(c) Khadga Prasad Sharma Oli
(d) Kul Bahadur Gurung

64. Who is the current FIFA president?
(a) Sepp Blatter (b) Gianni Infantino
(c) Issa Hayatou (d) Durgs

65. Who won the 2015 Australian Grand Prix?
(a) Louis Hamilton (b) Kimi Raikkonen
(c) Jenson Button (d) Sebastian Vettel

66. What are the waves that are used to penetrate solids and are used by doctors and at airports?
(a) Sound wave (b) X-rays
(c) Electro magnetic (d) Mechanical

67. If $(7x + 5)°$ and $(x + 5)°$ are complementary angles, then find value of x.
(a) 10 (b) 20 (c) 30 (d) 40

68. Rearrange the jumbled up letters in their natural sequence and find the odd one out.
(a) EARSUQ (b) ONGPOYL
(c) NAEGRCELT (d) RGETESNH

69. Choose the pair which is related in the same way as the words in the first pair from the given choices
Savage : Civilized :: ________ : ________
(a) Brutal: Heroic (b) Wild : Animal
(c) Dark : Light (d) Illiterate : Book

70. In a college, 25% of male faculties are same in number as 1/3rd of the female faculties. What is the ratio of male faculty to female faculty in that college?
(a) 4:3 (b) 3:4 (c) 2:3 (d) 3:2

71. If A denotes +, B denotes '–', C denotes '÷' D denotes '×' then the value of the expression 9 D 48 C 6 B 16 A 3 is
(a) 53 (b) 35 (c) 59 (d) 56

72. What is the process of slow cooling of hot glass called?
(a) Annealing (b) Humidifying
(c) Condensation (d) Decantation

73. Find the products : 0.5 x 0.05 x 0.005 x 500
(a) 0.0625 (b) 0.00625
(c) 0.06255 (d) 0.625

74. Boxing is related to Ring in the same Way as Tennis is related to
(a) Court (b) Ground
(c) Pool (d) Arena

75. Find the degree of the polynomial $8x^4 + 2x^2y^3 + 4$
(a) 4 (b) 5 (c) 0 (d) 1

76. In which Schedule to the Constitution of India is the list of States and Union Territories given?
(a) First Schedule (b) Second Schedule
(c) Fourth Schedule (d) Sixth Schedule

77. In a certain code, TABLE is written as GZYOV, then CHAIR can be written as
(a) XRZSI (b) XZSRI
(c) XSRZI (d) XSZRI

78. Milk of Magnesia is used as a
(a) Laxative (b) Pain killer
(c) Sedative (d) Antibiotic

79. In a number system, on dividing 11509 by a certain number, Mukesh gets 71 as quotient and 7 as remainder. What is the divisor?
(a) 132 (b) 172
(b) 182 (d) 162

DIRECTIONS (Qs. 80-82): *The table below depicts the Number of Books Sold by 5 cities during 5 months. Study the following table and answer the questions:*

Months	City A	City B	City C	City D	City E
June	213	200	195	253	229
July	156	208	216	187	175
August	177	197	185	181	215
September	220	145	235	265	231
October	253	188	278	243	249

80. If 30% of the total number of books sold by City B, D and E together in July were academic books, how many non - academic books were sold by the same Cities together in the same month?

(a) 379 (b) 389
(c) 399 (d) 309

81. What is the respective ratio between the total number of books sold by City A in July and September together and total number of books sold by City E in August and October together?

(a) 57:49 (b) 49:57
(c) 58:47 (d) 47:58

82. What is the average number of books sold by City C in July. September and October together?

(a) 243 (b) 242
(c) 234 (d) 224

83. Find the missing value denoted by '?'

3 : 243 :: 5 : ?

(a) 625 (b) 465
(c) 3125 (d) 425

84. If the standard deviation of a population is 3, what would be the population variance?

(a) 9 (b) 6 (c) 8 (d) 15

85. Below are given statements followed by two conclusions I and II. You have to take the given statements to be true even if they seem to be at variance from commonly known facts.

Statements:

Some buds are flowers.

All flowers are trees.

All trees are leaves.

Conclusions:

I. Some leaves are buds.

II. All flowers are leaves.

Decide which of the below options logically follows the given conclusions.

(a) Only Conclusion I follows
(b) Only Conclusion II follows
(c) Both I and II follow
(d) Neither I nor II follows

86. Find the LCM of the following fractions: 2/3, 8/9, 16/27, 32/81

(a) 32/81 (b) 81/32
(c) 32/3 (d) 11/41

87. In which state is Koyna dam located?

(a) Madhya Pradesh (b) Rajasthan
(c) Maharashtra (d) Gujarat

88. Which planet is the nearest in size to Earth?

(a) Mercury (b) Mars
(c) Venus (d) Saturn

89. The mean of a distribution is 15 and the standard deviation is 5. What is the value of the coefficient variation?

(a) 16.66% (b) 66.66%
(c) 33.33% (d) 100%

90. If S is the midpoint of a straight line PQ and R is a point different from S, such that PR = RQ, then

(a) $\angle PRS = 90°$ (b) $\angle QRS = 90°$
(c) $\angle PSR = 90°$ (d) $\angle QSR < 90°$

91. Who constructed the Hawa Mahal?

(a) Maharaja Bhagvat Singh
(b) Maharaja Jagatjit Singh
(c) Maharaja Sawai Pratap Singh
(d) Maharajah Jaswant Singh

92. If '>' means 'minus', '<' means plus, '*' means multipled by and # means 'divided by', then what would be the value of

27 < 81 # 9 > 6 =

(a) 32 (b) 30
(c) 36 (d) 25

93. Which king's story is the subject of the play Mudrarakshasa?

(a) Jaychand
(b) Chandra Gupta II
(c) Chandrapeeda
(d) Chandragupta Maurya

94. The amount of alcohol in two different medicines is 1.5% and 2.5% respectively. In what ratio they should be mixed such that amount of alcohol in the new mixture is 3.5%?

(a) 1:2 (b) 2:1
(c) 3:2 (d) None of the above

95. Who was responsible for building the Great wall of China?

(a) Qin Shi Huang
(b) Fa-Hien
(c) Xuanzang or Hiuen Tsang
(d) Yijing

96. Martin Crowe who passed away recently was the former cricket captain of which country?

(a) Australia (b) England
(c) New Zealand (d) South Africa

97. If 70% of 5/7th of a number is 90, find the number.

(a) 150 (b) 180
(c) 160 (d) 190

98. Which among the following is called quicksilver?

(a) Titanium (b) Mercury
(c) Platinum (d) Radium

99. Which of the following is a vertebrate?

(a) Kiwi (b) Sponges
(c) Star fish (d) Threadworm

100. Find the total simple Interest on ₹ 500 at 7% per annum, on ₹ 700 at 10% per annum and on ₹ 1000 at 4% per annum for 3 years.

(a) 435 (b) 500
(c) 700 (d) 1000

Hints & Solutions

1. (a) Cost price = Selling price $\times \frac{100}{100 + \text{profit\%}}$

$= 36 \times \frac{100}{100 + 20} = ₹30.$

When, selling price = ₹33

Profit = 33 – 30 = 3

Profit% = $\frac{3 \times 100}{30} = 10\%$

2. (a) Yokozuna is a honorary title for the highest ranking sumo wrestler.

3. (b) Mars, Venus and Jupiter are planet but comet is not a planet.

4. (b) UFO is any aerial phenomenon that cannot immediately be identified.

5. (b)

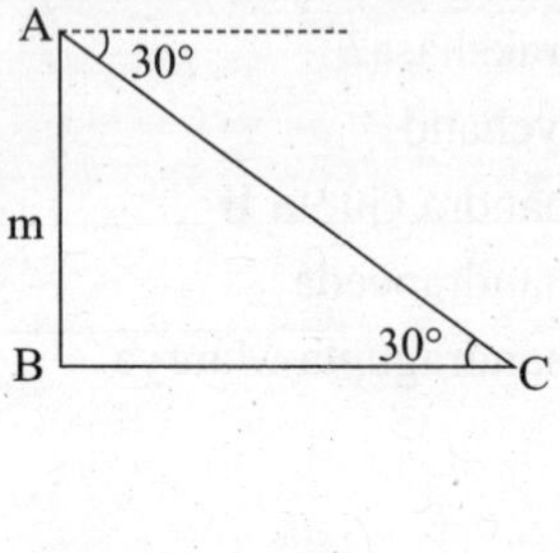

Let AB is the height of the tower = 20 m and ship is at point C.

$\angle ACB = 30°$

Now, $\tan 30° = \frac{AB}{BC}$

$\frac{1}{\sqrt{2}} = \frac{20}{BC} = BC = 20\sqrt{3}$

6. (c) Chand Bibi, is well known as the heroic defender of Ahmadnagar, married to Ali Adil Shahi.

7. (a) The UNO proclaimed Sept. 16 as the International Day for Preservation of the Ozone Layer to commemorate the Montreal Protocol on Substances that Deplete the Ozone Layer was signed.

8. (b) Benjamin Franklin invented bifocals—eyeglasses with two distinct optical powers.

9. (c) Reptiles are tetrapod animals in the class Reptilia, comprising of turtles, crocodilians, snakes, and lizards.

10. (a) Culture refers to the sum of human beings' life ways, their behaviour, beliefs, feelings, thought.

11. (c) Martin Cooper is regarded as the father of the cellular phone.

12. (a) A hypothesis is more than a wild guess but less than a well-established theory. It needs to go through a lot of testing before it gets labelled a theory.

13. (b)

14. (c) Ratio of angles = 1 : 4 : 7 (given)

$\therefore$ Ratio of greatest to smallest = 7 : 1.

15. (b) Sir Edwin Lutyens is known especially for his planning of New Delhi and his design of the President House there.

16. (c) Sum of 10 observation = 10 × 17 = 170

Let 11th observation is x

Then, mean of 11 observation = 16

ATQ, $16 \times 11 = 170 + x$

$= x = 176 - 170 = 6$

17. (a) The Battle of Plassey was a decisive victory of the East India Company over the Nawab of Bengal and his French allies on 23 June 1757, under Robert Clive.

18. (a) Work done by the two in two consecutive day $= \frac{1}{9} + \frac{1}{12} = \frac{4+3}{36} = \frac{7}{36}$

Work done in 10 days $\frac{7 \times 5}{36} = \frac{35}{36}$

19. (a) Let cost price is ₹ 100.

Then, Mark price $= 100 \times \frac{150}{100} = 150$

To get 10% profit, selling price

$= 100 \times \frac{100+10}{100} = 110$

Discount = 150 – 110 = 40

Discount% $= \frac{40}{150} \times 100 = 27\%$

20. (b) Let the required number be x.

Cost of 1 hair clip = ₹ $\frac{1}{7}$

Cost price of x numbering clips $= \frac{1}{7} \times x = \frac{x}{7}$

Selling price of x number of clips after 40% profit

$= \left(\frac{x}{7} \times \frac{40}{100}\right) + \frac{x}{7} = 1$

$\therefore \frac{40x}{700} + \frac{x}{7} = 1 \Rightarrow \frac{40x + 100x}{700} = 1$

$= \frac{140x}{700} = 1 \Rightarrow x = \frac{700}{140} = 5$

Hence, he has to sell 5 hair clips for a rupee.

21. (c) E = 5 (Letter's position in English alphabet)

GUN = 7 + 21 + 14 = 42

ROSE = 18 + 15 + 19 + 5 = 57

GATE = 7 + 1 + 20 + 5 = 33

22. (a) Valley of Flowers is a national park, in North Chamoli, in Uttarakhand and is known for its variety of flora. This richly diverse area is also home to rare and endangered animals.

23. (a) Let second number is x.

Then, third number is $\frac{x}{2}$

and first number is $\frac{x}{3}$

Average $= \frac{x + \frac{x}{2} + \frac{x}{3}}{3} = 66$

$\frac{11x}{18} = 66 = 108$

Hence, first number $= \frac{x}{3} = \frac{108}{3} = 36$

24. (b) Total length of circular path

$= \pi.d$, where d = diameter

Length of circular path $= \frac{22}{7} \times 28 = 88m$

As both are running in same direction

So, their relative speed = 48 – 40 = 8

Thence, time to cross each other $= \frac{88}{8} = 11$

25. (a)

26-28:

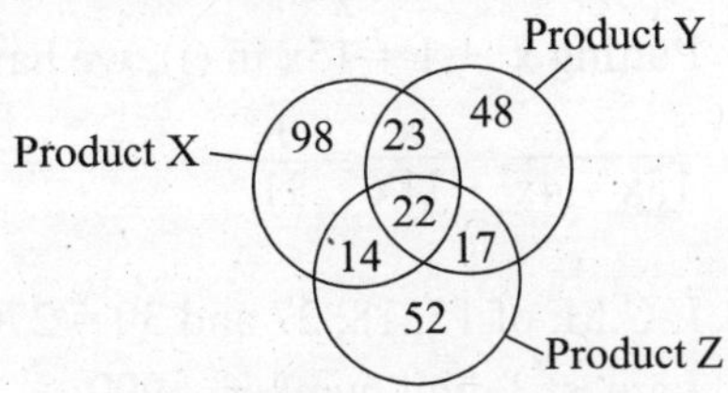

26. (a) From venn-diagram, village X is most popular

27. (c) Number of houses uses product Z only

$= 274 - 157 - 48 - 17 = 52$

28. (b) Required fraction that uses at least two products $= \dfrac{22 + 23 + 14 + 17}{274} = \dfrac{76}{274}$

29. (a) Let the length of the train is L m

As train and bike is running in the same direction, their relative speed = 90 – 36

= 54 kmph

$\therefore$ Distance travelled in 25 sec

$= \dfrac{54000}{3600} \times 25 = 375$ m

30.

E	F	M	I	J
↓ –1	↓ –1	↓ –1	↓ –1	↓ –1
D	E	L	H	I

Simply,

Hence, last letter is 'R'

31. (b) White cloths are good reflector of heat. Because light colours reflect maximum amount of heat and make us feel cool and hence. They are worn in summers.

32. (a)

9	:	27	::	81	:	729
↓		↓		↓		↓
$(3)^2$		$(3)^3$		$(9)^2$		$(9)^3$

33. (c) There were 565 princely states in the Indian subcontinent, apart from thousands of thakurs, taluqdars, zamindaris and jagirs.

34. (d) $\dfrac{5x}{5x^2 - 20x + 5} = \dfrac{5x}{5(x^2 - 4x + 1)}$

$\dfrac{x}{x^2 - 4x + 1}$ .....(i)

Again from $x + \dfrac{1}{x} = 15 \Rightarrow x^2 + 1 = 15x$

Putting $x^2 + 1 = 15x$ in (i), we have

$\dfrac{x}{15x - 4x} = \dfrac{x}{11x} = \dfrac{1}{11}$

35. (d)

36. (c) L.C.M. of 15, 18, 27 and 30 = 270.

Largest 3 digit number = 999

Now, we divide 999 by 270

We get as 89 remainder

999 – 89 = 810 is the largest 3 digit number divisible by 15, 18, 27 and 30.

37. (a) The Band-Aid was invented in 1920 by a Johnson & Johnson employee, Earle Dickson, for his wife, who frequently cut and burned herself while cooking.

38. (c) As given that , $x + \dfrac{1}{x} = 2$

By taking cube

$\Rightarrow \left(x + \dfrac{1}{x}\right)^3 = 2^3$

$\Rightarrow x^3 + \dfrac{1}{x^3} + 3\left[x + \dfrac{1}{x}\right] = 8$

$\Rightarrow x^3 + \dfrac{1}{x^3} + 3[2] = 8$

$\Rightarrow x^3 + \dfrac{1}{x^3} = 2$ ....(i)

Now taking square both side

$\Rightarrow \left(x^3 + \dfrac{1}{x^3}\right)^2 = 2^2$

$\Rightarrow x^6 + \dfrac{1}{x^6} + 2 = 4 \Rightarrow x^6 + \dfrac{1}{x^6} = 2$ ...(ii)

$\Rightarrow \left(x^6 + \dfrac{1}{x^6}\right)^3 = (x^6)^3 + \dfrac{1}{(x^6)^3} + 3\left[x^6 + \dfrac{1}{x^6}\right]$

[$\therefore$ By equation (2)]

$\Rightarrow x^{18} + \dfrac{1}{x^{18}} = 8 - 6 = 2$

So, the value of $(x^3 + 1/x^3) \div (x^{18} + 1/x^{18})$

$\Rightarrow 2/2 = 1$

39. (c) Time = March 9, 2010 to may 21, 2010

73 days $= \left(\dfrac{73}{365}\right)$ years.

C.I. $= \dfrac{p \times r \times t}{100} = \dfrac{100 \times 8.25 \times 73}{100 \times 365} =$ ₹33

40. (d)

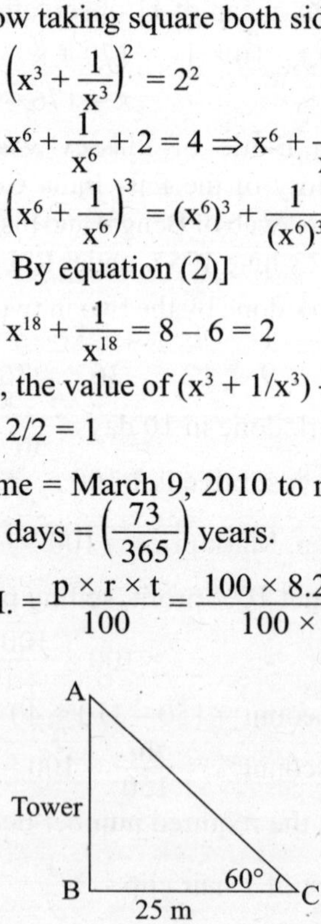

Let AB is a tower of height h.

From $\triangle$ ABC,

$$\tan 60° = \frac{AB}{BC} = \frac{AB}{25}$$

$$\sqrt{3} = \frac{AB}{25} \Rightarrow AB = 25\sqrt{3} \text{ m} = 43.3 \text{ m}$$

41. (b) Resolution refers to the number of pixels in an image. For example, an image that is 2048 pixels wide and 1536 pixels high (2048 x 1536) contains 3,145,728.

42. (a) A first generation are machine level languages used to program first-generation computers. Originally, no translator was used to compile or assemble the first-generation language.

43. (b) The fastest animal in the world is of course the cheetah.

44. (a) $16@4\$5\#72*8 = 16 + 4 \times 5 - 72 \div 8$

$= 16 + 20 - 9 = 27$

45. (c) Let present age of Rahul and Vikash are x and y years respectively.

Ratio of their ages before 4 years.

$$\frac{y-4}{x-4} = \frac{3}{5} \Rightarrow 3x - 5y = 8 \quad ...(i)$$

Ratio of their ages after 6 years.

$$\frac{y+6}{x+6} = \frac{4}{5} \Rightarrow 4x - 5y = 6 \quad ...(ii)$$

Applying (ii) (i), we get

Rahul's age = x = 8 + 6 = 14 years.

46. (a)

Letter	P	R	O	M	T	I	N
Code	3	6	5	4	8	9	7

Hence, code of MONITOR is 4579856.

47. (a) $9 + 8 \div 8 - 4 \times 9 = 9 \times 8 + 8 \div 4 - 9$

$= 72 + 2 - 9 = 65$

48. (a) Scott Kelly, and Russian Mikhail Kornienko, spent a total of 340 days living in space to understand how such long stints without gravity affect the human body.

49. (b) All knives are wedges, because of their ability to cut or split.

50. (c) **51. (c)**

52-54:

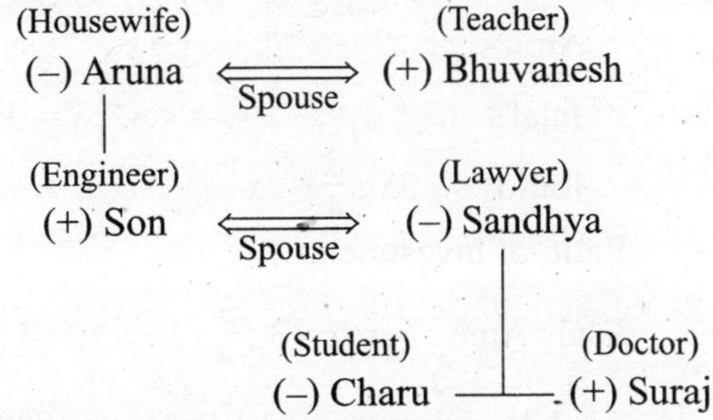

52. (d) Aruna is grand mother of Charu.

53. (b) Aruna is a housewife.

54. (c) Charu is grand daughter in the family.

55. (*)

56. (a) Vitamin deficiency causes diseases. Such as rickets, scurvy, night blindness, beriberi etc. Beriberi is not a viral infection, it is a disease caused by deficiency of vitamin B_1.

57. (b) Glaciers form when year-round, enough snow accumulates to transform into ice. Each year, new layers of snow compress the previous layers. This compression forces the snow to re-crystallize into grains. Gradually the grains get smaller, causing the snow to slowly compact and increase in density.

58. (a) Work done by one man in 1 day $= \frac{1}{80}$

Work done by 12 men in 1 day $= \frac{12}{80} = \frac{3}{20}$

Work done by 12 men and 16 women in 1 day $= \frac{1}{4}$

So, work done by 16 women in 1 day

$$= \frac{1}{4} - \frac{3}{20} = \frac{5-3}{20} = \frac{1}{10}$$

Work done, by 1 woman in 1 day

$$= \frac{1}{10 \times 16} = \frac{1}{160}$$

Hence, one woman alone will need 160 days to complete one work.

59. (b) Let Feroz's investment be = x

$\therefore$ Amit's " " $= \frac{3}{4}x$

$\therefore$ Jalal's " " $= 4 \times \frac{3}{4}x = 3x$

$\therefore$ Ratio $3x : \frac{3}{4}x : x$

Ratio of investment:

$$\text{Jalal : Amit : Feroz} = 3 : \frac{3}{4} : 1 \Rightarrow 12 : 3 : 4$$

$$\text{So, Jalal's share} = \frac{12}{(12+3+4)} \times 19000$$

$$= ₹\ 12000$$

60. (d)

61. (b) Bridge is different from other three stream, canal and river.

62. (d) Leakage in household gas cylinders can be detected because of the strong smell of ethyl mercepton mixed with L.P.G.

63. (c) **64. (b)** **65. (a)** **66. (b)**

67. (a) Sum of complementary angles = 90°

$(7x + 5) + (x + 5) = 90$

$8x + 10 = 90 \Rightarrow x = 10$

68. (d) EARSUQ — SQUARE,

ONGPOYL — POLYGON

NAEGRCELT — RECTANGLE

RGETESNH — GREENTS

Square, polygon and rectangle are geometrical fig. but greents is not a geometric fig.

69. (c) Savage is related to civilized in the same way dark is related to light.

70. (a) Let number of male and female faculties in the college are m and f.

$$\text{Then,} \quad m \times \frac{25}{100} = \frac{1}{3} \times f$$

$$\frac{m}{f} = \frac{100}{25 \times 3} = \frac{4}{3}$$

71. (c) $9D48C6B16A3 = 9 \times 48 \div 6 - 16 + 3$

$= 9 \times 8 - 16 + 3$

$= 72 - 16 + 3 = 59$

72. (a) Annealing is a temperature at which the glass is still too hard to deform, but soft enough for the stresses to relax.

73. (a) $0.5 \times 0.05 \times 0.005 \times 500 = 0.0625$

74. (a)

75. (b) $8x^4 + 2x^2y^3 + 4$

Degree of the polynomial is the highest power of any individual term

Here, $2x^2y^3$ has degree = 2 + 3 = 5

76. (a)

77. (d)

(20)	(1)	(2)	(12)	(5)
T	A	B	L	E
|	|	|	|	|
G	Z	Y	O	V
(20)	(1)	(2)	(12)	(5)

Alphabet position in reverse order.

Similarly,

(3)	(8)	(1)	(9)	(18)
C	H	A	I	R
|	|	|	|	|
X	S	Z	R	I
(3)	(8)	(1)	(9)	(18)

78. (a) Milk of Magnesia is magnesium hydroxide, used to treat constipation.

79. (d) Let divisor is x

Then, $71x + 7 = 11509$

$71x = 11502$

$$x = \frac{11502}{71} = 162.$$

80-82:

80. (c) Number of books sold by city B, D and E in July = 208 + 187 + 175 = 570

Number of academic book

$$= \frac{570 \times 30}{100} = 171$$

Hence, number of non-academic books

$= 570 - 171 = 399$

81. (d) Number of books sold by city A in July and September = 156 + 220 = 376

Number of books sold by city E in August and October = 215 + 249 = 464

$$\therefore \text{Required ratio} = \frac{376}{464} = \frac{47}{58}$$

82. (a) Average number of books sold by city C in July, September and October

$$= \frac{216 + 235 + 278}{3} = \frac{729}{3} = 243$$

83. (c) $3 : 243 :: 5 : 3125$ ($3 \xrightarrow{\times(3)^5} 243$, $5 \xrightarrow{\times(5)^5} 3125$)

84. (a) Variance = (Standard deviation)^2

$= (3)^2 = 9$

85. (c)

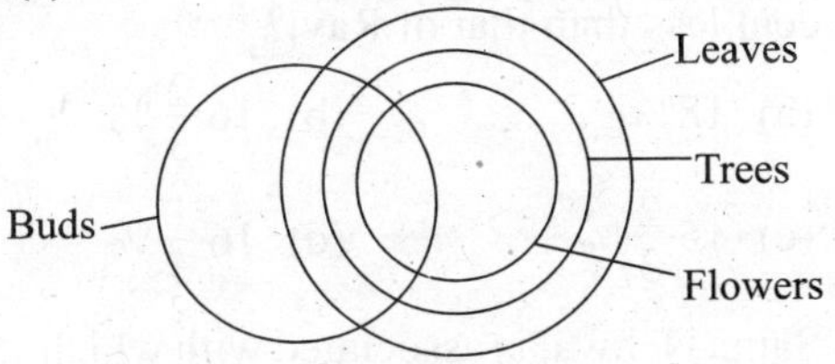

Both conclusion follow.

86. (c) LCM of Fractions $= \frac{\text{LCM of numerators}}{\text{HCF of denominators}}$

L.C.M. of $\frac{2}{3}, \frac{8}{9}, \frac{16}{27}, \frac{32}{81}$

$= \frac{\text{L.C.M. of 2, 8, 16 and 32}}{\text{H.C.F. of 3, 9. 27 and 81}} = \frac{32}{3}$

87. (c) The Koyna Dam is one of the largest dams in Maharashtra, constructed on Koyna River in Satara district, nestled in the Western Ghats on the state.

88. (c) Venus is like Earth in terms of mass and size, and closest to Earth, but the two planets are far from identical twins.

89. (c) Coefficient of variation $= \frac{\text{S.D.}}{\text{Mean}} = \frac{5}{15}$

$= \frac{1}{3} = 33.33\%$

90. (c)

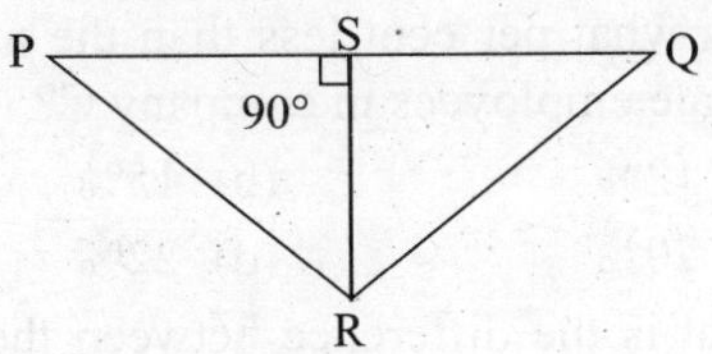

Here, PR = RQ

PRQ is isosceles triangle. and 'S' is the middle point of PQ $\therefore \angle QSR = \angle PSR = 90°$

91. (c) Hawa Mahal or the 'Palace Of The Winds' located in Jaipur in Rajasthan; is predominantly a high screen wall made of pink and red sandstone for royal women to get an eyeful of the street festivals and busy city life while remaining out of the view of public.

92. (b) After interchange the values.

$27<81\#9>6 = 27 + 81 \div 9 - 6$

$27 + 9 - 6 = 30$

93. (d) **94. (d)**

95. (a) It was the state Chu who first built the wall. To defend off the invasions from northern invaders, Emperor Qin Shi Huang had all the walls joined up. Thus, the Great Wall came into being.

96. (c)

97. (b) Let the number is n

Then, $n \times \frac{5}{7} \times \frac{70}{100} = 90.$

$n = \frac{90 \times 100 \times 7}{5 \times 70} = 180$

98. (b) The element mercury is also known as quicksilver for its mobility.

99. (a) A vertebrate animal has a backbone for body support. An invertebrate does not have a backbone. Kiwi habits and characteristics are so like a mammal that the bird is sometimes referred to as mammal.

100. (a) Total S.I.

$= \left(\frac{700 \times 10}{100} + \frac{1000 \times 4}{100} + \frac{500 \times 7}{100}\right) \times 3$

$= (35 + 70 + 40) \times 3 = 145 \times 3 = ₹\, 435$

RRB NTPC stage-I Solved Paper

Held On 16th April 2016 (Shift-I)

1. Which state in India is the highest producer of raw silk?

(a) Kerala (b) Andhra Pradesh
(c) Karnataka (d) Maharashtra

2. Mohan invested ₹ 1,00,000 in a garment business. After few months, Sohan joined him with ₹ 40,000. At the end of the year, the total profit was divided between them in ratio 3 : 1. After how many months did Sohan join the business?

(a) 3 (b) 2 (c) 4 (d) 5

3. If two complimentary angles are in the ratio of 4 : 5, find the greater angle.

(a) 40° (b) 50° (c) 60° (d) 30°

4. If HEAR is written as KJHA, then MILK can be written as

(a) PTNS (b) PNTS
(c) PNST (d) PTSN

5. The mean of 12 observations is 15. One more observation is included and the new mean becomes 16. The 13th observation is

(a) 20 (b) 24 (c) 26 (d) 28

6. Find the H.C.F. of $\frac{36}{51}$ and $3\frac{9}{17}$.

(a) $\frac{12}{17}$ (b) $\frac{15}{16}$
(c) $\frac{19}{21}$ (d) $\frac{12}{19}$

7. The third proportional of the numbers $(x-y)^2$, $(x^2-y^2)^2$ is

(a) $(x+y)^3(x-y)^2$ (b) $(x-y)^4(x-y)^2$
(c) $(x+y)^2(x-y)^2$ (d) $(x+y)^2(x-y)^3$

8. Find the value of 673.28 + 67.328 + 0.67328 + 6732.8 + 6.7328?

(a) 74808.1408 (b) 7480.78408
(c) 74808.2408 (d) 7480.81408

9. Which Indian state was declared a complete Digital State?

(a) Tamil Nadu (b) Kerala
(c) Maharashtra (d) Karnataka

10. If income of Ravi si 20% more than that of Ram, then income of Ram is how much per cent less than that of Ravi?

(a) 18% (b) $16\frac{2}{3}\%$
(c) $15\frac{2}{3}\%$ (d) $16\frac{1}{3}\%$

11. Saina Nehwal is associated with which sport?

(a) Tennis (b) Cricket
(c) Badminton (d) Gymnastics

DIRECTIONS (Qs. 12-14): *Based on the following table, answer the given questions.*

Data given in the table for the month of March, 2015

Company	Total number of employees	Number of female employees
A	5550	2410
B	3200	1860
C	2000	1600
D	2500	1220
E	4240	2600
F	3560	1240

12. The number of male employees in company D is what per cent less than the number of female employees in company C?

(a) 12% (b) 15%
(c) 20% (d) 22%

13. What is the difference between the number of male employees in company A and that in company F?

(a) 840 (b) 810
(c) 820 (d) 740

14. If in April 2015, the number of female employees in company E increased by 10% and the number of total employees in the company remained the same, what was the number of male employees?

(a) 1430 (b) 1420
(c) 1410 (d) 1380

15. RHYTM is related to MUSIC in the same way as DESIGN is related to

(a) ARCHITECT (b) BUILDING
(c) BEAUTY (d) SYMMETRY

16. In which country did the hotaki dynasty flourish?

(a) Sri Lanka (b) China
(c) Nepal (d) Afghanistan

17. Which of the following is a nitrogen-fixing bacteria?

(a) Salmonella (b) Rhizobium
(c) E. Coli (d) Pseudomonas

18. If $2x - \frac{1}{2x} = 5, x \neq 0$, then the value of $x^2 + \frac{1}{16x^2} - 2$ is

(a) $\frac{19}{4}$ (b) $\frac{23}{4}$
(c) $\frac{27}{4}$ (d) $\frac{31}{4}$

19. Based on the analogy given, find the missing pair from the given option

$\frac{3}{4} : 34 ::$ ________ : ________

(a) $\frac{3}{7} : 54$ (b) $\frac{4}{7} : 65$
(c) $\frac{3}{11} : 140$ (d) $\frac{4}{9} : 87$

20. In accordance to the Constitution, Protection of Life and Personal Liberty is granted under which Article?

(a) Article 20 (b) Article 21
(c) Article 22 (d) Article 23

21. Mayank, Deepak and Pawan each of them working alone can complete a work in 5, 10 and 15 days respectively. If all three of them work together to complete a work and earn ₹ 12,000. What would be Deepak's share of the earning.

(a) ₹ 2,000 (b) ₹ 6,000
(c) ₹ 4,000 (d) ₹ 3,000

22. Below are given statements followed by two conclusion I and II. You have to take the given statements to be true even if they seem to be at variance from commonly known facts.

Statements

I. All birds are trees.

II. All trees are papers. Some papers are books.

Conclusions

I. All birds are papers.

II. Some papers are birds.

Decide which of the below option logically follows the given conclusions.

(a) Both Conclusion I and II follows
(b) Neither Conclusion I nor II follows
(c) Only Conclusion I follows.
(d) Only Conclusion II follows.

23. If $10x^2 - 6xy + y^2 - 4x + 4 = 0$, then find the value of $(x + 2y)$.

(a) 10 (b) 20 (c) 14 (d) 18

24. What day of the week was it on 5th November, 1987, if it was Monday on 4th April, 1988?

(a) Monday (b) Friday
(c) Thursday (d) Sunday

25. The mean of a distribution is 20 and the standard deviation is 4. What is the value of the coefficient variation?

(a) 10% (b) 20%
(c) 40% (d) 60%

Directions (Q. Nos. 26-28) *Study the following information carefully and answer the questions given below it.*

There are six person in a family. Chithra is the

sister of Rakesh. Badhri is the brother of Eniya's husband. Dilip is the father of Arun and grandfather of Rakesh. There are two fathers, three brothers and a mother in the group.

26. How many male members are there in the family?

(a) Three (b) One
(c) Four (d) Two

27. A Which of the following is a group of brothers?

(a) Arun, Badhri, Dilip
(b) Arun, Badhri, Rakesh
(c) Badhri, Rakesh, Chithra
(d) Badri, Dilip, Rakesh

28. How is Rakesh related to Eniya?

(a) Son (b) Brother
(c) Uncle (d) Cousin

29. Choose the one which is different or odd from the following option.

(a) Lion (b) Tiger
(c) Horse (d) Giraffe

30. The number of students who passed in 2nd division is more than those in Ist division by

(a) 111 (b) 12
(c) 109 (d) 108

31. How many bones does a human baby have?

(a) 206 (b) 234
(c) 270 (d) 354

32. Based on the analogy given, find the missing number from the given options.

11 : 13 :: 17 : ______ ?

(a) 29 (b) 21 (c) 19 (d) 23

33. If the angles of a triangle are n the ratio of 2: 5:8, then find the value of the smallest angle?

(a) 36° (b) 18° (c) 12° (d) 24°

34. Ravish lost 20% by selling a radio set for ₹3072. What per cent will he gain by selling it for ₹4080?

(a) 5% (b) 7.50%
(c) 7.25% (d) 6.25%

35. Who received the Dinanath Mangeshkar award for 2015?

(a) Sanjay Leela Bhansali
(b) Ranveer Kapoor
(c) Anil Kapoor
(d) Amir Khan

Directions (Q. Nos. 36-38) *The following questions are based on the information given below:*

in a school of 4000 students, 3000 know English, 2000 know French and 500 know Hindi, 1500 know French and English, 300 know French and Hindi, 200 know English and Hindi and 50 know all the three languages.

36. How many do not know any of the three languages?

(a) 550 (b) 500
(c) 400 (d) 450

37. How many know only two languages?

(a) 450 (b) 500
(c) 1850 (d) 1580

38. How many know at least one language?

(a) 3500 (b) 3000
(c) 1850 (d) 3550

39. What is the average of first 30 multiples of 9?

(a) 142 (b) 138.5
(c) 139.5 (d) 143.5

40. Centigrade, is a unit of measurement of temperature named after whom?

(a) Kelvin
(b) Jean-Pierre Christin
(c) Marten Stromer
(d) Anders Celsius

41. If 'when' means '×'; 'she' means '÷', 'will' means '+' and 'come' means '–', then what will the value of '8 when 12 will 16 she 2 come 10'?

(a) 94 (b) 96 (c) 100 (b) 10

42. Which among the planets is orange in colour with white bands on it?

(a) Mars (b) Saturn
(c) Jupiter (d) Venus

43. Which bacterium is used to turn milk to curd?
(a) Streptomyces (b) Vibrio
(c) Lactobacillus (d) Spirilla

44. Who was the Railway Minister, presented the 2016 Rail Budget?
(a) Suresh Prabhu (b) Arun Jaitley
(c) Manoj Sinha (d) Jayant Sinha

45. What does SPM in environment mean?
(a) Suspended Pollution Mark
(b) Suspended Particulate Matter
(c) Suspended Particle Mode
(d) Suspended Particle Management

46. Rearrange the jumbled up letters to form a meaningful word and find the odd one out.
(a) ELMSL (b) ERHA
(c) IKNTH (d) SATTE

47. ₹ 10,000 is being compounded at 20% per annum. Calculate the amount after 2 years if the rate of interest is charged half yearly.
(a) ₹ 14,600 (b) ₹ 12,500
(c) ₹ 14,642 (d) ₹ 14,641

48. 'Satyashodhak Samaj' was founded by whom?
(a) Mahatma Gandhi
(b) Jyotirao Phule
(c) Dr BR Ambedkar
(d) Swami Vivekananda

49. If FHNPKMEG means GOLF, then what does RTSUHJBDJL stand for?
(a) HORSE (b) STICK
(c) PURSE (d) HOLES

50. If the standard deviation of a population is 4.5, what would be the population variance?
(a) 20.25 (b) 20 (c) 9 (d) 18

51. The tallest bridge in the world Millau Viaduct has been constructed over the river
(a) Seine (b) Tarn
(c) Durance (d) Loir

52. Ruchi invested ₹ 1600 at the rate of compound interest for 2 yr. She got ₹ 1764 after the specified period. Find the rate of interest.
(a) 4% (b) 5% (c) 10% (d) 8%

53. Who is the current supreme commander of Indian Defence Force?
(a) Narendra Modi
(b) Sumitra Mahajan
(c) Pranab Mukherjee
(d) Lt. Gen Dalbir Singh

54. If B = 2, K = 11; MAN = 1, SIN = 14, then what is the value of HOT?
(a) 7 (b) 0 (c) 1 (d) 22

55. Find the value of x if $0.08x + 0.04y = 10$ and $0.2(x - 1) + 0.4y = 24.8$
(a) 125 (b) 150
(c) 1.25 (d) 12.5

56. Who made the first chocolate bar?
(a) Nestle
(b) The Hershey Company
(c) Joseph Fry and Sons
(d) Pearson's

57. Find the LCM of 0.63, 10.5, 2.1,4.20
(a) 63 (b) 0.63
(c) 6.30 (d) 6300

58. In a certain time, a sum becomes 3 times at the rate of 5% per annum. At what rate of interest, the same sum becomes 6 times in same duration?
(a) 10% (b) 12%
(c) 12.5% (d) 15.5%

59. Based on the analogy given, find the missing word from the given options.
Foot : Toes :: Hand: ?
(a) Thumb (b) Palm
(c) Fingers (d) Nails

60. Who invented the pendulum clock?
(a) Galileo Galilei
(b) Thomas Alva Edison
(c) Frederick Jones
(d) Davidson

61. The simple interest at y% for 'y' years will be ₹ y on a sum. Find the principal amount.

(a) $100 \div y$ (b) $100 \times y$
(c) $100\ y^2$ (d) $100 \div y^2$

62. Choose the option that expresses the same relationship as the following.

Tobacco : Cancer

(a) Milk : Food (b) Bud : Flower
(c) Soil : Erosion (d) Mosquito : Malaria

63. Choose the odd one.

(a) Eyes (b) Nose
(c) Ears (d) Lungs

64. Find the remainder when 4^{23} divided by 3?

(a) 1 (b) 2 (c) 0 (d) 3

65. If TABLE is written as 84973 and CHAIR is written as 51462, then how is TEACHER coded?

(a) 8431532 (b) 8341532
(c) 8435132 (d) 8345132

66. Ramu can row 9 km/h in still water takes him twice as long to row up as row down. Find the rate of stream.

(a) 16 km/h (b) 8 km/h
(c) 3 km/h (d) 9 km/h

67. Neeraj's earning was decreased by 60% and after that subsequently increased by 60%. Find the final loss % on his earning?

(a) 12% (b) 36%
(c) 4% (d) 5%

68. Abus is running at a speed of 90km/h. What distance will it cover in 20 seconds?

(a) 500 m (b) 450m
(c) 180 m (d) 600 m

69. In what ratio should Darjeeling Tea costing ₹ 400 per kg be mixed with Assam Tea costing ₹ 300 per kg, so that by selling the mixture at ₹ 405 per kg, there is gain of 20%?

(a) 1 : 2 (b) 2 : 3
(c) 3 : 5 (d) 1 : 6

70. Consider the following statements and choose the correct options: When two straight lines intersect then,

1. Adjacent angles are supplementary
2. Opposite angles are supplementary

(a) Both 1 & 2 are incorrect.
(b) Both 1 & 2 are correct.
(c) 1 is incorrect and 2 is correct.
(d) 1 is correct and 2 is incorrect.

71. Which is the official language for Android development?

(a) Java (b) COBOL
(c) FORTRAN (d) Ada

72. The salary of a worker is first increased by 5% and then it is decreased by 5%. What is the change in his salary?

(a) 0.5% (b) 0.25% (c) 1% (d) 10%

73. Rearrange the jumbled up letters to form a meaningful word and find the odd one out.

(a) CEKRTCI (b) OHKCYE
(c) ESCSH (d) OTOFABLL

74. If BAG =71, then VICE =?

(a) 69 (b) 70 (c) 75 (d) 90

75. Who invented the mouse of a computer?

(a) John Backus (b) Charles Babbage
(c) Douglas Engelbart (d) Simon Colton

76. Which among the following is the brain of the computer?

(a) Software (b) Hardware
(c) CPU (d) Monitor

77. Who is the current Chief Election Commissioner of India?

(a) Syed Nasim Ahmed Zaidi
(b) Navin Chawla
(c) N. Gopalaswami
(d) A.K Jyoti

78. Compute the following series.

5, 11, 23, 47, 95, ?

(a) 198 (b) 194
(c) 191 (d) 185

79. Choose the missing number from the given alternatives.

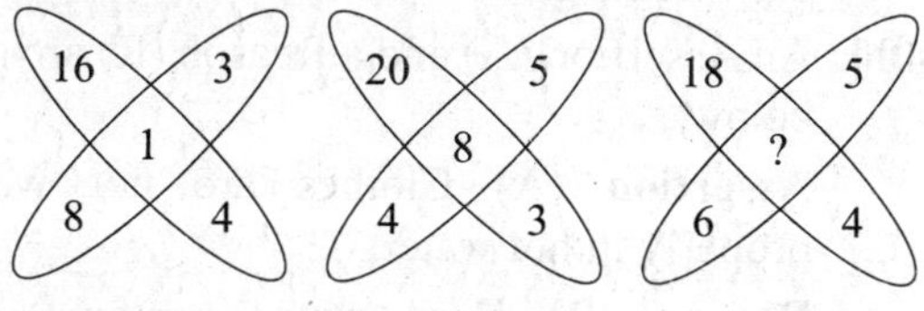

(a) 3 (b) 10
(c) 15 (d) 60

80. B is thrice as efficient as A and C is 0.75 times as efficient as A. What is the ratio of days taken by A,B and C. When they work individually

(a) 4 : 1 : 3 (b) 3 : 1 : 4
(c) 2 : 3 : 1 (d) 5 : 11 : 2

81. How many bio-geographical zones are there in India?

(a) 2 (b) 4 (c) 6 (d) 10

82. One of four words is a class to which the other three belong. Identify the class.

(a) Coal (b) Lignite
(c) Anthracite (d) Peat

83. Where did Rani Lakshmi Bai die fighting the British?

(a) Varanasi (b) Gwalior
(c) Morar (d) Jhansi

84. Which is the most powerful piece in a game of chess?

(a) King (b) Queen
(c) Rook (d) Knight

85. Odisha often faces natural disasters due to ________.

(a) earthquakes (b) cyclones
(c) rainfall (d) drizzle

86. If 20 – 10 means 200, 8 ÷ 4 means 12, 6 × 2 means 4, 20 + 10 = 2, then 100 – 10 × 1000 ÷ 1000 + 100 × 10 = ?

(a) 20 (b) 10
(c) 0 (d) 1

87. In a row of students, Anil is 7th from left, while Sunil is 18th form right. Both of them interchanged their positions such that Anil becomes 21st from left. What will be the total number of students in the class?

(a) 38 (b) 33 (c) 31 (d) 30

88. Who was the Chinese pilgrim who visited India during the Gupta period?

(a) Hiuen Tsang (b) Fa Hien
(c) I ching (d) Li Xiu

89. Atul can do a piece of work in 18 days, Aaravya is 50% more efficient than Atul. How much more time does Atul take than Aaravya to do the same piece of work?

(a) 12 (b) 6 (c) 18 (d) 10

90. If (x + a) is the HCF of $2x^2 + 5x - 12$ and $x^2 + x - 12$ then find the value of a.

(a) –3 (b) –2 (c) 4 (d) 5

91. Mohan is taller than Shyam but shorter than Ramesh. Ramesh is taller than Rajat but shorter than Gautam. If Shyam is taller than Rajat, then who is the shortest among all?

(a) Gautam (b) Rajat
(c) Shyam (d) Ramesh

92. The shadow of a tower on ground level is increased by 30 m, when the angle of depression by the sun changes from 60° to 30°. The height of the tower is?

(a) $12\sqrt{3}$ m (b) $17\sqrt{3}$ m
(c) $16\sqrt{3}$ m (d) $15\sqrt{3}$ m

93. Which of the below options is called a laughing gas?

(a) N_2O (b) CO_2
(c) H_2O (d) SO_2

94. What will be the measurement of the angle made by the hands of a clock when the time is 8 : 35?

(a) 32.4° (b) 37.5°
(c) 45° (d) 47.5°

95. Whois the current CEO of Flipkart?

(a) Ananth Narayanan (b) Mukesh Bansal
(c) Binny Bansal (d) Sachin Bansal

96. What is shape of the orbit of the planets?

(a) Round

(b) Straight line

(c) Elliptical

(d) Stretched out circles

97. What is the minimum value of 'Y' for which 267 Y 2 is divisible by 3?

(a) 2 (b) 1 (c) 0 (d) 5

98. Ram Naresh got two successive discounts, a bag with a list price of Rs. 400 is available at = 160. If the second discount is 20%, find the first discount.

(a) 40% (b) 30%

(c) 50% (d) 80%

99. Goecha La is a pass in which of the following Indian State.

(a) Sikkim (b) Assam

(c) Meghalaya (d) Uttarakhand

100. An Assertion (A) and a Reason (R) are given below,

Assertion (A) Clothes are not washed properly in hot water.

Reason (R) Hard water contains many minerals.

Choose the correct option.

(a) A is true but R is false.

(b) A is false but R is true.

(c) Both A and R are true and R is the correct explanation of A.

(d) Both A and R are true and R is not the correct explanation of A.

Hints & Solutions

1. (c) India is the second largest producer of silk in the world. India has the unique distinction of being the only country producing all the five kinds of silk namely Mulberry, Eri, Muga, Tropical Tasar and Temperate Tasar.

Karnataka is the largest producer of silk in India. The state produces an average of around 8,200 metric tonnes of silk every year, which is about one-third of the total silk production in India.

2. (b) Let Sohan has invested the amount for n months then, Ratio of their investment

$= 100000 \times 12 : 40000 \times n$

$= 30 : n$

We know that Ratio of investment = Ratio of Profit shares

So, $\frac{30}{n} = \frac{3}{1} \Rightarrow n = \frac{30}{3} = 10$ months

Hence, Sohan has invested after 2 months.

3. (b) Sum of complementary angles = 90°

$4x + 5x = 90 \Rightarrow 9x = 90$

$x = 10$

greater angle = $5 \times 10 = 50°$

4. (c) Similarly,

HEAR — KJHA MILK — PNST

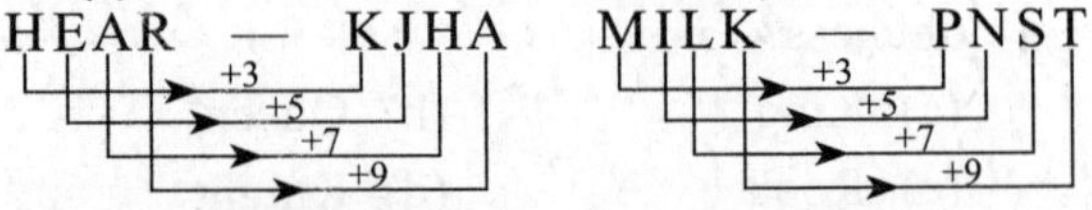

5. (d) 13th observation $= 13 \times 16 - 12 \times 15$

$= 208 - 180 = 28$

6. (a) H.C.F. of $\frac{36}{51} = \frac{12}{17}$ and $\frac{60}{17}$

$= \frac{\text{H.C.F. of 12 and 60}}{\text{L.C.M. of 17 and 17}} = \frac{12}{17}$

7. (b) Let the third proportional be P.

$\therefore (x - y)^2 : (x^2 - y^2)^2 :: (x^2 - y^2)^2 : P$

$\Rightarrow \frac{(x - y)^2}{(x + y)^2 (x - y)^2} = \frac{(x + y)^2 (x - y)^2}{P}$

$\Rightarrow (x + y)^4 (x - y)^2$

8. (d)

$$\begin{array}{r} 0673.28000 \\ 0067.32800 \\ 0000.67328 \\ 6732.80000 \\ 0006.73280 \\ \hline 7480.81408 \end{array}$$

9. (b)

10. (b) Let Ram's income is ₹ 100. Then Ravi's income is $100 + \frac{100 \times 20}{100} = ₹\ 120$

$\therefore$ Required percent $\frac{120 - 100}{100} \times 100\%$

$\Rightarrow \frac{20}{120} \times 100\ \% = 16\frac{2}{3}\ \%$

11. (c)

12. (c) Company D: male employee

$2500 - 1220 = 1280$

Company C female employee = 1600

Difference $1600 - 1280 = 320$

$\therefore \% = \frac{320}{1600} \times 100 = 20\%$

13. (c) Number of male employees in company A

$= 5550 - 2410 = 3140$

Number of male employees in company F

$= 3560 - 1240 = 2320.$

$\therefore 3140 - 2320 = 820$

14. (d) Number of female employees in company E in April 2015

$= 2600 \times \frac{(100 + 10)}{100} = 2860.$

$\therefore$ Number of male employees

$= 4240 - 2860 = 1380$

15. (b) RHYTM RYTHM is related to music like design related to building.

16. (d) The Hotaki dynasty was founded in 1709 by Mirwais Hotak at Kandahar, Afghanistan. It was made up of ethnic Afghans who belonged to the Hotak tribe of Pashtuns.

17. (b) Rhizobia are found in the soil and after infection, produce nodules in the legume where they fix nitrogen gas (N_2) from the atmosphere turning it into a more readily useful form of nitrogen.

18. (a) $2x - \frac{1}{2x} = 5$

Squaring both sides, we have

$$\left(2x - \frac{1}{2x}\right)^2 = (5)^2$$

$$\Rightarrow \quad 4x^2 + \frac{1}{4x^2} - 2 = 25$$

$$4x^2 + \frac{1}{4x^2} = 27$$

$$4\left(x^2 + \frac{1}{16x^2}\right) = 27$$

$$x^2 + \frac{1}{16x^2} - 2 = \frac{27}{4} - 2 = \frac{19}{4}$$

19. (b) $\frac{3}{5} : 34 :: \frac{4}{7} : 65.$

As $\frac{3}{5} \Rightarrow 3^2 + 5^2 = 9 + 25 = 34$

Similarly, $4^2 + 7^2 = 16 + 49 = 65$

20. (b) Article 21 guarantees the protection of life and personal liberty to every.

21. (*) Share of their earning = Ratio of their one day work

$$= \frac{1}{5} : \frac{1}{10} : \frac{1}{15} = \frac{1}{1} : \frac{1}{2} : \frac{1}{3}$$

$$= 6 : 3 : 2$$

Deepak's share in earning

$$= \frac{3}{(6 + 3 + 2)} \times 12000 = ₹\ 3272.7$$

22. (a) Conclusion I and II both follows.

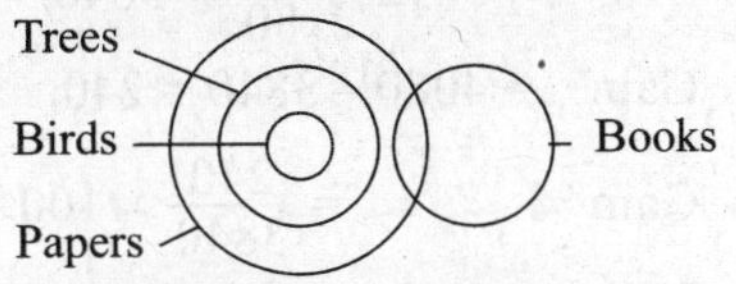

23. (c) $10x^2 - 6xy + y^2 - 4x + 4 = 0$

$9x^2 - 6xy + y^2 + x^2 - 4x + 4 = 0$

$(3x - y)^2 + (x - 2)^2 = 0$

this is possible, when, $3x - 4 = 0$ and $x - 2 = 0 \Rightarrow x = 2$

when, $x = 2$, $y = 3 \times 2 = 6$

Now, $(x + 2y) = (2 + 2 \times 6) = 2 + 12 = 14$

24. (c) As 4th April 1988 was Monday.

then, 5th November 1987 was Thursday.

25. (d) Co-efficient of Variation

$$= \frac{\text{S. D.}}{\text{Mean}} \times 100 = \frac{4}{20} \times 100 = 20\%$$

(26-28) :

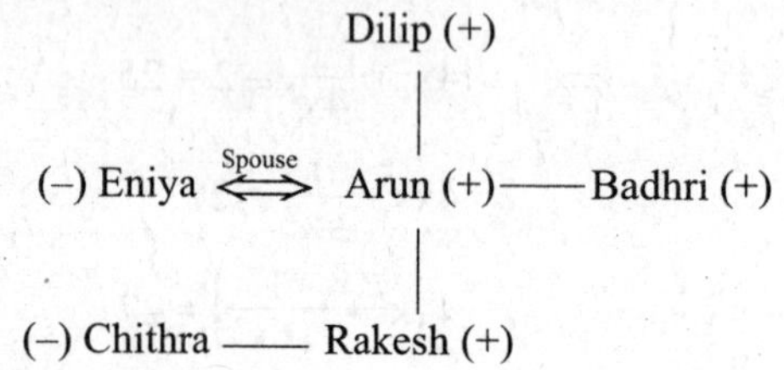

26. (c) Male members are Dilip, Arun, Badhri and Rakesh.

27. (b) Arun, Badhri and Rakesh are brothers.

28. (a) Rakesh is son of Eniya.

29. (c) Lion, Tiger and Giraffe are wild animals, where as horse is a domestic animal.

30. (*) **31. (c)**

32. (c) 13 is next prime number after 11. Like that

19 is next prime number after 17.

33. (d) Sum of the angles of a triangles = 180°

$2x + 5x + 8x = 180°$

$15x = 180° \Rightarrow x = 12$

Smallest angle $= 2 \times 12 = 24°$

34. (d) Cost price of the ratio

$$= 3072 \times \frac{100}{(100 - 20)}$$

$$= 3072 \times \frac{100}{80} = 3840.$$

Gain $= 4080 - 3840 = 240$

Gain % $= \frac{240}{3840} \times 100 = 6.25\%$

35. (c) Bollywood actor Anil Kapoor was conferred with prestigious Master Deenanath Mangeshkar Award 2015 by noted historian and writer Babasaheb Purandare on the occasion of the death anniversary of songstress Lata Mangeshkar's father.

(36-38) :

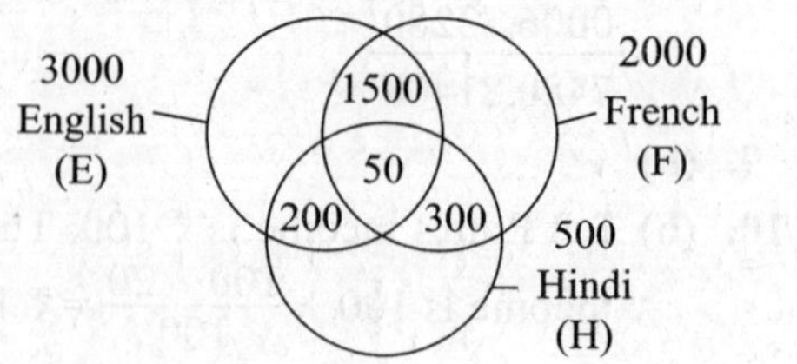

$n(E \cup F \cup H)$

$= n(E) + n(F) + n(H) - n(E \cap F) - n(F \cap H) - n(F \cap E) + n(E \cap F \cap H).$

$= 3000 + 2000 + 500 - 1500 - 300 - 200 + 50 = 3550.$

36. (d) Number of Students, who do not know any languages $= 4000 - 3550 = 450$.

37. (c) Number of students who know only two languages.

$= 1500 + 300 + 200 - 150 = 1850.$

38. (d) Number of students, who know at least one language $= n(E \cup F \cup H) = 3550$.

39. (c) Average

$$= \frac{9 + 9 \times 2 + 9 \times 3 + 9 \times 4 + ... 9 \times 30}{30}$$

$$= \frac{9(1 + 2 + 3 + ... + 30)}{30}$$

$$= \frac{9 \times 30 \times 31}{30 \times 2} = 139.5$$

40. (d) Centigrade, is a unit of measurement of temperature named after anders Celsius.

41. (a) 8 when 12 will 16 she 2 come 10

$= 8 \times 12 + 16 \div 2 - 10$

$= 8 \times 12 + 8 - 10$

$= 96 + 8 - 10 = 94.$

42. (c) Jupiter reflects many shades of white, red, orange, brown, and yellow. The colour change with storms and wind in the planet's atmosphere.

43. (c) Lactobacillus is the bacteria which is used to convert milk into curd by fermentation. The bacteria eats the sugar in the milk and produces lactic acid which then turns the milk proteins to curdle and gives the milk a tangy taste.

44. (a)

45. (b) Suspended particulate matter (SPM) are finely divided solids or liquids that may be dispersed through the air from combustion processes, industrial activities or natural sources.

46. (c) ELMSL — SMELL, ERHA — HEAR
IKNTH — THINK, SATTE — TASTE
Here, THINK is different from others.

47. (d) As interest is compounded half yearly,
then, $r = \frac{20}{2} = 10\%$,
time = 2 year = 4 half years
Amount $A = P\left(1+\frac{r}{100}\right)^t$.
$= 10000\left(1+\frac{10}{100}\right)^4$
$= 10000 \times \left(\frac{11}{10}\right)^4 = 11 \times 11 \times 11 \times 11$
$= 14641$

48. (b)

49. (b)

F H	N P	K M	E G
↓	↓	↓	↓
G	O	L	F

Similarly,

R T	S U	H J	B D	J L
↓	↓	↓	↓	↓
S	T	I	C	K

∴ The word is STICK.

50. (a) Population Variance (σ) = $(S.D.)^2$
$= (4.5)^2 = 20.25$.

51. (b)

52. (b) Let rate of interest is r % per year.
then, $1764 = 1600\left(1+\frac{r}{100}\right)^2$

$$\frac{1764}{1600} = \left(1+\frac{r}{100}\right)^2$$

$$\left(1+\frac{r}{100}\right) = \sqrt{\frac{1764}{1600}} = 1.05$$

$$\frac{r}{100} = 0.05 \Rightarrow r = 5\%$$

53. (c) **54. (a)**

55. (a) $0.08x + 0.04y = 10 \Rightarrow 0.8x + 0.4y = 100$
$0.4y = 100 - 0.8x$
Now, $0.2(x-1) + 0.4y = 24.8$
$0.2(x-1) + 100 - 0.8x = 24.8$
$100 - 0.2 - 24.8 = 0.8x - 0.2x$.
or, $0.6x = 75 \Rightarrow x = \frac{75}{0.6} = 125$.

56. (c)

57. (a) $0.63 = \frac{63}{100}, 10.5 = \frac{105}{10}, 2.1 = \frac{21}{10},$
$4.2 = \frac{42}{10}$
$\text{L.C.M.} = \frac{\text{L.C.M. of } 63, 105, 21, 42}{\text{HCF of } 100, 10, 10, 10}$
$= \frac{630}{10} = 63$.

58. (c) Interest = 3P – P = 2P,
where, P = Principal
then, time $= \frac{2P \times 100}{P \times 5} = 40$ years.
When, Amount becomes 6 times,
then, Interest = 6P – P = 5P
Now, Rate $= \frac{5P \times 100}{P \times 40} = 12.5\%$

59. (c) We have toes in four foot, like that we have fingers in our hands.

60. (a)

61. (a) Principal $= \frac{S.I \times 100}{\text{time} \times \text{rate}} = \frac{y \times 100}{y \times y} = \frac{100}{y}$

62. (d)

63. (d) Lungs is one of the internal parts of our body. Where as eyes, nose and ears are external parts of our body.

64. (a) Multiple of 4 divided by 3 Remainder

Multiple of 4	divided by	Remainder
4^1	3	1
$4^2 = 16$	3	1
$4^3 = 64$	3	1
4^{23}	3	1

Hence, all cases, we get remainder = 1.

65. (d)

Letter	T	A	B	L	E	C	H	I	R
Code	8	4	9	7	3	5	1	6	2

Hence, 'TEACHER's Code is '8345132'

66 (c) Let the speed of the stream is x km/hr

than, $2 \times \frac{d}{9+x} = \frac{d}{9-x} \Rightarrow 2(9-x)$

$= x + 9 \Rightarrow x = 3$ Km/hr.

67. (b) Let Neeraj's earning was ₹ 100.

After 60% decrease, it becomes

$= 100 - 100 \times \frac{60}{100} = 40$

After 60% increase, it becomes

$= 40 + 40 \times \frac{60}{100} = 40 + 24 =$ ₹ 64

$\% \text{ Loss} = \frac{(100-64)}{100} \times 100 = 36\%$

68. (a) Bus speed = 90 Km/hr

$= 90 \times \frac{5}{18} = 25$ m/sec.

Distance = Speed × time

$= 25 \times 20 = 500$ m

69. (c) let we mex x kg Darjeeling tea with y kg Assam tea.

then, ATQ

$(400x + 300y) \times \frac{120}{100} = 405(x + y)$

$(4x + 3y)\, 8 = 27(x + y)$

$32x + 24y = 27x + 27y$

$5x = 3y$

$\frac{x}{y} = \frac{3}{5}$

70. (d) Here, ∠ACB and ∠ACD are adjacent angles and ∠ACB + ∠ACD = 180°

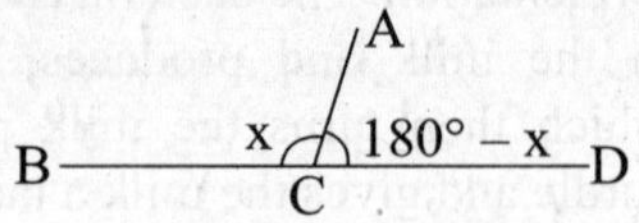

∴ ∠ACB = 180 – ∠ACD

Give, Adjacent angles are supplement

71. (a)

72. (b) let initial Salary was ₹ 10000.

then, 5% increases, new salary = $10000 \times \frac{105}{100} = 10500$.

Again, 5% decreases, new salary = $10500 \times \frac{95}{100} = 9975$

Decrease in salary = 10000 – 9975 = 25.

$\% \text{ Decrease} = \frac{25}{10000} \times 100 = 0.25\%$

73. (c) CEKRTCI → CRICKET;

OHKCYE → HOCKEY;

OTOFABLL → FOOTBALL;

where ESCSH → CHESS.

Here, CHESS is a indoor game, while, cricket, hockey and football are outdoor game.

74. (a)

B A G
| | |
25 26 20

= 25 + 26 + 20 = 71;

Letter's position in reverse alphabet

V I C E
| | | |
5 18 24 22

= 5 + 18 + 24 + 22 = 69

Letter's position in reverse alphabet

75. (c)

76. (c) The computer brain is a microprocessor called the central processing unit (CPU). The CPU is a chip containing millions of tiny transistors. It's the CPU's job to perform the calculations necessary to make the computer work -- the transistors in the CPU manipulate the data.

77. (a) Syed Nasim Ahmad Zaidi served as 20th Chief Election Commissioner of India. He is a retired I.A.S. officer of 1976 batch from the Uttar Pradesh cadre.

78. (c) 5 → 11 → 23 → 47 → 95 → **191**

$\times 2 + 1$ $\times 2 + 1$ $\times 2 + 1$ $\times 2 + 1$ $\times 2 + 1$

79. (a)

80. (b) According to the question,

when A suppose to finish the work in n days.

then B would finish the work in $\frac{n}{3}$ days.

and C would finish the work in $\frac{4}{3}$ n days.

their ratio = $n : \frac{n}{3} : \frac{4n}{3} = 3 : 1 : 4.$

81. (d) Biogeography is the study of the distribution of species (biology), organisms, and ecosystems in geographic space and through geological time. There are ten biogeographic zones in India.

1. Trans Himalayan zone.
2. Himalayan zone
3. Desert zone.
4. Semiarid zone.
5. Western ghat zone.
6. Deccan plateau zone.
7. Gangetic plain zone.
8. North east zone.
9. Coastal zone.
10. Islands

82. (a) Coal is an organic sedimentary rock that formed from the accumulation and preservation of plant materials, usually in a swamp environment million of year ago. The four types of coal include peat, lignite, bituminous, and anthracite, with anthracite being most desirable due to its high heat content.

83. (b) On June 18th 1858, Rani Lakshmibai of Jhansi, one of the most important figures of India's First War of Independence, died while fighting against the British in Gwalior.

84. (b) The queen is the most powerful piece in the game of chess. It is able to move any number of squares vertically, horizontally or diagonally.

85. (b)

86. (c) $20 - 10 = 20 \times 10 = 200$

$8 \div 4 \quad = 8 + 4 = 12$

$6 \times 2 \quad = 6 - 2 = 4$

$20 + 10 = 20 \div 10 = 2$

then, $100 - 10 \times 1000 \div 1000 + 100 \times 10$

$= 100 \times 10 - 1000 + 1000 \div 100 - 10$

$= 1000 - 1000 + 10 - 10 = 0$

87. (a) Total number of students in the row

= Anil's position in the row (after interchange) + from left end + Sunil's position from right end (before interchange) – 1 = 21 + 18 – 1 = 38.

88. (b) Fa Hien a Chinese Buddhist, was one of the pilgrims who visited India during the reign of the Gupta emperor Chandragupta II. He started his journey from China in 399 AD and reached India in 405 AD.

89. (b) Aaravya work efficiency $= x + \frac{x \times 50}{100}$

$= \frac{3}{2}x.$

Where, x is Atul's work efficiency.

So, time taken by Aaravya to finish the work = $18 \times \frac{2}{3} = 12$ days.

Difference in days = 18 – 12 = 6 days.

90. (c) $2x^2 + 5x - 12 = 2x^2 + 8x - 3x - 12$

$= (2x - 3)(x + 4)$

and $x^2 + x - 12 = x^2 + 4x - 3x - 12$

$= (x + 4)(x - 3)$

H.C.F. = Common factor = $(x + 4)$

Hence, a = 4

91. (b)

92. (d) Let AB be the tower of height h m.

then, ΔABC,

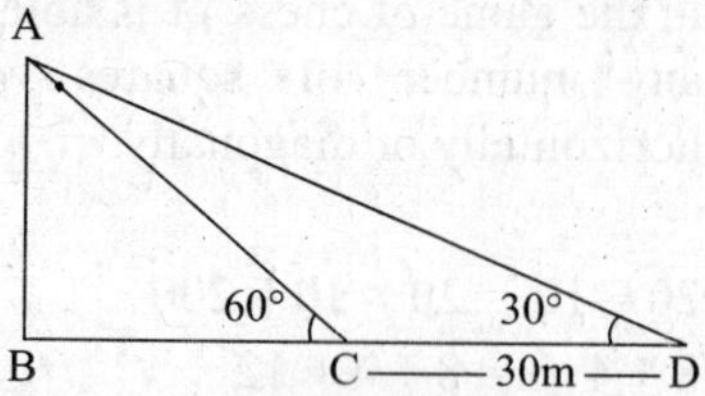

$$\tan 60° = \frac{AB}{BC} = \frac{h}{BC} \Rightarrow h = \sqrt{3}.BC.$$

From ΔABD, $\tan 30° = \frac{AB}{BC + CD}$

$$= \frac{\sqrt{3}.BC}{(BC + 30)}$$

$$\frac{1}{\sqrt{3}} = \frac{\sqrt{3}\,(BC)}{BC + 30}$$

$BC + 30 = 3BC \Rightarrow 2(BC) = 30$

$BC = 15$ m.

Hence, height of the tower = $15\sqrt{3}$ m.

93. (a)

94. (d) Angle made by hour hand in one hour.

$$= \frac{360}{12} = 30°$$

∴ Angle made by hour hand in 8:35 hour

$$= \left(8 + \frac{35}{60}\right) \times 30$$

$$= 240 + 17.5 = 257.5°$$

Angle made by minute hand in 1 minute

$$= \frac{360}{60} = 6°$$

∴ Angle made by minute hand in 35 minute = $6 \times 35 = 210°$

Hence, Angle between two hands

$= 257.5° - 210° = 47.5°$.

95. (d) Binny Bansal (born 1982/1983) is an Indian billionaire Internet entrepreneur. In 2007 he co-founded the e-commerce platform Flipkart with Sachin Bansal (no relation) and served as the chief operating officer until 11 January 2016 and was then promoted to chief executive officer (CEO).

96. (c) The planets'orbits are very nearly circular, but not quite. Each orbit has the shape of a slightly stretched-out circle, called an ellipse.

97. (b) Any number is divisible by 3, if sum of its digits would be divisible by 3

Sum of digits = $2 + 6 + 7 + y + 2$

$= 17 + y$

As 18 is divisible by 3.

So, $18 = 17 + y \Rightarrow y = 18 - 17 = 1$.

98. (c) Let first discount is x%

then, $400 \times \left(\frac{100 - x}{100}\right) \times \left(\frac{100 - 20}{100}\right) = 160$

$$400 \times \frac{(100 - x)}{100} \times \frac{80}{100} = 160$$

$$(100 - x) = \frac{160 \times 100 \times 100}{400 \times 80} = 50$$

$x = 100 - 50 = 50\%$

99. (a) Goecha La is a high mountain pass in Sikkim, India in the Himalaya range. The southeast face of Mt. Kanchenjunga, the world's third highest mountain, can be viewed from the pass, which is also a base camp for those aspiring to scale the mountain.

100. (d) Here (A) and (R) both are true.

Hard water contains many minerals and clothes are not washed properly in hot water.

RRB NTPC stage-I Solved Paper

Held On 16th April 2016 (Shift-III)

1. Who founded Twitter?
(a) Mark Zuckerberg (b) Tim Cook
(c) Noah Ark (d) Evan Williams

2. An Assertion (A) and a Reason (R) are given below.
Assertion (A): In India, females have higher life expectancy than the males.
Reason (R): Females receive a better diet.
Choose the correct option.
(a) A is true but R is false.
(b) A is false but R is true.
(c) Both A and R are true
(d) Both A and R are false.

3. Vikash purchased 5 bananas for Rs. 4 and sold 4 bananas for Rs. 5. Calculate his % profit?
(a) 55.56% (b) 53.25%
(c) 45.50% (d) 56.25%

4. Which State in India has the highest forest cover?
(a) Kerala (b) Madhya Pradesh
(c) Maharashtra (d) Bihar

5. Based on the analogy given, find the missing word from the given options.
Butter : Milk :: Book :
(a) Author (b) Paper
(c) Chapter (d) Printing

6. ___________ is a unit of length, roughly the distance from Earth to the Sun.
(a) Light years (b) Astronomical unit
(c) Kelvin (d) Joule

7. What is the name of the process where gas is directly converted to solids called?
(a) Sublimation (b) Deposition
(c) Condensation (d) Evaporation

8. In which city is the newly proposed AIIMS to be setup in Maharashtra?
(a) Nagpur (b) Mumbai
(c) Aurangabad (d) Pune

9. Which vaccine is primarily used against tuberculosis?
(a) BCG (b) DPT
(c) HiB (d) Varicella

10. Based on the analogy given, find the missing pair from the given options.
5 : 35 :: _____ : _____
(a) 11 : 55 (b) 7 : 49
(c) 3 : 24 (d) 9 : 45

11. Consider the following statement and select the correct option:
1. It is possible to draw at least 3 straight line from given 2 points.
2. If angle of one side is parallel to angle of other side than both the angles are neither equal nor supplementary.
(a) 1 and 2 both are not right.
(b) 1 and 2 both are right
(c) 1 is wrong and 2 is right.
(d) 1 is right and 2 is wrong.

12. An Assertion (A) and a Reason (R) are given below.
Assertion (A): Simla is colder than Delhi.
Reason (R): Simla is at a higher altitude as compared to Delhi.
Choose the correct option.
(a) A is true but R is false.
(b) Ais false but R is true.
(c) Both A and R are true and R is the correct explanation of A.
(d) Both A and R are true but R is not the correct explanation of A.

DIRECTIONS (Qs. 13-15): *Study the following information carefully and answer the questions given below it.*

There are six persons in a family - three males and three females. Out of these, there are two married couples and two persons who are unmarried. Each one of them likes different colour, viz. Blue, Red, Pink, Green, Yellow and White.

Seema, who likes Red colour, is Anitha's mother-in-law and Anitha is Raja's wife. Dinesh is Rohan's father and he does not like the blue colour or White colour. Bavya likes the Yellow colour and is Rohan's sister, who likes Pink colour, Raja does not use white colour.

13. Which of the following is one of the married couples?

(a) Rohan — Bavya (b) Dinesh — Bavya
(c) Dinesh — Seema (d) Rohan — Seema

14. Which of the following colours is liked by Anitha?

(a) White (b) Yellow
(c) Pink (d) Green

15. How is Rohan related to Seema?

(a) Brother (b) Son
(c) Father (d) None of these

16. If DRIVER is coded as 5 and BELIEVED is

(a) 9 (b) 7 (c) 11 (d) 8

17. Anil can do a piece of work in 14 days which Rohit can do in 21 days. They worked together for few days after which Anil left. If Rohit worked alone for 3 days, find the total number of days it took to complete the whole work.

(a) 31/5 (b) 51/5 (c) 21/5 (d) 13/5

18. Rearrange the jumbled up letters to form a meaningful word and find the odd one out.

(a) ESAEIDS (b) EAHLTH
(c) LISESNL (d) CKSESNS

19. If A:B = 3:4 and B:C = 6:5 then A:(A+C) is:

(a) 9 : 11 (b) 9 : 10 (c) 9 : 19 (d) 6 : 7

20. If two complimentary angles are in the ratio of 11:7, find the smaller angle.

(a) 35° (b) 55° (c) 45° (d) 25°

21. What does TCP stand for with respect to computer networks?

(a) Transmission Control Protocol
(b) Transfer Call Plan
(c) Transfer Control Process
(d) Transmission Call Protocol

22. 30 litres of salt solution contains 5% salt. How many litres of water must be added so as to get a resultant solution containing 3% salt?

(a) 20 *l* (b) 25 *l* (c) 30 *l* (d) 35 *l*

23. If DI JOB means CHINA, then the last letter of the word got by decoding KBQBO is

(a) I (b) A (c) M (d) N

24. Below are given statements followed by two conclusions I and II. You have to take the given statements to be true even if they seem to be at variance from commonly known facts.

Statements: All birds are tall. Some tall are peacocks.

Conclusions:

I. Some birds are peacocks.
II. Some peacocks are tall.

Decide which of the below options logically follows the given Statement.

(a) Both conclusions I and II follow
(b) Neither conclusion I nor II follows
(c) Only conclusion I follows
(d) Only conclusion II follows

25. If the length of the shadow of a vertical pole on the horizontal ground is √3 times its height then the angle of elevation

(a) 40° (b) 50° (c) 30° (d) 45°

26. On which river is the city Madurai situated?

(a) Cooum (b) Kaveri
(c) Vaigai (d) Pennar

27. Engineer is related to Engineering in the same way as Doctor is related to

(a) Medicine (b) Hospital
(c) Disease (d) Body

28. Which of the following Prime Ministers was awarded Bharat Ratna?
(a) V. P. Singh (b) Moraiji Desai
(c) Charan Singh (d) Manmohan Singh

29. How much salt is present in our body?
(a) 1% (b) 2% (c) 0.4% (d) 0.6%

30. What is the old name of Singapore:
(a) Temasek (b) Myanmar
(c) Ceylon (d) Bohemia

31. If the angles of a triangle are in the ratio of 2 : 5 : 8, then find the value of the largest angle.
(a) 36° (b) 96° (c) 84° (d) 60°

32. What is the name of the moon of Pluto?
(a) Charon (b) Ganymede
(c) Luna (d) Triton

33. If GOAT can be written as KSEX, then WOLF can be written as ____________.
(a) APJS (b) AJSP
(c) ASPJ (d) ASSJ

34. Find the unit digit in the given product $(4211)^{102} \times (361)^{52}$
(a) 3 (b) 1 (c) 4 (d) 7

35. The traffic lights at four different road crossings change after every 15 sec., 18 sec., 27 sec. and 30 sec. respectively. If they all change simultaneously at 6:10:00 hours, then at what time will they again change simultaneously?
(a) 6:14:30 hours (b) 6:40:00 hours
(c) 6:14:00 hours (d) 10:40:00 hours

36. The mean of a distribution is 21 and the standard deviation is 7. What is the value of the coefficient variation?
(a) 16.66% (b) 66.66%
(c) 33.33% (d) 100%

37. Michael Schumacher, a racing driver belongs to which country?
(a) USA (b) Germany
(c) Canada (d) Australia

38. Choose the one which is odd from the following options:
(a) Rupee (b) Lira
(c) Coin (d) Dinar

39. What was the element used in traditional thermometers which is highly toxic in nature?
(a) Carbon (b) Mercury
(c) Arsenic (d) Cadmium

40. Which of the following was built by the ancient Incas?
(a) City of Petra (b) Hagia Sophia
(c) Machu Picchu (d) Acropolis

41. In which year was the Aam Aadmi Party founded?
(a) 2010 (b) 2011 (c) 2012 (d) 2013

42. A spoon which looks bent is
(a) Reflection (b) Refraction
(c) Retention (d) Focus

43. Who discovered radioactivity?
(a) Max Planck
(b) James Clerk Maxwell
(c) Henri Becquerel
(d) Heinrich Hertz

44. What is special about a sword-billed hummingbird?
(a) It is the smallest bird in the world
(b) Its bill is longer than rest of its body
(c) It lives only in Antarctica
(d) It cannot fly

45. A boy running at 10/9th of his actual speed covers 39 km in 2 hours 20 minutes and 24 seconds. Find the actual speed of the boy (approx.).
(a) 15 km/hr. (b) 50 km/hr.
(c) 39 km/hr. (d) 150 km/hr.

46. Who devised the policy of Doctrine of Lapse?
(a) Lord Curzon (b) Lord Mountbatten
(c) Lord Dalhousie (d) Robert Clive

47. Sonam's age after eight years will be half of her father's age. Eight years ago the ratio of their ages was 1 : 3. Find the present age of Sonam's father.
(a) 48 (b) 56 (c) 36 (d) 65

48. Mohan earns a profit of 20% on selling a jean at 15% discount on printed price. The ratio of the cost price to printed price of the jean is
(a) 17:24 (b) 17:34
(c) 16:13 (d) 21:23

49. In accordance to the 18th Mercer Quality of Life study, which city in the World holds the first position as the best city to live in?
(a) Zurich (b) Vienna
(c) Sydney (d) Hyderabad

50. When was the battle of Chillianwala fought?
(a) 1865 (b) 1892
(c) 1849 (d) 1856

51. If 'W' means '×', 'X' means '–', "Y' means '+' and 'z' means '÷', then
28 Z 7 W 8 X 6 Y 4 = ?
(a) 30 (b) 3/2 (c) 32 (d) 34

52. If '<' stands for '–', '>' stands for '+', '+' stands for '×' and '@' stands for '÷' then what will be the value of 27 > 81 @ 9 < 6
(a) 32 (b) 33 (c) 30 (d) 35

53. If '×' means '–', '–' means '×', '+' means '÷', and '÷' means '+', then what will be the value for 15 – 2 + 900 + 90 × 100?
(a) 60 (b) – 60 (c) 0 (d) 1

54. A boy in a train notices that he can count 31 telephone posts in 60 seconds. The distance between two posts is 60 metres. Calculate the speed of the train?
(a) 90 km/hr (b) 108 km/hr
(c) 60 km/hr (d) 120 km/hr

55. Which of the following is a temple built out of marble by Vimal Shah?
(a) The Dilwara temple
(b) Brihadeeswarar temple
(c) Omkareswar temple
(d) Ranakpur Adinath temple

56. Who was the first Indian Badminton player to win the men's singles title at the All England Championship in 1980?
(a) Prakash Padukone (b) Pullela Gopichand
(c) Syed Modi (d) Chetan Anand

57. Who won the Academy award for documentary 'Amy' in 2016?
(a) Duke Johnson (b) Asif Kapadia
(c) Steven Spielberg (d) Georae Miller

58. What is income available with a person after deducting for taxes called?
(a) Disposable Income (b) Cash Income
(c) Salary (d) General Income

59. Which of the following was the first super computer developed in 1976?
(a) Acom Atom (b) Cray-1
(c) PCW (d) PET

60. The average of five consecutive even numbers is 40. What is the value of smallest of these numbers?
(a) 35 (b) 36 (c) 44 (d) 48

61. Which series is India's First Supercomputer developed in Pune?
(a) Vigyan (b) Param
(c) Dhanush (d) Shakti

62. A sum of money (P) doubles in 10 years. How much would it be in 20 years at the same rate of simple interest?
(a) P (b) 2P (c) 3P (d) 4P

63. If $(a + c + 1) = 0$. Then find the value of $(a^3 + c^3 + 1 - 3ac)$
(a) –1 (b) 1 (c) 2 (d) 0

64. Based on the analogy given, find the missing number from the given options.
49 : 81 :: 100 : ______
(a) 144 (b) 169 (c) 225 (d) 64

65. If $(x + y)^2 - xy = 0$, then find the value of $(x^3 - y^3) / (x - y)$.
(a) 2 (b) 3 (c) 0 (d) 5

66. One of four words is a class of which the other three belong. Identify the class.
(a) NOVELS (b) BOOKS
(c) POEMS (d) SHORT STORIES

67. A ladder is kept along a straight wall. The top of the ladder is at a distance of 9 m from the floor. When the bottom of the ladder is moved 3 m away then the two distances becomes equal. What is the length of the ladder?

(a) 16 m (b) 15 m (c) 20 m (d) 30 m

68. Who propounded the homeopathic principle of 'like cures like'?

(a) Hippocrates (b) Samuel Hahnemann
(c) Samuel Cockburn (d) George Vithoulkas

DIRECTIONS Qs. (69-71): *Study the following table carefully and answer the questions based on it.*

The following table shows the domestic sales of cars of five manufacturers from 2005 to 2010. (All the figures are in thousands)

Manu-facturer	2005	2006	2007	2008	2009	2010
L	440	480	470	500	520	510
M	400	410	415	415	420	430
N	380	390	390	400	420	495
O	360	380	400	415	440	500
P	480	440	440	420	425	435

69. During 2006. what is the approximate share domestic sales of cars of the manufacturer M?

(a) 19.5% (b) 10.5%
(c) 20.5% (d) 25.5%

70. During 2010, the sales of which manufacturer has shown the maximum percentage increase over the previous year?

(a) L (b) M (c) N (d) P

71. With respect to which of the following combinations, is the sales of cars the highest over the given period?

(a) L, 2009 (b) L, 2010
(c) L, 2008 (d) O, 2008

72. Which one of the following interchanges in signs and numbers would make the given equation correct? **3 + 5 – 2 = 4**

(a) + and –, 2 and 5 (b) + and –, 3 and 4
(c) + and –, 2 and 4 (d) + and –, 3 and 5

73. Which dynasty had its capital at Chittorgarh?

(a) Chauhan (b) Sisodia
(c) Hada (d) Rathor

74. With which sport is the term 'Freestyle' connected with?

(a) Tennis (b) Kho Kho
(c) Kabaddi (d) Swimming

75. Atul and Binay together complete a piece of work in 5 days. If Binay alone can complete the same work in 8 days, how many days can Atul take to complete the same work alone?

(a) 40/3 days (b) 20/3 days
(c) 9 days (d) 10 days

76. Below, an assertion (A) and a reason (R) is given.

Assertion (A): In India, a rapid increase in the users-of Smartphones is seen.

Reason (R): Best 3G and 4G services are available at low price.

Choose the right option.

(a) Ais correct but R is wrong.
(b) Ais wrong but R is correct.
(c) Both A and R are correct. R is the appropriate explanation of A.
(d) Both A and R are correct but — R is not the appropriate explanation of A.

77. Find the dividend if the divisor is (x + 2). quotient is (4x – 5) and the remainder is 12

(a) $4x^2 + 5x + 2$ (b) $4x^2 + 3x + 2$
(c) $4x^2 - 3x + 2$ (d) $4x^2 + 3x - 2$

78. Who is considered the greatest of the early Chola kings?

(a) Pulakeshi II (b) Rajasimha
(c) Karikala (d) Nandivarman

79. The mass per unit volume is called

(a) Force (b) Work
(c) Density (d) Pressure

80. The BRICS Development Bank is now called as
(a) Asia Development Bank
(b) World Bank
(c) New Development Bank
(d) New BRICS Bank

81. If MACHINE is coded as 19-7-9-14-15-20-11, how will you code DANGER?
(a) 10-7-20-13-11-24
(b) 13-7-20-11-10-25
(c) 11-7-20-16-11-24
(d) 13-7-20-9-11-25

82. What sum will produce the same interest in 9 years at the rate 8% simple interest as ₹ 800 produce in 3 years at 9% per annum?
(a) ₹ 100 (b) ₹ 125
(c) ₹ 150 (d) ₹ 110

83. Which among the following is not a qualification to become a Vice President of India?
(a) Citizen of India
(b) Above 35 years of age
(c) Possess the Membership of Lok Sabha
(d) Possess the Membership of Rajya Sabha

DIRECTIONS Qs. (84-86): *The following questions are based on the information given below:*

Out of a group of 60 students. 25 play Cricket, 30 play Football. 24 play Volleyball, 10 play Cricket and Football, 9 play Cricket and Volleyball, 12 play Volleyball and Football and 5 play all the three.

84. How many students play exactly two games?
(a) 7 (b) 13 (c) 5 (d) 16

85. How many students do not play any one of the games?
(a) 5 (b) 2 (c) 7 (d) 1

86. How many students play Cricket only?
(a) 11 (b) 13 (c) 8 (d) 5

87. Choose the pair which is related in the same way as the words in the first pair from the given choices Moon: Satellite:: Earth: ______
(a) Air (b) Planet
(c) Sun (d) Sea

88. Naveen purchased a gas cylinder and a stove for ₹ 4500. He sold the gas cylinder at a gain of 25% and the stove at a loss of 20%, still gaining 4% on the whole. Find the cost of the gas cylinder.
(a) ₹ 3600 (b) ₹ 2400
(c) ₹ 3000 (d) ₹ 2600

89. The name of our planet Earth originates from which language?
(a) Greek (b) Roman
(c) English (d) Sanskrit

90. Which of the following is a good source of Vitamin A?
(a) Cabbage (b) Carrot
(c) Regular Potato (d) Strawberry

91. In new government policy, the price of onion is raised by 35%. By what % should a person reduce onion consumption so that the expenditure on it does not increase?
(a) 25% (b) 29% (c) 26% (d) 33%

92. The mean of 10 observations is 13. Two more observations are included and the new mean becomes 14. The mean of two new observations is
(a) 19 (b) 18 (c) 17 (d) 16

93. If the standard deviation of a population is 6.5, what would be the population variance?
(a) 40.25 (b) 42.25
(c) 18.25 (d) 13

94. Rearrange the jumbled up letters to form a meaningful word and find the odd one out.
(a) ROUWBR (b) EDN
(c) OREO (d) ETNS

95. How many natural numbers between 15 and 85 are divisible by 7?
(a) 9 (b) 10 (c) 8 (d) 7

96. Who proposed the Scientific Management School of thought as opposed to the Administrative Management School of thought?
(a) Henry Fayol (b) Frederick Taylor
(c) Peter Drucker (d) Max Weber

97. Who discovered the ABO blood group system?
(a) Karl Roller (b) Maurice Hilleman
(c) Karl Landsteiner (d) Edward Jenner

98. Which value is closest to [5.168 x 4453 x 3.194 / 67.999 x 4224.017]
(a) 0.2 (b) 0.002
(c) 2 (d) 0.02

99. HCF of two numbers is 19 and their LCM is 665. If one of the number is 95, find the other.
(a) 19 (b) 133 (c) 190 (d) 77

100. Which of the following states in India has the highest area under mangroves?
(a) Gujarat (b) Andhra Pradesh
(c) Maharashtra (d) West Bengal

Hints & Solutions

1. (d)

2. (d) Here (A) and (R) both are false. In India, female have lower life expectancy than the males. Although, female needs a better diet, but they do not receive a better diet.

3. (d) Cost price of 1 banana $= \frac{4}{5}$

Selling price of 1 banana $= \frac{5}{4}$

$$\text{Profit\%} = \frac{\frac{5}{4} - \frac{4}{5}}{\frac{4}{5}} \times 100 = \frac{25-16}{16} \times 100$$

$$= \frac{9}{16} \times 100 = 56.25\%$$

4. (b) **5. (b)**

6. (b) Under the new astronomical unit the Earth-sun distance is 149,597,870,700 meters.

7. (b)

8. (a) The new AIIMS would be set up at Nagpur, Manglagiri in AP and Kalyani in West Bengal.

9. (a)

10. (b) 5 : 35 :: 7 : 49
(×7) (×7)

11. (a) 1. From two points, we can draw only one straight.
2. If angle of one side is parallel to angle of other side, then both the angles are equal.

12. (c) Shimla is at a higher attitude as compare to Delhi. So, Shimla is colder then Delhi.

13-15: Hence, married couples are Dinesh — Seema and Raja — Anita.

Family member	Colour	Relationship
Seema	Red	Dinesh's wife
Dinesh	Green	
Bavya	Yellow	Rohan's sister
Anita	White	Raja's wife
Raja	Blue	
Rohan	Pink	Dinesh's son

13. (c) Dinesh — Seema is a married couple.

14. (a) Anita likes white colour.

15. (b) Rohan is Seema's son.

16. (b) Number of letters in 'DRIVER' = 6
So, code of 'DRIVER' = 6 – 1 = 5
Similarly, Number of letters in 'BELIEVED' = 8
So, code of the word = 8 – 1 =7

17. (b) When they work together, the work completed in one day:

$$= \frac{1}{14} + \frac{1}{21} = \frac{3+2}{42} = \frac{5}{42} \text{ work}$$

Work finish by Rohit in 3 days

$$= \frac{3}{21} = \frac{1}{7} \text{ work}$$

Remaining work $= 1 - \frac{1}{7} = \frac{6}{7}$ work

Time required to finish $\frac{6}{7}$ work.

$$\frac{6}{7} \times \frac{42}{5} = \frac{36}{5} \text{ days}$$

Total time to finish the work $= \frac{36}{5} + 3$

$$= \frac{36+15}{5} = \frac{51}{5} \text{ days}$$

18. (*) ESAEIDS — DISEASE
EAHLTH — HEALTH
LISESNL — ILLNESS
CKSESNS —

19. (c) $A : B = 3x : 4x \Rightarrow 9x : 12x$
$B : C = 6x : 5x \Rightarrow 12x : 10x$
$A : B : C = 9x : 12x : 10x$
Now, $A : (A + C) = 9x : (9x + 10x)$
$= 9x : 19x = 9 : 19.$

20. (a) Sum of complimentary angles = 90°
$11x + 7x = 90°$
$18x = 90° \Rightarrow x = 5$
Hence, smaller angle $= 7x = 7 \times 5 = 35°$

21. (a) TCP/IP stands for Transmission Control and Internet Protocol, which is a set of networking protocols that allows two or more computers to communicate.

22. (a) Salt in 30L solution $= 30 \times \frac{5}{100} = 1.5$ L
Water $= 30 - 1.5 = 28.5$ L
Let us add x L of water.
Then, $(30 + x) \times \frac{3}{100} = 1.5$
$$30 + x = \frac{1.5 \times 100}{3}$$
$x = 50 - 30 = 20$ litres.

23. (d) DIJOB — CHINA

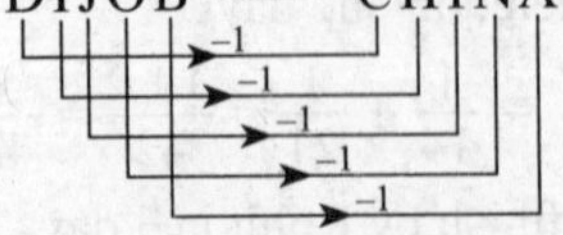

K B Q B O
↓–1 ↓–1 ↓–1 ↓–1 ↓–1
J A P A N

24. (d)

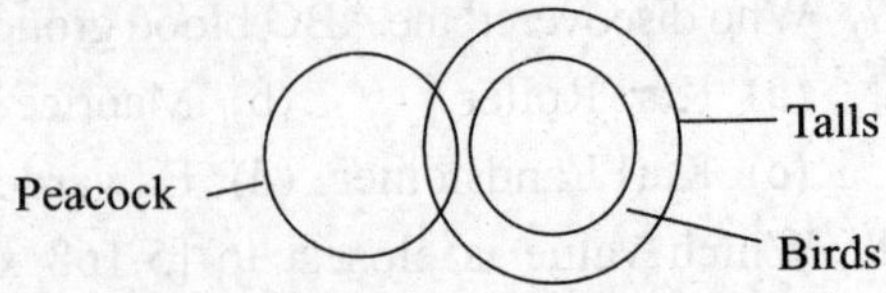

Here, only conclusion II follow.

25. (c)

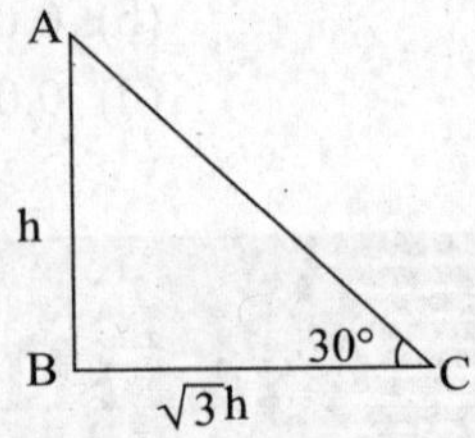

Let AB is a vertical pole of height h. and BC is its shadow of length $\sqrt{3}h$ and angle of elevation of the pole is θ
Now, in $\triangle ABC$,
$$\tan\theta = \frac{AB}{BC} = \frac{h}{\sqrt{3}h} = \frac{1}{\sqrt{3}}$$
$\tan\theta = \tan 30° \Rightarrow \theta = 30°$

26. (c) **27. (a)** **28. (b)**

29. (c) The human body contains around 0.4% sodium chloride of the body's weight.

30. (a)

31. (b) Sum of the angles of a triangle = 180°
$2x + 5x + 8x = 180 \Rightarrow 15x = 180 \Rightarrow x = 12$
$\therefore$ Largest angle $= 8 \times 12 = 96°$

32. (a) Charon, is the largest of the five natural satellites of the dwarf planet Pluto.

33. (c) G O A T
↓+4 ↓+4 ↓+4 ↓+4
K S E X
Similarly,
W O L F
↓+4 ↓+4 ↓+4 ↓+4
A S P J

34. (b) $(4211)^{102} \times (361)^{52}$
We know that $1 \times 1 = 1$
$1^m \times 1^n = 1$
So, last digit of the product = 1.

35. (a) L.C.M. of 15, 18, 27 and 30:

$15 = 3 \times 5$

$18 = 3 \times 3 \times 2$

$27 = 3 \times 3 \times 3$

$30 = 3 \times 2 \times 5$

$3 \times 3 \times 3 \times 2 \times 5 = 270$ sec.

= 4 min 30 sec

Hence, at 6 : 10 + 4 min 30 sec

= 6 : 14 : 30

All light change simultaneously.

36. (c) Coefficient of variation $= \frac{\text{S.D.}}{\text{Mean}} \times 100$

$= \frac{7}{21} \times 100 = 33.33\%$

37. (b)

38. (c) Rupee, Lira and Dinar are currency of different country, where coin is not a currency.

39. (b)

40. (c) Machu Picchu is a surviving example of Inca architecture.

41. (c)

42. (b) Refraction is bending of light wave as it passes from one medium to another due to which we saw spoon broken near water surface.

43. (c)

44. (b) The sword-billed humming bird is the only bird to have a beak longer than the rest of its body.

45. (a) Time = 2 hours 20 minutes 24 second

$= 2 \text{ hours} + \frac{20}{60} \text{ hour} + \frac{24}{3600} \text{ hour}$

$= \left(2 + \frac{1}{3} + \frac{1}{150}\right) = \frac{351}{150} \text{ hours}$

$\frac{10}{9} \times \text{Speed} = \frac{39}{\frac{351}{150}}$

$\therefore \text{Speed} = \frac{39 \times 150}{351} \times \frac{9}{10} = 15 \text{ km/hr.}$

46. (c) Dalhousie doctrined that in case a ruler of dependent state died childless, the right of ruling over the state reverted or 'lapsed' to the sovereign.

47. (b) Let Sonam's father age is x years. and Sonam's age is y years.

Then, $y + 8 = \frac{1}{2}(x + 8) \Rightarrow x - 2y = 8$....(i)

and, $\frac{y-8}{x-8} = \frac{1}{3} \Rightarrow x - 3y = -16$....(ii)

by subtracting (i) from (ii) we get,

$x = 3 \times 8 + 16 \times 2$

$\therefore$ Sonam's father's age = 56 years.

48. (a) Let cost price is x and print rate is y.

Then, $y \times \frac{85}{100} = x \times \frac{120}{100}$

$\therefore \frac{x}{y} = \frac{85}{120} = \frac{17}{24}$

49. (b) Vienna is the world's best city to live in; Baghdad is the worst.

50. (c) The Battle of Chillianwala was fought in January 1849 during the 2nd Anglo-Sikh War in the Chillianwala region of Punjab now part of Pakistan.

51. (a) 28z7w8x6y4 $= 28 \div 7 \times 8 - 6 + 4$

$= 4 \times 8 - 2 = 30.$

52. (c) 27>81@9<6 $= 27 + 81 \div 9 - 6$

$= 27 + 9 - 6 = 30.$

53. (b) $15 - 2 \div 900 + 90 \times 100$

$= 15 \times 2 + 900 \div 90 - 100$

$= 30 + 10 - 100 = -60$

54. (b) Total distance covered by crossing 31 posts $= 30 \times 60 = 1800$ m

Time t = 60 sec

Speed $= \frac{1800}{60}$ m/s

$= \frac{1800}{60} \times \frac{3600}{1000} = 108$ km/hr.

55. (a) **56. (a)** **57. (b)**

58. (a) Disposable personal income is the amount of money that households have available for spending and saving after income taxes have been accounted for.

59. (b)

60. (b) Let five consecutive even numbers are n, n + 2, n + 4, n + 6 and n + 8

Average

$$\frac{n+n+2+n+4+n+6+n+8}{5} = 40$$

$$\frac{5n+20}{5} = n + 4 = 40 \Rightarrow n = 36$$

61. (b) PARAM supercomputer was designed and assembled by C-DAC in Pune. The latest is PARAM SHIVAY. Parama means supreme in Sanskrit Language.

62. (c) Simple interest in 10 years = 2P – P = P.

So, $\text{rate} = \frac{\text{S.I.} \times 100}{P \times t} = \frac{P \times 100}{P \times 10} = 10\%$

Now, when rate = 10%, t = 20 years.

Then, $\text{S.I.} = \frac{P \times 10 \times 20}{100} = 2P$

Amount = 2P + P = 3P.

63. (d) We know that, when, a + b + c = 0

Then, $a^3 + b^3 + c^3 - 3abc = 0$

So, $a^3 + b^3 + (1)^3 - 2ab.(1) = 0$

64. (a) 49 : 81 :: 100 : 144

↓ ↓ ↓ ↓

$(7)^2$ $(9)^2$ $(10)^2$ $(12)^2$

65. (c) $(x + y)^2 - xy = 0$

$x^2 + y^2 + 2xy - xy = 0 \Rightarrow x^2 + y^2 + xy = 0$

Then,

$$\frac{(x^3 - y^3)}{(x - y)} = \frac{(x - y)(x^2 + y^2 + xy)}{(x - y)} = 0$$

66. (b) Books is different from other three: novels, poems and short stories.

67. (b)

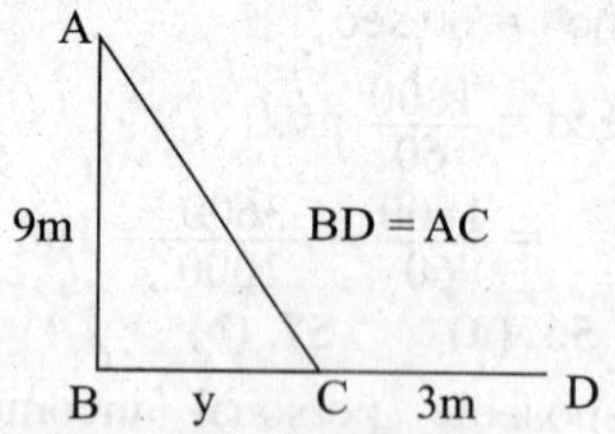

Let AC is the ladder.

Now, AB = 9 m. and BC = y m.

Then, $(9)^2 + (y)^2 = (y + 3)^2$

$81 + y^2 = y^2 + 9 + 6y$

$6y = 72 \Rightarrow y = 12$

∴ Length of the ladder = 12 + 3 = 15 cm.

68. (b) According to homeopathy, a substance which is capable of causing, is also capable of curing. The name was coined by its originator Samuel Hahnemann.

69-71: Total number of car sales during 2006 = 480 + 410 + 390 + 380 + 440 = 2100

69. (a) Approximate share of domestic sales of cars of manufacture M is

$$\frac{410}{2100} \times 100 = 19.5\%$$

70. (c) From table, we see that maximum % increase during 2010 over previous year for manufacturer is N.

71. (a) Sales of car the highest over the period is L, 2009.

72. (d) Given equation : 3 + 5 – 2 = 4

After interchange : 5 – 3 + 2 = 4

73. (b) **74. (d)**

75. (a) Number of days Atul take to complete the work alone. $= \frac{1}{\frac{1}{5} - \frac{1}{8}} = \frac{40}{8-5} = \frac{40}{3}$

76. (c) In India best 3G and 4G services are available at low price, cause for a rapid increase in the users of smart phones.

77. (b) Dividend = divisor × quotient + remainder

$= (x + 2) \times (4x - 5) + 12$

$= 4x^2 + 3x + 2.$

78. (*) Karikala, a Tamil Chola king conquered whole of India up to the Himalayas and constructed flood banks on river Kaveri. He is recognised as the greatest of the Early Cholas.

79. (c) Density is expressed in units of grams per cubic centimetre. e.g. the density of water is 1 gram per cubic centimetre.

80. (c) The New Development Bank, established by the BRICS states (Brazil, Russia, India, China and South Africa) to support public or private projects through loans, guarantees, equity participation and other financial instruments.

81. (a)

(12)	(1)	(3)	(8)	(9)	(14)	(5)
M	A	C	H	I	N	E
↓+6	↓+6	↓+6	↓+6	↓+6	↓+6	↓+6
19	7	9	14	15	20	11

Similarly,

(4)	(1)	(14)	(7)	(5)	(18)
D	A	N	G	E	R
↓+6	↓+6	↓+6	↓+6	↓+6	↓+6
10	7	20	13	11	24

82. (c) S.I. $= \frac{800 \times 3 \times 9}{100} =$ ₹ 108

Now, Sum $= \frac{108 \times 100}{9 \times 8} =$ ₹ 150

83. (c)

84-86:

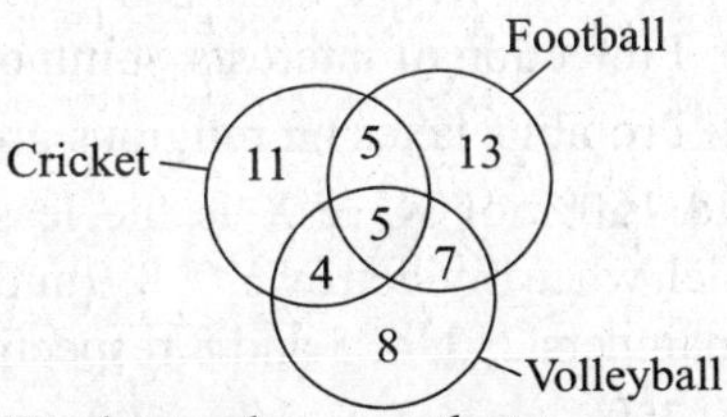

84. (d) Students play exactly two games = 5 + 4 + 7 = 16.

85. (c) Students not play any games = 60 – 21 – 13 – 11 – 8 = 7

86. (a) Students play cricket only = 25 – (5 + 5 + 4) = 25 – 14 = 11

87. (b) Moon is a satellite, like that Earth is a planet.

88. (b) Let cost price of gas cylinder is ₹ x.

Then, " " " stove = (4500 – x)

$$SP = CP\left[1 + \frac{\text{Gain\%}}{100}\right]$$

$$x \times \frac{100 + 25}{100} + (4500 - x) \times \frac{100 - 20}{100} = 4500 \times \frac{104}{100}$$

$$125x + 360000 - 80x = 468000$$

$$45x = 108000$$

∴ Cost price of gas cylinder, x = ₹ 2400.

89. (c) Earth is the only planet which wasn't named after a Greek or Roman god.

90. (b)

91. (c) Let price of 1 kg onion is ₹ 100.

Then, after raising the price by 35%

Price of onion $= 100 \times \frac{100 + 35}{100} = 135$

Now, In ₹ 135 any one can by 1000 gm onion

∴ In ₹ 100 " " $= \frac{1000}{135} \times 100$

= 740.7 gm.

∴ Decrease = 1000 – 740 = 260 gm.

= 26%

92. (a) Sum of 10 observation = 13 × 10 = 130

Sum of 12 observation = 14 × 12 = 168

Sum of last two observation = 168 – 130 = 38

Mean of last two observation $= \frac{38}{2} = 19.$

93. (b) Variance $= (\text{S.D.})^2 = (6.5)^2 = 42.25$

94. (*) ROUWBR — BURROW, EDN — DEN

OREO — , ETNS — NEST

95. (b) Number between 15 and 85 divisible by 7 : 21, 28, 35, 42, 49, 56, 63, 70, 77, 84.

96. (b) Taylor, a mechanical engineer observed that the owners and managers knew little about workshops. The scientific management movement produced revolutionary ideas such as employee training and implementing standardized best practices to improve productivity.

97. (c)

98. (a) $\frac{5.168 \times 4453 \times 3.194}{67.999 \times 4224.017} = 0.2555 = 0.2$

99. (b) Product of two number = L.C.M × H.C.F.

Number $= \frac{19 \times 665}{95} = 133$

100. (d) Mangrove wetland is considered highly productive. Gujarat hosts the second largest mangrove cover (1,140 sq km). The highest mangrove cover was in West Bengal which has an area of 2,114 sq km.

RRB NTPC stage-I Solved Paper

Held On 18th April 2016 (Shift-I)

1. Which is India's first defence satellite?
   (a) INSAT 2B (b) GSAT-7
   (c) GSAT 6 (d) IRS-1A
2. Below are given statements followed by two conclusions I and II. You have to take the given statements to be true even if they seem to be at variance from commonly known facts.
   Statements: A: All mothers are aunts.
   B: All aunts are ladies.
   Conclusions: I. All ladies are mothers.
   II. All ladies are aunts.
   Decide which of the below options logically follows the given Statement.
   (a) Only conclusion I follows
   (b) Only conclusion II follows
   (c) Both conclusions I and II follow
   (d) Neither conclusion I nor II follows
3. Which of the following ratio is greatest?
   (a) 7 : 15 (b) 15 : 23
   (c) 17 : 25 (d) 21 : 29
4. Choose the one which is odd from the following options.
   (a) Coffee (b) Rice
   (c) Tobacco (d) Sugarcane
5. The passenger reservation system of the Indian Railways is designed by
   (a) TCS (b) CRIS
   (c) Google (d) CMS
6. What is the chemical name of chalk?
   (a) Calcium Sulphate (b) Calcium Nitrate
   (c) Calcium Carbonate (d) Calcium Phosphide
7. What is the name of the book in Harry Potter series written by Jack Thome to be published in mid-2016?
   (a) Harry Potter and the Cursed Child
   (b) Harry Potter and the Deathly Hallows.
   (c) Fantastic Beasts and Where to Find Them
   (d) The Tales of Beedle the Bard.
8. If 3.5x = 0.07y, then find the result of [y – x/y + x]
   (a) 51/49 (b) 49/53
   (c) 49/51 (d) 53/57
9. Article 29 of the Constitution of India grants which of the following rights?
   (a) Protection in respect of conviction for offences
   (b) Traffic in human beings prohibited
   (c) Protection of interests of minorities
   (d) Prohibits taxes on religious grounds
10. Find 150% of X, if X is the least number which when divided by 6, 7, 8, 9 and 12 leaves remainders 2, 3, 4, 5 and 8 respectively.
    (a) 750 (b) 500
    (c) 1000 (d) 1200
11. For real a, b and c if $a^2 + b^2 + c^2 = ab + bc + ca$, then find the value of $(a + b + c)^2$
    (a) $9a^2$ (b) $81a^2$
    (c) $27a^2$ (d) $243a^2$
12. MATHEMATICS is related to NUMBERS in the same way HISTORY is related to
    (a) EVENTS (b) PEOPLE
    (c) WARS (d) DATES
13. In which year was Façebook started?
    (a) 2002 (b) 2004
    (c) 2008 (d) 2009
14. What is the chemical formula of Ozone?
    (a) O (b) O_2
    (c) O_3 (d) O_4
15. An Assertion (A) and a Reason (R) are given below.
    Assertion (A): Earthworms are not good for agriculture.

Reason (R): Earthworms break down the soil into fine particles and make it soft.

Choose the correct option.

(a) Ais true but R is false.
(b) Ais false but R is true.
(c) Both A and R are true and R is the correct explanation of A.
(d) Both A and R are false

16. What is the sound made by seal called?
(a) Bark (b) Moo
(c) Screech (d) Growl

17. Based on the analogy given, find the missing number from the given options. 7528 : 5306 :: 4673 : ?
(a) 2351 (b) 2541
(c) 2451 (d) 2531

18. If STUDENT is coded as 103, what is the code for SCHOOL?
(a) 72 (b) 27 (c) 37 (d) 73

19. If 'P' means 'divided by', "T' means 'add', M' means 'subtract' and 'D' means 'multiplied by', then what will be the value of the following expression?
12M12D28P7T15
(a) –21 (b) 15 (c) 30 (d) – 15

20. Who was the dentist who killed Cecil-the Lion in 2015?
(a) John Walker (b) Gary Crow
(c) Walter Palmer (d) Rupert Watson

21. The energy which we get from food is measured in
(a) Calories (b) Kelvin
(c) Tat (d) Amperes

22. How many litres of blood does an adult body have?
(a) 3 (b) 4 (c) 5 (d) 6

23. Who is known as the Father of video games?
(a) Karl Benz (b) Emile Berliner
(c) Rudolf Diesel (d) Ralph H. Baer

24. If Sunita earns 75/4% more than her boyfriend, find the approximate % her boyfriend earns less than Sunita.
(a) 16% (b) 14% (c) 25% (d) 11%

25. If the angles of a triangle are in the ratio of 2:3:7. Then find the ratio of the greatest angle to the smallest angle.
(a) 7 : 2 (b) 2 : 3
(c) 7 : 1 (d) 3 : 5

26. Which wood is used to make a cricket bat?
(a) Teak (b) Willow
(c) Bamboo (d) Rosewood

27. What of the given below devices converts chemical energy to electrical energy?
(a) Transformer (b) Battery
(c) Electric Generator (d) Wheel

28. An angle is 30 more than one half of its complement. Find difference between the greater and the smaller angles.
(a) 10° (b) 20° (c) 30° (d) 25°

29. What are the components of $(x^6 - x^4 - x^5 - x^4 + x^2 - 4)$?
(a) $(x - 1)$
(b) $(x + 1)$
(c) Both $(x - 1)$ and $(x + 1)$
(d) Neither $(x - 1)$ or $(x + 1)$

30. Who fought Ahmad Shah Abdali at the third battle of Panipat?
(a) Mughals (b) Lodhis
(c) Marathas (d) Khiljis

31. Which of the following is not a greenhouse gas?
(a) Carbon dioxide
(b) Methane
(c) Chlorofluorocarbons
(d) Oxygen

32. What are stars primarily made of?
(a) Oxygen and Hydrogen
(b) Hydrogen and Carbon
(c) Hydrogen and Helium
(d) Oxygen and Helium

33. On which date was the partition of India announced?
(a) 15th Aug 1947 (b) 3rd June 1947
(b) 17th July 1947 (d) 1st July 1947

34. Find the simple interest on ₹ 50 for 6 months at the rate of 10 paise per rupee per month.
(a) ₹ 35 (b) ₹ 40
(b) ₹ 25 (d) ₹ 30

35. Two numbers are in the ratio 5:6. When 6 is added to each, the ratio becomes 7:8 then the numbers are
(a) 10 & 12 (b) 20 & 24
(c) 15 & 18 (d) 5 & 6

36. If the given interchanges namely: signs + and + and numbers 2 and 4 are made in signs and numbers, which one of the following would be correct?
(a) $4 + 2 \div 6 = 1.5$ (b) $2 + 4 \div 6 = 8$
(c) $2 + 4 \div 3 = 3$ (d) $4 \div 2 + 3 = 4$

37. Stainless steel was invented by
(a) William Howard Livens
(d) Joseph Aspdin
(c) Harry Breadey
(d) James Dyson

38. If BORDER is coded as 579649, than ORDER can be coded as
(a) 79469 (b) 79649
(c) 76949 (d) 79667

39. The disease cirrhosis affects which organ in the body?
(a) Brain (b) Liver
(c) Heart (d) Kidney

40. The ratio between the speeds of two buses is 11:9. If the second bus runs 270 kms in 15 hours, then the speed of the first bus is?
(a) 23 km/hr (b) 11 km/hr
(c) 2 km/hr (d) 22 km/hr

41. Who presented the first Union Budget in 1947?
(a) Indira Gandhi
(b) Morarji Desai
(c) R. K. Shanmukham Chetty
(d) John Mathai

42. On which network was the first SMS sent?
(a) Airtel (b) Vodafone
(c) Verizone (d) Digicel

43. McAfee is a ______________?
(a) Anti-virus software
(b) Programming language
(c) Output device
(d) Computer device

44. An Assertion (A) and a Reason (R) are given below.
Assertion (A): In India judiciary is independent of the executive.
Reason (R): Judiciary favours the government and helps in the implementation of its plans.
Choose the correct option.
(a) A is true but R is false.
(b) A is false but R is true.
(c) Both A and R are true and R is the correct explanation of A.
(d) Both A and R are false

45. The product of the ages of Swati and Aparna is 120. If thrice the age of Aparna is more than Swati's age by 2 years, find the age of Swati.
(a) 18 (b) 20 (c) 24 (d) 16

46. A wholesaler sold a water purifier at a loss of 40%. If the selling price has been increased by ₹ 125. Then wholesaler will get the profit of 10%. What was the cost price of the purifier?
(a) ₹ 250 (b) ₹ 225
(c) ₹ 275 (d) ₹ 300

47. If IRON is written as GOKI, then KNIEF may be written as
(a) IKZEZ (b) IEKZZ
(c) IKEZZ (d) IZKEZ

48. Which tennis player has been awarded the Padma Bhushan award 2016?
(a) Sania Mirza (b) Leander Paes
(b) Mahesh Bhupathi (d) Rohan Bopanna

49. What does ATM stand for?
(a) Any Time Money
(b) Automated Teller Machine
(c) Automatic Talking Media
(d) Analog Time Machine

50. When Vijay sells 12 pens, he gains the selling price of 2 pens. Calculate his % profit?
(a) 15% (b) 20%
(b) 18% (d) 12%

51. To which dynasty did the famous patron of literature king Bhoja belong?
(a) Chalukya (b) Chola
(c) Paramara (d) Pala

52. Based on the analogy given, find the missing word from the given options.
Mother : Child :: Cloud : ?
(a) Rain (b) Thunder
(c) Water (d) Weather

53. If the standard deviation of a population is 7, what would be the population variance?
(a) 14 (b) 21 (c) 49 (d) 28

DIRECTIONS (Qs. 54-56): *Read the following Passage and answer the questions based on it.*

There are six members in a family. One couple has parents and their children in the family. Arjun is the son of Raju and Elamathi is the daughter of Arjun. Divya is the daughter of Rani who is the mother of Elamathi and Banu is the mother of Arjun.

54. How many female members are in the family?
(a) 2 (b) 3
(c) 4 (d) Cannot be determined

55. Which of the following pairs is the parents of the children?
(a) Raju & Banu (b) Arjun & Banu
(c) Raju & Rani (d) Arjun & Rani

56. What relationship Divya and Elamathi bear to each other respectively?
(a) Sisters
(b) Mother & Daughter
(c) Grandmother & Granddaughter
(d) Cannot be determined

57. A sum of ₹ 2000 at 40% per annum compounded annually. Calculate the interest for the third year at compound interest.
(a) 1500 (b) 1600
(c) 1568 (d) 1750

58. Who received the Man Booker Prize in 2015 for his novel 'A brief history of seven killings'?
(a) Marlon James (b) Richard Flanagan
(c) Arvind Adiga (d) E.O. Wilson

DIRECTIONS (Qs. 59-61): *The following questions are based on the information given below:*

An advertising agency finds that, of its 170 clients, 115 read Indian Express, 110 read The Hindu and 130 read Times of India. Also 85 read Indian Express and Times of India, 75 read Indian Express and The Hindu, 95 read The Hindu and Times of India and 70 read all the three.

59. How many read only The Hindu?
(a) 5 (b) 10 (c) 25 (d) 35

60. How many read Indian Express and Times of India but not The Hindu?
(a) 10 (b) 20 (c) 15 (d) 30

61. How many read only Indian Express?
(a) 15 (b) 25 (c) 5 (d) 10

62. For what value of C_2, the system of equation $6x + 2y = 2$ & $3x + y = C_2$, will be coincident?
(a) 4 (b) 0 (c) 2 (d) 1

63. What is the increase in the number of workdays under the rural job guarantee scheme (MNREGA) in drought-affected areas?
(a) 10 (b) 25 (c) 40 (d) 50

64. By dividing 14528 by a certain number, Suresh gets 83 as quotient and 3 as remainder. What is the divisor?
(a) 165 (b) 185
(c) 195 (d) 175

DIRECTIONS (Qs. 65-67): *Read the following table carefully and answer the questions given below:*

The percentage change in sales of six departmental stores from 2010 to 2012 is shown in the following table:

Store	Percentage Change	
	From 2010 to 2011	From 2011 to 2012
P	+ 20	– 20
Q	– 20	+ 9
R	+ 5	+ 12
S	– 7	– 15
T	+ 17	– 8
U	+ 21	+ 9

65. Sales in store P amounted to ₹ 80 lakhs in 2010. What was the sales amount of the same store in 2012?
(a) 76.8 lakhs (b) 78.6 lakhs
(c) 80 lakhs (d) 74 lakhs

66. In store T the sales for 2011 amounted to what percentage of the sales for 2012?
(a) 113 (b) 109 (c) 105 (d) 101

67. In 2012 which of the stores had greater sales than any other stores?
(a) R (b) P (c) T (d) Q

68. Sunil and Gopal are partner in a business. Sunil invests ₹ 20,000 for 9 months and Gopal invests ₹ 30.000 for 12 months. Find the share of Sunil from the total profit of ₹ 60,000.
(a) ₹ 15000 (b) ₹ 18000
(c) ₹ 25000 (d) ₹ 20000

69. The mean of a distribution is 11 and the standard deviation is 5. What is the value of the coefficient variation?
(a) 45.45% (b) 35.35%
(c) 25.25% (d) 55.55%

70. The mean of 14 observations is 11. One more observation is included and the new becomes 12. The 15th observation is
(a) 20 (b) 24 (c) 26 (d) 28

71. Five women can do a work in thirty six days. If the ratio between the capacity of a man and a woman is 3:1, then find how many days it will take 5 men to complete the same work?
(a) 12 days (b) 15 days
(c) 18 days (d) 108 days

72. Who conferred the title of 'Gurudev' on Rabindranath Tagore?
(a) Mahatma Gandhi
(b) Pandit Nehru
(c) Lala Lajpat Rai
(d) Bal Gangadhar Tilak

73. If NCLAGJ stands for PENCIL, then AMJMSP stands for
(a) ERASER (b) PAPERS
(c) KOLOUR (d) COLOUR

74. If (sinA + cosA)/(sinA – cosA) = 5/4, the value of $(\tan^2A + 1)/(\tan^2A - 1) = ?$
(a) 41/40 (b) 12/13
(c) 40/41 (d) 3/5

75. If 15 persons can do a job in 30 days, then 30 persons with twice the efficiency can do the same job in how many days?
(a) 7 (b) 3.5 (c) 5 (d) 7.5

76. If two complementary angles are in the ratio of 2:3, find the ratio of square of smaller angle to square of greater angle.
(a) 3 : 2 (b) 9 : 11
(b) 4 : 5 (d) 4 : 9

77. What denotes offering several products for sale as one combined product?
(a) Advertisement (b) Product mix
(c) Product bundling (d) Differentiation

78. Which was the capital of the first Sri Lankan kingdom?
(c) Jaffna (b) Polonnaniwa
(c) Anuradhapura (d) Kandy

79. $\sin^6A + \cos^6A - 1$ is equal to
(a) $-3\sin^2A\cos^2A$ (b) $1 - 3\sin A\cos A$
(c) $1 + 3\sin^2A\cos^2A$ (d) 0

80. In the following expression ‘α’ stands for ‘$>$’; ‘β’ stands for ‘$<$’; ‘γ’ stands for ‘not greater than’: ‘δ’ stands for ‘not less than’; and ‘μ’ stands for ‘$=$’.

If 3C δ 2A and B α C, then which of the following statement is true?

(a) 3B μ 2A (b) B μ A

(b) 3B α 2A (d) 2A α 3B

81. Which of the following is a bad conductor of heat?

(a) Wood (b) Diamond

(b) Water (d) Mica

82. Choose the pair which is related in the same way as the words in the first pair from the given choices

Mosquito : Malaria ::______ : ______

(a) Housefly : Food (b) Road : Accident

(c) Soil : Erosion (d) Tobacco : Cancer

83. Where will the 2022 Commonwealth Games be played?

(a) Glasgow (b) Durban

(c) Gold Coast (d) New Delhi

84. Rearrange the jumbled up letters in their natural sequence and find the odd one out.

(a) LAFC (b) UKCGIDLN

(c) RILNIGHE (d) BCU

85. Sita starts to calculate sum of all odd natural numbers less than 72. What result does she get?

(a) 1196 (b) 1296

(c) 1331 (d) 1276

86. On an average how many times does lightning strike the Earth?

(a) 100 times per second

(b) 100 times per day

(c) 1000 times per day

(d) 100 times per hour

87. An Assertion (A) and a Reason (R) are given below.

Assertion (A): We feel comfortable in hot and humid climate.

Reason (R): Sweat evaporates faster in humid climate.

Choose the correct option.

(a) A is true but R is false.

(b) A is false but R is true.

(c) Both A and R are true and R is the correct explanation of A.

(d) Both A and R are false

88. Rearrange the jumbled up letters in their natural sequence and find the odd one out.

(a) UTNA (b) EINEC

(c) OMEHRT (d) ROBEHRT

89. Which is the form of market where there is lack of competition?

(a) Monopoly

(b) Oligopoly

(c) Perfect competition

(d) Marketisation

90. One of four words is a class to which the other three belong. Identify the class.

(a) Hawaii (b) Cubav

(c) Island (d) Greenland

91. Based on the analogy given, find the missing pair from the given options.

32 : 13 ::______ : ______

(a) 51 : 36 (b) 83 : 121

(c) 71 : 81 (d) 47 : 65

92. Find the LCM of 0.36, 2.72, 0.12 and 1.44

(a) 24.48 (b) 2448

(c) 2.448 (d) 244.8

93. Which of the following is called ‘The queen of Arabian sea’?

(a) Mumbai

(b) Thiruvananthapuram

(c) Kochi

(d) Surat

94. What is the name of the castle that was built in honour of world renowned composer Richard Wagner?
(a) Balmoral Castle
(b) Neuschwanstein Castle
(c) Conwy castle
(d) Rronborg

95. Select the correct set of symbols which will fit in the given equation? **5 0 3 5 = 20**
(a) +, –, + (b) ×, +, ×
(c) –, +, × (d) ×, ×, ×

96. Evaporation of water from leaves of a plant is called
a) Transpiration (b) Respiration
(c) Perspiration (d) Evaporation

97. How do you know Yarlung Tsangpo better?
(a) Ganges (b) Brahmaputra
(c) Mahanadi (d) Sutlej

98. The famous Sanchi Stupa was commissioned by
(a) Bindusara
(b) Ashoka
(c) Chandragupta Maurya
(d) Kanishka

99. How long will Ramesh take to run round a square park of edge 50 metres, if he runs at the rate of 18 km/hr?
(a) 40 sec (b) 20sec
(c) 80sec (d) 160 sec

100. Ramesh sold a phone at a loss of 5%. Had he sold it for = 200 more, he would gave gained 15%. To gain 25%, he should sell it for :
(a) ₹ 1175 (b) ₹ 1150
(c) ₹ 1225 (d) ₹ 1250

Hints & Solutions

1. (b) India's maiden defence satellite made for the Navy by the ISRO, is an advanced multi-band, state-of-the-art GSAT-7. It was launched by an European rocket, to improve space-based communications and intelligence gathering over oceanic region and the country's landmass.

2. (d)

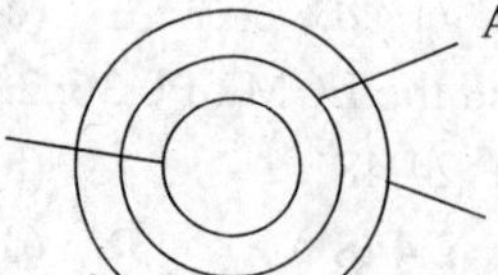

Neither conclusion I nor II follow.

3. (d) $\frac{7}{15} = 0.467, \frac{15}{23} = 0.65, \frac{17}{25} = 0.68,$
$\frac{21}{29} = 0.72$ Hence, $\frac{21}{29}$ is greatest.

4. (b)

5. (b) The Centre for Railway Information Systems (CRIS) designs, develops, implements and maintains information systems of Indian Railways.

6. (c) Calcium carbonate is a common substance found in rocks as limestone, and is the main component of pearls and the shells of marine organisms, snails, and eggs. It is medicinally used as a calcium supplement or as an antacid.

7. (a) Harry Potter and the Cursed Child is a British two-part stage play written by Jack Thorne based on an original story by Thorne, J. K. Rowling and John Tiffany.

8. (c) $3.5x = 0.07y \Rightarrow \frac{y}{x} = \frac{3.5}{0.07} = 50$
Now, $\frac{y-x}{y+x} = \frac{50-1}{50+1} = \frac{49}{51}$

9. (c) Article 29 protects the interests of the minorities having a distinct language, script, religion or culture it mandates that no discrimination would be done to them.

10. (a) L.C.M. of 6, 7, 8, 9 and 12 = 504

Remainder in each case = (6 – 2) = 4

(7 – 3) = 4, (8 – 4) = 4, (9 – 5) = 4, (12 – 8) = 4

So, X = 504 – 4 = 500

Now, $500 \times \frac{150}{100} = 750.$

11. (a) $(a+b+c)^2 = a^2 + b^2 + c^2 + 2ab + 2bc + 2ca$

$\because ab + bc + ca = a^2 + b^2 + c^2$ ...(given)

$= a^2 + b^2 + c^2 + 2(a^2 + b^2 + c^2)$

$\therefore (a + b + c)^2 = 3(a^2 + b^2 + c^2)$ ...(i)

Again from, $a^2 + b^2 + c^2 = ab + bc + ca$

Multiplied both side by 2

$2a^2 + 2b^2 + 2c^2 – 2ab – 2bc – 2ca = 0$

$(a – b)^2 + (b – c)^2 + (c – a)^2 = 0$

$\therefore a = b = c.$

Hence, $(a + b + c)^2 = 3(a^2 + b^2 + c^2) = 9a^2$

12. (a) As Mathematics is related to numbers like that History is related to events.

13. (b) Facebook was founded by Mark Zuckerberg, Eduardo Saverin, Dustin Moskovitz, and Chris Hughes, students at Harvard University.

14. (c)

15. (b) Earthworms are important soil animals that maintain the fertility of the soil. They restore soil nutrients, improve soil structure, allow water and air to enter the soil more freely.

16. (a) A seal makes a sound that is a mixture of a bark and an eerie whaling sound.

17. (c) 7528 : 5306 :: 4673 : 2451

7528 → 5306 (– 2222); 4673 → 2451 (– 2222)

18. (a)

S	T	U	D	E	N	T
19	20	21	4	5	14	20

Letter's position in alphabet

19 + 20 + 21 + 4 + 5 + 14 + 20 = 103

Similarly,

SCHOOL = 19 + 3 + 8 + 15 + 15 + 12 = 72

19. (a) 12M12D28P7T15 $= 12 – 12 \times 28 \div 7 + 15$

$= 12 – 12 \times 4 + 15$

$= 12 – 48 + 15 = –21$

20. (c) Cecil (c. 2002-2015) was a lion who lived in the Hwange National Park North, Zimbabwe. He was being studied and tracked by a research team of the University of Oxford as part of a long-term study. On the night of 1 July 2015, Cecil was wounded with an arrow by Walter Palmer.

21. (a) One calorie is equal to 4.184 joules, a unit of energy. The calories listed on a food package are actually kilocalories (1000 calories = 1 kilocalorie).

22. (c) The average adult has 4.5 to 5.5 litres of blood in their body. 5-6 years old, children also have about the same amount of blood. Since their bones, muscles and organs don't weigh as much, their blood makes up a larger percentage of their body weight.

23. (d) Ralph Henry Baer was a German inventor, game developer, and engineer. He is considered "the Father of Video Games".

24. (a) Let Sunita's boyfriend earning is ₹ 100

Then, Sunita's earning $= 100 + \frac{100 \times 75}{4 \times 100}$

$= \frac{475}{4} = 118.75$

Approx. % her boyfriend earn less then her $= \frac{118.75 \times 100}{118.75} \times 100 = 16\%$

25. (a) Sum of the angles of a triangle = 180°

$2x + 3x + 7x = 180$

$12x = 180 \Rightarrow x = 15$

Ratio of greatest angle to smallest angle

$= \frac{7 \times 15}{2 \times 15} = \frac{7}{2}$

26. (b) The bat is traditionally made from willow

wood, treated with unboiled linseed oil, which has a protective function.

27. (b) A battery stores electrical energy in the form of chemical energy, and converts that energy into electricity.

28. (a) Sum of complement angle = 90°

Let one angle is x, then other angle is (90 – x)

$$x - \frac{1}{2}(90 - x) = 30$$
$$2x - 90 + x = 60$$
$$3x = 150 \Rightarrow x = 50°$$
$$90 - x = 90 - 50 = 40°$$

Difference = 50 – 40 = 10°

29. (d) Let $f(x) = (x^6 - x^4 - x^5 - x^4 + x^2 - 4)$

For x = 1,

$$(1)^6 - (1)^4 - (1)^5 - (1)^4 + (1)^2 - 4 = -5$$

For x = –1,

$$(-1)^6 - (-1)^4 - (-1)^5 - (-1)^4 + (-1)^2 - 4 = -3$$

∴ (x + 1) is not a component of f(x)

30. (c) The 3rd Battle of Panipat took place in 1761 at Panipat, near Delhi, between Maratha forces and invading forces of the King of Afghanistan, Ahmad Shah Abdali, supported by two Indian allies—the Najib-ud-daulah, of the Doab region and Shuja-ud-Daula of Awadh.

31. (d)

32. (c) Stars are made of very hot gases. These gases are mostly hydrogen and helium, the two lightest elements. Stars shine by burning hydrogen into helium in their cores, and later in their lives create heavier elements.

33. (b) Lord Mountbatten, the last viceroy, announced the Partition Plan on 3 June 1947, declaring that the British would transfer power to the Indian and Pakistani governments by mid-August 1947.

34. (d) r = 10%, t = 6 months, P = 50

$$\text{A.I.} = \frac{P \times r \times t}{100} = \frac{50 \times 10 \times 6}{100} = ₹\,30$$

35. (c) Let the two numbers are 5x and 6x.

$$\frac{5x + 6}{6x + 6} = \frac{7}{8} \Rightarrow 8(5x + 6) = 7(6x + 6)$$
$$42x - 40x = 48 - 42 \Rightarrow 2x = 6 \Rightarrow x = 3$$

∴ Numbers : 5 × 3 = 15,

6 × 3 = 18

36. (b) $2 + 4 \div 6 = 8$

After interchange $\Rightarrow 4 \div 2 + 6 = 2 + 6 = 8$

37. (c) Harry Brearley of UK is credited with inventing the first true stainless steel, which had a 12.8% chromium content.

38. (b)

Letter	B	O	R	D	E
Code	5	7	9	6	4

Hence, ORDER code is 79649.

39. (b) Cirrhosis is a chronic disease of the liver. If the damage is not stopped, the liver gradually loses its ability to carry out its normal functions.

40. (d) Speed of second bus $= \frac{\text{distance}}{\text{time}}$

$$= \frac{270}{15} = 18 \text{ kmph.}$$

Ratio of speed = 11 : 9

Now, $\frac{\text{Speed of first bus}}{\text{Speed of second bus}} = \frac{11}{9}$

$$\frac{\text{Speed of first bus}}{18} = \frac{11}{9}$$

Speed of first bus $= \frac{11}{9} \times 18 = 22$ kmph

41. (c)

42. (b) The first SMS message was sent over the Vodafone GSM network in UK on 3 December 1992, from Neil Papworth of Sema Group using a personal computer to Richard Jarvis of Vodafone using an Orbitel 901 handset. The text of the message was "Merry Christmas."

43. (a) McAfee AntiVirus Plus is a next generation security for your computer that detects and blocks viruses and malware.

44. (a)

45. (a) Let Swati's age is x years

Then, Aparna's age is $\frac{120}{x}$ year

$$\frac{120}{x} \times 3 = x + 2$$

$$360 = x^2 + 2x \Rightarrow x^2 + 2x - 360 = 0$$

$$(x + 20)(x - 18) = 0 \Rightarrow x = 18, -20$$

Hence, Swati's age = 18 years.

46. (a) Let cost price of purifier is ₹ x.

Selling price = $x \times \left(\frac{100 - 40}{100}\right) = 0.6x$

New selling price = (0.60x + 125)

Then, profit% = 10%

So, $0.6x + 125 = x \times \left(\frac{100 + 10}{100}\right) = 1.1x.$

$(1.1x - 0.6x) = 125$

Hence, cost price $x = \frac{125}{0.5} =$ ₹ 250.

47. (c) I R O N

↓−2 ↓−3 ↓−4 ↓−5

G O K I

Similarly,

K N I E F

↓−2 ↓−3 ↓−4 ↓−5 ↓−6

I K E Z Z

48. (a)

49. (b) ATM is Automated Teller Machine. It's a specialized computer that makes it convenient to manage your money. All ATMs allow you to withdraw money, and many allow you to make deposits.

50. (b) Vijay cost price = 12 − 2 = 10 pen cost price

So, Vijay gain = $\frac{2}{10} \times 100 = 20\%$ gain.

51. (c) Bhoja was a king from the Paramara dynasty around the Malwa region in central India. His kingdom extended from Chittor in the north to upper Konkan in the south, and from the Sabarmati River in the west to Vidisha in the east.

52. (a) Every child has come out from its mother like that every rain has come out from cloud.

53. (c) Variance = $(S.D.)^2 = (7)^2 = 49$

54. (c) There are four female members: Banu, Rani, Elamathi and Divya.

55. (d) Arjun and Rani are spouse and parent of the two children.

56. (a) Elamathi and Divya are sisters.

57. (c) Interest for 3 years:

$$C.I. = P\left[\left(1 + \frac{r}{100}\right)^t - 1\right]$$

$$= 2000\left[\left(1 + \frac{40}{100}\right)^3 - 1\right]$$

$$= 2000[(1.4)^3 - 1] = 2000\,[1.744 - 1]$$

= ₹ 3488

Now, interest for 2 years.

$$= 2000\left[\left(1 + \frac{40}{100}\right)^2 - 1\right]$$

$$= 2000[(1.4)^2 - 1] = 2000\,[1.96 - 1]$$

= ₹ 1920

∴ Interest for 3rd year

= 3488 − 1920 = 1568.

58. (a) Jamaican author Marlon James won the Man Booker Prize for his novel 'A Brief History of Seven Killings' inspired by the attempted assassination of Bob Marley in the 1970s.

59-61:

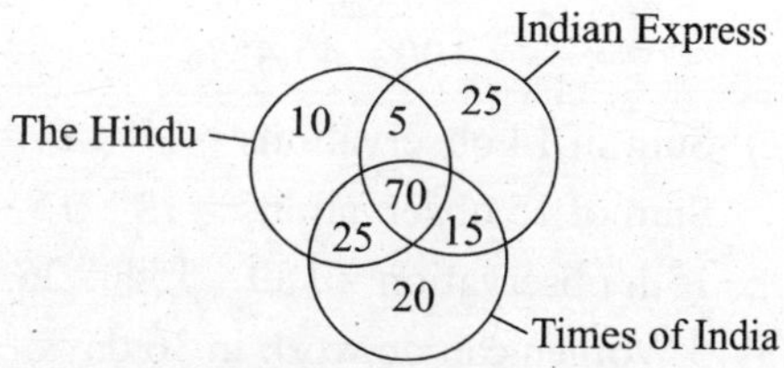

59. (b) 10 clients read only the Hindu.

60. (c) 15 clients read Indian Express and Times of India but not the Hindu.

61. (b) 25 clients read only Indian Express.

62. (d) $6x + 2y = 2 \Rightarrow 3x + y = 1$ ...(i)

and $3x + y = C_2$ ...(ii)

From (i) and (ii), two equation coincident if

$a_1 = a_2$, $b_1 = b_2$ and $c_1 = c_2$

$\therefore C_2 = 1.$

63. (d)

64. (d) Let divisor is d

Then, dividend = divisor × Quotient + Remainder

$14528 = d \times 83 + 3$

$\text{dividend} = \frac{14528 - 3}{83} = 175$

65. (a) Sale of P in 2012

$= 80 \times \frac{120}{100} \times \frac{80}{100} = 76.8$ lakhs.

66. (b) Let sales of store T is ₹ 100 lakhs

$\text{Sales of store T in 2011} = 100 \times \frac{117}{100} = 117$

$\text{Sales of store T in 2012} = 117 \times \frac{92}{100} = 107.64$

$\text{Required percent} = \frac{117}{107.64} \times 100 = 109\%$

67. (d) In 2012, store Q had greater sales than any other stores.

68. (d) Ration of investment

Sunil : Gopal = 20000 × 9 : 30000 × 12

= 2 × 3 : 3 × 4 = 1 : 2

Sunil's share in profit

$= \frac{1}{1+2} \times 60000 = 20000$

69. (a) $\text{Coefficient of variation} = \frac{\text{S.D.}}{\text{Mean}} \times 100$

$= \frac{5}{11} \times 100 = 45.45\%$

70. (c) Sum of 14 observations = 11 × 14 = 154

Sum of 15 observations = 12 × 15 = 180

15th observation = 180 – 154 = 26.

71. (a) 5 Women can do work in 36 days.

1 woman can do work in 36 × 5 days

So, 1 man " " $= \frac{36 \times 5}{3} = 60$ days

Hence, 5 men " $= \frac{60}{5} = 12$ days.

72. (a)

73. (d)

N	C	L	A	G	J
↓+2	↓+2	↓+2	↓+2	↓+2	↓+2
P	E	N	C	I	L

Similarly,

A	M	J	M	S	P
↓+2	↓+2	↓+2	↓+2	↓+2	↓+2
C	O	L	O	U	R

74. (a) $\frac{(\sin A + \operatorname{Cos} A)}{(\sin A - \cos A)} = \frac{5}{4}$

$= 4(\sin A + \cos A) = 5(\sin A - \cos A)$

$= 5\sin A - 4\sin A = 4\cos A + 5\cos A$

$= \sin A = 9\cos A \Rightarrow \tan A = 9.$

Now, $\frac{\tan^2 A + 1}{\tan^2 A - 1} = \frac{(9)^2 + 1}{(9)^2 - 1} = \frac{82}{80} = \frac{41}{40}$

75. (d) 15 persons can do the work in 30 days

Then, 30 persons can " $= \frac{30 \times 15}{30} = 15$

As efficiency of person is double.

So, 30 persons can do the work in $= \frac{15}{2}$

= 7.5 days

76. (d) Ratio of smaller to greater angle = 2 : 3.

Ratio of their square = $(2)^2 : (3)^2 = 4 : 9$

77. (c) Product bundling is the sale of two or more products in combination as a package.

78. (c) The Anuradhapura, was the first kingdom in ancient Sri Lanka by Sinhalese people. Founded by King Pandukabhaya in 377 BC, the kingdom's authority extended throughout the country.

79. (a) $\sin^6 A + \cos^6 A - 1 = (\sin^2 A)^3 + (\cos^2 A)^3 + (-1)^3$

Here $a = \sin^2 A$, $b = \cos^2 A$ and $c = -1$

New, $a + b + c = \sin^2 A + \cos^2 A - 1 = 1 - 1 = 0$

As, $a + b + c = 0$, Then $a^3 + b^3 + c^3 = 3abc$

$\therefore \sin^6 A + \cos^6 A - 1 = 3\sin^2 A.\cos^2 A\,(-1)$

$= -3\sin^2 A.\cos^2 A$

80. (c) $3C\ \delta\ 2A = 3C \geq 2A$...(i)

and $B\ \alpha\ C = B > C$...(ii)

Equation (ii), can be written as

$3B > 2A = 3B\ \alpha\ 2A.$

81. (a) Wood is a poor conductor of heat and other forms of energy because it does not have free electrons that scatter about to conduct different forms of energy like metals and other strong conductors do.

82. (d) Malaria is caused due to mosquito bite like that one of the causes for cancer is tobacco chucking.

83. (b) **84. (c)**

85. (b) Sum of odd number less then 72

$S = 1 + 3 + 5 + 7 \text{------} 71$

$= \frac{36}{2}[1 + 71] = \frac{36 \times 72}{2} = 1296$

86. (a) About 100 lightning bolts strike the Earth's surface every second That's about 8 million per day and 3 billion each year.

87. (d) Here both (A) and (R) is false. We feel uncomfortable in hot and humid climate. Because sweat evaporates slower in humid climate.

88. (d)

89. (a) A monopoly exists when a specific person or enterprise is the only supplier of a particular commodity. Oligopoly consists of a few sellers dominating a market. Monopolies are characterized by a lack of economic competition to produce the good or service; a lack of viable substitute goods, and the possibility of a high monopoly price that leads to a high monopoly profit.

90. (c)

91. (d) 32 : 13 :: 47 : 65

$(3)^2 + (2)^2$ $(4)^2 + (7)^2$

92. (a) L.C.M. of 0.36, 2.72, 0.12 and 1.44.

or, $\frac{36}{100}, \frac{272}{100}, \frac{12}{100}$ and $\frac{144}{100}$

or, $\frac{9}{25}, \frac{68}{25}, \frac{3}{25}$ and $\frac{36}{25}$

$\text{L.C.M.} = \frac{\text{L.C.M of } 9, 68, 3, 36}{\text{H.C.F. of } 25, 25, 25, 25}$

$= \frac{612}{25} = 24.48$

93. (c) Known as the Queen of the Arabian Sea, Kochi was an important spice trading centre on the west coast of India. Occupied by the Portuguese in 1503, Kochi was the first of the European colonies in colonial India.

94. (b) The magnificent castle in Bavaria, Germany , was built by King Ludwig II aka "Fairytale King" in 1886. The Neuschwanstein Castle is located in the Alps in Bavaria and has an amazing view, gazing the Hohenschwangau valley.

95. (c) $5 - 0 + 3 \times 5 = 5 + 15 = 20.$

96. (a) Transpiration is essentially evaporation of water from plant leaves.

97. (b) The Brahmaputra River is one of the last free-flowing rivers emanating from the Tibetan Plateau. Originating as the Yarlung Tsangpo River, it flows across southern Tibet through the Himalayas and into India and Bangladesh before merging with the Ganges and emptying into the Bay of Bengal.

98. (b) The Great Stupa at Sanchi is one of the oldest stone structures in India, and an important monument of Indian Architecture. It was originally commissioned by the emperor Ashoka in the 3rd century BCE. Its nucleus was a simple hemispherical brick structure built over the relics of the Buddha.

99. (a) Perimeter of the square = distance to be run

$= 4 \times 50 = 200 \text{ m}$

$\text{Speed} = 18 \text{ km/hr} = 18 \times \frac{5}{18} = 5\text{m/sec.}$

$\text{Time} = \frac{200}{5} = 40 \text{ second.}$

100. (d) Let cost price of the phone is x.

Then, selling price at 5% loss

$= \frac{95}{100}x = 0.95x$

$0.95x + 200 = x \times \frac{115}{100}$

$1.15x - 0.95x = 200$

$0.2x = 200 \Rightarrow x = 1000$

To get 25% profit selling price

$= 1000 \times \frac{125}{100} = ₹\ 1250$

RRB NTPC stage-I Solved Paper

Held On 19th April 2016 (Shift-I)

1. If **'summer it hot'** it coded as **'de fe ba'** and **'come cold summer'** as **'ja ha ba'** and **'winter is cold'** as **'pa ja de'** then **'come hot winter'** is coded as ________.

(a) de ba ja (b) fe ba pa
(c) ba pa ha (d) pa ha fe

2. What is the minimum number to be subtracted from 6321, which makes it completely divisible by 14?

(a) 8 (b) 12 (c) 7 (d) 11

3. Jahangir was the ________ Mughal emperor of India.

(a) 3rd (b) 4th (c) 5th (d) 6th

4. If P means '÷' R means '×', Q means '+' and S means '–', then

48 P 8 Q 6 R 9 S 31 = ?

(a) 60 (b) 29 (c) 31 (d) 54

5. ________ granted charter to East India Company to establish trading posts in India in 1600.

(a) Queen Elizabeth I
(b) Queen Elizabeth II
(c) King George V
(d) King George VI

6. Ramdas invested Rs. 90000 in a cosmetic business. After few months. Shyamdas joined him with Rs. 30000. At the end of the year, the total profit was divided between them in ratio 4 : 1. After how many months did Shyamdas joined business?

(a) 4 (b) 3 (c) 1 (d) 6

7. Methane is known as ________.

(a) Laughing gas
(b) Tear gas
(c) Marsh gas
(d) Non-greenhouse gas

8. Hawa Mahal in Jaipur is constructed using

(a) White and green marble
(b) Granite
(c) Red and Pink sandstone
(d) Normal rocks

9. If the angles of a triangle are in the ratio of 1 : 2 : 3, then find the value of the largest angle.

(a) 30° (b) 60°
(c) 90° (d) 120°

10. Read the given statements carefully and answer the question.

Statement: Though the school bags policy has been announced, it is not clear how many schools arc following it. The state Government is also clueless whether schools have implemented the rules.

Which of the following is true according to the given statement?

(a) School bags policy has been implemented by the Government.
(b) Schools are not interested in following the rules.
(c) There is no monitoring system.
(d) State Government is not interested in follow-up.

11. The concept of the game of ________ is eliminating an opponent by touching.

(a) Kho Kho (b) Kabaddi
(c) Judo (d) Kalari

12. The mean of 22 observations is 10. Two more observations are included and the new mean becomes 11. The mean of two new observations is

(a) 19 (b) 20 (c) 21 (d) 22

13. An angle is 10° more than one third of its complement. Find the greater angle.

(a) 30° (b) 60° (c) 45° (d) 75°

14. Neelam and Manisha starting from the same place run at a rate of 7 kmph and 9 kmph respectively. What time will they take to be 12 km apart. If they run in the same direction?

(a) 3 hours (b) 6 hours
(c) 12 hours (d) 9 hours

15. Delhi metro covers a distance in 40 minutes, if it runs at a speed of 48 kmph on an average. Find the speed at which the train must run to reduce the time of journey to 32 minutes.

(a) 60 kmph (b) 50 kmph
(c) 70 kmph (d) 80 kmph

16. The mean of a distribution is 13 and the standard deviation is 7. What is the value of the coefficient variation?

(a) 50% (b) 76.77%
(c) 53.85% (d) 38.88%

17. A car stops on applying brakes mainly due to ______________ force.

(a) Gravitational (b) Centripetal
(c) Frictional (d) Centrifugal

18. Statements followed by some conclusions are given below.

Statements:

1. Knowledge is not a skill. It is learning and experience.
2. The illiterate are not those who cannot read and write but those who cannot learn.

Conclusions:

I. Those who cannot read and write are literate.
II Knowledge and skill are two different things.

Find which of the given conclusions logically follows from the given statements.

(a) Only conclusion I follows.
(b) Only conclusion II follows.
(c) Both I and II follow.
(d) Neither I nor II follows.

19. Statements followed by some conclusions are given below.

Statements:

1. Depleting natural resources is a major concern in our country.
2. Unless we go for renewable energy sources in a big way, increase in population being a heavy burden on the energy resources, will reduce the quality of life.

Conclusions:

I. Depleting resources impacts quality of life.
II. Use of renewable energy sources is a solution to counter increase in population.

Find which of the given conclusions logically follows from the given statements.

(a) Only conclusion I follows.
(b) Only conclusion II follows.
(c) Both I and 11 follow.
(d) Neither I nor 11 follows.

20. Quartz used in clocks is ______________.

(a) Nitrogen silicate (b) Silicon dioxide
(c) Sodium silicate (d) Calcium silicate

21. The head of the state in India is the ________

(a) Prime Minister
(b) President
(c) Parliament
(d) Chief Justice of India

22. Name the type of government in Bangladesh.

(a) Islamic Republic
(b) Parliamentary Democracy
(c) Federal Republic
(d) Constitutional Monarchy

23. Which pair is not exactly similar to the other three pairs?

(a) Principal : School
(b) Pages : Note book
(c) Letters : Word
(d) Students : Class

24. Which Indian state shares its borders with the maximum number of other Indian states?

(a) Manipur (b) West Bengal
(c) Assam (d) Uttarakhand

25. ____________ does not refer to the game of playing card.

(a) Bridge (b) Blackjack

(c) Squash (d) Solitaire

26. ____________ was appointed as one of the Goodwill Ambassadors by UNDP in March 2016,

(a) Ashley Judd (b) Michelle Yeoh

(c) Merrick Garland (d) Hillary Clinton

27. Is the process of absorption of moisture from air.

(a) Deliquescence (b) Capillary action

(c) Absorption (d) Osmosis

28. The process of optimization fat content in milk is called ____________.

(a) Vitamin fortification

(b) Pasteurization

(c) Standardization

(d) Homogenization

29. Bird : Wings :: Fish: ?

(a) Gills (b) Head

(c) Fins (d) Legs

30. An assertion (A) and a reason (R) are given below.

Assertion (A): Perennial rivers originate from the Himalayas.

Reason (R): The fountains in the Himalayas feed the rivers.

Choose the correct option.

(a) Both A and R are true and R is the correct explanation of A

(b) Both A and R are true, but R is not the correct explanation of A

(c) A is true, but R is false

(d) A is false, but R is true

31. Find the missing (?) in the series:

3, 75 13, 21, 31, ?

(a) 41 (b) 42 (c) 43 (d) 44

32. Which state has the second highest number of seats in the Lok Sabha?

(a) Uttar Pradesh (b) Andhra Pradesh

(c) West Bengal (d) Bihar

33. If **TABLE = RYZJC**, then **CHAIR** ______.

(a) AFZHQ (b) AFYGP

(c) FAGYP (d) ZFAHQ

34. Find the odd pair out.

(a) Nitrogen & oxygen : Air

(b) Sulphur & Phosphorous : Match stick

(c) Hydrogen & Oxygen : Water

(d) Magnesium & Silver : Stainless steel

35. ____________ was the first Geographical Indication (GI) tagged product in India.

(a) Darjeeling Tea (b) Solapuri Chaddar

(c) Nagpur Orange (d) Orissa Ikat

36. Freezing point of water is ____________.

(a) 40° F (b) 42° F

(c) 34° F (d) 32° F

37. ADGJ, CFIL, EHKN, ____________.

(a) FILO (b) HKNQ

(c) DGJM (d) GJMP

38. If the rate of interest is 8% per annum and Rs. 10000 lent at the compound interest half yearly then calculate the equivalent simple rate of interest for the first year?

(a) 8.16% (b) 9%

(c) 7% (d) 10%

39. 'docx' file is created with

(a) Spreadsheet (b) Powerpoint

(c) Word processor (d) Paint

40. Evaluate (35/2)% of 800 gm – (45/2) % of 400 gm

(a) 50 gm (b) 150 gm

(c) 100 gm (d) 80 gm

41. 12 men finished 1/4 part of whole work in 6 days. Find the number of additional men required to complete the job in next 6 days.

(a) 36 (b) 12 (c) 18 (d) 24

42. B is the brother of C. D is the sister of B. F is the sister of E who is the son of C. K is the husband of C. How is D related to F?

(a) Maternal Aunt (b) Mother
(c) Sister (d) Niece

43. ____________ does not belong to the twelve zodiac signs.

(a) Ophiuchus (b) Aquarius
(c) Libra (d) Pisces

44. Rearrange the jumbled letters to make meaningful words and then select the one which is different.

(a) ENIMSAJ (b) DLOGIRAM
(c) TORRAC (d) REWOLFNUS

45. Taxonomy is basically related to ____________.

(a) Biodiversity
(b) Tax structure
(c) A branch of astronomy
(d) Study of human behaviour

46. Ramesh purchased a memory card at a price of Rs. 625 including the sales tax. The rate of sales tax is 25%. If the seller has made a gain of 50%. then the cost price of the memory card is:

(a) ₹ 333 (b) ₹310
(c) ₹ 350 (d) ₹ 360

47. The shadow of a standing tower of height $25\sqrt{3}$ m is found to be 50 m longer when the sun's elevation changes from 60° to X°. Find the measure of X.

(a) 45° (b) 30° (c) 75° (d) 90°

48. 30 persons can finish a job in 20 days. After 6 days how many persons should leave the job, so that work is completed in a total of 26 days?

(a) 9 (b) 12 (c) 8 (d) 7

49. An investor invested 1/2 of his capital at 5%, 1/4 at 10% and rest at 8%. If his income after 2 years is ₹ 2800, find the capital amount

(a) Rs. 10000 (b) Rs. 15000
(c) Rs. 20000 (d) Rs. 12000

50. The distance between the two poles of length 16 m and 9 m, is X m. If two angles of elevation of their respective top from the bottom of the other are complementary to each other then the value X is:

(a) 10m (b) 15m
(c) 16m (d) 12m

51. ____________ is not a constituent of tooth paste.

(a) Abrasive (b) Fluoride
(c) Lubricant (d) Surfactant

DIRECTIONS (Qs. 52-54): *Consider the following information and answer questions based on it.*

Suresh is taller than Ramesh who is shorter than Rakesh. Jinesh is taller than the shortest person but shorter than Rakesh. Pritesh is taller than Suresh but shorter than Jinesh.

52. Who is the shortest?

(a) Rakesh (b) Ramesh
(c) Pritesh (d) Suresh

53. If Jayesh who is taller than Suresh joins the group, who will be fourth, if they are arranged in a descending order?

(a) Jayesh
(b) Jinesh
(c) Pritesh
(d) Cannot be determined

54. Which statement, among the following, is correct?

(a) Suresh is taller than Jinesh.
(b) Pritesh is shorter than Rakesh
(c) Jinesh is taller than Rakesh.
(d) Ramesh is taller than Pritesh.

55. If **VOTER** = **41352**, **HEATER** = **743654**, **TEASER** = **645834**, which number represents S?

(a) 1 (b) 5 (c) 8 (d) 7

56. Pointing to a man, a woman said "he is the brother of the daughter of my husband's wife". What is the woman to the man?

(a) Son (b) Mother
(c) Father (d) Sister

57. Triangle PQR is such that PR = 7.5 cm and triangle PQR is similar to triangle XYZ. If XY = 18 and YZ = 12 cm then find the ratio of PQ : QR

(a) 1 : 2 (b) 3 : 2
(c) 4 : 5 (d) 5 : 2

58. The planet Pluto was discovered in the year...

(a) 1925 (b) 1930
(c) 1935 (d) 1940

59. Two numbers are in the ratio 3 : 5. If each number is increased by 10, the ratio becomes 5 : 7. The smaller number is :

(a) 8 (b) 12 (c) 15 (d) 18

60. In. 1955, ____________ was renamed as State Bank of India.

(a) Bank of Bengal
(b) Bank of Bombay
(c) Bank of Madras
(d) Imperial Bank of India

61. Two vessels contain milk and water in the ratio 2:3 and 7:5. Find the ratio in which the contents of the two vessels have to be mixed so that the ratio of milk and water in the new mixture is equal.

(a) 2 : 1 (b) 1 : 2
(c) 3 : 2 (d) 2 : 3

62. Find the value of 335 * 335 – 165 * 165?

(a) 20000 (b) 65000
(c) 85500 (d) 27500

63. Which one is not generally used as a fruit?

(a) Strawberry (b) Grapes
(c) Pear (d) Tomato

64. 'Make in India Week' was launched in ____________ from 13th to 18th February 2016.

(a) Bhubaneswar (b) Udaipur
(c) Mysuru (d) Mumbai

65. If **Chennai : Tamil Nadu**, the ____________ : **Jharkhand**

(a) Raipur (b) Ranchi
(c) Dhanbad (d) Durgapur

66. Read the given statements carefully and answer the question.

Most people get their own cars to office. The number of vehicles on road is increasing day by day. It leads to traffic congestion and adds to the ever-increasing air pollution issues. As a result, respiratory problems are on a rise. People should, as far as possible, take public transport or do car pooling.

Which of the following situations better fits the above statement?

(a) People are becoming rich day by day and hence buying more cars.
(b) People can go to the shopping malls in cars but not to office.
(c) Respiratory problems doesn't affect the people who use public transport.
(d) More number of vehicles on road leads to traffic congestion.

67. The famous forbidden city is in ____________.

(a) France (b) Italy
(c) China (d) USA

68. Rate of heat conduction in solids does not depend on ____________.

(a) Density of the material
(b) Dimensions of the material
(c) Friction
(d0 Electronic configuration

69. As per tiger census of 2014, tiger population in India was estimated at ____________.

(a) 1411 (b) 1706
(b) 2226 (d) 1906

70. ____________ was the theme for World Wetland Day in 2016.

(a) Sustainable Livelihoods
(b) Wetlands take care of water
(c) Wetlands for our future
(d) Wetlands and Agriculture

71. L is K's sister. M is the father of K. N and O are brothers. L is the mother of O. How is K related to N?

(a) Maternal Uncle (b) Brother
(c) Nephew (d) Cannot be determined

72. _______________ is used in refrigeration.
(a) Chlorofluorocarbon
(b) Carbon dioxide
(c) Nitrogen peroxide
(d) Ammonium oxide

73. If $(x^2 + I/x^2) = 6$, then find the value of $(10x - 10/x)$
(a) +/– 15 (b) +/– 20
(c) +/– 30 (d) +/– 40

74. Halley's comet is expected to return to the vicinity of earth in the year...
(a) 2086 (b) 2061
(c) 2041 (d) 2026

75. Asymmetric Digital Subscriber Line (ADSL) is _______________ technology.
(a) a wireless data communication
(b) a wired data communication
(c) amateur radio communication
(d) satellite communication

76. Who was appointed as the Defense Minister when the 16 Lok Sabha was formed in 2014?
(a) Venkaiah Naidu
(b) Ravi Shankar Prasad
(c) Manohar Parikkar
(d) Suresh Prabhu

77. If '÷' means '+', '+' means '÷', and '–' means '×'. then **25 ÷ 25 + 5 ÷ 2 – 15 = ?**
(a) 0 (b) –12 (c) 60 (d) 45

78. If **SMART = 31524**, **MARBLE = 428376** and **EAT = 537**, then **STABLE = ?**
(a) 618537 (b) 253678
(c) 453678 (d) 243678

79. Choose the odd one out
(a) Optical disc (b) Magnetic Storage
(c) Solid State Drive (d) Petabyte

80. Which one is not true with 'backup'?
(a) Exact copy of computer files.
(b) It is part of business continuity plan.
(c) PCs do not require regular back up.
(d) Offsite and on-site backup are more beneficial.

81. If the standard deviation of a population is 9.5, what would be the population variance?
(a) 19 (b) 90.25
(c) 81.25 (d) 93.25

82. Find the largest 6 digit number which is completely divided by 71.
(a) 999965 (b) 999954
(c) 999964 (d) 999974

83. The first, all women two wheeler public transportation service in India was started in
(a) Gurgaon (b) Noida
(c) Chennai (d) Bengaluru

84. If $(a - 1/a) = 3/4$, Find the value of $(a^3 - 1/a^3)$.
(a) 164/31 (b) 171/64
(c) 171/32 (d) 164/37

85. Find the greatest number which on dividing 3050 and 5200 leaves remainders 7 and 9 respectively.
(a) 149 (b) 111
(c) 153 (d) 179

DIRECTIONS (Qs. 86-88): *The following table represents the human resource profile of a global company.*

Consider the table and answer questions based on it.

Country	No. of offices	Male		Female		Total
		Class I	Class II	Class I	Class II	
US	20	150	50	70	35	305
UK	15	115	40	65	20	240
India	10	125	25	45	90	285
Canada	10	80	30	50	10	170

86. The percentage of male employees in India to the total number of employees of the company is
(a) 11% (b) 15.5% (c) 15% (d) 20%

87. Total number of employees in the company is

(a) 950 (b) 960
(c) 995 (d) 1000

88. The ratio of female employees of US to Canada is

(a) 4 : 7 (b) 7 : 4
(c) 21 : 17 (d) 21 : 29

89. The period of Dominion of India refers to

(a) Pre-partition day
(b) Pre-Independence day
(c) Post Republic day
(d) Independence day to Republic day

90. Who won the man of the match award in the 2016 Asia Cup T20 held in Bangladesh?

(a) Bhuvaneshwar Kumar
(b) Virat Kohli
(c) Shikhar Dhawan
(d) R Ashwin

91. What is the average of first 25 multiples of 11?

(a) 152 (b) 147 (c) 143 (d) 134

92. If 2x (x + y + z) = 250, 2y (x + y + z) = 100, 2z (x + y + z) = 100. Then find the value of (3x + 6y + 15z).

(a) 110 (b) 95 (c) 85 (d) 69

93. Kakori train robbery took place in the year

(a) 1923 (b) 1924
(c) 1925 (d) 1926

94. By selling an article for Rs. 979, a shopkeeper bears a loss of 11%. If shopkeeper sells that article for Rs. 1232, then the profit % is:

(a) 12% (b) 21% (c) 11% (d) 14%

95. The HCF and LCM of two numbers are 45 and 270 respectively. If the ratio of the two numbers is 2:3 and smaller of the two numbers is X. then find X?.

(a) 2025 (b) 4225
(c) 8100 (d) 18225

96. Inflammation of the mucous membrane is called

(a) Bronchitis (b) Hepatitis
(c) Iritis (d) Gastritis

DIRECTIONS (Qs. 97-99): *Consider the following information and answer the questions based on it.*

Out of 200 kids, 20 wanted to see only the galaxy, 25 wanted to see only stars, 30 wanted to see only planets, 50 wanted to see stars, planets and moon, 25 wanted to see both moon and galaxy, 25 wanted to see only moon and the remaining did not want to see anything.

97. In all, how many kids did not want to see only the galaxy?

(a) 130 (b) 100 (c) 155 (d) 125

98. In all, how many kids wanted to see the moon?

(a) 50 (b) 75 (c) 100 (d) 120

99. How many kids wanted to see at least 2 objects?

(a) 50 (b) 25 (c) 75 (d) 55

100. Manish purchased mobile phone and got 50% concession on the marked price of the phone and sold it for Rs. 8100 with 35% profit on the price he bought. What was the marked price?

(a) ₹ 8000 (b) ₹ 12000
(c) ₹ 10000 (d) ₹ 9000

Hints & Solutions

1. (d) Summer is hot — de fe ba
come cold Summer — ja ha ba
winter is cold — pa ja de

Hence, code for 'come hot winter' is 'pa ha fe'.

2. (c) 6321 ⇒ Divide by 14 ⇒ Remainder = 7

$\therefore$ 6321 = 6314 + 7

Hence, minimum number to subtract = 7.

3. (b) Jahangir (1569-1627) s/o emperor Akbar was the fourth Mughal emperor of India.

4. (b) $48P8Q6R9S31 = 48 \div 8 + 6 \times 9 - 31$

$= 6 + 54 - 31 = 29.$

5. (a)

6. (b) Ratio of investment = Ratio of profit share

Let Shyamdas invested for month n.

Then, $\frac{90000 \times 12}{30000 \times n} = \frac{4}{1}$ $\quad \therefore n = 9$

Hence, Syamdas join the business after 12 – 9 = 3

7. (c) Methane (Marsh Gas) is produced when vegetation decomposes (anaerobic digestion) naturally in marshes, swamps, and bogs.

8. (c) Hawa Mahal made with the red and pink sandstone, sits on the edge of the City Palace, Jaipur, and extends to the women's chambers. Built in 1799 by Maharaja Sawai Pratap Singh.

9. (c) Sum of angles of a triangle = 180°

$x + 2x + 3x = 180$

$6x = 180 \Rightarrow x = 30$

Largest angle $3 \times 30 = 90°$

10. (c) According to the given statement, there is no monitoring system.

11. (a)

12. (d) Sum of 22 observations = 22 × 10 = 220

Sum of 24 observations = 24 × 11 = 264

Sum of last 2 observations = 264 – 220 = 44

Mean of two observation = $\frac{44}{2} = 22.$

13. (b) Let one angle is x, then complement angle = (90 – x)

$\because \quad x - \frac{1}{3}(90 - x) = 10$

$3x - 90 + x = 30$

$4x = 120 \Rightarrow x = 30°$

Larger angle = 90 – 30 = 60°

14. (b) Neelam and Manisha running in same direction.

So, relative speed = 9 – 7 = 2 kmph.

Required time = $\frac{12}{2}$ = 6 hours.

15. (a) Distance covered in 40 minutes

$= 48 \times \frac{40}{60} = 32$

Required speed = $\frac{32}{\frac{32}{60}}$ = 60 km/hr

16. (c) Coefficient of variation = $\frac{\text{S.D.}}{\text{Mean}} \times 100$

$= \frac{7}{13} \times 100 = 53.85\%$

17. (c) Friction force resists motion between two touching and moving surfaces. When you apply brakes, it creates friction between the brake pads and discs; and, therefore, slows down or stops the car.

18. (b) Knowledge is not a skill. It is learning and experience. Knowledge and skill are two different things.

19. (c) Depleting natural resources is a major concern in our country. Use of renewable energy sources is a solution to counter increase in population.

20. (b) A quartz clock uses an electronic oscillator regulated by a quartz crystal to keep time. This crystal oscillator creates precise frequency. So, quartz clocks are more accurate than mechanical clocks.

Quartz is piezoelectric that accumulates electrical charge when subjected to stress.

21. (b) The president is the head of the state and commander-in-chief of the Armed Forces. The position is largely a ceremonial one and executive powers are de facto exercised by the prime minister.

22. (b) Bangladesh is a parliamentary democracy.

23. (a)

24. (c) Assam and Chhattisgarh share border with 7 states. Assam bordering states – West Bengal, Arunachal Pradesh, Nagaland, Manipur, Mizoram, Tripura and Meghalaya.

25. (c) Squash is a ball and racquet sport played by two or four players in a four-walled court with a small, rubber ball.

26. (b) The Malaysian star Michelle Yeoh was appointed UNDP Goodwill Ambassador in 2016 to raise awareness and mobilize support for the sustainable development goals to end poverty by the year 2030.

27. (a) Deliquescence - substance absorbs moisture from the atmosphere.

28. (c) Milk sold to the consumers is standardized with different fat content. Whole milk, (semi)-skimmed, and buttermilk have different fat content in them.

29. (c) Birds fly with the help of wings, like that fish can swim with the help of fins.

30. (c) Here (A) is true but (R) is false. Perennial rivers mostly originate from the Himalayas.

31. (c) 3, 7, 13, 21, 31, 43

(+4, +6, +8, +10, +12)

32. (d)

33. (b)

T A B L E
↓−2 ↓−2 ↓−2 ↓−2 ↓−2
R Y Z J C

Similarly,

C H A I R
↓−2 ↓−2 ↓−2 ↓−2 ↓−2
A F Y Z P

34. (d) Stainless steel is an alloy, made up of iron steel with chromium, nickel, molybdenum, silicon, aluminium and carbon.

35. (a) Darjeeling tea is the first GI tagged product in India. GI sign tells about the regional origin of the product.

36. (d) The freezing point of water is 32°F and boiling point is 212°F (at standard atmospheric pressure).

37. (d) A D G J, (+3 +3 +3) C F I L, (+3 +3 +3)

E H K N, (+3 +3 +3) G J M P, (+3 +3 +3)

38. (a) $1000\left[1+\frac{4}{100}\right]^2 - 1000 = \frac{1000 \times r \times 1}{100}$

$(1.04)^2 - 1 = \frac{r}{100} \Rightarrow r = 8.16\%$

39. (c) DOC/DOCX are document format used by Microsoft. Both are open, but DOCX is more efficient and creates smaller, less corruptible files.

40. (a) $\frac{35}{2 \times 100} \times 800 - \frac{45}{2 \times 100} \times 400$

$140 - 90 = 50$ gm.

41. (a) 12 men complete work in 6 days $= \frac{1}{4}$th

So, 12 " " whole work in $6 \times 4 = 24$

To complete whole work in 6 days, number of men required $= 12 \times 4 = 48$ men.

So, additional men required $= 48 - 12 = 36$

42. (a) + = male and − = female

(−)D —— (+)B —— (−)C ⟺ K(+) (Spouse)

(+)E —— F(−) (below C)

So, D is maternal aunt of F.

43. (a) Ophiuchus is a large constellation straddling the celestial equator.

44. (c)

45. (a) In biology, taxonomy means 'arrangement'. It is the science of naming, defining and classifying organisms on the basis of shared characteristics.

46. (a) Let cost price of money card is ₹ x.

S.P. $= x \times \frac{150}{100} = \frac{3}{2}x$

Sale tax $= \frac{3}{2}x \times \frac{25}{100} = \frac{3}{8}x$

$\therefore \frac{3}{2}x + \frac{3}{8}x = 625$

$\left(\frac{4 \times 3 + 3}{8}\right)x = 625$

$\frac{15}{8}x = 625 \Rightarrow x = \frac{625 \times 8}{15} = ₹\ 333$

47. (b)

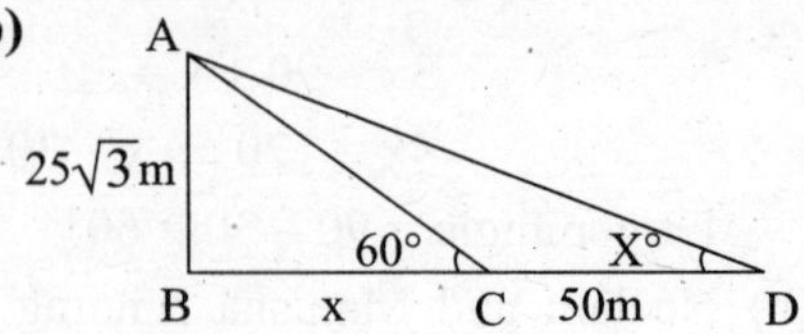

Let BC is the shadow of the tower = x

Then, In $\triangle$ ABC,

$\tan 60 = \frac{25\sqrt{3}}{x} \Rightarrow x = \frac{25\sqrt{3}}{\sqrt{3}} = 25$ m

$\therefore$ BC = 25 m

In $\triangle$ ABD, $\tan X = \frac{AB}{BD} = \frac{25\sqrt{3}}{25 + 50}$

$= \frac{25\sqrt{3}}{75} = \frac{25\sqrt{3}}{25 \times 3} = \frac{\sqrt{3}}{\sqrt{3} \times \sqrt{3}} = \frac{1}{\sqrt{3}}$

$\tan X = \frac{1}{\sqrt{3}} \Rightarrow X = 30°$

48. (a) Total work = 30 × 20

Work done in 6 days = 30 × 6

Remaining work = 30 × 14

Let x people left the work $\Rightarrow$ 30 × 14 work is to be done by (30 – x) people

$\Rightarrow 30 \times 14 = (30 - x) \times 20$

Number of men required

$(30 - x) = \frac{30 \times 14}{20} = 21.$

So, number of men = 30 – 21 = 9 men

49. (c) ATQ, Let capital is ₹ P.

$\frac{P \times 5 \times 2}{2 \times 100} + \frac{P}{4} \times \frac{10 \times 2}{100} + \frac{P}{4} \times \frac{8 \times 2}{100} = 2800$

$\frac{20P}{400} + \frac{20P}{400} + \frac{16P}{400} = 2800 \Rightarrow P = 20000$

50. (d)

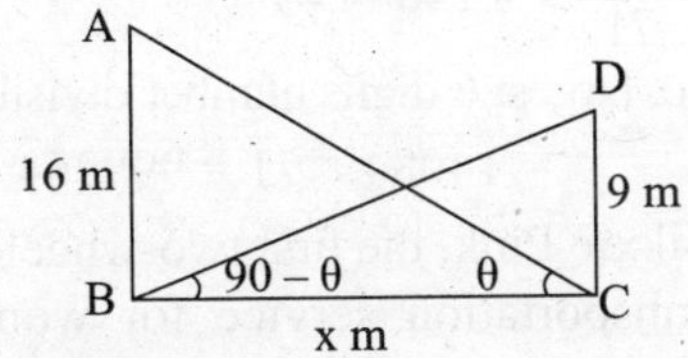

From $\triangle$ ABC,

$\tan\theta = \frac{AB}{BC} = \frac{16}{x}$ ....(i)

From $\triangle$ BCD,

$\cot(90 - \theta) = \frac{BC}{CD} = \frac{x}{9}$

$\tan\theta = \frac{x}{9}$ ...(ii)

From (i) and (ii) ,

$\frac{16}{x} = \frac{x}{9} \Rightarrow x^2 = 144 = 12$ m.

51. (c) A lubricant is used to reduce friction between surfaces in contact; reduces the heat generated when the surfaces move.

52-54:

Ramesh < Suresh < Pritesh < Jinesh < Rakesh

Shortest | Tallest

52. (b) Ramesh is shortest.

53. (d) Here Jayesh is taller then Suresh but that is not enough data to give the answer.

54. (b) Pritesh is shorter then Rakesh.

55. (c) From (i), (ii) and (iii)

We get that code of 'S' is '8'.

56. (b) That woman is the mother of that man.

57. (b) As $\triangle$ PQR and $\triangle$ XYZ are similar, then.

$\frac{PQ}{XY} = \frac{QR}{YZ} = \frac{PR}{XZ} \Rightarrow \frac{PQ}{18} = \frac{QR}{12}$

$= \frac{PQ}{QR} = \frac{18}{12} = \frac{3}{2}$

58. (b) In 1930, Tombaugh discovered the tiny, distant planet Pluto.

59. (c) Let two numbers are 3x and 5x.

ATQ,

$\frac{3x + 10}{5x + 10} = \frac{5}{7} \Rightarrow 7(3x + 10) = 5(5x + 10)$

$21x + 70 = 25x + 50$

$4x = 20 \Rightarrow x = 5$

So, smaller number = 3 × 5 = 15.

60. (d) In 1955, the government of India and RBI assumed joint ownership of Imperial Bank of India, and renamed it State Bank of India.

61. (a) Let quantity of milk in two vessels is 2x and 3x and quantity of water in two vessels be 7y and 5y respectively.

Then, $\frac{2x + 7y}{3x + 5y} = 1$

$2x + 7y = 3x + 5y \Rightarrow 2y = x$

$\therefore \frac{x}{y} = \frac{2}{1}$

62. (c) $335 \times 335 - 165 \times 165 = (335)^2 - (165)^2$

$= (335 + 165)(335 - 165)$

$= 500 \times 170 = 85000$

63. **(d)** Tomatoes are considered vegetables by nutritionists. Botanically, a fruit is a ripened flower ovary and contains seeds. Tomatoes, zucchinis are all edible fruits.

64. **(d)** The six-day long week saw the participation from 1,500 foreign companies and business delegations from 65 countries. Showcased the potential of design, innovation and sustainability across India's manufacturing sectors.

65. **(b)** Channai is the capital of Tamil Nadu, like that Ranchi is the capital of Jharkhand.

66. **(d)** The best situation fits in the above statement is more number of vehicles on the road leads to traffic confection.

67. **(c)** The Forbidden City is a palace in Beijing, China. It houses the Palace Museum, and was the imperial palace from the Ming to the end of the Qing dynasty.

68. **(c)** Rate of heat conduction in solids does not depend on friction.

69. **(c)**

70. **(a)** Sustainable Livelihoods is the theme for World Wetlands Day in 2016.

71. **(d)** + = male and – = female

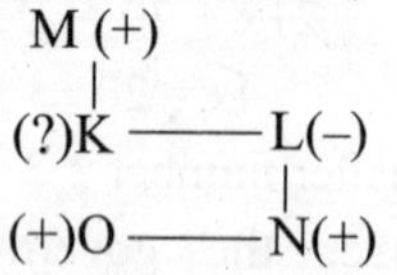

As gender of K is not given. So, we can not find the relation between K and N.

72. **(a)** Chlorofluorocarbon (CFC) refrigerants were commonly used before 1995.

73. **(b)** $x^2 + \frac{1}{x^2} = 6 \Rightarrow x^2 + \frac{1}{x^2} - 2 = 4$

$= \left(x - \frac{1}{x}\right)^2 = (2)^2 \Rightarrow x - \frac{1}{x} = \pm 2$

Now,

$10 - \frac{10}{x} = 10\left(x - \frac{1}{x}\right) = 10\,(\pm 20) = \pm 20$

74. **(b)** Halley's Comet is a 'periodic' comet and returns to Earth's vicinity every 75 years. The last time it was here was in 1986, and it is projected to return in 2061.

75. **(b)** Asymmetric digital subscriber line (ADSL) is a digital subscriber line (DSL) technology that enables faster data transmission over copper telephone lines.

76. **(c)** Manohar Parikar was Chief Minister of Goa. He also served as Defence Minister.

77. **(c)** $25 \div 25 + 5 \div 2 - 15 = 25 + 25 \div 5 + 2 \times 15$

$25 + 5 + 30 = 60.$

78. **(a)** From question, we have in

SMART = 31524 ...(i)

MARBLE = 428376 ...(ii)

EAT = 537 ...(iii)

From (i), (ii) and (iii) A = 3

From (i) and (iii) T = 5, E = 7

From (i) and (ii), S = 1, M or R = 2 or R

$\therefore$ STABLE = 618537

79. **(d)** Here peta byte is different from other three optical disc, magnetic storage and solid state drive.

80. **(c)**

81. **(b)** Variance = $(\text{S.D.})^2 = (9.5)^2 = 90.25$

82. **(c)** Largest 6 digits number = 999999

on dividing by 71, we get

$\frac{999999}{71} = 14084.49$

So, largest 6 digits number divisible by 71

$= 14084 \times 71 = 999964$

83. **(a)** Bikxie Pink, the first two-wheeler public transportation service for women was started by a couple Divya Kalia and Mohit Sharma.

84. **(b)** $\left(a - \frac{1}{a}\right) = \frac{3}{4}$, Then,

$a^3 - \frac{1}{a^3} = \left(a - \frac{1}{a}\right)\left(a^2 + \frac{1}{a^2} + 1\right)$

$= \frac{3}{4}\left[\left(a - \frac{1}{a}\right)^2 + 3\right]$

$= \frac{3}{4}\left[\left(\frac{3}{4}\right)^2 + 3\right] = \frac{3}{4} \times \frac{57}{16} = \frac{171}{64}$

85. **(d)** Numbers is H.C.F. of (3050 – 7) and (5200 – 9)

= H.C.F. of 3043 and 5191 = 179

86. (c) Make employees in India = 125 + 25 = 150

Total employees of company = 305 + 240 + 285 + 170 = 1000

% of male employees = $\frac{150}{1000} \times 100 = 15\%$

87. (d) Total number of employees in the company = 1000.

88. (b) Female employees in US = 70 + 35 = 105

Female employees in Canada = 50 + 10 = 60

Required ratio = $\frac{105}{60} = \frac{21}{12} = \frac{7}{4}$

89. (d) India was an independent dominion in the British Commonwealth of Nations between 15 August 1947 and 26 January 1950. It was created by the Indian Independence Act 1947 and was transformed into the Republic of India by the promulgation of the Constitution of India in 1950.

90. (c)

91. (c) Average = $\frac{11(1 + 2 + 3 \text{ ------} + 25)}{25}$

$= \frac{11 \times 25 \times 26}{25 \times 2} = 143$

92. (b) $2x(x + y + z) + 2y(x + y + z) + 2z(x + y + z) = 250 + 100 + 100$

$= (x + y + z)(2x + 2y + 2z) = 450$

$= 2(x + y + z)^2 = 450$

$= (x + y + z)^2 = 225 \Rightarrow x + y + z = 15$

Now, $2x(15) = 250 \Rightarrow x = \frac{25}{3}$

$2y(15) = 100 \Rightarrow y = \frac{10}{3}$

$2z(15) = 100 \Rightarrow z = \frac{10}{3}$

Now, $3x + 6y + 15z =$

$= \frac{25}{3} \times 3 + \frac{10}{3} \times 6 + \frac{10}{3} \times 15$

$= 25 + 20 + 50 = 95.$

93. (c) The Kakori case was a train robbery that took place in 1925 during the Indian Independence Movement against the British Government. The robbery was organised by Hindustan Republican Association (HRA).

94. (a) Cost price of the article

$= 979 \times \frac{100}{(100 - 11)} = 1100$

Profit = 1232 – 1100 = 132

Profit% = = 12%

95. (c) Let two numbers are 2x and 3x.

Then, product of numbers = L.C.M. × H.C.F.

$2x \times 3x = 270 \times 45$

$6x^2 = 12150 \Rightarrow x^2 = 2025$

$x = 45$

Hence, smaller number = 2x = 2 × 45 = 90

Now, $(90)^2 = 8100$

96. (a) Bronchitis is an inflammation of the lining of the airways that connect the windpipe to the lungs.

97-99:

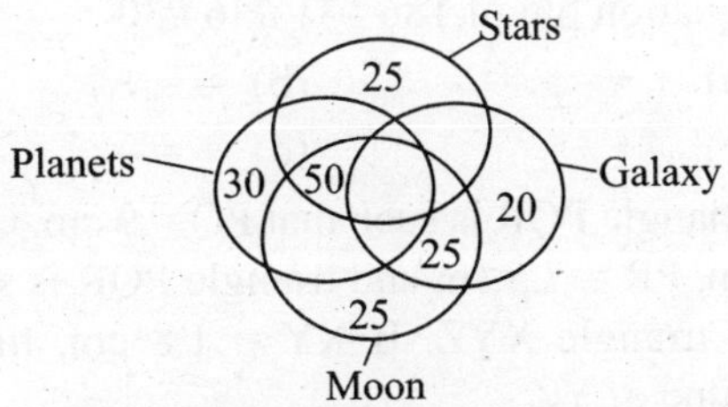

Total number of kids, who wanted to see stars or planets or galaxy or moon = 25 + 30 + 20 + 25 + 25 + 50 = 175

97. (c) Kids who didn't want to see only galaxy

= 175 – 20 = 155

98. (c) Kids who wanted to see the moon

= 25 + 25 + 50 = 100

99. (c) Kids who wanted to see at least 2 object.

= 25 + 50 = 75

100. (b) Let marked price is ₹ x.

Then, cost price = $x \times \frac{50}{100} = \frac{x}{2}$

$\Rightarrow \frac{x}{2} \times \left(\frac{100 + 35}{100}\right) = 8100$

$x = \frac{8100 + 200}{135} = ₹\ 12000$

RRB NTPC stage-I Solved Paper

Held On 19th April 2016 (Shift-II)

1. If **'how are you'** is written as **'ne kl se'** and **'where are you'** as **'ne bl se'** and **'you were here'** as **'ke ne jo'**, then **'how you here'** is written as
(a) ke kl ne (b) se ne kl
(c) ne bl ke (d) bl se ne

2. ____________ is not a type of heat transfer.
(a) Diffusion (b) Reflection
(c) Convection (d) Radiation

3. International Women's day is celebrated on _____ March every year.
(a) 6th (b) 7th (c) 8th (d) 9th

4. Replace # sign with the mathematical operators '+', '÷', '–' or = to get balanced equation out of 186 #31 #36 #30
(a) + ÷ = (b) – = +
(c) – + ÷ (d) ÷ = –

5. Triangle PQR is such that PQ = 9 cm, QR = 6 cm, PR = 7.5 cm and triangle PQR is similar to triangle XYZ. If XY = 1.8 cm, find the value of YZ.
(a) 15 cm (b) 18 cm
(c) 12 cm (d) 9 cm

6. ________ is used as a stabilizer in ice cream.
(a) Gelatin (b) Sugar
(c) Milk (d) Strawberry

7. The major ingredient of sweetened soft drink is
(a) Carbonated water (b) Hydrochloric acid
(c) Phosphoric acid (d) Caffeine

8. ₹ 10000 is being compounded at 20% per annum. Calculate the amount after 2 years if rate of interest is charged half yearly.
(a) ₹ 10041 (b) ₹ 14641
(c) ₹ 12000 (d) ₹ 13660

9. Pakistani film industry is known as ________
(a) Pollywood (b) Lollywood
(c) Kollywood (d) Mollywood

10. The mean of a distribution is 18 and the standard deviation is 4.5. What is the value of the coefficient of variation?
(a) 50% (b) 25% (c) 100% (d) 75%

11. If $a^3 + b^3 + c^3 - 3abc = 0$, then find the value of $(a^2/bc + b^2/ac - 3)$.
(a) $-c^2/ab$ (b) $-c^2/bc$
(c) $-c^3/ba$ (d) $-c/a$

12. Pointing to a woman, I said that her brother's only son is the brother of my wife. How is the woman related to me?
(a) Father-in-law's sister
(b) Mother-in-law
(c) Sister-in-law
(d) Sister

13. Which of the following states does not share a border with Myanmar?
(a) Assam (b) Mizoram
(c) Nagaland (d) Manipur

14. Geographical Indication (GI) is related to ____________ having unique geographic origin and evolution over centuries.
(a) Hills (b) Mountain ranges
(c) Plains (d) Products

15. In March 2016 Election Commission of India declared assembly elections in _____ states scheduled for April May 2016.
(a) 3 (b) 7 (c) 5 (d) 6

16. 10 persons can do a job in X days. If 20 persons with twice the efficiency can do the same job in 5 days, then find the value of X?
(a) 40 (b) 15 (c) 20 (d) 30

17. P can do a piece of work in 60 days & Q can do the same work in 50 days. Find the ratio of working efficiencies of P to Q.
(a) 1/3 (b) 6/5 (c) 5/6 (d) 4/5

18. A kite is flying at a height of 50m. If the length of string is 100m then the inclination of string to the horizontal ground in degree measures is:

(a) 90 (b) 45 (c) 60 (d) 30

19. Retinol is mainly related to ________

(a) Vitamin A (b) Vitamin B
(c) Vitamin D (d) Vitamin E

20. A lady said that father of Rahul's father is my father. How is the lady related to Rahul?

(a) Mother (b) Paternal aunt
(c) Sister (d) Niece

21. Bollywood actor ________ has been selected for the 47th Dadasaheb Phalke Award for 2015.

(a) Dilip Kumar (b) Manoj Kumar
(c) Rajinikanth (d) Anupam Kher

22. Read the given statement carefully and answer the question.

A group of people getting together casually without prior planning and in a relaxed manner is called informal gathering.

Which of the following situations better fits the above statement?

(a) A group celebrates every month on salary day.
(b) Invitees gather on the occasion of wedding reception.
(c) Soon after the release of mark list, top 10 rankers gather to greet each other.
(d) People gather to witness beating retreat at Wagah border in Amritsar.

23. Sleep apnea is related to ________ while sleeping.

(a) walking (b) talking
(c) snoring (d) smiling

24. Boiling point of water is ________.

(a) 210°F (b) 212°F
(c) 214°F (d) 208°F

25. Circumvent : Bypass : : Comprehensible :

(a) Understandable (b) Unclear
(c) Grasping (d) Apprehend

26. Find the sum of first 8 odd prime numbers.

(a) 77 (b) 98 (c) 75 (d) 100

27. If a = 2b/3, b = 2c/3, and c = 2d/3, then find the ratio of b and d:

(a) 8/9 (b) 4/9 (c) 4/3 (d) 5/27

28. Window's 10 is

(a) an utility software.
(b) a browser.
(c) an application software.
(d) an operating system.

29. One of the techniques used for desalination of sea water is

(a) Filtration (b) Distillation
(c) Evaporation (d) Condensation

DIRECTIONS (Qs. 30-32): *The following table represents the number of fans of stars MSD, VK, RD and SR in different areas of a town. Consider the information and answer the following questions based on it.*

	Area 1	Area 2	Area 3	Area 4
VK	2500	1700	2300	5000
MSD	3000	3000	4000	3100
RD	1500	3500	4500	5200
SR	1500	4000	3500	2500

30. What is the difference between the numbers of fans of Area 2 to that of Area 3?

(a) Area 2 has 2200 more fans
(b) Area 2 has 2100 less fans
(c) Area 3 has 2200 more fans
(d) Area 3 has 2200 less fans

31. What is the difference between the total number of fans of SR and MSD?

(a) 1500 (b) 1600
(c) 3000 (d) 3200

32. In all. Who has the highest number of fans?

(a) VK (b) MSD
(c) RD (d) SR

33. Echocardiogram is more closely related to
(a) Doppler effect (b) Zeeman effect
(c) Photoelectric effect (d) Magnetic effect

34. Statements followed by some conclusions are given below.

Statements:

1. Compulsive online shopping has become a common behaviour among youngsters.
2. This is evident from most of those seeking counselling for de-addiction.

Conclusions:

I. All youngsters are addicted online shopping.
II. All youngsters seek counselling for de-addiction.

Find which of the given conclusions logically follows from the given statements.
(a) Only conclusion I follows
(b) Only conclusion II follows
(c) Both I and II follow
(d) Neither I nor II follows

35. In a mixture 25 litres, the ratio of milk and water is 4:1. How many litres of milk must be added to make the ratio 16:1?
(a) 21 (b) 25 (c) 60 (d) 36

36 World Wetland day is celebrated every year on _____ February.
(a) 2nd (b) 3rd (c) 4th (d) 5th

37. Night blindness : Sight :: _______ : speech
(a) Talk (b) Stutter
(c) Speak (d) Lecture

38. Davis Cup 2015 final was held in
(a) UK (b) Australia
(c) Belgium (d) Argentina

39. Mohan starts to calculate sum of all odd natural number less than 83. What result does he get?
(a) 1456 (b) 1681 (c) 1437 (d) 1671

40. 'Start' menu in a standard personal computer is
(a) Part of the hardware
(b) A set of options and commands
(c) Nothing but the status bar
(d) Network related

41. If the mathematical operator '÷' means '×', '+' means '–', '×' means '+' and '–' means '÷', then **24 + 48 – 12 × 4 ÷ 2 = ?**
(a) 6 (b) –6 (c) 16 (d) 28

42. Avalanche : Ice :: Volcano :
(a) Lava (b) Sand
(c) Heat (d) Earth

43. The process of reducing the milk fat globules size to allow them to stay evenly distributed in milk is called __________.
(a) Standardization (b) Pasteurization
(c) Homogenization (d) Fortification

44. __________ was the 3rd Mughal Emperor of India.
(a) Humayun (b) Akbar
(c) Aurangzeb (d) Jahangir

45. Velocity of a car does not depend on
(a) Speedometer
(b) Change in direction
(c) Change in speed
(d) Change in acceleration

46. The Colosseum, known as the Flavran amphitheater, is located in __________.
(a) Venice (b) Rome
(c) Milan (d) Vatican City

47. Mukesh got series of discount 30%, 25%, 15% on his shirt. Find out the single equivalent discount.
(a) 52.34% (b) 38.35%
(c) 55.38% (d) 57.38%

48. In March 2016 National Green Tribunal imposed an initial compensation of Rs. 5 Crore on ______________ for tampering with the Yamuna river's flood plains.
(a) Kalki Avatar Foundation
(b) Art of Living Foundation
(c) Emissaries of Divine Light
(d) Sant Nirankari Mission

49. The ancient Indian legal document 'Manusmriti' was written in ________.

(a) Tamil (b) Hindi
(c) Sanskrit (d) Bengali

50. Find the missing (?) in the series:

...., FHJ, KMO, PRT, ?

(a) UVZ (b) UXZ
(c) UVW (d) UWY

51. India won the 2016 Asia Cup T20 held in Bangladesh by ________ wickets.

(a) 7 (b) 6 (c) 5 (d) 8

52. Kakori train robbery was organized by the ________ in 1925.

(a) Swaraj Party
(b) Indian National Congress
(c) Anushilan Samiti
(d) Hindustan Republican Association

53. The mean of 20 observations is 19. One more observation is included and the new mean becomes 20. The 21th observation is:

(a) 20 (b) 30 (c) 40 (d) 42

54. Golconda Fort was built during ________.

(a) Vijayanagara Empire
(b) Qutb Shahi dynasty
(c) Satavahana dynasty
(d) Hoysala Dynasty

55. Provincial Autonomy was provided by ______

(a) The Government of India Act 1935
(b) The Montague-Chelmsford Report
(c) The Government of India Act 1919
(d) The Indian Independence Act 1947

56. Who is number 1 in the Forbes 2016 ranking of World's billionaires?

(a) Warren Buffet (b) Amancio Ortega
(c) Bill Gates (d) Carlos Slim Helu

57. In a factory, 60 workers can stitch 120 m of clothes in 7 days, what length of clothes can be stitched by 70 workers in 5 days?

(a) 100 m (b) 90 m
(c) 85 m (d) 110 m

58. Which one reveals, more appropriately, functioning of the heart?

(a) Electrocardiogram (b) Echocardiogram
(c) Stethoscope (d) Lipid profile

59. Given that $(a^2 + b^2) = 60$, then find the value of $(a + b)^2 + (a - b)^2$.

(a) 90 (b) 120
(c) 140 (d) 150

60. Mother of K's father is the sister of G. S is the daughter of G. How is S related to K's father?

(a) Cousin sister
(b) Mother
(c) Paternal Aunt
(d) Cannot be determined.

61. A balloon is connected to a meteorological station by a cable of length 130 m. inclined at 60° to the horizontal. Find the height of the balloon from the ground. Assume that there is no slack in cable.

(a) 110.32 m (b) 173 m
(c) 163.25 m (d) 112.58 m

62. Orbital period of Halley's comet is ______ years.

(a) 25 (b) 50 (c) 75 (d) 100

63. Find the greatest number which on dividing 1580 and 3800 leaves remainders 8 and 1 respectively.

(a) 262 (b) 131 (c) 65.5 (d) 393

64. Which one is not the cause of kidney stone formation?

(a) Drinking more water
(b) Diabetic mellitus
(c) Taking nuts rich in oxalate
(d) Eating lot of stone forming foods

65. If the angles of a triangle are in the ratio of 2:3:5, then find the ratio of the greatest angle to the smallest angle.

(a) 7 : 2 (b) 5 : 2
(c) 5 : 3 (d) 3 : 5

66. The annual financial statement prepared under article 112 of the Indian Constitution is called ________.
(a) Public account
(b) Consolidated account
(c) Budget
(d) Revenue account

67. Ram travels 4/9th of the total journey by bus. 5/18th by rail and the remaining 10 km on foot. Find the distance of total journey.
(a) 42 km (b) 90km
(c) 36km (d) 18km

68. If a = 5, b = 4, c = 8 then find the value of $(a^3 + b^3 + c^3 - 3abc)/(ab + bc + ca - a^2 - b^2 - c^2)$.
(a) 15 (b) 17 (c) – 17 (d) – 15

69. The average age of a batch of 19 members is 24 years. If the age of the faculty be included, then the average increases by 4 months. What is the age of the faculty?
(a) 35 years (b) 30 years 8 months
(c) 37 years 4 months (d) 32 years 8 months

70. Courtroom : Judge :: Stadium : ________.
(a) Landlord (b) Organizer
(d) Referee (d) Promoter

71. The tennis star, ________ was provisionally suspended after testing positive for banned drugs during Australian open 2016.
(a) Maria Sharapova (b) Serena Williams
(c) Ana Ivanovic (d) Andy Murray

DIRECTIONS (Qs. 72-74): *Consider the following information and answer the questions based on it.*

Out of the 75 birders, 15 wanted to see only sunbird. 10 wanted to see only flycatcher, 12 wanted to see both sunbird and nuthatch, 15 wanted to see only bee-eater, 13 wanted to see both sunbird and bee-eater, 5 wanted to see both flycatcher and nuthatch and the remaining wanted to see only nuthatch.

72. The difference between the birders who want to see sunbird and those who want to see flycatcher is
(a) 12 (b 25 (c) 30 (d) 15

73. How many birders wanted to see only one bird?
(a) 30 (b) 40 (c) 45 (d) 50

74. The ratio of birders who like nuthatch to those who like bee-eaters is
(a) 11/14 (b) 10/7
(c) 11/20 (d) 30/8

75. Find the missing (?) in the series:
9, 4, 16, 6, 36, 9, 81, ?
(a) 12 (b) 10 (c) 11 (d) 13

76. Charles Wilkinson's English version of Bhagavad Gita was first published in the year
(a) 1685 (b) 1725
(c) 1785 (d) 1885

77. A sum of money of ₹1000 is lent out in two parts in such a way that the interest on one part at 10% per annum for 5 years is equal to another at 5% for 10 years. Calculate the sum lent out at 5%.
(a) ₹ 500 (b) ₹ 800
(c) ₹ 1000 (d) ₹ 1200

78. In a certain code, **329** means **'you are bad'**, **419** means **'bad is good'** and 195 means 'nothing is bad' ________ represents 'good'.
(a) 9 (b) 4 (c) 1 (d) 3

79. Any online 'demo' is ________
(a) An interactive presentation
(b) A non-interactive presentation
(c) Not a sequential presentation
(d) An active user interface

80. In a certain code, **324** means **'are you alright'**. **783** means **'you come home'** and **9271** means **'we are at home'**. Which digit represents 'come'?
(a) 8 (b) 9 (c) 7 (d) 3

81. The game of football is also referred to as ________.
(a) Rugby (b) Poker
(c) Soccer (d) Ping-Pong

82. Rearrange the jumbled letters to make meaningful words and then select the one which is different.

(a) OMESU (b) ROTINOM
(c) RETIAW (d) RETNTRP

83. Find the odd pair out.

(a) Nitrogen : Air
(b) Hydrogen : Water
(c) Uranium : Coins
(d) Sulphur : Match stick

84. Neeraj purchased few shirts for his shop at cost prices ranging from ₹ 400 to ₹ 550 and sold at prices ranging from ₹ 450 to ₹ 650. What is the maximum profit that might be made in selling 10 shifts?

(a) ₹ 2800 (b) ₹ 2500
(c) ₹ 2400 (d) ₹ 2000

85. As per historical astronomy there are ________ zodiac divisions.

(a) 9 (b) 10 (c) 11 (d) 12

86. How much is the maximum % discount that Sheela can offer to her customer on her Marked Price so that she sells her product at no profit or loss, if she had already marked her product by 25% more than the cost price?

(a) 25% (b) 20% (c) 30% (d) 40%

87. If the standard deviation of a population is 10, what would be the population variance?

(a) 100 (b) 30 (c) 5 (d) 20

88. An assertion (A) and a reason (R) are given below.

Assertion. (A): Electric wires are generally made of copper.

Reason (R): Copper is a good conductor of electricity.

Choose the correct option.

(a) Both A and R are true and R is the correct explanation of A
(b) Both A and R are true, but R is not the correct explanation of A
(c) A is true, but R is false
(d) Ais false, but R is true

89. Ram is thrice as fast as Mohan and Mohan is twice as fast as Sohan. The distance covered by Sohan in 42 minutes will be covered by Mohan in:

(a) 18 minutes (b) 21 minutes
(c) 20 minutes (d) 22 minutes

90. An angle is 60° more than one fifth of its complement. Find the smaller angle in degrees.

(a) 65° (b) 35° (c) 25° (d) 45°

DIRECTIONS (Qs. 91-93): *Consider the following information and answer questions based on it.*

Seven coloured bottles— brown, blue, black, violet, white, indigo and purple are kept in a row, in random order, from left to right such that the —

1. White and purple bottles are not at either extremes.
2. Brown bottle is to the immediate right of violet bottle and to the immediate left of the white bottle.
3. White, violet and brown bottles are not at the center.
4. Black bottle is to the immediate left of purple bottle.
5. Blue bottle is neither second last nor at either extremes.

91. Bottles at the extreme right and left ends are

(a) Violet and purple (b) Indigo and violet
(c) Black and indigo (d) Black and violet

92. Which bottle is at the center of the row?

(a) Black bottle (b) Indigo bottle
(c) Blue bottle (d) Purple bottle

93. Which of the following statement is correct?

(a) Indigo bottle is to the immediate left of the purple bottle.
(b) Blue is to the immediate right of the purple bottle.
(c) There are at least five bottles between brown and black.

(d) Black bottle is to the immediate right of the blue bottle.

94. Statements followed by some conclusions are given below.

Statements:

1. Demand and supply determine the prices of goods and services.
2. When there are too many buyers, prices are pushed up and too many sellers push down prices.

Conclusions:

I. Buyers and sellers determine the prices.

II. Price discovery is market driven.

Find which of the given conclusions logically follows from the given statements.

(a) Only conclusion I follows
(b) Only conclusion II follows
(c) Both I and II follow
(d) Neither I nor II follows

95. Find the value of 6 + 11 + 16 + 21 +...... + 71.

(a) 539 (b) 561 (c) 661 (d) 639

96. The astronomer who discovered planet Pluto was ____________

(a) Sylvain Arend (b) Joseph Asbrook
(c) Edwin Hubble (d) Clyde Tombaugh

97. Read the given statements carefully and answer the question.

Statement: the main reasons behind cyber criminals using international phone numbers to cheat the public, by asking their secured credit card details are

(i) it is easy to convince people and

(ii) it is difficult to trace the calls coming from foreign countries.

Which of the following is true according to the given statement?

(a) There are only two reasons behind such calls.
(b) People have full faith in foreign calls.
(c) It is not possible to trace foreign calls.
(d) Cyber criminals prefer international calls to cheat gullible people.

98. Three numbers are in the ratio of 3:5:10 and LCM is 630. Find their HCF.

(a) 21 (b) 42 (c) 63 (d) 36

99. 3 years ago, the ratio of Maya's and Shikha's age was 5:9 respectively. After 5 years, this ratio would become 3 : 5. Find present age of Maya?

(a) 40 (b) 45 (c) 43 (d) 53

100. If **'god is fair'** = **'ge se fa'**, **'who is god'** = **'ge we fa'** and **'you are god'** = **'ne le fa'**, which code does represent 'is'?

(a) se (b) ge (c) fa (d) we

Hints & Solutions

1. (a) how are you — ne kl se

where are you — ne bl se

you where here — ke ne jo

Hence, 'how you here' — 'kl ne ke'.

2. (b) **3. (c)**

4. (d) 186#31#36#30 = 186 ÷ 31 = 36 – 30

= 6 = 6.

5. (c) As $\triangle$ PQR and $\triangle$ XYZ are similar, then.

$$\frac{PQ}{XY} = \frac{QR}{YZ} = \frac{PR}{XZ}$$

$$\frac{9}{18} = \frac{6}{YZ} \Rightarrow YZ = \frac{6 \times 18}{9} = 12 \text{ cm.}$$

6. (a) The stabilizers (gelatin) are usually polysaccharide food gums responsible for adding viscosity to the mix and the unfrozen phase of the ice cream.

Without the stabilizers, the ice cream would become coarse and icy.

7. (a) A soft drink contains carbonated water, a sweetener, and a natural or artificial flavouring. The sweetener may be a sugar, high-fructose corn syrup, fruit juice, or some combination of these. They are about 90 percent water.

8. (b) $\text{C.I.} = P\left(1+\frac{r}{100}\right)^t$

$= 10000\left(1+\frac{20}{200}\right)^4 \Rightarrow 10000(1.1)^4$

$= 10000 \times 1.4641 = ₹\ 14641$

9. (b)

10. (b) Coefficient of variation $= \frac{\text{S.D.}}{\text{Mean}} \times 100$

$= \frac{4.5}{18} \times 100 = 25\%$

11. (a) $a^3+b^3+c^3-3abc=0 \Rightarrow a^3+b^3-3abc=-c^3$

$\frac{a^3+b^3-3abc}{abc} = \frac{-c^3}{abc}$

Now, $\frac{a^2}{bc}+\frac{b^2}{ca}-3=-\frac{c^2}{ab}$

12. (a) Woman's brother's only son is the brother of my wife ⇒ woman's brother is my father-in-law.

∴ Woman is father-in-law's sister.

13. (a) Northeast Indian states that share the border with Myanmar are Arunachal Pradesh, Nagaland, Mizoram, and Manipur.

14. (d) A geographical indication (GI) is a sign used on products which corresponds to a specific geographical location or origin certifying that the product possesses certain qualities; is made by traditional methods; or enjoys a certain reputation.

15. (c)

16. (c) 20 persons can do work in 5 days

Then, 10 persons " " $= 5 \times 2 = 10$ days

Now, efficiency of 10 persons are half then, time required $= 10 \times 2 = 20$ days.

17. (c) $\frac{\text{P working efficiency}}{\text{Q working efficiency}} = \frac{\text{P's one day work}}{\text{Q's one day work}}$

$= \frac{\frac{1}{60}}{\frac{1}{50}} = \frac{5}{6}$

18. (d)

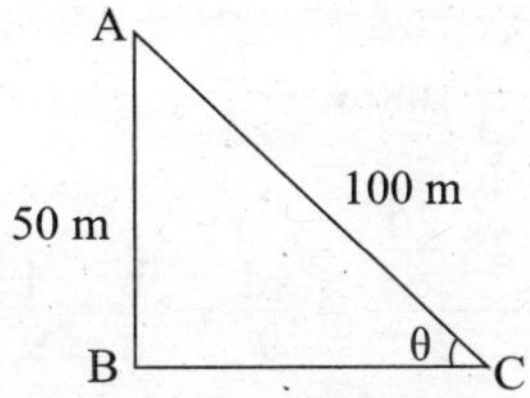

Let AC is the length of the string 100 m and AB is the kite height 50 m.

Then, inclination

$\sin\theta = \frac{AB}{AC} = \frac{50}{100} = \frac{1}{2} = \sin 30°$

$\sin\theta = \sin 30° \Rightarrow \theta = 30°$

19. (a) Vitamin A is important for growth and development, for the maintenance of the immune system and good vision.

20. (b) Rahul's father is brother of that lady, so that lady paternal aunt of Rahul.

21. (b) Veteran Bollywood star Manoj Kumar, known for his patriotic films Purab Aur Paschim, Upkar and Kranti, was the 47th recipient of the prestigious Dadasaheb Phalke award, the highest official recognition in Indian cinema, in 2015.

22. (c)

23. (c) About one-half of people who snore loudly have obstructive sleep apnea (no respiration for short periods). While you sleep, the muscles of your throat relax, your tongue falls backward, and your throat becomes narrow and "floppy causing apnea".

24. (b) The boiling point of water is 100°C or 212°F at 1 atmosphere of pressure.

Water boils at a lower temperature as you go higher on a mountain, and boils at a higher temperature if you increase atmospheric pressure.

25. (a) Circumvent : Bypass :: Comprehensive : Understandable are pair of synnomioxs word.

26. (b) Sum of first 8 odd prime numbers

$3 + 5 + 7 + 11 + 13 + 17 + 19 + 23 = 98.$

27. (b) $b = \frac{2c}{3}$ and $c = \frac{2d}{3}$

$$b = \frac{2 \times \frac{2d}{3}}{3} = \frac{4d}{9} \Rightarrow \frac{b}{d} = \frac{4}{9}$$

28. (d)

29. (b) Distillation is commonly used method of desalination. It is a phase separation method whereby saline water is heated to produce water vapour, which is then condensed to produce freshwater.

30-32:

30. (b) Difference = No. of fans of Area3 – No. of fans of Area2

= 14300 – 12200 = 2100

31. (b) Total number of fans of SR = 11500

Total number of fans of MSD = 13100

Difference = 13100 – 11500 = 1600.

32. (c) No. of fans of VK = 11500

No. of fans of MSD = 13100

No. of fans of RD = 14700 ...highest number

No. of fans of SR = 11500

33. (a) An echocardiogram, is a sonogram of the heart. Echocardiography uses Doppler ultrasound to create images of the heart.

34. (d) Here neither conclusion I nor II follows.

35. (c) Initially milk in 25 litres $= 25 \times \frac{4}{5} = 20$

water in 25 litres = 25 – 20 = 5

Let x litres of milk added now.

$$\Rightarrow \frac{20 + x}{5} = \frac{16}{1}$$

$x = 16 \times 5 - 20 = 80 - 20 = 60$ litres

36. (a)

37. (b) Due to night blindness, we can not see object clearly like that due to stutter, we can not speak clearly.

38. (c) The 2015 Davis Cup was the 104th edition of the Davis Cup, a tournament between national teams in men's tennis.

39. (b) Number of odd number less then 83

$= \frac{82}{2} = 41$

We know, sum of n odd numbers $= n^2$

$= (41)^2 = 1681$

40. (b)

41. (d) $24 + 48 - 12 \times 4 \div 2 = 24 - 48 \div 12 + 4 \times 2$

$= 24 - 4 + 8 = 28$

42. (a)

43. (c) Homogenization reduces the milk fat globules to less than 1.0 μm which allows them to stay evenly distributed in milk.

44. (b) Muhammad Akbar, the 3rd Mughal emperor, reigned from 1556 to 1605, succeeded his father, Humayun, under a regent, Bairam Khan, who helped expand and consolidate Mughal domains in India.

45. (a)

46. (b) The Colosseum in Rome, Italy, is a large amphitheatre that hosted events like gladiatorial games.

47. (c) Single discount

$$\left[1 - \left(1 - \frac{30}{100}\right)\left(1 - \frac{25}{100}\right)\left(1 - \frac{15}{100}\right)\right] \times 100$$

$$\left[1 - \frac{70}{100} \times \frac{75}{100} \times \frac{85}{100}\right] \times 100\%$$

$[1 - 0.44625] \times 100\% = 55.375\%$

48. (c) The National Green Tribunal fined Rs 5 crore on the Art of Living foundation for the damage caused to the environment, ecology, biodiversity and aquatic life of the Yamuna river, because of their 3 day cultural festival.

49. (c)

50. (d) U W Y, F H J, K M O, P R T

(each: +2, +2)

51. (d)

52. (d) Kakori Case was a train robbery that took place between Kakori, near

Lucknow, on 9 August 1925 during the Indian Independence Movement against the British Government. The robbery was conceived by freedom fighters Ram Prasad Bismil and Ashfaqullah Khan who belonged to the HRA

53. (c) Sum of 20 observations = 20 × 19 = 380

Sum of 21 observations = 21 × 20 = 420

$\therefore$ 21th observation = 420 – 380 = 40

54. (b) In 1507 AD Quli Qutub Shahi fortified and modified the Golconda fort as a structure for defence.

55. (a) Government of India Act 1935 under the British Act of Parliament.

56. (c) Bill Gates was again on top as the world's richest person on FORBES' 30th annual ranking of the world's billionaires.

57. (a) 60 workers in 7 days stich 120m of cloth.

$\therefore$ 1 worker " " " $\frac{120}{60}$ " "

$\therefore$ 1 " 1 day " $\frac{120}{60 \times 7}$ "

$\therefore$ 70 " 5 days " $\frac{120}{60 \times 7} \times 70 \times 5$

$= 100$ m.

58. (b) Echocardiography or echo, is a painless test that uses sound waves to create moving pictures of the heart. Echo can pinpoint areas of heart muscle that aren't contracting well because of poor blood flow or injury from a previous heart attack. A type of echo, Doppler, shows how well blood flows through your heart's chambers and valves.

59. (b) $a^2 + b^2 = 60$ then, $(a + b)^2 + (a - b)^2$

$= a^2 + b^2 + 2ab + a^2 + b^2 - 2ab$

$= 2(a^2 + b^2) = 2\,(60) = 120$

60. (a) Mother of K's father is the sister of S's father.

Hence, S is K's father sister.

61. (d)

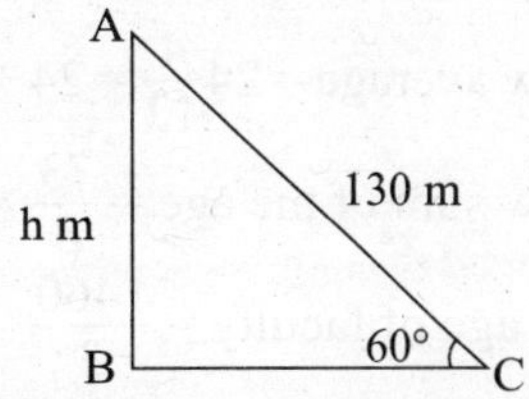

Let balloon height from the ground is AB = h m.

AC = length of cable = 130 m

In $\triangle$ABC, $\sin 60 = \frac{AB}{AC} = \frac{h}{130}$

$h = 130 \times \sin 60 = 65\sqrt{3} = 112.58$

62. (c) Halley's Comet is the most famous comet. It is a "periodic" comet that returns to Earth's vicinity about every 75 years. The last time it was here was in 1986, and it is projected to return in 2061.

63. (b) Required number = H.C.F of (150 – 8) and (3800 – 1)

= H.C.F. of 1572 and 3799

Now, $1572 = 2 \times 2 \times 3 \times 131$

$3799 = 29 \times 131$

$\therefore$ H.C.F = 131

64. (a) A kidney stone is a hard mass of minerals and salts that form in the kidneys. Certain foods and drinks contain chemicals that can lead to these stones.

65. (b) As the angle ratio is given, so greatest to smallest angle ratio = 5 : 2.

66. (c)

67. (c) Let total distance is x km

Then, distance travels by foot

$= x - \frac{4x}{9} - \frac{5x}{18} = \frac{(18 - 8 - 5)x}{18} = \frac{5x}{18}$

$\frac{5x}{18} = 10 \Rightarrow 5x = 180 = 36$ km

68. (c) $\frac{a^3 + b^3 + c^3 - 3abc}{(ab + bc + ca - a^2 - b^2 - c^2}$

$= -\frac{(a + b + c)(a^2 + b^2 + c^2 - ab - bc - ca)}{(a^2 + b^2 + c^2 - ab - bc - ca)}$

$= -(a + b + c) = -(5 + 4 + 8) = -17$

69. (b) Total age of the batch = 19 × 24 = 456

New average $= 24\frac{4}{12} = 24 + \frac{1}{3} = \frac{73}{3}$ years

New sum of the age $= \frac{73}{3} \times 20 = \frac{1460}{3}$

So, age of faculty $= \frac{1460}{3} - 456$

$= \frac{1460 - 1368}{3} = \frac{92}{3}$

30 years 8 months.

70. (c) In a courtroom, judge decision is the final decision like that in a stadium, referee decision is taken as a final decision.

71. (a) Maria Sharapova was provisionally banned from tennis after she tested positive at the Australian Open for a banned drug that she had been taking for 10 years for health reasons.

72-74:

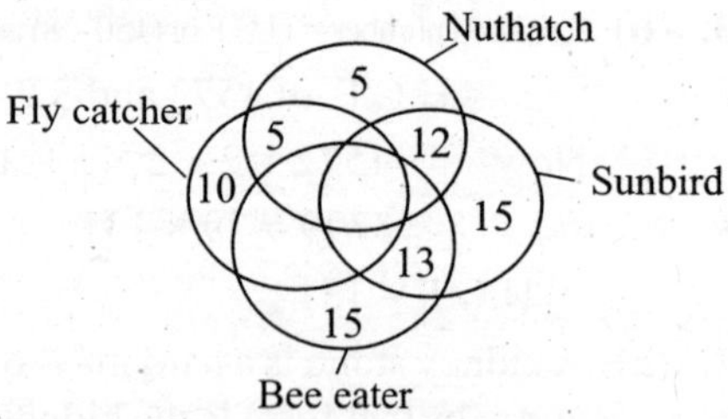

72. (b) No. of birders that wanted to see. Sunbird

= 15 + 12 + 13 = 40

Fly catcher = 10 + 5 = 15

Difference = 40 – 15 = 25

73. (c) No. of birders that wanted to see only one bird = 15 + 15 + 10 + 5 = 45

74. (a) Number of birders who like nuthatch

= 5 + 5 + 12 = 22

Number of birders who like bee-eaters

= 15 + 13 = 28

Required ratio $= \frac{22}{28} = \frac{11}{14}$

75. (d)

+2   +3   +4

9 , 4 , 16, 6, 36, 9 , 81, 13

×4   ×6   ×9

76. (c) Charles Wilkins, in 1785, did the first translation in English prose, of the classic epic poem of Hinduism, the Bhagavad-gita. He characterised it as 'a performance of great originality, of sublimity of conception, reasoning, and diction almost unequalled'.

77. (a) ATQ $\frac{x \times 5 \times 10}{100} = \frac{(1000 - x) \times 10 \times 5}{100}$

x = 1000 – x ⇒ 2x = 1000 ⇒ x = ₹ 500

78. (b) you are [bad] = 3 2 [9]

[bad] △is good = 4 △1 [9]

nothing △is [bad] = △1 [9] 5

79. (b)

80. (a) are [you] alright = [3] 2 4

[you] come △home = △7 8 [3]

we are at △home = 9 2 △7 1

81. (c) Football, also known as soccer, is played by 250 million players in over 200 countries, making it the world's most popular sport.

82. (c)

83. (c) Uranium : Coins is different from other three, as Nitrogen, Hydrogen and Sulphur are constituents of air, water and match stick.

84. (b) For maximum profit

C.P. of one shirt = ₹ 400

S.P. " " = ₹ 650

Net profit on 10 shirt = (650 – 400) × 10

= ₹ 2500

85. (d) An astrological age is a time period that parallels major changes in the development of Earth's inhabitants, relating to culture, society, and politics. There are twelve astrological ages corresponding to the twelve zodiacal signs. Advocates believe that when one cycle of the twelve astrological ages is completed, another cycle begins.

86. (b) Let cost price is ₹ 100,
then market price ₹ 125
For no profit, no loss, selling price = cost price = 100
Discount = 125 – 100 = 25

$$\text{Discount\%} = \frac{25}{125} \times 100 = 20\%$$

87. (a) Variance = $(S.D.)^2 = (10)^2 = 100$.

88. (a) Electric wire are made of copper as it is good conductor of electricity.

89. (b) Mohan is twice as fast as Sohan, so, time taken to distance covered by Mohan

$= \frac{1}{2} \times$ time taken by Sohan

$= \frac{1}{2} \times 42 = 21$ minutes

90. (c) Let two angle are θ and (90 – θ).

$$\theta - \frac{1}{5}(90 - \theta) = 60$$

$$\theta + \frac{\theta}{5} - 18 = 60$$

$$\frac{6\theta}{5} = 78 \Rightarrow \theta = \frac{78 \times 5}{6} = 65^\circ$$

Complementary angle = 90 – θ = 25°

91-93: Arrangement of bottle in a row.
Voilet, Brown, White, Blue, Black, Purple, Indigo.

91. (b) Indigo — extreme right, Voilet — extreme left

92. (c) Blue bottle — at the centre.

93. (d) Black bottle is to the immediate right of Blue.

94. (c) Buyers and sellers determine the prices of goods and services when buyers increases, then price increases and vice-versa. Price discovery is market driven.

95. (a) 6 + 11 + 16 + 21 + ...+ 71
Here, $71 = 6 + (n - 1) \times 5 \Rightarrow 65 = (n - 1)5$
$(n - 1) = 13 \Rightarrow n = 14$

Now, sum of above series $= \frac{n}{2}(a + l)$

$$= \frac{14}{2}(6 + 71)$$

$$= 539$$

96. (d) Clyde William Tombaugh was an American astronomer. He discovered Pluto in 1930, the first object to be discovered in what would later be identified as the Kuiper belt.

97. (d) It is true that cyber criminals prefer international calls to cheat gulliable people as it is difficult to track the call and they convincingly cheat the people.

98. (a) Let the three number are 3x, 4x and 10x.
Then L.C.M. of 3x, 4x and 10x = 30x
30x = 630 ⇒ x = 21
H.C.F. of 3x, 4x and 10x = x
H.C.F. = 21.

99. (c) Let persent age of Maya and Shikha are x and y.
From question ,

$$\frac{x - 3}{y - 3} = \frac{5}{9} \Rightarrow 9x - 5y = 12 \quad ...(i)$$

and $$\frac{x + 5}{y + 5} = \frac{3}{5} \Rightarrow 5x - 3y = -10 \quad ...(ii)$$

From (i) and (ii), we have
27x – 25x = 36 – (–50)
2x = 86 ⇒ x = 43
Hence, present age of Maya = 43 years.

100. (b) [god] △is fair — △ge se [fa]
who △is [god] — △ge we [fa]
you are [god] — ne le [fa]
Hence, code for 'is' — 'ge'

RRB NTPC stage-I Solved Paper

Held On 27th April 2016 (Shift-III)

1. Introducing a man, Shamita said, "He is the only son of my mother's mother." How is Shamita related to the man?

(a) Mother (b) Aunt
(c) Sister (d) Niece

2. If 2x + 3 = 9 then find the value of 3x + 2

(a) 12 (b) 16 (c) 13 (d) 11

3. Radish is an example of:

(a) bulb (b) root
(c) tuber (d) fruit

4. Pointing to a man in a photograph, Gunjan said, "His mother's only daughter is my mother." How is Gunjan related to that man?

(a) Nephew (b) Sister
(c) Wife (d) Niece

5. One should use porcelain and not containers in a microwave oven because...

(a) Charge may accumulate on the metal surface and there is danger of getting a shock.
(b) Porcelain vessels are better conductors of heat and thus food gets cooked quickly.
(c) Metal containers might undergo chemical reaction leading to spoilage of food.
(d) Porcelain vessels are cheaper than the metal containers.

6. Thomas Cup is associated with which of the following sports?

(a) Hockey (b) Badminton
(c) Football (d) Cricket

7. When was the ASLV used in India for the first time?

(a) 1980 (b) 1987
(c) 1994 (d) 2000

8. Three clocks are designed to alarm in every hour, two hours and three hours respectively. If they all alarmed together three hours before, then after how many hours will they next alarm together?

(a) 3 hours (b) 6 hours
(c) 2 hours (d) 1 hours

9. Name the international independent agency whose key activities include scientific research, education, development & monitoring of anti-doping capacities and code in all sports and all countries.

(a) International Body Against Doping
(b) World Anti-Doping Agency
(c) Play true, Play safe
(d) International Body for Sports Ethics

10. Winner of Mixed doubles category in Wimbledon, 2015 is ______________.

(a) Sania Mirza & Leander Paes
(b) Serena Williams & Roger Federer
(c) Martina Hingis & Leander Paes
(d) Serena Williams & Novak Djokovic

11. Insert the missing character depicted by

18	24	32
12	4	16
3	?	4
72	112	128

(a) 2 (b) 3 (c) 4 (d) 5

12. India has designed and developed pilotless target aircrafts named ______________ and made successful test flights of its unmanned air vehicle (UAV).

1. Nishant
2. Lakshya
3. Astra

(a) Only 2 (b) Only 1
(c) Only 2 and 3 (d) Only 1 and 2

13. Which of the following branch of medical science deals with the study and treatment of the liver?

(a) Helcology (b) Hepatology
(c) Heterology (d) Geriatrics

DIRECTIONS (Qs. 14-16): *Study the bar chart and answer the questions based on it.*

Production of Pesticides by Coromandal International Ltd. Company (in 1000 tonnes)

Production (in 1,000 tonnes)

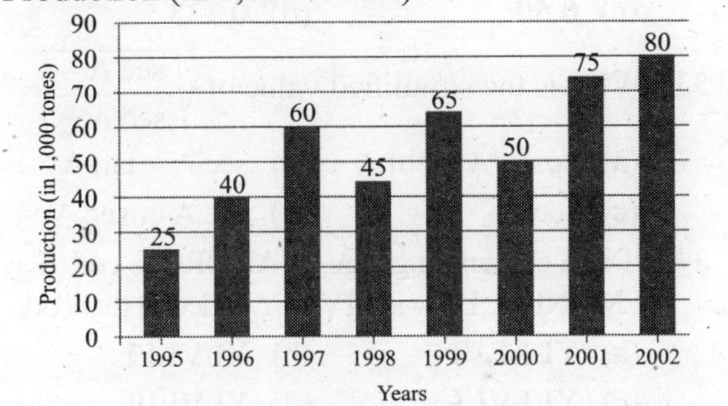

14. The average production of 1996 and 1997 was exactly equal to the average production of which of the following pairs of years?

(a) 2000 and 2001 (b) 1999 and 2000
(c) 1998 and 2000 (d) 1995 and 2001

15. In which year was the percentage increase in production as compared to the previous year the maximum?

(a) 2002 (b) 2001
(c) 1997 (d) 1996

16. What was the percentage increase in production of Pesticides in 2002 compared to that in 1995?

(a) 320% (b) 300%
(c) 220% (d) 200%

17. The President of India, Pranab Mukheijee presented the 24th Saraswati Sammaan for the year 2014 to:

(a) Govind Mishra (b) Sugathakumari
(c) M Veerappa Moily (d) Dilip Parulekar

18. ______________ is one of the states of matter obtained by cooling a gas of very low density to extremely low temperatures.

(a) Gas
(b) Plasma
(c) Bose-Einstein Condensate (BEC)
(d) Plasma Condensate

DIRECTIONS (Qs.19-21): *Study the following figure and answer the questions given below.*

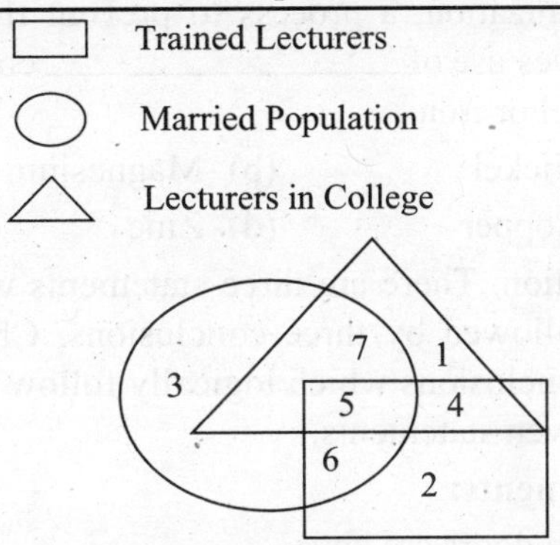

19. By which number, the trained unmarried lecturers in the college are represented?

(a) 6 (b) 5 (c) 7 (d) 4

20. If Ravenshaw college management requires only married trained lecturers for teaching, What is represented by the number 7?

(a) Married lecturers in the college
(b) Trained lecturers
(c) Unmarried trained lecturers
(d) Married trained lecturers

21. By which number, the trained married lecturers in the college are represented?

(a) 7 (b) 6 (c) 5 (d) 4

22. Four pairs of words are given below out of which three are alike in some manner and one is different. Which is different from the rest?

(a) Steel : Utensils (b) Bronze : Statue
(c) Duralumin : Aircraft (d) Wood : Rails

23. Find the least number that must be subtracted from 98534, to get a number exactly divisible by 824.

(a) 484 (b) 478 (c) 422 (d) 375

24. 20 pens and 46 pencils were purchased for Rs. 235. If the average price of a pencil is Rs. 2.50 then calculate the average price (in Rs.) of a pen.

(a) 6 (b) 4 (c) 8 (d) 12

25. Belur Math is located in

(a) West Bengal (b) Maharashtra

(c) Uttar Pradesh (d) Tamil Nadu

26. Galvanization, a process to prevent rusting involves use of ________________ coating to steel or iron.

(a) Nickel (b) Magnesium

(c) Copper (d) Zinc

27. Direction: There are three statements which are followed by three conclusions. Choose the conclusions which logically follow from the given statements.

Statements:

All the doors are keys.

All the keys are bats.

Some clocks are bats.

Conclusions:

1. Some bats are doors.
2. Some clocks are keys.
3. All the keys are doors.

(a) Only (1) and (2) (b) Only (1)

(c) Only (2) (d) Only (1) and (3)

28. Insert the missing character depicted by ?'

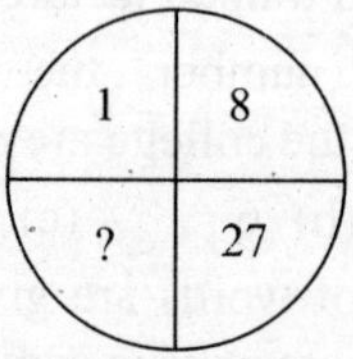

(a) 41 (b) 64 (c) 35 (d) 61

29. If $\sqrt{5} = 2.236$; then $\sqrt{5}/2$ is

(a) 1.851 (b) 1.118

(c) 2.236 (d) 1.782

30. Which state of India produces the highest quantity of Jute?

(a) Bihar (b) Odisha

(c) West Bengal (d) Jharkhand

31. Which of the following languages was not included in the 8th schedule of Indian Constitution through 92nd amendment act?

(a) Maithili (b) Bodo

(c) Santhali (d) Kannada

32. A table tennis player, lost 12 games out of 18 games played. Calculate the games won in terms of decimal.

(a) 0.667 (b) 0.067

(c) 0.50 (d) 0.333

33. What is the simplified value of $\sqrt{\dfrac{\sec A - 1}{\sec A + 1}}$?

(a) cosec A – cot A (b) sec A – tan A

(c) $\sec^2 A$ (d) sec A cosec A

34. If in a certain language, MANURE is coded as EMRNUA, How is LIVELY coded in that code.

(a) YLLEVI (b) YLVLEI

(c) YLLVEI (d) YLVLIE

35. The value of (0.00000729/0.00000027) is

(a) 0.27 (b) 0.027

(c) 2.7 (d) 27

36. If a/b = 1/4; b/c =1/8 and a = 2 then the value of c is

(a) 8 (b) 16 (c) 32 (d) 64

37. The value of $\cos 0°$ is

(a) 0 (b) Infinite

(c) not defined (d) 1

38. Read the statement and select a conclusion from the given alternatives:

Statement:

Company 'X' had asked its employees to declare income and assets but it has been strongly opposed by the employees' his/her union and no employee is going to declare his her income.

Conclusions:

I. The employees of the company 'x' do not seem to have any additional income besides their salary.

II. The employees' union want all the senior officer to declare their income first.

(a) only conclusion I follows.
(b) only conclusion II follows.
(c) either I or II follows.
(d) neither I nor II follows.

39. Prime Minister Narendra Modi has released two commemorative coins of denominations Rs. 125 & Rs. 10 as a mark of tribute to whom?

(a) Abdul Kalam
(b) Mahatma Gandhi
(c) Dr. Rajendra Prasad
(d) B. R.Ambedkar

40. If in an investment, Ramesh gains 50% more profit than Hemant, then by what percentage profit of Hemant is less than the profit of Ramesh.

(a) 50% (b) 25%
(c) $33\frac{1}{3}\%$ (d) $66\frac{2}{3}\%$

41. __________ soils are red in colour and not suitable for agriculture found along the Tamil Nadu, Odisha and small part of Chhotanagpur and Meghalaya.

(a) Alluvial Soil (b) Red Soil
(c) Laterite Soil (d) Regur Soil

42. Complete the Figure X from the given alternatives 1, 2, 3, 4.

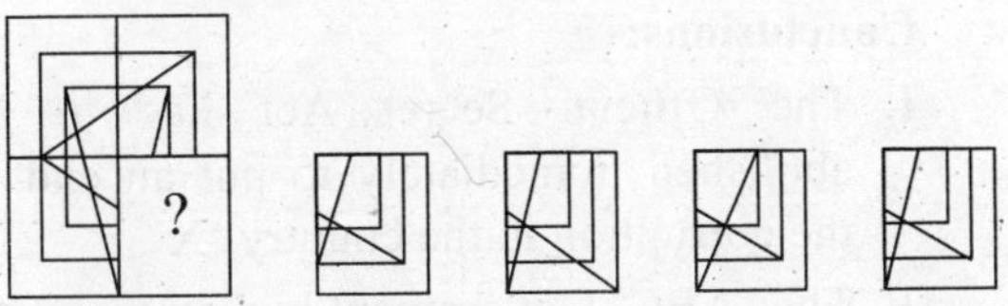

(X) (1) (2) (3) (4)

(a) 1 (b) 2 (c) 3 (d) 4

43. If on a marked price, the difference of selling prices with a discount of 30% and two successive discounts of 20% and 10% is ₹ 72, then the marked price (in rupees) is

(a) 3,600 (b) 3,000
(c) 2,500 (d) 2,400

44. Name the device used to connect computers for communication via telephone lines.

(a) HUB (b) Switch
(c) Repeater (d) MODEM

45. Factors of $x^2 + 7x + 10$ are

(a) $(x-5)(x-2)$ (b) $(x+5)(x+2)$
(c) $(x-5)(x+2)$ (d) $(x-4)(x+2)$

46. Who among the following is known as the Father of Civil Services in India?

(a) Lord Cornwallis
(b) Warren Hastings
(c) Lord Wellesley
(d) Lord William Bentinck

47. In terms of environmental studies, CER refers to:

(a) Certified Emission Reductions
(b) Capped Emission Repository
(c) Certified Emission Repository
(d) Capped Emission Reductions

48. World climate conference popularly known as COP-21 (2015) was held in __________.

(a) New York (b) London
(c) Paris (d) Berlin

49. Gitesh took a loan for 4 years at 5% Compound Interest. If the total interest paid was Rs. 431.01, Calculate the principal.

(a) Rs. 2000 (b) Rs. 2050
(c) Rs. 2100 (d) Rs. 2150

50. A, B and C can complete the work in 4, 5 and 6 hours respectively. If they all work together and receive Rs. 777 as wages, then find the share of a

(a) Rs. 300 (b) Rs. 315
(c) Rs. 326 (d) Rs. 175

51. A shopkeeper purchased a pen drive of marked price Rs. 1000 at successive discounts of 10% & 15% respectively. He spent Rs. 35 on packaging and sold it on Rs. 1000. Calculate the Gain percent.

(a) No Gain (b) 25% (c) 30% (d) 35%

52. In a certain code language, if EXECUTE is coded as 5351695 and SCRIPT is coded as 714279, then EXIST will be coded as?

(a) 23579 (b) 97532
(b) 23597 (d) 53279

53. Complete the Figure X from the alternatives 1, 2, 3, 4.

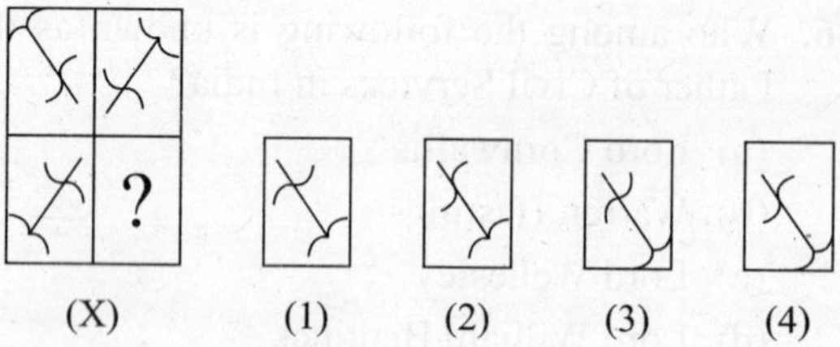

(a) 1 (b) 2 (c) 3 (d) 4

54. Rampal told Arjun, 'Yesterday I defeated the only brother of the daughter of my grandmother.' Whom did Rampal defeat?

(a) Son (b) Father
(c) Brother (d) Father-in-law

55. Battle of Gulnabad was led by Mahmud Hotaki and fought in the year ________.

(a) 1770 (b) 1722
(c) 1712 (d) 1702

56. Apollo-11, the first artificial satellite that landed humans on moon, was launched in which year?

(a) 1975 (b) 1968
(c) 1969 (d) 1958

57. The smallest number that is completely divisibly by 6, 8, 12 and 16 is

(a) 48 (b) 24 (c) 64 (d) 80

58. Name the committee appointed in 1986 by Rajiv Gandhi on "Revitalisation of Panchayati Raj Institution for Democracy & Development".

(a) Ashok Mehta Committee
(b) LM Singhvi Committee
(c) G.V.K Rao Committee
(d) Balwant Rai Mehta Committee.

59. ________ are a mountain range that runs almost parallel to the western coast of the Indian peninsula, and is one of the eight "hottest hotspots" of biological diversity in the world, sometimes called the "Great Escarpment of India".

(a) Eastern Ghats (b) Western Ghats
(c) Himalayas (d) Satpura Range

60. A man, rowing a boat, covers a distance of 16 km in two hours downstream. He covers half the distance in same amount of time when rowing upstream. Calculate the speed of the stream.

(a) 4 km/hr (b) 2 km/hr
(c) 3 km/hr (d) 1 km/hr

61. Match the Correct Memory Units.

(a) 4 bit (p) 1 MB
(b) 1024 KB (q) 1 byte
(c) 1024 TB (r) 1 nibble
(d) 8 bit (s) 1 PB

(a) a-r, b-p, c-s, d-q (b) a-p, b-s, c-q, d-r
(c) a-r, b-s, c-q, d-p (d) a-r, b-q, c-s, d-p

62. Read the statement and select a conclusion from the given alternatives:

Statement:

The Official Secret Act (OSA) enacted by the 'ABC' Government in the year 1930 seems to be one of the major sources of corruption in the country 'X'.

Conclusions:

I. The Official Secret Act has to be abolished immediately to put an end to the corruption in the country 'X'.

II. The 'ABC' Government had an intention of encouraging corruption in the Government offices.

(a) only conclusion I follows.
(b) only conclusion II follows
(c) either I or II follows.
(d) neither I nor II follows

63. After whom is the Amrut Yojana scheme named? (initiative to meet the nutrition needs of pregnant, lactating women in the tribal areas)

(a) Mahatma Gandhi (b) Abdul Kalam

(c) B R Ambedkar (d) Indira Gandhi

64. Find the maximum area of a rectangular field which is surrounded by a rope of 400 m.

(a) 5000 m^2 (b) 6250 m^2

(c) 4000 m^2 (d) 10000 m'^2

65. Read the statements and select a conclusion from the given alternatives:

Statement:

The minimum qualification for this job is M TECH.

However, candidates who have appeared for the final year of M TECH can also apply.

Conclusions:

I. All candidates who have yet to post graduate will be there in the list of selected candidates.

II. All candidates having M TECH as their minimum qualification will be there in the list of selected candidates.

(a) only conclusion I follows.

(b) only conclusion II follows.

(c) either I or II follows.

(d) neither I nor II follows

66. If $19x^2 = 100^2 - 90^2$, then find the value of x

(a) 10 (b) 9 (c) 11 (d) 12

67. ________ a professional Tennis player, became the new goodwill ambassador for the UN Fund for Children.

(a) Sania Mirza (b) Serena Williams

(c) Roger Federer (d) Novak Djokovic

68. Rahul and Raghav are 110 km apart from each other and they started horse-riding towards each other at same time at a speed of 20 km/hr. and 24 km/hr. After how many hours of riding will they be at a distance of 22 km?

(a) 1 hour (b) 1 hour 30 min

(c) 2 hours (d) 2 hours 30 min

69. The lady who played an important role in the awakening of Indian women to their right for independence and who is also known as Nightingale of India is —

(a) Vijaya Lakshmi Pandit

(b) Durga Bai Deshmukh

(c) Sarojini Naidu

(d) Madam Bhikaiji Cama

70. A man buys 10 oranges for Rs. 3 and sells 8 for Rs, 3. Calculate his gain percent.

(a) 20% (b) 25% (c) 27% (d) 30%

71. A motorist knows four different routes from Jaipur to Bhangarh. From Bhangarh to Alwar he knows three different routes and from Alwar to Carlisle he knows two different routes. How many routes does he know from Jaipur to Carlisle?

(a) 12 (b) 24 (c) 48 (d) 60

72. The expenses of a person increases by Rs. 50000 for every month in February and March. If his expenses in January was Rs. 50000, Calculate his average expenditure (in Rs.) from January to March.

(a) 100000 (b) 150000

(c) 75000 (d) 50000

73. An example of Full Duplex communication channel.

(a) Radio Broadcasting

(b) Television Broadcasting

(c) Walkie-Talkie

(d) Telephone conversation

74. Ravi, Rohan and Rajesh alone can complete a work in 10, 12 and 15 days respectively. In how many days can the work be completed, if all three work together?

(a) 4 days (b) 5days

(c) 3 days (d) 8 days

75. In an examination, student gets on average 76 marks. The total marks for five subjects is 500. His marks in 4 subjects are mentioned; calculate the marks obtained by the student in Mathematics marked as "X" in the table below.

Subject	Maths	English	Sanskrit	Science	Social Science
Marks Obtained	X	87	83	78	57

(a) 80 (b) 83 (c) 72 (d) 75

76. If Selling Price is Rs. 72 & Gain Percentage = 20%, calculate the Cost Price.

(a) Rs. 60 (b) Rs. 58
(c) Rs. 61 (d) Rs. 59

77. Complete the given series
15, 155, 1545, 15455 ....

(a) 154545 (b) 15555
(c) 154555 (d) 155454

78. What fraction of 2 hours is 12 seconds?

(a) 1/200 (b) 1/300
(c) 1/400 (d) 1/600

79. Who has been appointed as first-ever Ombudsman (Ethics officer) of BCCI?

(a) Justice A. P. Shah
(b) Justice Anil R. Dave
(c) Justice Dipak Misra
(d) Justice Jagdish Singh Khehai

80. Insert the missing character depicted by ? .

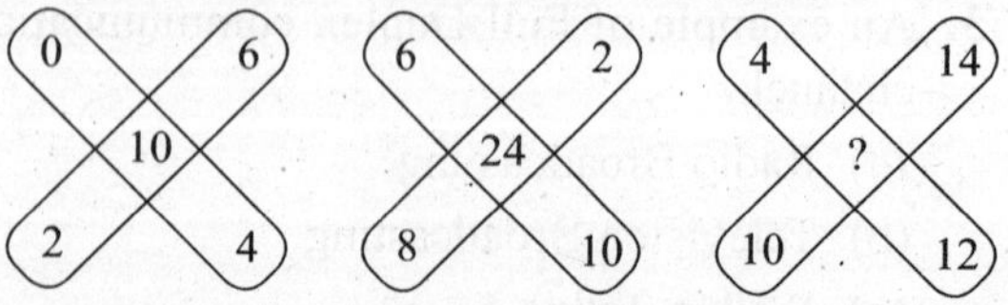

81. If the average age of 20 students in Class I is 10 years and average age of 25 students in Class II is 12 years, find the average age (in years) of all students.

(a) 11 (b) 11.111
(c) 10.50 (d) 10.85

82. Which part of the human brain is the centre for intelligence, memory and emotions?

(a) Hypothalamus (b) Cerebrum
(c) Corpus Callosum (d) Mid Brain

83. Two numbers are in ratio 3 : 4. When 3 is subtracted from both the numbers, the ratio becomes 2 : 3. Find the sum of the numbers.

(a) 16 (b) 20 (c) 21 (d) 22

84. If @ stands for +, $ stands for –, % stands for ×, > stands for ÷. Then what is the value of 48 > 4 $ 8 % 2@8

(a) 12 (b) –8 (c) –4 (d) 4

85. Calculate the principal if an amount of Rs. 441 is received on compound interest at the rate of 5% per annum after 2 years.

(a) Rs. 400 (b) Rs. 390
(c) Rs. 380 (d) Rs. 350

DIRECTIONS (Qs. 86-88): *Answer the questions based on the following information:*

Six colleagues are sitting in a circle and are facing the center of the circle. Diana is between Puskar and Padma. Priyanka is between Mahesh and Lucky. Puskar and Mahesh are opposite to each other.

86. Who are the neighbours of Mahesh?

(a) Puskar and Diana
(b) Diana and Priyanka
(c) Priyanka and Padma
(d) Lucky and Priyanka

87. Who is just right to Padma?

(a) Diana (b) Lucky
(c) Puskar (d) Priyanka

88. Who is sitting opposite to Priyanka?

(a) Puskar (b) Diana
(c) Padma (d) Lucky

89. Directions:

There are three statements which are followed by four conclusions. Choose the conclusions which logically follow from the given statements

Statements:

Some cups are pins.
Some pins are covers.
All the covers are pens.

Conclusions:

1. Some pens are pins.

2. Some covers are cups.
3. No cup is pin.
4. Some pins are cups.

(a) Only (1) and (2) (b) Only (2) and (4)
(c) Only (2) and (3) (d) Only (1) and (4)

90. A man is 3 years older than his wife and four times as old as his son. If the son becomes 15 years old after 3 years, what is the present age of the wife?

(a) 60 years (b) 51 years
(c) 48 years (d) 45 years

91. If sin θ = 40/41, then cot θ is

(a) 40/9 (b) 9/40
(c) 9/41 (d) 41/9

92. If the sum of LCM and HCF of two numbers is 60 and their LCM is 30 more than their HCF, then the product of two numbers will be.

(a) 625 (b) 675
(c) 525 (d) 575

93. If in a certain language, SCARCE is coded as CSRAEC, how is STABLE coded in that code?

(a) TBSAEL (b) BTSAEL
(c) BTELSA (d) TSBAEL

94. Direction:

There are three statements which are followed by four conclusions. Choose the conclusions which logically follow from the given statements

Statements:

Some images are answers.

Some answers are videos.

All the videos are poems.

Conclusion:

(1) Some videos are answers.
(2) Some poems are images.
(3) All the images are poems.
(4) Some poems are answers.

(a) Only (1) and (2) (b) Only (1) and (4)
(c) Only (1) and (3) (d) Only (2) and (4)

95. In a certain code language, if CHECK is coded as 97294 and QUERY is coded as 51238, then CHERRY will be coded as?

(a) 729833 (b) 972338
(c) 792338 (d) 338972

96. Human blood platelets releases ________ which helps in clotting of blood.

(a) prothrombin (b) fibrin
(c) fructose (d) sucrose

97. Light can travel ________ km in a year.

(a) 5 billion (b) 10 billion
(c) 5 trillion (d) 10 trillion

98. What was the major decision that took place in 1987 Montreal Conference?

(a) Developed countries will completely ban CFC production by 2000
(b) Developed countries will completely ban CFC production by 2010
(c) Developing countries will completely ban CFC production by 2000
(d) Developing countries will completely ban CFC production by 2020

99. The major objective of INSAT series satellites is to facilitate.

(a) TV relay to remote areas
(b) mobile network in remote areas
(c) internet services
(d) mapping locations through GPS

100. A good cricket fielder while catching a fast moving ball moves his hand along with the ball because.

(a) He decreases the time of contact therefore increasing the force of contact.
(b) He increases the time of contact thereby reducing the force of contact.
(c) He is afraid to take the ball and thus takes his hand out.
(d) He decreases the time of contact therefore reducing the force of contact

Hints & Solutions

1. **(d)** Mother's mother only son is her mother's brother. So she is his niece.

2. **(d)** $2x + 3 = 9 \Rightarrow 2x = 9 - 3 \Rightarrow x = \frac{6}{2} = 3$
Now, $3x + 2 = 3\,(3) + 2 = 9 + 2 = 11$

3. **(b)** Radish is an edible root vegetable consumed throughout the world, mostly eaten raw as a crunchy salad vegetable.

4. **(d)** Gunjan is the niece of that man.

5. **(a)**

6. **(b)** The Thomas Cup, is an international badminton competition.

7. **(b)** The Augmented Satellite Launch Vehicle (ASLV), made its maiden flight on 24 March 1987, and its final flight on 4 May 1994.

8. **(a)** L.C.M. of 1, 2 and 3 = 6 hours. So, they all alarm together at the interval of 6 hours. Hence, they next alarm together after 3 hours.

9. **(b)** The World Anti-Doping Agency's key activities include scientific research, education, development of anti-doping capacities, and monitoring of the anti-doping policies in all sports.

10. **(c)**

11. **(b)**

18	24	32
12	14	16
3	3	4
$18 \div 3 \times 12$	$24 \div 3 \times 14$	$32 \div 4 \times 16$
72	112	128

12. **(d)** UAN named Nishant is capable of performing aerial reconnaissance of the battlefield to locate targets at long distances behind enemy lines.

13. **(b)** Hepatology is the study, prevention, diagnosis and management of diseases of liver, gallbladder, biliary tree and pancreas.

14. **(d)** Average production of 1996-97
$= \frac{40 + 60}{2} = 50$
and average protection of 1995 and 2001
$= \frac{25 + 75}{2} = 50$

15. **(d)** Percentage increase in production in
$1996 = \left(\frac{40 - 25}{25}\right) \times 100 = \frac{15}{25} \times 100 = 60\%$
Which is maximum.

16. **(c)** Required percentage increase
$= \left(\frac{80 - 25}{25}\right) \times 100 = \frac{55}{25} \times 100 = 220\%$

17. **(c)**

18. **(c)** A Bose–Einstein Condensate is formed by cooling a gas of extremely low density, to ultra-low temperatures close to absolute zero (-273.15°C).

19-21:

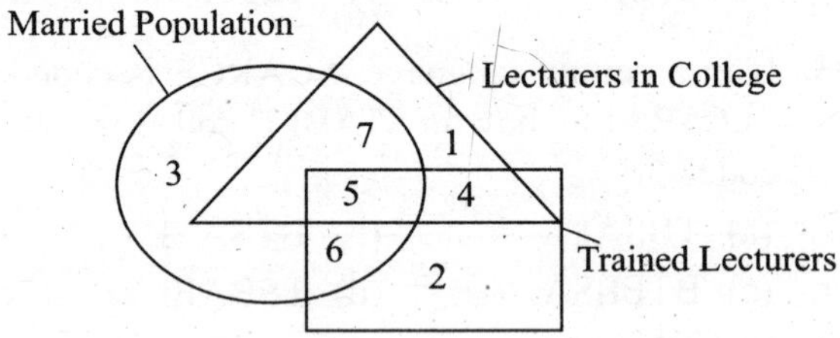

19. **(d)**

20. **(a)** Married lecturer in the college.

21. **(c)** 5 represent trained married lecturer in the college.

22. **(d)** Steel is used to make utensils, Bronze is uses to make statue like that duralumin is uses to make. Aircraft, but woods are not uses to make rail.

23. **(b)** $\frac{98534}{824} = 119.58$
So, least number $= 98538 - 824 \times 119$
$= 98538 - 98056 = 478$

24. **(a)** Let average price of a pen is ₹ x.
Then, $20x + 46 \times 2.5 = 235$
$20x + 115 = 235$
$20x = 120 \Rightarrow x = 6.$

25. (a) Belur Math is the headquarters of the Ramakrishna Mission, founded by Swami Vivekananda. It is located on the west bank of Hooghly River, West Bengal.

26. (d) Galvanization is the process of applying a protective zinc coating to steel or iron, to prevent rusting.

27. (b)

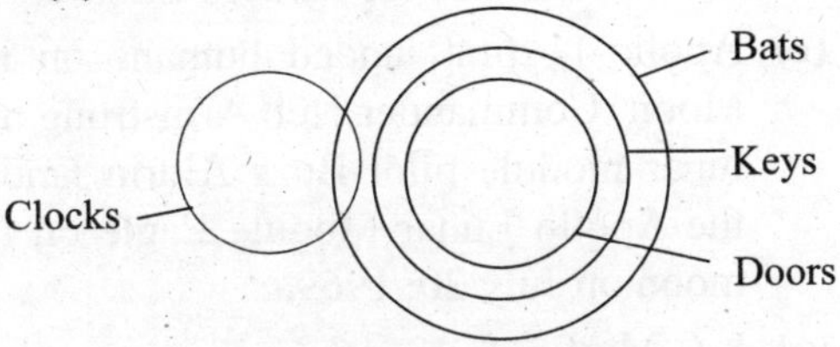

Only conclusion I follow.

28. (b)

$1 = (1)^3$	$8 = (2)^3$
$64 = (4)^3$	$27 = (3)^3$

29. (b) $\sqrt{5} = 2.236$

$$\frac{\sqrt{5}}{2} = \frac{2.236}{2} = 1.118$$

30. (c) West Bengal tops the list of jute producing states with 8969 thousand bales of Jute production in the year 2014-15.

31. (d) The 8th schedule of Indian Constitution lists the official languages of India.

32. (d) $\frac{\text{game won}}{\text{total game}} = \frac{6}{18} = \frac{1}{3} = 0.333$

33. (a) $\sqrt{\frac{\sec A - 1}{\sec A + 1}} = \sqrt{\frac{\frac{1}{\cos A} - 1}{\frac{1}{\cos A} + 1}} = \sqrt{\frac{1 - \cos A}{1 + \cos A}}$

$$= \sqrt{\frac{(1 - \cos A)(1 - \cos A)}{(1 - \cos A)(1 + \cos A)}}$$

$$= \sqrt{\frac{(1 - \cos A)^2}{(1 - \cos^2 A)}}$$

$$= \frac{(1 - \cos A)}{\sin A} = \operatorname{cosec} A - \cot A$$

34. (c) M A N U R E — E M R N U A

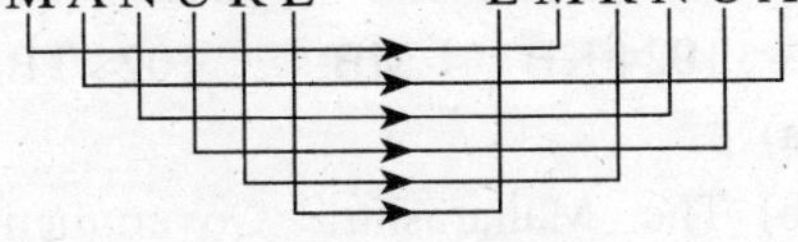

Similarly,

L I V E L Y — Y L L V E I

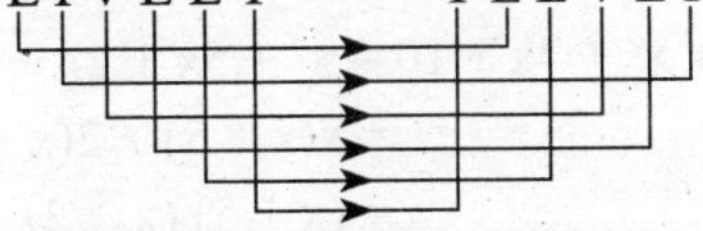

35. (d) $\frac{0.00000729}{0.00000027} = \frac{729}{27} = \frac{9 \times 9 \times 9}{9 \times 3} = 27$

36. (d) $\frac{a}{b} = \frac{1}{4}$ and $\frac{b}{c} = \frac{1}{8}$

Now, $\frac{a}{b} \times \frac{b}{c} = \frac{1}{4} \times \frac{1}{8} \Rightarrow \frac{a}{c} = \frac{1}{32}$

$c = 32a = 32 \times 2 = 64$

37. (d) $\cos 0° = \sqrt{1 - \sin^2 0} = \sqrt{1 - 0} = 1.$

38. (d) None of the conclusion, follow the instruction.

39. (d) Prime Minister Modi released two commemorative '10-rupee' and '125-rupee' coins, on 125th birth anniversary of Dr B.R. Ambedkar.

40. (c) Let Hemant gain is ₹ 100, then Ramesh gain is $100 + 100 \times \frac{50}{100} = 150$

Hemant profit in comparison to Ramesh

$$= \left(\frac{150 - 100}{150}\right) = \frac{50}{150} \times 100 = 33\frac{1}{3}\%$$

41. (c) Red soil is derived from crystalline rock. It is poor growing soil, low in nutrients and humus and difficult to cultivate because of its low water holding capacity.

42. (d)

43. (a) Let marked price is ₹ x.

Then, selling price $= x \times \frac{100 - 30}{100} = 0.7x$

Again, price after two discount

$$= x \times \left(\frac{100 - 20}{100}\right) \times \left(\frac{100 - 10}{100}\right)$$

$= x \times 0.8 \times 0.9 = 0.72x$

ATQ, $0.72x - 0.7x = 72$

$0.02x = 72$

$$x = \frac{72 \times 100}{2} = 3600$$

44. (d) A digital subscriber line modem is used to connect a computer or router to a telephone line to provide digital subscriber line service for connectivity to the Internet.

45. (b) $x^2 + 7x + 10 = x^2 + 5x + 2x + 10$
$= x(x + 5) + 2(x + 5)$
$= (x + 5)(x + 2)$

46. (a) Warren Hastings founded Civil Services and Cornwallis reformed, modernised and rationalised it. Hence, he is known as the 'Father of Civil Service in India'.

47. (a) A carbon credit is a permit allowing the holder company, to emit CO_2 or other greenhouse gases. A developing nation could receive these credits for supporting sustainable development initiatives.

48. (c)

49. (a) Let the principal is ₹ P.

Now, $C.I. = P\left[\left(1 + \frac{r}{100}\right)^t - 1\right]$

$431.01 = P\left[\left(1 + \frac{5}{100}\right)^4 - 1\right]$

$431.01 = P\left[\left(\frac{21}{20}\right)^4 - 1\right]$

$P = \frac{431.01 \times (20)^4}{(21)^4 - (20)^4} = \frac{431.01}{0.216} = 2000$

50. (b) Share of A : Share of B : Share of C

$\frac{1}{4} : \frac{1}{5} : \frac{1}{6} = 15 : 12 : 10$

$\therefore$ Share of A $= \frac{15}{15 + 12 + 10} \times 777$

$= \frac{15}{37} \times 777 =$ ₹ 315.

51. (b) Shopkeeper's cost price of a pen drive

$= 1000 \times \frac{90}{100} \times \frac{85}{100} = 765$

Packing cost = 35

gross cost price = 765 + 35 = 800.

Selling price = 1000

$\text{Profit\%} = \left(\frac{1000 - 800}{800}\right) \times 100$

$= \frac{200}{800} \times 100 = 25\%$

52. (d)

Letter	E	X	C	U	T	S	R	I
Code	5	3	1	6	9	7	4	2

Hence, code of EXIST is 53279.

53. (d)

54. (b) Brother of the daughter of grandmother means father. Hence, Rahul defeated his father.

55. (b) The Battle of Gulnabad was fought between the forces from Hotaki Dynasty and the army of the Safavid Empire.

56. (c) Apollo-11 first landed humans on the Moon. Commander Neil Armstrong and lunar module pilot Buzz Aldrin landed the Apollo Lunar Module Eagle on the moon on July 20, 1969.

57. (a) L.C.M of 6, 8, 12, 16

2	6, 8, 12, 16
2	3, 4, 6, 8
2	3, 2, 3, 4
3	3, 1, 3, 2
	1, 1, 1, 2

$\therefore$ L.C.M. $= 2 \times 2 \times 2 \times 2 \times 3 = 48$

58. (b)

59. (b) The western ghats are a mountain range that run parallel to the western coast of Indian peninsula. It is a UNESCO world heritage site and hottest hot-spots of biological diversity in the world. It is called the Great Escarpment of India.

60. (b) Let speed of the boat is x km/hr and speed of stream is y km/hr.

Now, $x + y = \frac{16}{2} \Rightarrow x + y = 8$ ...(i)

And $x - y = \frac{8}{2} \Rightarrow x - y = 4$ ...(ii)

From (i) and (ii) we have

Speed of stream, y = 2 km/hr.

61. (a) We know that 1 nibble = 4 bit

8 bit = 1 byte, 1024 B = 1 KB,

1024 KB = 1 MB, 1024 TB = 1 PB

62. (a)

63. (b) The Maharashtra Government on 3 November 2015 approved a revised scheme, named APJ Abdul Kalam Amrut Yojna, for pregnant and lactating women in the tribal areas of the state.

64. (d) Perimeter of the rectangle = length of rope

$2(L + B) = 400 \Rightarrow L + B = 200$

For maximum area L = B.

$L + L = 200 \Rightarrow L = 100$

Now, Area $= L \times L = 100 \times 100 = 10000\ m^2$

65. (d) The criteria given in the statement is for the eligibility of the job and not the criteria to select a candidate.

Hence, neither conclusion I nor II follow.

66. (a) $19x^2 = 100^2 - 90^2 = (100 - 90)(100 + 90)$

$19x^2 = 10 \times 190 \Rightarrow x^2 = 100 \Rightarrow x = 10$

67. (d) Novak Djokovic was made the new goodwill ambassador for the UN Fund for Children, joining a roster of athletes and celebrities to hold this post.

68. (c) Both are riding in the opposite direction, so, their relative speed = 20 + 24 = 44 km/hr.

Let after t hr. distance between two remains 22 km.

Then, $44 \times t + 22 = 110$

$44t = 88 \Rightarrow t = 2$ hours

69. (c)

70. (b) Cost of each orange $= \dfrac{3}{10}$

Selling price of each orange $= \dfrac{3}{8}$

Gain percent $= \dfrac{\frac{3}{8} - \frac{3}{10}}{\frac{3}{10}} \times 100$

$= \dfrac{3}{3 \times 4} \times 100 = 25\%$

71. (b) Number of different routes from

Jaipur to Bhangarh = 4

Bhangarh to Alwar = 3

Alwar to Carlisle = 2

So, total number of different routes from Jaipur to Carlisle = 4 × 3 × 2 = 24

72. (a) Expenses in January = ₹ 50000

" " February = 50000 + 50000

" " March = 100000 + 50000

Average expenses

$= \dfrac{50000 + 100000 + 150000}{3} = \dfrac{300000}{3}$

= ₹ 100000

73. (d) A full-duplex device is a telephone, in which parties at both ends of a call can speak and be heard by the other party simultaneously.

74. (a) Time required to complete the whole work, when they all work together

$= \dfrac{1}{\frac{1}{10} + \frac{1}{12} + \frac{1}{15}} = \dfrac{1}{\frac{6 + 5 + 4}{60}}$

$= \dfrac{60}{15} = 4$ days

75. (d) Average marks $= \dfrac{X + 87 + 83 + 78 + 57}{5}$

$76 = \dfrac{X + 305}{5} \Rightarrow X + 305 = 380$

$X = 75$

76. (a) Cost price = selling price $\times \dfrac{100}{100 + \text{Gain\%}}$

$= 72 \times \dfrac{100}{100 + 20} = \dfrac{72 \times 100}{120} =$ ₹ 60

77. (a) 15, 155, 1545, 15455, 154545

× 10 + 5, × 10 – 5, × 10 + 5, × 10 – 5

78. (d) 2 hours = 2 × 3600 sec.

Now, $\dfrac{12}{2 \times 3600} = \dfrac{1}{600}$

79. (a)

80. (c) (6 + 4 + 2 + 0) – 2 = 10,

(2 + 10 + 8 + 6) – 2 = 24,

(14 + 12 + 10 + 4) – 2 = 38

81. (b) Total age of 20 students of class I = 20 × 10 = 200

" " 25 " class II = 25 × 12 = 300

Average age of all the students

$= \dfrac{200 + 300}{20 + 25} = 11.11$ years

82. (b) Cerebrum performs higher functions like interpreting touch, vision, hearing, speech, reasoning, emotions, learning, and fine control of movement.

83. (c) Let the two numbers are 3x and 4x.

$$\frac{3x-3}{4x-3}=\frac{2}{3}\Rightarrow 3(3x-3)=2(4x-3)$$

$$=9x-9=8x-6\Rightarrow x=3$$

Sum of two numbers $=(3+4)x=7\times 3=21$

84. (d) $48>4\$8\%2@8=48\div 4-8\times 2+8$

$$=12-16+8=4$$

85. (a) Let the principal is P

Then, $A=P\left[\left(1+\frac{r}{100}\right)^{t}\right]$

$$441=P\left[\left(1+\frac{5}{100}\right)^{2}\right]\Rightarrow 441=P\left(\frac{21}{20}\right)^{2}$$

$$P=\frac{441\times 20\times 20}{21\times 21}=₹\,400$$

86-88: Sitting arrangement of six friends in a circle is like this:

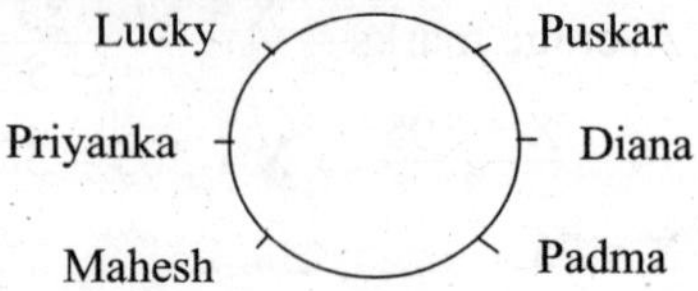

86. (c) Priyanka & Padma

87. (a) Diana **88. (b)** Diana

89. (d)

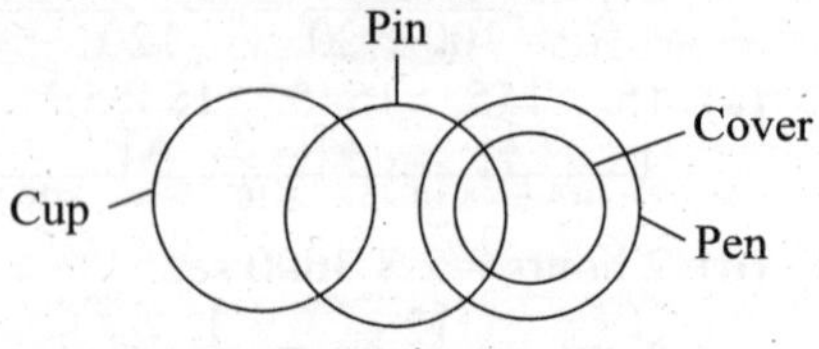

Only conclusion I and 4 follows.

90. (d) Let the present age of his wife is x years.

Then, men's age = (x + 3)

Son's age $=\frac{(x+3)}{4}$

$$\Rightarrow \frac{(x+3)}{4}+3=15$$

$$\frac{(x+3)}{4}=12\Rightarrow x=48-3=45 \text{ years.}$$

91. (b) $\sin\theta=\frac{40}{41}$, $\cos\theta=\sqrt{1-\sin^2\theta}$

$$=\sqrt{1-\left(\frac{40}{41}\right)^2}=\frac{9}{41}$$

$$\text{Now, }\cot\theta=\frac{\cos\theta}{\sin\theta}=\frac{\frac{9}{41}}{\frac{40}{41}}=\frac{9}{40}$$

92. (b) Let two numbers are such that, their L.C.M. and H.C.F. are x and y.

Then, $x+y=60$ ...(i)

and $x=y+30\Rightarrow x-y=30$ ....(ii)

Squaring and subtracting (i) and (ii)

$$(x+y)^2-(x-y)^2=(60)^2-(30)^2$$

$$4xy=(60+30)(60-30)\Rightarrow xy=675$$

93. (d) S C A R C E

C S R A E C

Similarly S T A B L E

T S B A E C

94. (b)

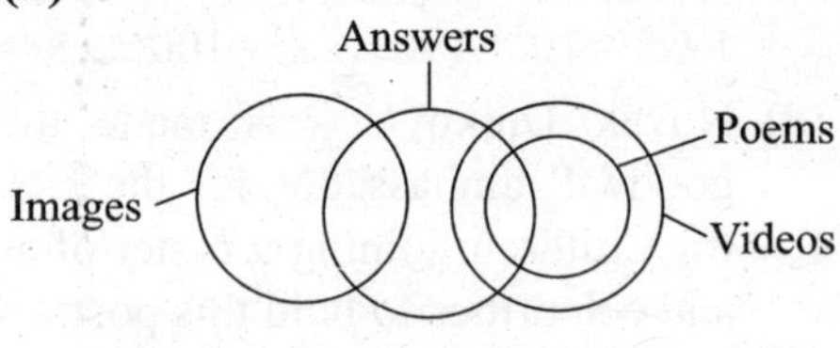

Only conclusion I and 4 follows.

95. (c)

Letter	C	H	E	K	Q	U	R	Y
Code	9	7	2	4	5	1	3	8

Hence, code of 'CHERRY' is '972338'

96. () Coagulation: Prothrombin is transformed into thrombin by clotting factor X or prothrombinase; thrombin then acts to transform fibrinogen, into fibrin, which, in combination with platelets, forms a clot.

97. (d) It is the distance that light travels in one year. It moves at a velocity of about 300,000 km per second. So in one year, it can travel about 10 trillion km.

98. (a)

99. (a) The Indian National Satellite (INSAT) provides services to television broadcasting, telecommunications, satellite news-gathering, weather forecasting, disaster warning, search and rescue operations.

100. (b)